MUSIC, SOUND,
AND TECHNOLOGY
IN AMERICA

MUSIC, SOUND, AND TECHNOLOGY IN AMERICA

· ·

A Documentary History of Early Phonograph, Cinema, and Radio

Edited by **Timothy D. Taylor,**
Mark Katz, and Tony Grajeda

Duke University Press
Durham and London
2012

© 2012 Duke University Press

All rights reserved.

Printed in the United States of America on acid-free paper ∞

Typeset in Minion by Tseng Information Systems, Inc.

Library of Congress Cataloging-in-Publication Data and

republication acknowledgments appear on the last printed

page of this book.

Like water, like gas, like the electrical current coming from afar into our homes responding to our needs in return for almost no effort, so we will be supplied with visual or audible images, appearing and disappearing with the least gesture, almost a sign, only to leave us again the same way as they came.

—**Paul Valéry**, "La Conquête de l'ubiquité," in *Pièces sur l'art*, 1928–1934

Contents

Playing to the Pictures

Performative Accompaniment

The Organist of the Picture Palace

Conducting and Scoring to the Movies

Taste, Culture, and Educating the Public

Part III. Radio

General Introduction   Timothy D. Taylor

Music Technologies in Everyday Life

Few films or novels better capture the transition from quiet, small-town American life in the early twentieth century to the hustle and bustle of urban life in the 1920s than King Vidor's silent film *The Crowd* (1928). The film opens in a small town on Independence Day 1900 with the birth of Johnny Sims. The baby's proud father tells the doctor, "There's a little man the world is going to hear from all right, Doctor. I'm going to give him every opportunity." The next scene is set in 1912: "Johnny Sims reached the age of twelve. He recited poetry, played piano and sang in a choir . . . so did Lincoln and Washington!" Young boys sit on a fence, discussing their aspirations. Johnny says, "My Dad says *I'm* goin' to be somebody big!" But then a horse-drawn ambulance appears in front of the Sims house. The boys run there, finding that the whole town has turned out because of the death of Johnny's father. Young Johnny is told he will have to be the man in the family now. The film then cuts to New York City in 1921, where John has come to realize his potential. Vidor's camera cranes dramatically up a skyscraper and through an office window, revealing at first a sea of identical desks before zooming in to show John at his. Life in the demoralizing, homogenizing city takes its toll on John: he is ruled by the clock in his drab office as he struggles to be "somebody big." He gets married and endures both the death of his daughter and his wife's threats to leave him. To win her back, he buys her a bunch of flowers, all he can afford. Bereft of words, he puts on a phonograph recording of "There's Everything Nice about You." His wife relents, and the two go to a vaudeville show with their son. The last shot of the film begins with a medium close-up of the couple's happy faces, slowly zooming out until they are lost in the crowd.

The Crowd depicts many of the transitions and anxieties Americans experienced in the early twentieth century: the shift from rural or small-town life to cities; the fear of being lost in the crowd; the fear that opportunity will never really present itself; the rise of mass culture. Such feelings and anxieties were produced or exacerbated by many of the great technological changes that were occurring in America in this period, changes that contributed to a general sense that Americans were living in a new era with a faster, even bewildering, pace — the "modern tempo." Electricity, the airplane, the automobile, the telephone, the phonograph, the radio, and the motion picture all helped contribute to a sense that modernity was exhilarating, frightening, and wholly new.

As Vidor's film shows, the decade that best represented these changes was the 1920s, for it witnessed the modernization of cultural forms and communication technologies in the meteoric rise of radio and the advent of sound film.[1] For people living in the 1920s, the decade represented a greater break with the past than anyone could remember. The writer and historian Frederick Lewis Allen began *Only Yesterday*, his history of the 1920s, with a comparison to the previous decade, devising a fictitious couple, Mr. and Mrs. Smith, and describing what their lives were like in 1919. Women's dresses extended to ankle length, they wore their hair long and rarely smoked, and most automobiles were open rather than covered and had to be started with a hand crank. When Mr. and Mrs. Smith went to a tea dance at a local hotel in 1919, they might have heard a new jazz band instead of the usual orchestra, though there were no saxophones in those orchestras yet. When the Smiths stayed home, they might have read one of the latest novels of the day, but they most certainly did not listen to the radio — for radio was something only hobbyists were tinkering with at the time.[2]

Commodification, Consumption, and the Rise of Mass Culture

While the decade of the 1920s was probably the most tumultuous of all those represented in this collection, it was part of a broader shift that Americans were experiencing in the late nineteenth century and the early twentieth: they were entering a world of mass culture, in which goods — including cultural goods such as sound recordings, films, and more — were produced and consumed on a scale previously unknown. The transition to a consumer economy was facilitated by the rise of new forms of payment, or deferred payment, such as credit and installment-plan purchasing ("buy now, pay later" was a slogan introduced by the automobile industry around 1915),[3] by new forms of retail, such as department stores and chain stores, and by the rise of the advertising industry.[4] The slow conversion of the American economy from being primarily production-oriented to consumption-oriented was described by a distributor of packaged meat this way in 1920: "Mass selling has become almost the universal rule in this country, a discovery of this decade of hardly less importance than the discovery of such forces as steam and electricity."[5] This volume captures the slow transition toward a consumer society by focusing on the modernization of sound in general and music in particular, describing the processes by which music evolved from something that people primarily made for themselves or heard live to a commodity and object of consumption.[6]

Music and sound technologies were part of this shift, and indeed the phonograph (preceded by the player piano) introduced a new mode in the commodification of music: it became something that one purchased as *sound*.[7] Musical sound as a commodity was of course aided by devices to reproduce or transmit it. In the mid-1920s sales of phonographs and radios increased greatly; sales of radio sets rose from $60 million in 1922 to $358 million in 1924.[8] Movie attendance was similarly on the rise. A survey by the Bureau of Labor Statistics on the cost of living among working families in Chicago found that more than half of the family amusement budget was spent on movies; even people in that city receiving public assistance attended movies regularly.[9] By the mid-1920s fifty million Americans went to the movies each week, about half the population at the time, and attendance doubled by 1930 with the advent of the talkies.[10]

Along with the wide-scale adoption of these new technologies in the 1920s, this decade also witnessed the rise of new popular magazines for radio fans, phonograph record buyers, and film buffs. This massive popular press, well represented in the readings, gave listeners information about their favorite musicians and stars, sponsored contests and conducted polls to survey the preferences of audiences, and printed fan letters about their favorite stars, music, and films. These magazines helped create a star system that we now take for granted but in fact was a historical construction of the early twentieth century.

The advent of the phonograph, the sound film, and the radio played an important part in this larger shift in American life. Families and neighbors listened together to records; large audiences convened many times daily in movie houses; nationwide thousands, eventually millions, shared live musical or theatrical performances over the radio. Perhaps more than the other technologies represented in this volume, radio imparted a feeling of connectedness, since everyone listening in knew that others were hearing the same programs at the same time. As one commentator wrote in 1923, "How easy it is to close the eyes and imagine the other listeners in little back rooms, in kitchens, dining-rooms, sitting-rooms, attics; in garages, offices, cabins, engine-rooms, bunga-lows, cottages, mansions, hotels, apartments; one here, two there, a little com-pany around a table away off yonder, each and all sitting and hearing with the same comfort just where they happen to be."[11] The writer goes on about mem-bers of the far-flung audience, united in time and in their pleasure at hearing music coming out of their radios.[12]

The phonograph, the sound film, and the radio emerged around the same time as Frederick Winslow Taylor's "scientific management" techniques that rationalized work and Henry Ford's assembly-line manufacturing that made work repetitive, alienating, and dull, as in *The Crowd*. This banalization of work heightened the importance of consumption as a leisure activity and an escape.

Additionally, the movement from rural to urban areas, where the majority of Americans had come to reside by the 1920s, meant that many Americans were living in an environment in which they were surrounded by a crowd of strangers, a condition that was compounded by unprecedented waves of immi-gration. The anonymity of existence in the city, like that of Vidor's John Sims, coupled with the rising importance of consumption over production and the growth of mass culture, provoked a good deal of anxiety among many Ameri-cans, who feared that they were losing their individuality to the masses. As early as 1909, a magazine writer despaired, "We *are* a mass. As a whole, we have lost the capacity for separate selfhood."[13]

The advertising industry, becoming a major force in American culture in this period by selling not only goods but a new consumption-oriented mode of existence, took seriously its role as an arbiter of this new, mass national cul-ture: *Printers' Ink*, the main trade magazine for the advertising industry before the Second World War, wrote in 1938 that in the 1920s advertisers had failed to realize just what their power was, for mass production had "made it not only possible but imperative that the masses should live lives of comfort and leisure; that the future of business lay in its ability to manufacture customers as well as products."[14] The distinct but overlapping developments of the recording indus-try, the movie industry, and broadcasting all fueled the modern notion of mass audiences as great multitudes of customers, and the advent of radio in the 1920s especially proved a huge boon to advertisers, who were quick to sponsor programs that hawked their products.

At the same time, however, many intellectuals and artists were disturbed by the rise of mass culture and the threats to individuality that they thought it represented, fearing that the repetition of great works of music on the radio or phonograph would lead to their trivialization through superficial listening, as many represented in this volume argue. But they were in the minority. As we all know now, with our infatuation with iPods, TiVo, and other gadgets, the culture industry was successful in recruiting people into the world of purchasing music, educating them to relate to music as consumers more than as producers.

Mediated Music in Everyday Life

Consuming music as sound meant that people were making music less while permitting it to enter their homes with the newest devices. This was a long transitional period, in which people would interact with the phonograph and radio as though they were musical instruments. Many Americans greeted the advent of these devices with mixed feelings in the first half of the twentieth century. What we have captured in this volume are the attitudes of everyday people toward these new technologies, particularly when they began to employ them in their everyday lives. The questions that concern us, among others, are the following: How did people find uses for the new technologies? Are those uses the same that scientists and engineers envisioned? How did a technology that seemed at first like a strange gadget or a fad become so integral to everyday life? Other questions concern the controversies surrounding new technologies. How were they championed or opposed? Finally, we investigate music and people's relationships to it. How did people react to music when they could no longer see the musicians? How did these technologies change the way people learned music, whether as listener or performer? How was the previously clear distinction between the production and consumption of music blurred by these new technologies? How did the phonograph and radio change people's relationship to live music? How did the combination of music and film introduce and inflect new meanings to familiar musical works?

To address these and other questions, our collection brings together primary sources chronicling the development and subsequent uses of technologies, primarily in America, that profoundly shaped people's relationship to music before the Second World War. It begins in the late nineteenth century with the rise of the phonograph and moves through the growth of radio and talking pictures in the 1920s, thus covering roughly seventy years in the development of these three important music and media technologies.

The volume concludes with the end of the Second World War, by which point all three technologies had matured and been integrated into everyday American life. By the time of the arrival of television in the late 1940s and early 1950s (or, for that matter, the World Wide Web in the 1990s), American culture had already been shaped by and had adapted to the phonograph, radio, and sound film. It was these earlier technologies that had helped to introduce the notion that one didn't have to make one's own music or go out to hear it, but could enjoy it at home when one wanted. Furthermore, both radio and the phonograph established new economic and legal standards regarding broadcasting and copyright law. More recent technologies, such as television and the Internet, rather than representing communication revolutions, instead were built upon existing structures formed alongside earlier technologies.[15] Indeed, we would argue that these early years of the phonograph, radio, and sound film are in some ways at least as important socially and culturally as many developments afterward.

For any technology, people may find uses that its inventors didn't foresee. It is striking, for example, that neither the phonograph nor radio was developed primarily for musical purposes. The radio grew out of telephone technologies, and the phonograph was originally used as a dictation device. That these inventions became important musical devices speaks to what Jonathan Sterne has called "plasticity," the use of technology for purposes not imagined in the laboratory.[16]

Additionally, we believe that it is essential to view new technologies not so much as foreign to social or private life but as devices, when they gain a foothold, that help people continue to do what they have always done, but perhaps in new ways, whether faster, slower, or more efficiently. The idea that people adapt technologies to their own uses is found in the sociologist Claude Fischer's study of the telephone, which makes insightful arguments about how new technologies do not change everything, do not "determine the basic character of [American] life." "The telephone," he writes, "did not radically alter American ways of life; rather, Americans used it to more vigorously pursue their characteristic ways of life."[17] Or as the anthropologist Marilyn Strathern writes more generally, "However transformative and innovative [new technologies] are, they work on what is already there, what already gives shape to people's lives."[18]

And it is the same for the music technologies represented in this volume: people often use them to do what they were already doing. A woman recalling life in Little Sicily in Chicago in the 1920s said of the phonograph that on Saturday nights her neighbors would "play all these Italian records and they would dance."[19] In other words, the phonograph helped these immigrants be Italians in America, not merely passive consumers of American mass culture. At the same time, however, just as one could argue that the telephone did play a significant role in changing people's communicative relationships to each other, sound technologies also played a role in changing people's relationships to music. The point here is to try to conceptualize the introduction of these new technologies not as "changing everything" on the one hand or as simple tools for listening to music on the other, but as entering social life in the first half of the twentieth century in a complex and ever-changing dynamic.

By adopting these and other perspectives, this volume contributes to a small but fast-growing body of literature by musicologists and ethnomusicologists that is shedding light on the development of important music and audio technologies.[20] In addition, there are two new fields that study sound in general, sometimes including music: Science and Technology Studies (STS) and Sound Studies.[21] This volume is part of the new interest in sound reproduction technologies, and is especially indebted to those works concerned with what not only inventors and musicians but everyday users made of new music technologies.[22]

Reading What Follows

This collection is divided into three parts: sound recording, cinema, and radio. The documents were chosen not only for their descriptions of new technologies, but for what they reveal about music and how it was mediated to everyday users. To this end, a variety of sources are used, including those written by inventors or composers; other publications and genres are also represented, such as the popular press, advertisements, fiction, sheet music, fan letters, and business documents—whatever illuminates people's changing relationships to music. Since this volume is primarily about how these technologies gained acceptance in real people's lives, it begins with the advent of these technologies and concludes with their maturation, their full-fledged participation in Americans' everyday lives. For the most part, the documents are thematically rather than chronologically arranged, which helps highlight the various issues surrounding the introduction and use of these technologies.

While most of the documents contained here can be read for the information they purvey, we believe that they should all be read ethnographically—one can read them for what they reveal about people's attitudes and ideas about a particular technology and music, with questions such as the following: Why did a publication see fit to publish a story on a particular subject? Who was the intended audience? What were the underlying assumptions of the article? By reading this way, it is possible to begin to understand just how people were feeling and thinking about these technologies and the changes they were bringing to everyday people's lives. Just as we have our own reactions to, and discussions of, the latest and most pleasurable kind of technology, so too did people in the 1920s or other historical periods long before our own.

We believe that a volume of documents on these technologies serves two important purposes. The first is to make these fascinating and diverse sources—many little-known, unpublished, or difficult to find—easily available to students, scholars, and other interested readers. The second reason is more intellectual. We have gathered these writings to demonstrate that these three technologies—and the songs, symphonies, and movies produced with them—are profoundly shaped by social, cultural, and historical forces. We believe that these technologies cannot be understood without also understanding their relationship with real people in real places in real historical moments. Given that sound recording, radio, and film are still with us today and as deeply influential as ever, these documents not only open a window onto the past but can help us understand our continued and close relationship with mediated sound and music.

Editorial Note

For ease of reading, all spellings and punctuation have been modernized (e.g., "to-morrow" is spelled "tomorrow"). Typographical and spelling errors in original publications have been corrected; in unpublished materials such as fan letters, original spellings and punctuation have been retained.

PART I. SOUND RECORDING

SOUND RECORDING

Introduction   Mark Katz

Imagine encountering recorded music for the first time. Say, for example, that
you enter a room that is empty except for a smallish box sitting on a table, and
emanating from it is a human voice—singing. In the world of this thought experiment, music had always been—until now—experienced live; this is therefore a wholly unprecedented encounter. What, then, might your reaction be?
How would you explain a voice without a body? You might believe yourself the
victim of a ventriloquist's hoax. You might conclude that you are in the presence
of magic, whether good or evil. You might question your sanity. Perhaps you
would be, in the words of the composer Arthur Sullivan, "astonished and somewhat terrified." This is how Sullivan (of Gilbert and Sullivan fame) described
his reaction to a demonstration in 1888 of Thomas Edison's still relatively new
invention, the phonograph, which he fittingly preserved on a recording cylinder
that night, well over a century ago.[1]

Amazement and even fear were not uncommon reactions to the technology
of sound recording in the late nineteenth century and the early twentieth. The
reason is simple, but crucial: recorded music is very different from live music.
Live music exists only in the moment; recordings, however, capture those fleeting sounds and preserve them on physical media. With recording technology,
music could be disseminated, manipulated, and consumed in ways that had
never before been possible. When recorded, music comes unmoored from its
temporal origins. It can be heard after its original performance and repeated
almost indefinitely. The technology is therefore a kind of magic, for it grants
immortality and allows the dead to communicate with the living. It is these
distinctive aspects of recorded sound—these changes in the materiality and

temporality of music—that early users of the technology responded to; their reactions, in turn, led to profound changes in the way music came to be created and experienced.[2]

The advent of sound recording can be understood, according to the scholar Patrick Feaster, as "one of those moments of crisis . . . in which the preexisting constellation of technologies of communication is thrown out of equilibrium and then gradually reconfigured as a stable niche is carved out for the newcomer."[3] That loss of equilibrium is exactly what makes the early history of sound recording (and indeed, radio and film) so fascinating, and the documents reproduced here reveal how users of the technology struggled to make sense of wholly new ways of experiencing sound and, in particular, music.

The first three documents reproduced here are the oldest in this volume, and offer early predictions about the phonograph when its possibilities were as open as they were unsettled. I give the first word to Thomas Edison, who, although speaking as the phonograph's inventor, understood that he had no privileged information when it came to the future of his creation. When reading this document it is important to understand that Edison did not set out to invent a device for recording and reproducing music.[4] Working with two existing technologies, the telephone and the telegraph, he and his assistants were seeking a way to preserve spoken messages.[5] The first working phonograph, which assistant John Kruesi built in 1877 from Edison's sketches, was an elegantly simple device that used no electricity. Recordings were made by (necessarily) shouting into a mouthpiece (or "speaking diaphragm") while turning a crank attached to a metal cylinder. A needle, conveying the sound vibrations of the voice, inscribed a thin sheet of tinfoil wrapped around the cylinder. The tinfoil "record" could then be played back by turning the crank as the needle tracked the grooves indented in the foil; this action reversed the conveyance of sound from the foil to the needle to the "reproducing diaphragm," essentially a small speaker (see figure 1).[6]

What might strike us today as particularly remarkable about the earliest phonographs (and most phonographs built before the mid-1920s) is that no electricity was involved—for the most part sound was captured and reproduced mechanically.[7] The years between 1877 and 1925 mark a distinctive period in the history of sound recording, known collectively as the acoustic era. In 1925 the acoustic era was effectively brought to a close with the widespread introduction of microphones, which ushered in what came to be known as the electrical era. (It was not until the 1970s that the technology entered yet a new phase—the digital era.) Most of the documents that follow come from the acoustic era, and this is no accident. The demands of listening to and creating music in the

Figure 1. Thomas Edison's tinfoil phonograph, 1877. Photograph courtesy of the Thomas Edison National Historical Park, West Orange, New Jersey.

acoustic era were considerable, and it is during these years that we see most clearly how users came to terms with the phonograph. In fact, roughly half the documents here come from the decade between 1916 and 1926, a period that we might consider the technology's adolescence, and it was indeed a time that combined rapid growth with frequent introspection and anxiety.[8]

As Edison makes clear in his article from 1878, "The main utility of the phonograph [is] for the purpose of letter writing and other forms of dictation."[9] Specifically, he was thinking about business correspondence, the idea being that the phonograph—essentially a dictation device—would render secretaries and clerks redundant, with sheets of tinfoil (later, wax cylinders) replacing old-fashioned paper letters.[10] In general, the recording of speech was seen as the main function of the phonograph, and indeed it was commonly referred to as a "talking machine." Edison, however, did allow that his invention might have other uses. Music was one of them, though it placed fourth on Edison's list of possibilities. It might seem odd to us today that he did not see music as a more obvious avenue, but he was hardly alone. The article from the *New York Times* in 1877 that follows Edison's essay here fancifully explores the metaphor of bottling human speech, comparing record collecting to the stewardship of fine wines. It envisages "a well-stocked oratorical cellar" of cylinders preserving the speeches and sermons of prominent figures of the day. Music is not even mentioned. It was more than a decade before music came to be considered a viable option for the technology. This was due to a number of factors, including the failure of Edison's business phonograph venture, the development of coin-operated machines (which encouraged the use of the phonograph as an entertainment device in public gathering places),[11] and technological advances such as Emile Berliner's invention of the flat disc and its player, the gramophone, patented in 1887.[12] (At first, the term "gramophone" specifically referred to a disc-playing machine as distinct from the cylinder-playing phonograph. Later, after disc machines became standard, the terms became more or less interchangeable, generically referring to record players.) Music was more difficult to record than speech, and it was not until 1889 that the first commercial recordings were produced. When Philip Hubert (see item 3) predicted in 1893 that the phonograph would play a "tremendous role . . . in the future of music and musicians," he was making a fairly new claim, though of course he could not have guessed just how prominent this role would be. As Edison admitted in his essay, "In the case of an invention of the nature and scope of the phonograph, it is practically impossible to indicate [its potential] today, for tomorrow a trifle may extend it almost indefinitely."[13]

The documents that follow reveal a variety of perspectives on the musical potential of sound recording as users explored its possibilities in this period of disequilibrium. Except for the first and final groups, all the documents fall into categories connected with one of three musical activities: listening, performing, and composing. In music scholarship, composing is traditionally privileged above performing and listening. Listeners, however, were by far the largest group of phonograph users, and the group most deeply affected by recorded music, so it is with them that we begin.

A century ago it was necessary to learn how to listen to the phonograph. This process entailed both emulating certain aspects of the experience of live music and exploiting the distinctive possibilities of phonographic listening. Early commentators delighted in imagining unusual uses of the phonograph, whether playing recordings at weddings or funerals, using the machine as a ventriloquist to fool bystanders, or surreptitiously recording conversations.[14] An example of the last is given in the comic song "Susan, Dear Sue (The Phonograph Song)" (1901, item 8), in which a secretary holds her fickle employer to his promise of marriage when she confronts him (in court!) with phonographic evidence that he cannot refute (see figure 2).

Such uses of the phonograph were uncommon, and in reality most listeners

Figure 2. "Susan, Dear Sue (The Phonograph Song)." Words by Jas. O'Dea and Arthur Gillespie. Music by Herbert Dillea. New York: Witmark, 1901.

took a more cautious approach to the technology. Consider the simple fact that with recordings one hears music but does not see musicians. This was an unsettling experience for many early listeners who, as a music critic explained in 1923, "cannot bear to hear a remarkably life-like human voice issuing from a box. They desire the physical presence. For want of it, the gramophone distresses them."[15] The industry, of course, wanted to avoid producing such cognitive dissonance and often used advertisements to convince the public that the visual experience of music was not completely lost in the process of recording. Some ads boasted that their recordings were so lifelike that listeners could practically see the performers; many depicted the recorded musicians standing next to the machines, sometimes in ghostly outlines, sometimes in miniature, sometimes as life-size figures mingling with listeners (see figure 3).[16]

Another suggestion for visualizing live performance is found in an instruction sheet given to visitors of Edison phonograph shops (1916, item 4). Customers were asked to take the "Edison Realism Test," the purpose of which was to recreate the emotional impact of live performance for the phonograph listener. Such painstaking directions for listening to a record seem unnecessary, even comical. But it is clear from Edison's instructions, and from many phonograph ads of the time, that sightless listening was far from the "natural" activity we now take for granted.

Solitary listening was another facet of the phonographic experience that challenged early users. Consider the question posed by Orlo Williams in an article in the British journal *Gramophone* (1923, item 6). How would you react, he asked, if you were to discover a friend listening to recorded music alone? His answer, which will likely strike modern readers as fanciful, was this: such an activity would be evidence of an unwell mind, whether caused by mental instability or substance abuse. To make sense of this statement we have to understand that before the days of sound recording, it had been for the most part neither practical nor desirable to hear music alone. Music had always accompanied social and communal events; solitary listening, therefore, contradicted centuries of tradition and challenged long-held notions about the function of music. Williams, however, was exhorting readers to accept and even embrace solitary listening, and in this tension between tradition and novelty we witness the process by which listeners came to terms with what was often called "canned music."

Not all listeners immediately accepted these new possibilities, and many resisted. One was W. C. Shott of New Philadelphia, Ohio, who complained to Thomas Edison in 1921 that representatives of his phonograph company were

The best friend of a hostess is the Victrola

The hostess who has a Victrola never need worry about how the evening will "go".

Is there an awkward moment after the guests leave the dinner table? A Victrola will "break the ice".

Do the young people get tired of general conversation? A Victrola will furnish the latest dance music and set their feet to sliding.

Does someone mention a melody from the latest opera? Let us try it on the Victrola.

Always there is the Victrola—the treasure house of entertainment in reserve—never obtrusive but always ready.

Is your home like this? It might be—so easily.

There are Victors and Victrolas in great variety of styles from $10 to $500, and any Victor dealer in any city in the world will gladly demonstrate them to you.

Victor Talking Machine Co., Camden, N. J., U. S. A.

Berliner Gramophone Co., Montreal, Canadian Distributors

Figure 3. Advertisement for Victrola, *Collier's* 52 (4 October 1913), back cover. Collection of Mark Katz.

offering public demonstrations of secular music on Sundays, and thus "disregarded the divine command to keep the Lord's day" (item 10). Generally, however, instead of resisting the technology outright, listeners adapted to this new mode of musical experience by drawing upon existing practices and traditions. In the earliest years, phonograph owners often enjoyed listening to recordings of their own making. Cylinder machines were typically capable of both recording and playback, and the industry even encouraged amateur recordings, as in the National Phonograph Company's charming pamphlet *How We Gave a Phonograph Party* (1899, item 7); thousands of such recordings still exist as evidence of these gatherings.[17] Group listening was practiced in other ways as well. For example, in 1905 Grinnell Brothers Music Parlors of Detroit invited patrons to evening musicales, with music furnished by a phonograph; such concerts were not at all uncommon in the first decades of the century.[18] Phonograph societies, which arose in England in the second decade of the century and later spread to the United States and continental Europe, sponsored concerts that brought music lovers together to listen to recorded music.[19] These concerts were much like traditional ones: they were held in recital or concert halls, programs were distributed, the dress was formal, and the pieces were greeted with applause. The only striking difference was that in these concerts the audience sat facing machines rather than musicians. Outdoor phonograph concerts were also in vogue for a time. In 1909, for example, an audience of over forty thousand gathered in Heaton Park in Manchester, England, for a free concert of recordings by the tenor Enrico Caruso.[20]

Phonograph concerts were also given in private homes. In 1905 a writer in the *Talking Machine News* told of hosting a well-attended "phonograph entertainment" at his home. He described a varied program—much like the typical potpourri concert of the time—and noted that encores were demanded of several pieces.[21] In 1912 the German phonograph journal *Die Stimme seines Herrn* suggested several thematic phonograph programs for home gatherings, including birthdays, confirmations, weddings—even stag parties (*Herrenabend*).[22] And in 1921 an American literary magazine reported that home concert impresarios would even "go to the length of . . . maintaining as rigid a discipline against talking during the music as if Caruso or Rachmaninoff were there in person."[23] Note that all the examples of phonograph concerts cited above took place in the first two decades of the century. Such formal events became less common in the 1920s and beyond, suggesting that listeners were becoming sufficiently accustomed to the phonograph to explore new ways of using it.

As evidence of the phonograph's increasing assimilation into the modern home, we can also point to the great popularity of dancing to recorded music. In fact, the so-called dance craze that pervaded the United States and Europe from 1910 to 1930 was often attributed to sound recording. As the American journal *Music Monitor and World* argued in 1914, "The revival of dancing is undoubtedly due in large measure to the influence of the player-piano and the phonograph."[24] The British magazine *Gramophone* made the claim even more strongly a few years later: "Few people will deny that the dance craze, which now holds everyone literally in its grip, owes nearly everything to the gramophone."[25] The connection was fairly simple: with recordings it was possible to dance at home, cheaply, and at one's convenience. As Pauline Partridge explained in her article "The Home Set to Music" (1924, item 9), "An informal dancing party can be given with no preparation more difficult than rolling up the rugs and calling in the neighbors." Moreover, those who wanted to learn to dance but feared public embarrassment could practice their steps in private, whether alone or with a trusted partner. Countless advertisements encouraged home dancing, and as early as 1914 the Victor Talking Machine Company published pamphlets that served as dance manuals-cum-record catalogues.[26] The appeal of domestic dancing was even reflected in popular songs of the day, such as "They Start the Victrola (And Go Dancing around the Floor)."[27] (Victrola was a brand name of a variety of phonographs made by the Victor Talking Machine Company. Victrolas were so popular that the name came to be used generically to refer to any type of record player.)

In the second decade of the century the phonograph began to spread from the home to the school, and particularly in the United States educators quickly embraced the possibilities of recorded music. At the time, American music education was undergoing a revolution, one that promoted a new ideal known as appreciation—generally understood as the intelligent enjoyment of music, typically classical music, as a listener.[28] Recorded music was seen as an excellent way to promote music appreciation, for by this time sturdy, portable, and relatively cheap phonographs were available, making it possible to bring the classics (or "good music," as it was often called) to all the nation's children. (Later, as we will see in part II of this volume, radio was to assume an important role in the music appreciation movement.) Two articles reproduced here (items 11 and 12) give a sense of the phonograph's role in primary education and the enthusiasm with which the technology was generally received. Annie Pike Greenwood's "The Victor in the Rural School" shows how one young teacher brought music (and discipline) to the children of Milner, Idaho. The article so impressed the prominent educator and longtime editor of the *Journal of Education*, A. E. Winship, that he visited Greenwood and later wrote this in praise of the phonograph: "I yield to no one in my appreciation of the rural mail service, and of the rural telephone, but I place above either and both of them in the service for God and humanity the possibilities of the instrument which will evermore thrill country life with the richest music of the greatest masters."[29] The second article explains the phenomenon of the music memory contest, which C. M. Tremaine introduced in 1916 as a way of using sound recordings to help children learn the masterworks of classical music. The music memory contest quickly caught on, and by 1926 schools in more than fourteen hundred cities were participating.[30] While the phenomenon seems to have peaked just before the Depression hit, contests are still being held today, their goals and format much the same as they had been in the early twentieth century.[31]

As recorded music came to have an increasing presence in the lives of millions of men and women, we see issues of gender coming to the fore in the phonographic discourse.[32] An article in 1931 in the American journal *Disques*, for example, repeats two stereotypes that to the author and apparently many others were entirely unproblematic: "That men are notoriously fascinated by small mechanical details is a securely established fact. Women, as everybody knows, take little or no interest in mechanical things." The upshot of these "facts" is quite clear: "Well, then, is it any wonder that hundreds of men suddenly became profoundly interested in the phonograph?"[33] Yet the facts were not quite so clear. As the documents reprinted here reveal, many early-twentieth-century women were deeply interested in the phonograph, while men often had to be coaxed into accepting the technology.

The industry clearly recognized the importance of women customers. In 1919 a study commissioned by the Sonora Phonograph Company showed that women purchased players more than twice as often as men and, when accompanied into stores by men, remained the primary decision makers.[34] Gladys Kimmel's article for the trade magazine *Talking Machine Journal* (1919, item 15) divides women customers into three categories, offering detailed suggestions to phonograph dealers for interacting with each type. Phonograph companies were major advertisers in the first decades of the twentieth century, and every significant American magazine carried ads, often full-page and in color. Many were clearly aimed at women, appearing in publications like *Good Housekeeping* and *Ladies' Home Journal*. Some touted the convenience and versatility of the phonograph, which could be used for educating children and entertaining adults. Others claimed that the technology could add a touch of culture and class to the average home. A full-page Victrola advertisement in 1913 in the weekly *Collier's* sent this message through text as well as image (see figure 3). The illustration offers a glimpse into a luxurious salon that few readers would have ever encountered. A group of opera characters comes to life to form a receiving line, greeted by the elegantly dressed hostess standing near a conspicuously placed high-end Victrola. The text, however, addresses women of more modest means, who would likely not wear gowns to entertain and were certain to take an interest in knowing that they too could—through the magic of the Victrola—have a taste of the good life for as little as ten dollars.

Fewer phonograph advertisements were aimed specifically at men. While it may have been, as the earlier-cited *Disques* article suggested, that men of the time were often mechanically inclined, the phonograph industry seemed to believe that fewer were musically inclined as well. Perhaps for good reason: in the early twentieth century devotion to music was hardly thought to exemplify manliness—to show too great an interest in music was often to risk being seen as "sissy" or "soft."[35] Ads directed at men often attempted to convince them that it was acceptable to enjoy music through the phonograph, particularly as a form of socializing with other men. According to an ad in 1905, "Every young man should have an Edison Phonograph." "Here is your opportunity," it explained, "to become a good fellow, and make your rooms the merriest rendezvous in town."[36] An Aeolian-Vocalion ad in 1916 offered another approach (item 14). It touted the Graduola, a simple volume control device operated by pulling or pushing a knob attached to a cable; the "slender tube terminating in a handle," as the ad describes it, in turn opened or closed a set of internal shutters inserted within the machine's horn. The protagonist of the advertisement goes with his wife to play bridge at the Joneses, after which he is introduced to the Graduola. Upon trying it out while a record of the sentimental song "Ben Bolt" plays, he immediately loses his prejudice against phonographs and miraculously becomes a musician. Whether intended or not, there seems to be a homoerotic subtext here, as the unnamed businessman handles the swelling, phallic Graduola with glorious trembling. At a distance of more than ninety-five years, however, one can only speculate on how such copy might have been interpreted at the time.

The letters that appeared in the British journal *Gramophone* and its American counterpart *Phonograph Monthly Review* (items 16–19) capture an early episode in a continuing conversation about women as phonograph and record enthusiasts. The opening salvo, from the pseudonymous Scrutator, poses the question "Where are the ladies?," asking for women readers to contribute their "charming prattle" to the magazine. Following this condescending but apparently well-meaning letter comes true misogyny from a phonograph dealer writing as T.A.F. Several women, all using their full names, responded with varying degrees of indignation. One of them, Dorothy Fisher, was an American reader who wrote not to *Gramophone* but to the *Phonograph Monthly Review*, sparking further letters and generating a transatlantic debate. Taken together, these documents reveal a complex gendering of the technology in the early twentieth century, one that both reinforced and resisted common stereotypes.[37]

At the same time the phonograph found itself in the middle of the so-called battle of the sexes, it also played a role in less metaphorical battles, as soldiers fighting abroad brought record players and discs with them by the thousands. Items 20–22 offer a look at the role of the phonograph in the Great War, specifically from the American perspective.[38] "Talking Machines Are 'Essentials'" (1917), the title of an article from the trade magazine *Talking Machine Journal*, offers an impassioned plea on behalf of the industry in the early days of America's involvement in the war. With factories from across the manufacturing spectrum being repurposed for the war effort, the author argued that phonographs and recordings (and thus the factories that produce them) were in fact essential for the morale of the soldiers and those on the home front.[39] The anonymous author needn't have worried. Although many record plants were converted or partially converted, the war years saw a tremendous boom in sales. According to census figures, between 1914 and 1919 the value of America's phonograph production rocketed from just over $27 million to just under $159 million; as one historian of the phonograph observed, "Americans had gone on a phonograph binge."[40]

Mr. Vivian Burnett, composer and lyricist of "When I Hear That Phonograph Play" (item 21), was not a career composer but rather a journalist and, for a time, an associate editor at *Talking Machine Journal*. (He may well have been the author of "Talking Machines Are 'Essentials.'") Illness kept him out of the war, but he found another way to serve. In 1918 he organized a "National Phonograph Records Recruiting Corps" of fifteen thousand volunteers to collect "slacker" records to send to soldiers in the training camps and overseas.[41] At the time, a slacker was someone who evaded military service, so this was a clever way to encourage patriotic phonograph owners to donate discs. (Figure 4 reproduces one of the posters advertising the record drive.) That same year he articulated his support for the necessity of recorded music during wartime in another way: through song. "When I Hear That Phonograph Play" is a sentimental piece for voice and piano that invokes the power of recorded music to connect distant loved ones. Burnett's work on behalf of the soldiers drew a good deal of positive

Figure 4. "Poster exhorting Americans to donate unused ("slacker") records to soldiers," 1918. Courtesy of the University of North Carolina, Chapel Hill, Rare Book Collection.

press, though it likely never overshadowed his real claim to fame. As a child he was the inspiration for the main character of a wildly popular book written by his mother, Frances Hodgson Burnett: *Little Lord Fauntleroy*.[42]

Although Burnett did not write his song from firsthand experience, the accounts of soldiers listening to records on the front, even in the trenches, reveal that for many, records were indeed "essentials." The article "Phonographs on the Firing Line" (1919, item 22) vividly relates the value that soldiers placed upon their battered record players and their worn and scratched discs.

While the primary literature richly documents the attitudes and practices of consumers, whether mothers, teachers, or soldiers, there is much less material from the perspective of those who made the records. (For example, there are few if any guides or manuals analogous to those that later appeared for performers and composers involved with radio.) From what accounts we do have, however, it is clear that the recording studio of the early twentieth century was not a congenial venue for making music. The room was usually cramped and hot, with the musicians playing for an audience of engineers and, before the ad-

Figure 5. Rosario Bourdon conducting the Victor Salon Orchestra, c. 1920. Photo courtesy of the Behring Center, Smithsonian Institution, Washington.

vent of the microphone in 1925, a large acoustic recording horn (or many such devices — sometimes up to a dozen horns were used in a recording session). We can understand, then, why even very experienced performers sometimes suffered "phonograph fright" in their recording sessions.[43] The insensitivity of the horn and the short recording time of cylinders and 78 rpm discs (generally between two minutes and four-and-a-half minutes) significantly affected how the musicians performed. Seating for ensembles was dictated by how well or poorly the instruments projected sound; the results, as can be seen in figure 5, rarely resembled what one might see on a concert stage.

Some instruments did not project well enough and were often altered or replaced. Figure 5 shows several Stroh violins, the most noticeable being played by the performer in the foreground. Patented in 1899 by Augustus Stroh, the instrument dispensed with the wooden body of the violin, replacing it with a conical metal horn; a second smaller horn pointed toward the musician's left ear (in a way presaging the use of headphones by studio musicians). The sound was quite powerful and hard to distinguish from a traditional violin when heard on early recordings.[44] There were no Stroh basses, and in the early years of recording the tuba often sat in for the big fiddle. Jazz recording sessions rarely used snare or bass drums; percussion was often limited to woodblocks, cowbells, or washboards, which had a concentrated, easily distinguished sound. Soloists, whether singers or instrumentalists, stood right in front of the horn and had to rein in their fortissimos, lest they "blast" the needle out of the groove, and had to replace their pianissimos with mezzofortes simply to be heard. As Yvonne de Treville notes in her article "Making a Phonograph Record" (1916, item 24), some recording sessions included what she called a "gentle pusher," a studio employee who, standing directly behind her, pushed her toward the horn or pulled her away when she sang too softly or too loudly.

Because of the permanence of recordings and their limited playing time, a session in the studio was often a tense, carefully planned affair. In the days before magnetic tape became widely available (c. 1948) there was no splicing or patching—if a cylinder or side of a disc was to hold a whole piece or movement, it had to be played from start to finish without interruption. The musicians were required to start and end exactly on cue, with absolute silence before and after. As the vignette from *Violinist* magazine makes clear (1910, item 23), recording sessions demanded an extremely low tolerance for error. In her memoirs, the Australian soprano Nellie Melba recalled a session in 1906: "After making what I believe would have been the most beautiful record, I stumbled backwards over a chair, and said 'Damn' in an all too audible voice. That 'damn,' when the record was played over, came out with a terrible clarity, making me feel much as a sinner must on the Day of Judgment."[45] Many an early recording was ruined by similarly intemperate exclamations. Jazz players had a further concern: as the drummer Baby Dodds explained in his memoirs (excerpted in item 25), musicians recording in the acoustic era could never play in the studio exactly as they did in a club, where they could extend their solos and play multiple choruses as they saw fit. Dodds also recounts the now legendary story of the 1923 recording of "Dippermouth Blues," in which the banjoist Bill Johnson yelled, "Play that thing!" when Dodds forgot to come in, immortalizing the line that later became part of the song in their subsequent performances.[46]

As Dodds and the American conductor Edwin McArthur explain (1941, item 26), not all of the differences between live and recorded music arose from the technical limitations of the equipment. As mentioned, one fact of recording is that the performers and listeners cannot see one another. Dodds lamented this and wondered how it could be that recordings became so popular given this mutual invisibility. McArthur, in his article, argued that the lack of the visual component required slightly faster tempos and tighter phrasing. Given all the travails the musicians describe, it seems a wonder that so much music managed to make it out of the recording studio alive. Yet even the most famous and respected musicians of the day—the opera star Enrico Caruso, the violinist Fritz Kreisler, or the pianist Ignacy Paderewski, for example—quickly accepted the technology, seeing its value to their careers, and left recordings that are cherished to this day. Perhaps it is true, as McArthur suggested, that the harsh conditions forced musicians to rise to the occasion.[47]

While a certain wariness about sound recording characterizes the writings of professional performers, commentators were generally more sanguine about the technology when it came to teaching young musicians. In 1916 the influential American music journal *Etude* asked prominent educators to discuss their experience with and opinion of the use of "mechanical instruments" in music pedagogy (item 27). ("Mechanical instruments" included not only the phonograph but the player piano, and it should be noted that the latter had a more prominent role in the musical life of the early twentieth century than is generally realized today.) Ten responses were published, and collectively they reveal the excitement, and to a lesser extent trepidation, that many felt about the pedagogical impact of technology. Several of the respondents spoke of using records to inspire their pupils and to serve as models for their performances. The noted voice teacher Oscar Saenger went further and published a course of vocal study in which the student listened to and then imitated various exercises on several specially made discs; item 28 reproduces instructions and photographs from the volume for soprano.[48] Although one of the repeated criticisms of the phonograph was that it would discourage performance (more on this below), for these teachers, at least, there was nothing mutually exclusive about music appreciation and musical activity.

While even the most famous performers of the early twentieth century quickly accepted the phonograph, this was not the case with composers, particularly of classical music. Turn-of-the-century catalogues listed only a few recent works of popular music, such as Joseph Flanner's "A Hot Time in the Old Town" (composed 1896), Joseph Howard's "Hello, Ma Baby" (1899), and several marches by John Philip Sousa. New classical music was even scarcer, and most of the best-known composers were not represented on disc until after about 1910.[49] With the exception of Sousa's famous critique of mechanical music (1906, item 33, discussed below) and some brief positive comments from the English composer Edward Elgar,[50] few composers wrote publicly about sound recording before the 1920s, another indication of their relative lack of engagement with the technology. When composers started publishing their thoughts on recording, their opinions ran the gamut. The French composer Vincent d'Indy, for example, argued in 1927, "Music and machines can have no rapport, for music draws its life from expression whereas the machine is fundamentally inexpressive," while his Swiss colleague Arthur Honegger offered the opposite opinion in 1928: "I am sincerely convinced that the future of music lies in the development of mechanical instruments."[51] Others, such as Béla Bartók and Igor Stravinsky—classical composers who recorded a number of their own works—were more ambivalent (see Stravinsky's account in item 30 of his experiences in the recording studio).[52] In item 29 the American experimentalist composer Henry Cowell suggests ways in which composers could use the phonograph as a creative, and not simply re-creative, tool. The documents that follow Cowell's essay (items 31 and 32) explore the idea of the phonograph as a compositional tool in greater depth. They offer intriguing possibilities: Carol-Bérard encourages composers to incorporate recorded noises into their works, an idea that anticipated both *musique concrète* and digital sampling,[53] while Stravinsky calls for future composers to write specifically for the phonograph. At the time these were written (1929–30), the technology was simply not capable of realizing such far-seeing ideas. Yet these articles offer more than optimistic speculation, for they reiterate two common themes in the discourse of modernist composition: first, the notion of giving composers control over the execution of their works, while conversely reducing or eliminating the role of the independent performer, and second, the idea of using technology to expand the sound resources available to composers. Thus, while the specific proposals in these writings might have been ahead of their time, the goals and values they represented certainly expressed the zeitgeist.[54]

The final documents in part I (items 33–37) represent the debate over the value of recorded music, particularly in the United States. John Philip Sousa, the famous bandleader and composer of march music, saw the phonograph as a direct threat both to musical amateurs and to professionals: the former would have no incentive to make music themselves, while the latter would find their livelihoods threatened (especially given the vagueness of copyright laws at the time).[55] Writing almost twenty-five years later, Joseph Weber, the president of the American Federation of Musicians, echoed many of Sousa's concerns but addressed newer technological threats as well, such as the recent introduction of sound film, a development that led to the practical extinction of the cinema orchestra in fairly short order. The Portland City Council document from 1907 offers an example of the many ordinances that sought to circumscribe the use of phonographs and graphophones (another type of record player), machines that many (like Sousa and Weber) saw as destroyers of the peace. The ordinance, however, did not pass.

Sousa's article was much discussed at the time and remains the most oft-cited writing from these debates. Yet while the phonograph had its detractors, its proponents were numerous, varied, and vocal, espousing the belief that this technology, as *Etude* magazine claimed in 1922, would "help America become a truly musical nation."[56] From a modern vantage point the rhetoric of both sides may seem overheated, but neither should be dismissed, for they reveal deeply held values. For many detractors, recorded music represented the loss of the old ways and the attendant dehumanization of American society, while champions of the phonograph exhibited a common strain of utopianism, one that endowed technology with the ability to achieve a perfect society. Thus, these last documents—and indeed, all those reproduced here—open a window into a time of disequilibrium that the phonograph both reflected and helped create.

SOUND RECORDING

Readings   Compiled by Mark Katz

Predictions

1. Thomas A. Edison, "The Phonograph and Its Future"
North American Review 126 (1878), 530–36

Of all the writer's inventions, none has commanded such profound and earnest attention throughout the civilized world as has the phonograph. This fact he attributes largely to that peculiarity of the invention which brings its possibilities within range of the speculative imaginations of all thinking people, as well as to the almost universal applicability of the foundation principle, namely, the gathering up and retaining of sounds hitherto fugitive, and their reproduction at will.

From the very abundance of conjectural and prophetic opinions which have been disseminated by the press, the public is liable to become confused, and less accurately informed as to the immediate result and effects of the phonograph than if the invention had been confined to certain specific applications, and therefore of less interest to the masses. The writer has no fault to find with this condition of the discussion of the merits and possibilities of his invention; for, indeed, the possibilities are so illimitable and the probabilities so numerous that he—though subject to the influence of familiar contact—is himself in a somewhat chaotic condition of mind as to where to draw the dividing line. In point of fact, such line cannot with safety be defined in ordinary inventions at so early a stage of their development. In the case of an invention of the nature and scope of the phonograph, it is practically impossible to indicate it today, for tomorrow a trifle may extend it almost indefinitely.

There are, however, certain stages in the developing process which have thus far been actually reached; certain others which are clearly within reach; and others which, though they are in the light of today classed as possibilities, may tomorrow become probable, and a little later actual achievements. It is the intention of the writer in this article to confine himself to the actual and the probable, to the end that a clearer conception of the immediate realizations of the phonograph may be had. He concedes to the public press and the world of science the imaginative work of pointing out and commenting upon the possible. It is in view of the liberal manner in which this has already been done, and the handsome treatment he has received at their hands, that he for the first time appears *in propria persona*[1] to discuss and comment upon the merits of one of his own inventions.

In order to furnish a basis upon which the reader may take his stand, and accept or combat the logic of the writer in his presentment of the probabilities of the phonograph, a few categorical questions are put and answers given upon the essential features of the principle involved:

1. Is a vibrating plate or disk capable of receiving a complex motion which shall correctly represent the peculiar property of each and all the multifarious vocal and other sound-waves?

   The telephone answers affirmatively.

2. Can such complex movement be transmitted from such plate, by means of a single embossing-point attached thereto, to effect a record upon a plastic material by indentation, with such fidelity as to give to such indentations the same varied and complex form; and, if so, will this embossing-point, upon being passed over the record thus made, follow it with such fidelity as to retransmit to the disk the same variety of movement, and thus effect a restoration or reproduction of the vocal or other sound-waves, without loss of any property essential to producing upon the ear the same sensation as if coming direct from the original source?

   The answer to this may be summed up in a statement of the fact that, by the application of power for uniformity of movement, and by attention to many seemingly unimportant and minor details, such as the *form* and material of the embossing-point, the proper *dampening* of the plate, the character of the material embossed, the formation of the mouth-piece over the plate, etc., the writer has at various times during the past weeks reproduced these waves with such degree of accuracy in each and every detail as to enable his assistants to read, without the loss of a word, one or more columns of a newspaper article unfamiliar to them, and which were spoken into the apparatus when they were not present. The only perceptible loss was found to be in the quality of the utterance—a non-essential in the practical application of the apparatus. Indeed, the articulation of some individuals has been very perceptibly improved by passage through the phonograph, the original utterance being mutilated by imperfection of lip and mouth formation, and these mutilations eliminated or corrected by the mechanism of the phonograph.

3. Can a record be removed from the apparatus upon which it was made, and replaced upon a second without mutilation or loss of effective power to vibrate the second plate?

This is a mere mechanical detail, presenting no greater obstacle than having proper regard for the perfect interchangeableness of the various working parts of the apparatus—not so nice a problem as the manufacture of the American watch.

4. What as to facility of placing and removing the record-sheet, and as to its transportation by mail?

But ten or fifteen seconds suffice for such placing or removal. A special envelope will probably be required for the present, the weight and form of which, however, will but slightly increase the cost of postage.

5. What as to durability?

Repeated experiments have proved that the indentations possess wonderful enduring power, even when the reproduction has been effected by the comparatively rigid plate used for their production. It is proposed, however, to use a more flexible plate for reproducing, which, with a perfectly smooth stone point—diamond or sapphire—will render the record capable of from 50 to 100 repetitions, enough for all practical purposes.

6. What as to duplication of a record and its permanence?

Many experiments have been made, with more or less success, in the effort to obtain stereotypes of a record. This work has been done by others, and, though the writer has not as yet seen it, he is reliably informed that, very recently, it has been successfully accomplished. He can certainly see no practical obstacle in the way. This, of course, permits of an indefinite multiplication of a record, and its preservation for all time.

7. What are the requisite force of wave impinging upon the diaphragm and the proximity of the mouth to the diaphragm to effect a record?

These depend in a great measure upon the volume of sound desired in the reproduction. If the reproduction is to be made audible to an audience, considerable force is requisite in the original utterance; if for the individual ear, only the ordinary conversational tone (even a whisper has been reproduced). In both cases the original utterances are delivered directly in the mouthpiece of the instrument. An audible reproduction may, however, be had by speaking at the instrument from a distance of from two to three feet in a loud tone. The application of a flaring tube or funnel to collect the sound waves and the construction of an especially delicate diaphragm and embossing-point, etc., are the simple means which suggest themselves to effect this. The writer has not as yet given this stage of the development much attention, but sees no practical difficulty in gathering up and retaining a sectional part of the sound waves diffused about the original source, within a radius of, say, three feet (sufficiently removed not to be annoying to a speaker or a singer).

The foregoing presentment of the stage of development reached by the several essential features of the phonograph demonstrates the following *faits accomplis*:

1. The captivity of all manner of sound-waves heretofore designated as "fugitive," and their permanent retention.
2. Their reproduction with all their original characteristics at will, without the presence or consent of the original source, and after the lapse of any period of time.
3. The transmission of such captive sounds through the ordinary channels of commercial intercourse and trade in material form, for purposes of communication or as merchantable goods.
4. Indefinite multiplication and preservation of such sounds, without regard to the existence or non-existence of the original source.
5. The captivation of sounds, with or without the knowledge or consent of the source of their origin.

The probable application of these properties of the phonograph to the various branches of commercial and scientific industry presently indicated will require the exercise of more or less mechanical ingenuity. Conceding that the apparatus is practically perfected in so far as the faithful reproduction of sound is concerned, many of the following applications will be made the moment the new form of apparatus, which the writer is now about completing, is finished. These, then, might be classed as actualities; but they so closely trench upon other applications which will immediately follow, that it is impossible to separate them: hence they are all enumerated under the head of probabilities, and each specially considered. Among the more important may be mentioned: Letter-writing and other forms of dictation, books, education, reader, music, family record; and such electrotype applications as books, musical boxes, toys clocks advertising and signaling apparatus, speeches, etc., etc.

Letter-writing.—The apparatus now being perfected in mechanical details will be the standard phonograph, and may be used for all purposes except such as require special form of matrix, such as toys, clocks, etc., for an indefinite repetition of the same thing. The main utility of the phonograph, however, being for the purpose of letter writing and other forms of dictation, the design is made with a view to its utility for that purpose.

The general principles of construction are a flat plate or disk, with spiral groove on the face, operated by clockwork underneath the plate; the grooves are cut very closely together, so as to give a great total length to each inch of surface—close calculation gives as the capacity of each sheet of foil, upon which the record is had, in the neighborhood of 40,000 words. The sheets being but ten inches square, the cost is so trifling that but 100 words might be put upon a single sheet economically. Still, it is problematical whether a less number of grooves per inch might not be the better plan—it certainly would for letters—but it is desirable to have but one class of machine throughout the world; and as very extended communications, if put upon one sheet, could be transported more economically than upon two, it is important that each sheet be given as great capacity as possible. The writer has not yet decided this point, but will experiment with a view of ascertaining the best mean capacity.

The practical application of this form of phonograph for communications is very simple. A sheet of foil is placed in the phonograph, the clockwork set in motion, and the matter dictated into the mouthpiece without other effort than when dictating to a stenographer. It is then removed, placed in a suitable form of envelope, and sent through the ordinary channels to the correspondent for whom designed. He, placing it upon his phonograph, starts his clock-work and *listens* to what his correspondent has to say. Inasmuch as it gives the tone of voice of his correspondent, it is *identified*. As it may be filed away as other letters, and at any subsequent time reproduced, it is a perfect *record*. As two sheets of tin foil have been indented with the same facility as a single sheet, the "writer" may thus *keep a duplicate* of his communication. As the principal of a business house or his partners now dictate the important business communications to clerks, to be written out, they are required to do no more by the phonographic method, and do thereby *dispense with the clerk*, and *maintain perfect privacy* in their communications.

The phonograph letters may be dictated at home, or in the office of a friend, the *presence* of a stenographer *not being required*. The dictation may be as rapid as the thoughts can be formed or the lips utter them. The recipient may listen to his letters being read at a rate of from 150 to 200 words per minute, and at the same time busy himself about other matters. Interjections, explanations, emphasis, exclamations, etc., may be thrown into such letters, *ad libitum*.

In the early days of the phonograph, ere it has become universally adopted, a correspondent in Hong Kong may possibly not be supplied with an apparatus, thus necessitating a written letter of the old-fashioned sort. In that case the writer would use his phonograph simply as a dictating-machine, his clerk writing it out from the phonograph at leisure, causing as many words to be uttered at one time as his memory was capable of retaining until he had written them down. This clerk need not be a stenographer, nor need he have been present when the letter was dictated, etc.

The advantages of such an innovation upon the present slow, tedious, and costly methods are too numerous, and too readily suggest themselves, to warrant their enumeration, while there are no disadvantages which will not disappear coincident with the general introduction of the new method.

Dictation.—All kinds and manner of dictation which will permit of the application of the mouth of the speaker to the mouth-piece of the phonograph may be as readily effected by the phonograph as in the case of letters. If the matter is for the printer, he would much prefer, in setting it up in type, to use his ears in lieu of his eyes. He has other use for them. It would be even worthwhile to compel witnesses in court to speak directly into the phonograph, in order to thus obtain an unimpeachable record of their testimony.

The increased delicacy of the phonograph, which is in the near future, will enlarge this field rapidly. It may then include all the sayings of not only the witness, but the judge and the counsel. It will then also comprehend the utterances of public speakers.

Books.—Books may be read by the charitably inclined professional reader, or by such readers especially employed for that purpose, and the record of each book used in the asylums of the blind, hospitals, the sick-chamber, or even with great profit and amusement by the lady or gentleman whose eyes and hands may be otherwise employed; or, again, because of the greater enjoyment to be had from a book when read by an elocutionist than when read by the average reader. The ordinary record-sheet, repeating this book from fifty to a hundred times as it will, would command a price that would pay the original reader well for the slightly-increased difficulty in reading it aloud in the phonograph.

Educational Purposes.—As an elocutionary teacher, or as a primary teacher for children, it will certainly be invaluable. By it difficult passages may be correctly rendered for the pupil but once, after which he has only to apply to his phonograph for instructions. The child may thus learn to spell, commit to memory, a lesson set for it, etc., etc.

Music.—The phonograph will undoubtedly be liberally devoted to music. A song sung on the phonograph is reproduced with marvelous accuracy and power. Thus a friend may in a morning-call sing us a song which shall delight an evening company, etc. As a musical teacher it will be used to enable one to master a new air, the child to form its first songs, or to sing him to sleep.

Family Record.—For the purpose of preserving the sayings, the voices, and *the last words* of the dying member of the family—as of great men—the phonograph will unquestionably outrank the photograph. In the field of multiplication of original matrices, and the indefinite repetition of one and the same thing, the successful electrotyping of the original record is an essential. As this is a problem easy of solution, it properly ranks among the probabilities. It comprehends a vast field. The principal application of the phonograph in this direction is in the production of

Phonographic Books.—A book of 40,000 words upon a single metal plate ten inches square thus becomes a strong probability. The advantages of such books over those printed are too readily seen to need mention. Such books would be listened to where now none are read. They would preserve more than the mental emanations of the brain of the author; and, as a bequest to future generations, they would be unequaled. For the preservation of languages they would be invaluable.

Musical Boxes, Toys, etc.—The only element not absolutely assured, in the result of experiments thus far made, which stands in the way of a perfect reproduction at will of Adelina Patti's[2] voice in all its purity, is the single one of quality, and even that is not totally lacking, and will doubtless be wholly attained. If, however, it should not, the musical-box, or cabinet, of the present will be superseded by that which will give the voice and the words of the human songstress.

Toys.—A doll which may speak, sing, cry, or laugh may be safely promised our children for the Christmas holidays ensuing. Every species of animal or mechanical toy—such as locomotives, etc.—may be supplied with their natural and characteristic sounds.

Clocks.—The phonographic clock will tell you the hour of the day, call you to lunch, send your lover home at ten, etc.

Advertising, etc.—This class of phonographic work is so akin to the foregoing that it is only necessary to draw attention to it.

Speech and Other Utterances.—It will henceforth be possible to preserve for future generations the voices as well as the words of our Washingtons, our Lincolns, our Gladstones, etc., and to have them give us their present "greatest effort," in every town and hamlet in the country, upon our holidays.

Lastly, and in quite another direction, the phonograph will *perfect the telephone*, and revolutionize present *systems of telegraphy*. That useful invention is now restricted in its field of operation by reason of the fact that it is a means of communication which leaves no record of its transactions, thus restricting its use to simple conversational chit-chat, and such unimportant details of business as are not considered of sufficient importance to record. Were this different, and our telephone conversation automatically recorded, we should find the reverse of the present status of the telephone. It would be expressly resorted to as a means of perfect record. In writing our agreements we incorporate in the writing the summing up of our understanding—using entirely new and different phraseology from that which we used to express our understanding of the transaction in its discussion, and not infrequently thus begetting perfectly innocent causes of misunderstanding. Now, if the telephone, with the phonograph to record its sayings, were used in the preliminary discussion, we would not only have the full and correct text, but every word of the whole matter capable of throwing light upon the subject. Thus it would seem clear that the men would find it more advantageous to actually separate a half mile or so in order to discuss important business matters, than to discuss them verbally, and then make an awkward attempt to clothe their understanding in a new language. The logic which applies to transactions between two individuals in the same office applies with the greater force to two at a distance who must discuss the matter between them by the telegraph or mail. And this latter case, in turn, is reinforced by the demands of an economy of time and money at every mile of increase of distance between them.

"How can this application be made?" will probably be asked by those unfamiliar with either the telephone or phonograph.

Both these inventions cause a plate or disk to vibrate, and thus produce sound waves in harmony with those of the voice of the speaker. A very simple device may be made by which the one vibrating disk may be made to do duty for both the telephone and the phonograph, thus enabling the speaker to *simultaneously transmit and record his message.* What system of telegraphy can approach that? A similar combination at the distant end of the wire enables the correspondent, if he is present, *to hear it while it is being recorded.* Thus we have a mere passage of words for the action, but a complete and durable record of those words as the result of that action. Can economy of time or money go further than to annihilate time and space, and bottle up for posterity the mere utterance of man, without other effort on his part than to speak the words?

In order to make this adaptation, it is only requisite that the phonograph shall be made slightly more sensitive to record, and the telephone very slightly increased in the vibrating force of the receiver, and it is accomplished. Indeed the "Carbon Telephone," invented and perfected by the writer, will already well-nigh effect the record on the phonograph; and, as he is constantly improving upon it, to cause a more decided vibration of the plate of the receiver, this addition to the telephone may be looked for coincident with the other practical applications of the phonograph, and with almost equal certainty.

The telegraph company of the future—and that no distant one—will be simply an organization having a huge system of wires, central and sub-central stations, managed by skilled attendants, whose sole duty it will be to keep wires in proper repair, and give, by switch or shunt arrangement, prompt attention to subscriber no. 923 in New York, when he signals his desire to have private communication with subscriber no. 1001 in Boston, for three minutes. The minor and totally inconsequent details which seem to arise as obstacles in the eyes of the groove-traveling telegraph-man wedded to existing methods will wholly disappear before that remorseless Juggernaut—"the needs of man"; for will not the necessities of man surmount trifles in order to reap the full benefits of an invention which practically brings him face to face with whom he will; and, better still, doing the work of a conscientious and infallible scribe?

2. "The Phonograph"

New York Times, 7 November 1877, 4

The telephone was justly regarded as an ingenious invention when it was first brought before the public, but it is destined to be entirely eclipsed by the new invention of the phonograph. The former transmitted sound. The latter bottles it up for future use. The telephone can furnish us with Talmage's sermons[3] drawn directly from the wood, so to speak; but, with the aid of the phonograph, the same sermons can be stored away in the cellar, to be brought out years hence with their tones unimpaired by age, and their loudest yells as piercing and pervasive as ever. It may seem improbable that a hundred years hence people will be able to hear the voice of Wendell Phillips in the act of delivering an oration, but the phonograph will render it possible to preserve for any length of time the words and tones of any orator. It is unnecessary to explain the mechanical construction of the phonograph, but it may be said on general terms that if an orator empties his voice into the hopper of a phonograph, it will remain silent until some one sets a similar machine in motion, when the voice will instantly make itself audible, and will repeat in exact order the words of its former proprietor.

It is evident that this invention will lead to important changes in our social customs. The lecturer will no longer require his audience to meet him in a public hall, but will sell his lectures in quart bottles, at fifty cents each; and the politician, instead of howling himself hoarse on the platform, will have a pint of his best speech put into the hands of each one of his constituents. A large business will, of course, be done in bottled sermons, and many weak congregations which are unable to pay a regular Pastor will content themselves with publicly opening a bottle of "Dr. Tyng," "Dr. Crosby," or some other popular ministerial brand, but the practice of personal preaching will be continued, since in no other way can a weekly opportunity be afforded to ladies for mutual bonnet inspection.

Another result will doubtless be a large consumption of orators at public dinners and in the home circle. Whether a man has or has not a wine cellar, he will certainly, if he wishes to be regarded as a man of taste, have a well-stocked oratorical cellar. In stocking his cellar he will lay in several dozen of "Bob Ingersoll," or of "Senator Conkling," especially the celebrated Rochester vintage of the latter, for the use of those of his political friends who require strong stimulants. As a pleasant and palatable table orator, he will select dry "Mark Twain," or possibly "Beecher," although the latter has rather too much body. "Sparkling Cox," and "Effervescing Frothingham" would be appropriate for evening parties, and "George William Curtis" would unquestionably be very popular as a sweet and not too stimulating cordial. The connoisseur of orators will become in time as great a bore as the connoisseur of wines. He will be constantly saying to his guests "Try a little of that 'Anna Dickinson.' I fancy you will admit that it is very nice, though, perhaps, a little too dry for an uneducated taste. It cost me $48 a dozen, and is far superior to any 'Gail Hamilton' now in the market"; or, "I want you to give me your honest opinion of that 'Evarts.' I got a dozen of it at a bargain the other day, and I flatter myself that it is the genuine thing." The medical profession will prescribe orations instead of medical stimulants, and persons suffering from physical weakness will be told to take half a bottle of this or that orator at dinner, and a wine-glassful of "Ben. Butler" before going to bed. The use of bottled orators will, of course, be carried to excess by weak or vicious persons, and it is sad to think to what wrecks men and women will reduce themselves by consuming, say three or four bottles of "Holland" or "Talmage" daily. This, in its turn, will lead to the formation of temperance societies, the aim of which will be to pass a prohibitory law forbidding the sale of all varieties of bottled orators, and making no distinction between the pernicious "Citizen Swinton" and the mild and innocuous "Hayes." Whether bottled orations can be adulterated by unprincipled dealers remains to be seen, but we may be sure that, if adulteration is practicable, it will be as difficult to buy a dozen of any pure native or foreign orator as it is to buy any pure champagne or madeira.

There is good reason to believe that if the phonograph proves to be what its inventor claims that it is, both book making and reading will fall into disuse. Why should we print a speech when it can be bottled, and why should we learn to read when, if some skillful elocutionist merely repeats one of "George Eliot's" novels aloud in the presence of a phonograph, we can subsequently listen to it without taking the slightest trouble? We shall be able to buy Dickens and Thackeray by the single bottle or by the dozen, and rural families can lay in a hogshead of "Timothy Titcomb" every Fall for consumption during the Winter. Instead of libraries filled with combustible books, we shall have vast storehouses of bottled authors, and though students in college may be required to learn the use of books, just as they now learn the dead languages, they will not be expected to make any practical use of the study. Blessed will be the lot of the small boy of the future. He will never have to learn his letters or to wrestle with the spelling-book, and if he does not revere the name of the inventor of the phonograph, he will be utterly destitute of all gratitude.

3. Philip G. Hubert Jr., "What the Phonograph Will Do for Music and Music-Lovers"

Century Magazine, May 1893, 152–54

Looking at the phonograph from the point of view of a person professionally interested in music, I cannot see room for doubting the tremendous role which this extraordinary invention is to play in the future of music and musicians. Few people seem to realize that the phonograph, even in its present stage—which is admitted to be one of imperfection as compared with what may be expected before many years have passed—has really title to be called a musical instrument. My own skill with the phonograph is certainly not that of an expert, and yet I get no little enjoyment from the dance-music and the operatic fantasias which it reels off in the evening for the amusement of the family, which people less pampered than I am in the matter of music are filled with enthusiasm over its performances. It is really music, and not a mere suggestion of music. The different instruments employed are perfectly distinct, while the time is of course perfect. Taking, for instance, a chord of the piano, not only are the notes of the chord heard, but the after-vibrations, lasting for several seconds. When a small funnel is used to magnify the sound, every person in a large room can hear distinctly, and the music is almost loud enough to be used for dancing. In one of the phonograms, as the wax cylinders are called, the rounds of applause, the hand-clapping, the pounding of canes upon the floor, which followed the spirited performance of a popular melody at Mr. Edison's Orange laboratory,[4] have been allowed to appear, making most people start with amazement as, after the last chords have died away, come these sharp cries of "Bravo!" and the confused rattle of the applause from the audience.

Such being the case—and every musician familiar with the musical doings of the phonograph will admit that the foregoing is a moderate statement—what may the phonograph, as a music-maker and -teacher, not do for the world? Bear in mind that these phonograms do not deteriorate by constant use, the same music coming out the hundredth time as perfectly as the first;[5] also that, by the duplication through a special electrotyping process, facsimiles of a good phonogram can be made in large numbers at almost nominal cost. If each phonogram turned out required the actual performance of music for its production, the output would be restricted and costly; it would be like setting anew the type for every copy of a book. Again, if the phonogram could be used only a few times, as was the case with the zinc-foil sheets used in the crude form of the instrument, the apparatus would remain a toy for the rich. Conceding its power of musical reproduction by means of wax cylinders, which are both cheap and lasting, the imagination may run riot without exhausting the field opened before one. Besides giving musical pleasure past present computation to the million, it will do wonders for the musician. First, it will offer the composer a means of indicating his wishes concerning time and expression compared with which the metronome and all printed directions and expression-marks of the present are but the clumsiest of makeshifts. Secondly, it will become a great teacher of music, as even the phonographic echo of the piano, of singing, or of orchestral work, will be sufficient to furnish pupils with precise models. In the third place, it offers a means for solving tone problems too delicate for the powers of the human ear, and heretofore beyond solution.

At Herr von Bülow's farewell concert in this country, two years ago, a phonograph was employed to make a record of the whole concert, and particular care was taken with Beethoven's symphony, the "Eroica."[6] The learned conductor left the country before the phonograms, the results of the evening's work, could be prepared for his hearing, but these results surprised and delighted a host of musical experts. Musicians of repute have confessed to me that, whereas they had looked upon the stories concerning the phonograph's musical achievements with incredulity, what they heard far surpassed the promises made by the advocates of the invention, and showed possibilities for the device as a help to the musician of the future which would set every musician a-dreaming. It may be granted without discussion that the phonographic record of our music will give for all future time the exact wishes of our composers and performers with regard to *tempi*, shades of expression, phrasing, dynamic gradations, and all the niceties of the interpretation which no written marks, however minute, can begin to convey. The metronome has until now been the only means of marking the time or pace at which a composition is intended to be played by the composer. As contrasted with the phonographic guide to correct time, it is crude enough. The worst phonograph will at least give a faithful record of the exact time of a piece, and for every bar—in fact, the exact length of every note in the score. The experiments made with the records of piano-playing show that, so far as accuracy is concerned, no limit can be placed upon its possibilities as an echo. Every minute change of time, every shade of expression, is heard in the echo as plainly as in the original. It is no exaggeration to say that an expert can distinguish between the playing of two pianists as reproduced in the phonograph.

There are certain things about piano-playing—indeed, about all musical performances—that cannot be taught. Pianists, violinists, and singers are apt to surpass themselves under certain conditions, due perhaps to the applause of a great audience, perhaps to peculiar personal conditions favorable to artistic expression. Effects are produced which escape analysis, and cannot be reproduced at will or for the benefit of pupils. The artist may not ever be able to do again what has been done once, and the exact elements or constituents of an effect are lost. The niceties of phrasing cannot be indicated by written marks; they must be left to the musical instinct or intelligence of the singer or player: yet expressive phrasing constitutes an important element of all fine musical work. The half-dozen notes of a bar may each one have a different length and different power, and yet be all alike on paper. If we can obtain at a trifling cost a perfect echo of any musical performance, it is highly probable that, when the phonograph is found in every house, a phonographic version of every piece of music will accompany the printed sheet. The latter will give the actual notes, while the phonogram will give the reading of some great player. Or, perhaps, inasmuch as the phonograms can be reproduced for almost nothing, the readings of half a dozen artists will follow the printed page. For instance, the music-shops might sell with Beethoven's pianoforte concertos the phonographic readings for the same concertos by [Anton] Rubinstein, [Hans von] Bülow, and [Camille] Saint-Saëns. The whole need not cost more than a few cents, so far as the phonograms are concerned.

Some persons have expressed a fear lest the wide distribution of an apparatus capable of echoing all sorts of music, in a more perfect fashion than any music-box, might lead to the gradual extinction of piano-playing or violin-playing except for purposes of public exhibition, the phonographic echo of some great performer's work being so much superior to what most people could hope to accomplish. It seems to me that the contrary would be the result. Cheap phonographs, giving more or less perfect echoes of music, might make superfluous the painful attempts—painful to others as well as to herself—of the unmusical young woman to master impossibilities. To the person of real musical instinct and capacity, the wealth of good music would certainly prove an incentive. When the phonograph goes everywhere, and phonographic music is cheap, the housewife can listen to Rubinstein as she darns the stockings in the evening, and get superb lessons at the great fountains of musical art, if she has any taste that way. There is no reason to suppose that it will be any more difficult to record a performance of [Richard Wagner's] "Die Meistersinger" than a recitation by [the French actor Benoît-Constant] Coquelin, or a Beethoven symphony under Bülow's baton. There is a good time coming for the poor man of good taste.

An interesting question, perhaps to be solved by means of the phonograph, concerns the differences between a good and a bad performance, whether of a piano piece or of an opera. It has often been remarked that a particular performance "would not go." In the case of a soloist's work, failure to produce the desired effect might be attributed to the shortcomings of the soloist. But operas and plays sometimes fail signally when, according to all rules, they ought to succeed. Every music-lover will remember certain performances which ought to have been superb, but were nothing of the kind. Operagoers of the city of New York will be pretty sure to cite the memorable performance of [Charles Gounod's opera] "Faust" which opened the Metropolitan Opera-House in the autumn of 1883—memorable because of its bitter disappointments. A faithful phonographic record of that performance contrasted with a record of some of the succeeding successful performances of "Faust" by the same artists might disclose interesting features. It might show that success, or artistic effect, lay in taking one part of this chorus a trifle slower and another part a trifle faster, in emphasizing the bass part here or the soprano part there.

A few years ago there was a performance of Wagner's "Tristan and Isolde" that was also curiously ineffective. The opera had already been given half a dozen times that season with remarkable success; it was the musical achievement of the winter. A repetition was announced for the last night of the year, and the house was well filled. The singers were those who had already made so great a success in Wagner's masterpiece—Fräuleins [Lilli] Lehmann and [Marianne] Brandt, Herren [Albert] Niemann, [Emil] Fischer, and [Adolf] Robinson. The conductor was Herr [Anton] Seidl. Yet long before the evening was over people wondered what the matter was. It may be suspected that the audience was tired out with Christmas shopping, and that the singers, finding no response to their efforts, grew discouraged and careless; the anti-Wagnerite may hint that after six performances of "Tristan," the long-suffering public turned upon its persecutors. But every one cannot have been tired out that New Year's eve. Every one's dinner cannot have gone wrong. Whatever the cause, whether the trouble was in the auditors or the performance, Herr Seidl was thoroughly discontented with the results, and one devoted Wagnerite, who had been known to rave over "Tristan" by the hour, said to me as we passed out of the Opera-House, "I feel as if I do not care to hear 'Tristan' again for the next ten years." A fortnight later there was another performance of "Tristan," which was as conspicuous for success as the one just mentioned had been for failure. A careful comparison of the phonographic records of these two performances might have shown wherein the fault lay. As the sublime is very near the ridiculous, so the impressive performance may be very near the dismal failure—only the phonograph, with its minute and faithful record, faithful beyond the power of human perceptions, can tell us how near.

The phonograph as a musical educator offers encouragement to the composer. His work, if it has value, will be known to millions where now it is known to thousands, and it will not take a generation for its worth to be recognized. It was not until twenty years after the production of "Tristan" that we New-Yorkers were enabled to hear its wondrous beauties; and the masterwork of the high priest of musical art, Wagner's "Nibelung" trilogy,[7] was not heard here until more than ten years after all musical Europe had been ringing with it. In a very few years I fully expect to receive from Europe not only written accounts of the new operas of Berlin, Vienna, and Paris, but phonograms enabling me to hear them from end to end. As the wide distribution of literature which followed the cheap books of modern times has helped the author to a living income, so this wide distribution of music through the phonograph will probably do the same thing for the composer of good music. Then the future Wagner may perhaps receive as much for the composition of a music-drama as the author of another "Silver Threads Among the Gold"[8] gets for his gibberish—which has not been the way in our day.

The Listener and the Phonograph

Learning to Listen

4. Edison Realism Test
Broadside, c. 1916

EDISON REALISM TEST

1. State what kind of voice (soprano, tenor, etc.,) or kind of musical instrument you wish to hear.
2. Sit with your back to the instrument.
3. Spend two minutes looking through the scrapbook[9] which will be handed to you by demonstrator.
4. Then select one of the clippings at random and read it carefully.
5. Having read the clipping, recall the last time you heard the kind of voice or instrument which you have asked to hear. Picture the scene. When it is clearly in your mind, say to the demonstrator, "I am ready."
6. About forty-five seconds after the music begins, close your eyes and keep them closed for a minute or more. Then open your eyes for fifteen seconds but do not gaze at your surroundings. After this, close your eyes again and keep them closed until the end of the selection.

Result You should get the same emotional reaction experienced when you last heard the same kind of voice or instrument.

If you do not obtain this reaction at the first test, it is due to the fact that you have not wholly shaken off the influence of your surroundings. In that case you should repeat the test until you are no longer influenced by your surroundings.

5. "Illustrated Song Machine"

Talking Machine World, October 1905, 33

The new illustrated song machine of the Rosenfield Manufacturing Co. is bound to meet with great success and be widely sought after by all the parlors in the country, for it is just what the public has wanted since the first automatic machine was placed on the market, and the listener drew a mind's picture as the words and music were repeated to him. This and more is accomplished by the machine, for as the song progresses, each phrase is illustrated by beautiful reproductions in transparent colors, with all the delicate shadow of nature. The whole is gotten up with great taste and will be from every standpoint an attraction well worthy of consideration.

"Illustrated Song Machine"

Talking Machine World, November 1905, 33

One of the greatest marvels of the age is the illustrated song machine manufactured by Rosenfield Manufacturing Co., of New York, which is winning its way into a large measure of favor for arcades, cafes and all public places. An idea for the demand of these instruments may be estimated from the fact that over two thousand are already in use. They have proven tremendously popular, and the reason is obvious. The combination of beautiful illustrations which tell the story of the song, makes a valuable adjunct to the song itself. And this is what the machine does. The most delicate shades of nature are shown in the reproductions, and the entire forms one of the most attractive specialties placed on the market in many a day. In New York the Surprise Vaudeville Co., the People's Vaudeville Co., the Auditorium, the Decomo Co., and others handle hundreds of them, and as it is in New York, so is it elsewhere. To operate this machine a storage battery is not necessary. By simply connecting this machine to an electric lighting circuit the machine is ready for operation. It is generally conceded that it is one of the greatest money makers ever placed on the market and is worthy of investigation.

6. Orlo Williams, "Times and Seasons"

Gramophone, June 1923, 38–39

Since it may be assumed in these days that nearly everybody has a gramophone, there is some point in speculating a little upon the morals and decencies, the times and seasons, for gramophoning. The instrument, of course, will lend itself to almost any vagary. One man might keep it in his bedroom and turn it on as he leapt from his couch to drown the singing of the matutinal lark, and another might prefer to keep it in the bathroom to discourage his own tendency to sing while sponging. But to illustrate as strongly as possible that moralities and decencies *are* involved I have only to propound the question—should one play the gramophone immediately after breakfast?

Here, I think, we touch one of the ingrained superstitions of the Englishman, that music, except for the purpose of scales and exercises, is not decent at such an early hour of the day. Yet the idea has probably grown, not from the indecency, but from the impossibility, of such diversions for the worker. With outward horror, but with secret envy, let us imagine a man so unfortunate as to be wealthy, unambitious, unencumbered, comfortable and provided with a gramophone. He comes down to breakfast at half-past nine: he skims the headlines of his paper over the kidneys and reads the feuilleton over his marmalade. Then, if I am right, he lights a large but mild cigar, sinks into an armchair, and rings for the butler to set the gramophone going. "My dear fellow . . ." you say in expostulation, "how absurd . . . how could anybody . . . I mean . . . can't you see?" I apologise. Imagination, yours at any rate, boggles at the thought: yet what I see in all alluring clearness, is a gentleman tastefully attired, smoking in an easy but not too soft a chair, while at ten o'clock on a sunny morning, he listens to the voice of [opera singer Enrico] Caruso issuing from a little cupboard in a mahogany cabinet. The villain! The *embusqué!* The renegade! But there he is, and I cannot for the life of me see what is to prevent a sufficiently lazy and independently minded man from being in this enviable position. There is a passage in one of Baron Corvo's books which describes how he hired a band of Italian musicians to play him an *aubade* while he ate a breakfast of fruits in his Italian villa. You say "how charming!" when you read it, not observing the Baron's bad taste in choosing an air of [Pyotr Ilich] Tschaikowsky's for such a place and occasion: yet you would condemn an English gentleman, who cannot so easily hire serenaders, from giving himself a similar pleasure after his eggs and bacon. "Pho!" you will exclaim. "Wotherspoon. The sort of feller who plays the gramophone after breakfast!" Your audience will understand what you mean, and Wotherspoon's reputation will be gone forever. But I praise Wotherspoon, if such a man exist, and pray that he may continue to play the gramophone after breakfast to show how little, in a philosopher's estimation, public opinion is to be valued.

Again, to show how ridiculous our inhibitions are, let me ask what you would say, if, on visiting a lady or gentleman, you found her or him solitary, listening to the music of his own gramophone. You would think it odd, would you not? You would endeavour to dissemble your surprise; you would look twice to see whether some other person were not hidden in some corner of the room, and if you found no such one would painfully blush, as if you had discovered your friend sniffing cocaine, emptying a bottle of whisky, or plaiting straws in his hair. People, we think, should not do things "to themselves," however much they may enjoy doing them in company: they may not even talk to themselves without incurring grave suspicion. And I fear that if I were discovered listening to the Fifth Symphony [of Beethoven] without a chaperon to guarantee my sanity, my friends would fall away with grievous shaking of the head. But, when science and enterprise have put so much pleasure within our reach as a gramophone and a selection of good records will give, you will find it hard to convince me by logic, or mere vociferation, that music in solitude is indecent. If I may read alone, I may turn on the gramophone alone: for a record is but another book, and why must I have company to enjoy it? Two persons, I admit, is the ideal number: but my reason for this opinion is no higher one than a distaste for winding up and changing the needles myself.

And so, in the matter of gramophones, let us try to free ourselves from these trammels of convention, which would confine the use of the gramophone to the first half hour of after dinner plethora. There is music to be had for all times and seasons. I would turn on something hopeful after breakfast like the minuet from Mozart's Symphony in E flat, or a madrigal by the English Singers; after tea I would be ruminative and romantic with a chamber concert of strings or Gervase Elwes singing the *Shropshire Lad* with his rich English quality. Caruso, [Amelita] Galli-Curci and the rest will be for the last hours of the day when the mind is lazily receptive. And then, sometimes for a week or more, the machine shall be silent, so that I may come fresh to my records and find new pleasures in them. Yes, one may as well be intelligent. Your gramophone is not a toy, and will use you as you use it. The perfect gramophonist has imagination. He knows no stereotyped times and seasons, but when the spirit says "Now," he seizes the minute and knows what record will be the magic interpreter of his mood, whether it be spring-like among daffodils, while the kettle's boiling, or autumnal and brooding under a harvest moon; whereas some will put on the Scherzo of [Felix Mendelssohn's] the *Midsummer Night's Dream* after a beefsteak pudding. Times and seasons matter, indeed, but in a deeper sense.

The Phonograph in Everyday Life

7. *How We Gave a Phonograph Party*
New York: National Phonograph Company, 1899

It was Charlotte's plan. The idea struck her suddenly (they always do come to her that way) during an evening we were spending over at the Openeer's. Young Mrs. Openeer had asked us to dine with them and play whist; but after dinner Mr. Openeer started one of his Phonographs so that we could hear an opera we had been talking about, and cards were entirely forgotten. It was delightful. They had lots of the wax records — almost a complete score of the opera in question. The talk naturally turned on how it was all done, for it seemed perfectly wonderful. So he showed us all about it, and that's how Charlotte's inspiration came.

"I have it, I have it," she whispered excitedly the moment we left the house, and she almost pushed me down the steps in her eagerness. "We will give a Phonograph Party, and it will be the newest and most delightful thing out," and she straightway unfolded the whole scheme as we crossed the street to our house. By the time we had climbed up to our room the schedule was complete. I must say that Charlotte is a quick and ready thinker. Her plan was fine. You see, she teaches mathematics in the high school, while I have only a kindergarten class. She thought the idea and I completed the practical arrangements; and between us we planned an entertainment which I am sure will be long remembered by our friends as a very happy evening.

We sent out our invitations the very next day, for Wednesday evening of the following week. To Beverly Dunlap's we added a line "Bring your Cornet." To Alice Blank's "Please bring your Banjo" postscript and Nat Browton's a "clarinet" item. Charlotte had a violin and I a guitar, which, with the piano (fortunately an upright), would give a variety of instrumental music for the occasion. In each of the other notes, we wrote the mystifying words, "Please bring your voice."

To Mr. and Mrs. Openeer's invitation Charlotte insisted on adding (as a matter of form only she explained to me), "Please bring your Phonographs"; for we had already enlisted their cooperation, and Mr. Openeer had entered into our plan with enthusiasm. He loaned us not one, but two Phonographs "for convenience sake" said he, "one for recording and one for reproducing. Saves the bother of changing speakers and horns." He also insisted on furnishing us with a plentiful supply of smooth wax cylinders or blanks as they are called; at the same time offering us his services as an expert should we need him.

The next few days saw us busy at every spare moment. First we tried and experimented in every possible way with the Phonograph, making record after record, until we found out just how to do it. It's wonderfully simple if you only know how—(like everything else in this world for that matter). Mr. Openeer offered to teach us, but we wanted to find out all by ourselves; and we did very nicely by following the printed instructions which he furnished us. Then we had refreshments to prepare. Charlotte gave way to my ideas in this matter, and my kindergarten training suggested that we get some jelly glasses that were just the right size, two and a half inches across and four inches deep. Into these we packed our ice cream after we made it, so that each guest should have a "frozen record" just like that great fib of Baron Munchausen's.[10] We also made ginger snaps in the shape of a [phonograph] horn, by fashioning a cake cutter out of a strip of tin. All our plans matured beautifully, except that Charlotte scorched two whole pans of ginger snaps, and let some salt get into the ice cream tins; Charlotte was never good at those things.

Every one of our guests came on Wednesday evening; every one of them as curious as an original Eve (or Adam) and every one of them delighted on learning what was in prospect. We commenced right away with the cornet. It makes a fine loud record, and we wanted to start off auspiciously. We had placed our Recording Phonograph high up on a small table on top of a larger table, so that the horn was about on a level with Mr. Dunlap's head, as he stood ready to play. The shape of the horn too, makes some little difference. Mr. Openeer loaned us his recording horn for our party. It was fully two feet long and shaped with a cone. It had no flare or bell on the end, which was about 6 or 7 inches across. Our equipment was really quite perfect. The second Phonograph stood on one end of the large table and was fitted with a reproducing diaphragm or speaker as they call it. It also had a small fourteen-inch bell shaped horn, which shape seems to spread the sound better than the other. I attended to the machine, put on a new blank and started it, while Charlotte started each performer. At the close of each record taking, I stopped the machine, took off the record and put it on the reproducing Phonograph, and we all heard what had just been played into the other machine, reproduced with startling and marvelous exactness.

I will say right here that a single Phonograph with two speakers and a bell-shaped horn would have been all that was absolutely necessary. The only advantage of having two Phonographs was that it saved the delay (a very small matter) of changing the recording speaker for the reproducer after each record was made.

As directed by Charlotte, Mr. Dunlap stood about 5 feet away, and played directly into the horn. He gave a short aria from [William Vincent Wallace's opera] "Maritana," playing it with considerable volume and with even, well sustained notes, with but little attempt at expression. He used only half his record in a minute and a half, so Charlotte whispered, "Do you know any bugle calls?" (Dunlap was in camp at Jacksonville all through the war.) His laughing answer "Do I know any bugle calls by heart? Well rather!" made us all laugh too. It was wonderful the way he made his cornet fairly talk.

> I can't get 'em up
> I can't get 'em up
> I can't get 'em up
> In the morning.

His attempt ended in a storm of applause, which was repeated a few minutes later when I changed his record to the other Phonograph and reproduced it. First came the aria, loud and clear and distinct. Then a pause of a few seconds. Then a big manly voice said, "Do I know any bugle calls by heart? Well rather!" How we all shouted! It did sound so funny. Then came his bugle call and a faint clapping of hands and then our real applause. Our first record was a success!

Then Nat Browton played his clarinet; and the reproduction was so perfect that we could actually hear his breathing. Those quick little gasps for breath that I for one had never particularly noticed, until the reproduction of the record called it to my attention. He played directly into the horn, and as close to it as he could.

Then we had several vocal solos. Each singer stood close to the horn, with the face almost within the opening. Charlotte cautioned them all to sing rather loud and be particularly careful to draw back the head while taking any high notes. Our bass and baritone artists made highly successful records. Our tenor sang "The Holy City" most beautifully, but his voice lacked that peculiar quality necessary for Phonograph record making. The tones of his voice were like the invisible rays of the spectrum beyond the violet; it seemed impossible to record them. Charlotte discoursed learnedly about the number of vibrations per second caused by his high C—about a thousand I think she said.

Mr. Openeer lessened his discomfiture by remarking that a Phonograph tenor was an exceedingly rare phenomenon. "As rare as a Phonograph soprano" he added bowing to Mrs. Openeer who was our next performer, "and although my wife has a beautiful voice I have never yet taken a really good record of it."

We made a passably fair record of Mrs. Openeer's fine soprano voice by draping the opening of the horn with mosquito netting; but it wasn't real good and we had to put it in the same class with the tenor's; and also with Charlotte's violin record, which came next on the programme. The amateur will do well to avoid the sorrow that is almost inevitable in attempting to make a record of a high tenor, a soprano or a violin.

The most effective records we made during the entire evening were two chorus records. All stood close together in a bunch about three feet from the horn and sang "Marching through Georgia" and it came out fine. Our success led us to try another "Onward Christian Soldiers" and it was every bit as good. The piano accompaniments of all our records were very good indeed. In every case the piano stood about three feet distant, with its open back towards the Phonograph. A square or a grand piano is not so well adapted for this accompaniment work, although a solo may be recorded very nicely by bringing the horn close up to the raised cover of the instrument.

We now removed our recording Phonograph from its lofty perch, to accommodate our banjoists and also those of our guests who were to make talking records, and preferred to sit rather than stand. The banjo should be played as close to the horn as is possible. We made several capital records, so loud and natural as to tone quality that I would defy anyone listening with eyes shut or in the next room to tell the difference.

The talking records were mostly all good too. The performers were cautioned to speak very distinctly, sounding the S's and soft C's with particular emphasis. Some of them caused lots of merriment when they were reproduced, owing to the funny and irrelevant side remarks of the speakers; most of whom had never talked into a Phonograph, and seemed to forget that the machine would catch and repeat all that was said.

Last of all came the ginger snap horns and the "frozen records." The tenor declared that these were the best of all. He may have been perfectly honest, (for they were real good) or it may have been gross flattery; or yet again his failure may have made him a little jealous of the others. But, somehow, I didn't exactly like his remark. I think on the whole, while perfectly polite and courteous to Charlotte and me, his hostesses, what he said simply proved the proverb, "the way to a man's heart is through his stomach"; for the rest of us unanimously agreed, not even counting in our "frozen records," that our Phonograph Party had been a grand success.

8. Jas O'Dea, Arthur Gillespie, and Herbert Dillea, "Susan, Dear Sue (The Phonograph Song)"

New York: Witmark, 1901

She was an artful typewriter,
He was her boss and in love;
Oft-times he used to delight her
Calling her dearie and dove;
Once with a phonograph near her,
Set to record all he'd say,
With graces that made him revere her,
She caused him to plead in this way:

CHORUS
Sue, Sue, Susan, dear Sue;
I'm in love dear, with you;
Your name, Susan, won't do;
Link it with mine, dear, forever.
When you're typing away
On my heartstrings you play
Be mine, dear, from today
And I will part from you never.

Soon that sweet courtship made weary,
He who had sworn to be true;
And when he went back on dearie,
Susan, dear Susie, did Sue
Artful Sue got all she sued for,
When as a witness in court
She brought on the phonograph record,
And here's what it had to report:

CHORUS
Sue, Sue, Susan, dear Sue;
I'm in love dear, with you;
Your name, Susan, won't do;
Link it with mine, dear, forever.
When you're typing away
On my heartstrings you play
Be mine, dear, from today
And I will part from you never.

9. Pauline Partridge, "The Home Set to Music"

Sunset, November 1924, 68, 75–76

In the days of the Brussels carpet and the kerosene lamp, the parlor stove and the patent rocker, music was a solemn formality, usually undertaken upon occasions of importance only and led up to by hours of trembling preparation on the part of the performer. Music in those years of innocence was a matter of long and sometimes unwilling training, and naturally the range of "selections" was limited.

Then along came the phonograph, or "talking machine," crowding the half-hearted amateur from the parlor floor perhaps, but putting music, real music, good music, into the American home for the first time in history.

The old argument against mechanical music is swept aside and silenced forever by the answer, forestalling further criticism, that mechanical music is music perfectly produced, whether it be vocal or instrumental. Your neighbor's choice may not be yours, and the fault, if it be a fault, may lie in the taste of the individual, but of its kind, whether it is the banjo or a quartette, it is the best that artistic talent and modern manufacture working together can produce.

The gracious response of the phonograph is untiring. No cajolery is necessary to persuade it to give of its richest treasure, it is never temperamental, needs no thanks, wishes no praise.

It will run for hours on end for dancing, keeping perfect, unvarying time, and in the rests between dances turn from jazz to opera with no comments or apologies for either.

The home has many moods from grave to gay and music must suit them all if it is to mean what it should. The older generation prefers the songs of its youth, and it is easy to slip back across the years with the notes of the old-time songs on the modern instruments. Familiar and well-loved hymns are here too; for Christmas, the splendid carols, "Oh, Little Town of Bethlehem," "Holy Night," "While Shepherds Watched their Flocks by Night," all beautifully done by voices that give the sweet old words new tenderness and feeling.

The home is many sided and not the least important angle from which it should be considered is its influence upon family and community life. Dancing, one of the most healthful and joyous of diversions if properly indulged in, has been to a great extent reclaimed from the public dance hall and returned to the home through the accessibility of good music. An informal dancing party can be given with no preparation more difficult than rolling up the rugs and calling in the neighbors, while the best orchestras in the world, Paul Whiteman's, Art

Hickman's, [Zez] Confrey's, and [Frank] McKee's, are on call with their sweeping, caressing, imperative music that will not be denied until every foot is tapping and every body swaying with the rhythm. Music like this binds the family together through its shared pleasures, and a strongly united family is one that talks the same language when it comes to fun and relaxation.

An education in music has quite a different interpretation today from its meaning twenty-five years ago. An ability to play a musical instrument depends on inherent talent, combined with opportunity, desire, perseverance and ambition. On the other hand a very thorough knowledge of the best in music is possible to every person, to every home. A familiarity with the operas, at least with the well-known arias so that they are recognizable when heard, is easily achieved and well repays the effort—if it is an effort.

The centers where opera is given are not many, widely scattered across a continent, accessible to a comparative and fortunate few, but the same music by the same artists with the same orchestras accompanying them may be heard in the most isolated homes at the most remote points.

It is an unforgettable experience to have heard [Enrico] Caruso in opera, but it is an experience that cannot now be repeated. Yet Caruso will live for succeeding generations through the records of his singing preserved in all its full golden beauty, its tenderness and passion.

Not to know Wagner is overlooking one of the great influences on opera. The majestic "Pilgrims' Chorus" from "Tannhauser," the "Fire Music" from "Walkure," "Elsa's Dream" from "Lohengrin" and the "Swan Song," that poignant despairing cry of the human heart, give some small idea of the grandeur and glory of his music.

Right here is the place to add a recipe which is as valuable esthetically as any of those on the opposite page are materially. Take the occasion of the first open fire of the season on the hearth of the home you have set to music. Light the fire and allow it to burn until the clear flames are leaping. Of course, if you have some driftwood powder it may be added for good measure but it is not essential. Put the "Fire Music" record on the phonograph and put out all lights in the room. Sit in the firelight and watch the flames while the record is played. Observe how the flames keep time to the music. Apparently they are dancing to its rhythm. Until you have tried this recipe you can have no adequate understanding of what Wagner accomplished in this particular composition. Of course the result is also excellent when the recipe is tried out of doors, with a portable phonograph and a campfire.

In the lighter French and Italian operatic music the exquisite "Depuis Le

Jour" from [Gustave Charpentier's] "Louise," the passionate tenderness of "My Heart at Thy Sweet Voice" from [Camille Saint-Saëns's] "Samson and Delilah," the Prologue to [Ruggero Leoncavallo's] "Pagliacci," are only a scattered few of the hundreds of selections that are gradually becoming familiar to modern America.

But a broad knowledge of music does not confine itself to the opera. By means of the phonograph any instrument can be brought into the home and the ear trained to a perfect interpretation while the senses are delighted.

There are other uses for the talking machine where it does indeed talk: physical exercises for developing a healthy beautiful body put to music and languages taught through the ear, undoubtedly an excellent method; but its greatest service lies in taking into the average home the great music of the world—and leaving it there.

This service of the phonograph in the home has been greatly reinforced by the development of the radio. In the first stages of radio programs, phonograph records were used but these were soon abandoned because the listeners-in often had the records available in the home and the copyright element entered, beside. Direct production was demanded. Original programs, direct from musicians, are now a feature of the activities of broadcasting stations. There is connection by direct wire with hotel dance orchestras, too, and it is possible, by means of the loud speaker, to dance at home to elaborate jazz emanations from over the hills and far away. If the radio program does not happen to fit your dance program, the phonograph is always the handmaid to the dance impulse, serving at a moment's notice. Between the two, the worship of Terpsichore is secure.

The radio merely reinforces, it does not displace the phonograph, any more than the motion picture or the lecturer displaces the library. We enjoy the ingenious setting of the film and we rejoice also in a finely illustrated travel book or in rereading one of the great stories by a favorite author. The book and the record make up the library of the modern home. Indeed, the record takes the place of the printed music which perhaps nobody in the household could play. Added to the delight of listening to the direct word or musical note by radio there is the satisfaction of possession, the ability to command at will the words or the music best beloved, the power of encore, you might say. And furthermore the phonograph remains entrenched against displacement because there are heights to which the radio can never aspire while the "box office," sordid fact of life, continues to appeal to the creative and artistic talent of the world. The motion-picture drama is a form of limited broadcast but it rests upon the box office. There is no ticket-window, however, to "the desert and illimitable air." Copyrights and royalties are far more difficult to navigate upon the ether waves. Therefore, even while they are living and in the pride of their performance, the great ones of the musical world must still be sought out through the box office or secured for private entertainment in the home through payment of royalty on the individual record. And afterward, of course, when their actual performance is hushed forever, the echoes of their music will still come from the phonograph. So far as we can now foresee, these echoes will not come by radio. There have been many persons who have delivered literary compositions purporting to be such echoes from great authors but we have never heard of any who delivered music in this manner.

All of which is diverting speculation. The facts at hand are marvelous enough. By phonograph and radio our homes are set to music; the music of the present, ephemeral perhaps but tingling with the spirit of the moment; the music of the past, the deathless portion of it, preserved for all time.

10. Thomas A. Edison, Inc., questionnaire and responses, 1921
Collection of the University of Michigan Libraries, Ann Arbor

LABORATORIES OF

THOMAS A. EDISON

ORANGE, NEW JERSEY

Will you do this?

It will take, perhaps, fifteen minutes of your time.

I have no right to ask you to do so—but you are a music lover, and I believe you will spare the time.

We want to learn the favorite tunes of twenty thousand representative people, who own New Edisons.

Please tell us your real honest to goodness favorites. I want to record them for you, if they have not already been recorded.

Tell us just what tunes you like best, and if possible, tell us why.

There are spaces below for twenty tunes. Give us your favorites in the order of your preference.

A stamped and addressed envelope is enclosed for your reply. May I not hear from you promptly?

THOMAS A. EDISON.

Mr. Edison:

The following are my favorite tunes:

NAME OF TUNE / Have we recorded it? / Have you a RE-CREATION[11] of it? / What is the number of the RE-CREATION? / WHY DO YOU LIKE THE TUNE?

[Excerpts from the survey responses follow, along with tables listing the first five songs the respondents mentioned.]

. . . . .

[V. W. Benedict[12]
Iron Mountain, Wyoming
11 January 1921]

I have one of your $265[13] Diamond Disc [phonographs] and have not heard anything that can compare with it in volume of sound and tone. I have about fifty of your Re-Creations and want more. We are out in the mountains here 40 miles north of Cheyenne living in box cars. But our train men and others admit the New Edison sure has a soul.

. . . . .

Excerpt from survey response by V. W. Benedict

NAME OF TUNE	Have we recorded it?	Have you a RE-CREATION of it?	What is the number of the RE-CREATION?	WHY DO YOU LIKE THE TUNE?
Finnegans Jambori*	Yes/cylinder	No	Don't know	Humorous
Turkey in [the] Straw	—	—	50605	—
Dixie-Medley-Banjo	—	—	50195	Very fond of old melodies
Arkansaw [*sic*] Traveler	—	—	50195	Humorous
[Arkansas Traveler] Returns	—	—	—	—

* I.e., "Down at Finnegan's Jamboree." This was not a music record per se, but a vaudeville sketch that included music.

[Phillip S. Gibbons
Milton, Oregon
21 February 1921]

It is only fair to say that in selecting over 140 records for our Edison we have, with the above [listed songs] taken on some jazz[,] some of the so-called higher class instrumental music, some fox-trots and more or less of the new war tunes and still newer song hits which to our mind are in a good many cases misses. We have acquired quite a few that are not occupying much of our time[,] for instance Old Bill Bailey, and Cupids In The Briny[;] the singer is good but the subject is suggestive and to our mind is unfit where there are children in the home. What few we have of the so called higher class records have been played extensively, and we have done our darndest [to] learn to like them and sometimes some of our more highly advanced relatives drop in and go into spasms of joy on hearing them and discourse learnedly about them but we are afraid we will never properly appreciate them for instance whenever we hear Mr. Spalding,[14] it makes us feel uneasy, we feel as if he may bust something before he gets done, and the arias or whatever you call them that your higher class singers go into voice convolutions over make us think they are going in for an awful lot of agony. Christine Miller[15] is plenty good enough for us, but possibly after two or

Excerpt from survey response by Phillip S. Gibbons

NAME OF TUNE	Have we recorded it?	Have you a RE-CREATION of it?	What is the number of the RE-CREATION?	WHY DO YOU LIKE THE TUNE?
Nearer My God To Thee	Yes	x		Family funeral tune
When The Roll is Called Up Yonder	x	x		Because it is scared and has stirring rhythm
Close to Thee	x	x		Beauty of diction
Work for the Night is Coming	x	x		It appeals of [timeless?] values
Throw Out the Life Line	x	x		It is a prayer of faith

three thousand years our progeny may get far enough advanced to appreciate what we fail to understand.

. . . . .

[Ed C. Shaw
Tarentum, Pennsylvania
31 January 1921]

Now that I have partly replied to your request of other side of this sheet, will you kindly reply to mine?

Why is it your Records or Re-Creations Warp, and why do they Crack? Now I have several cracked and so Warped that I can't play them at all.

When I bought your Machine and Records I was told the Re-Creations were Indestructible and would be replaced if above defects occurred.

How about this?

Also why is it that your Re-Creations are so noisy, that is, scratchy sounding?

Now don't ans[wer] and say it is the Reproducer or Sound Box because they [the records] have been tried on 6 or 8 different machines with the same result.

Excerpt from survey response by Ed C. Shaw

NAME OF TUNE	Have we recorded it?	Have you a RE-CREATION of it?	What is the number of the RE-CREATION?	WHY DO YOU LIKE THE TUNE?
Believe me if all those endearing Charms. Orchestra	No	No	No	On account of it[s] smooth melody
Underneath the Stars Violin	"	"	"	Thrill of expression. Artistic
Silver Threads Among the Gold Tenor	"	"	"	
Rosary Tenor or Baritone	"	"	"	Think it more suitable for said voices
Ben Bolt Soprano or Tenor	"	"	"	

The Phonograph I have is among the first 2 or 3 that came to this town and the motor is as good as new for I have made it a point to keep it well oiled[—]there is not a jerk or rattle to it. It is a $200.00 machine and as good as new but for the above mentioned faults. I have practically quit buying your Re-Creations. I use an attachment and buy Victor + Columbia Records.

If you can grant the time please answer stating if you will replace cracked + warped Re-Creations?

. . . . .

[Response to Mr. Shaw from an unnamed member of Edison's Record Service Department, 10 February 1921:]

Mr. Edison wishes us to acknowledge with thanks receipt of questionnaire that you so kindly filled out. The information supplied will prove of value.

We regret far more than you possibly can the fact that so many RE-CREATIONS listed in our catalogue are missing from stock in the case of both jobber and dealer, as well as here at the laboratories, but this situation is one that is gradually righting itself and we feel confident it will be but a short time only, until you will be able to secure service that will merit fullest approval.

The facts are these: We had accurately forecasted a large increase in our business, but during the past year a demand wholly beyond expectations developed and despite everything we could do to increase production, our efforts up to quite recently were negligible, but satisfactory progress is now being made and catalogued numbers that have not been in stock for months past are now coming thru and going forward to all sections.

The RE-CREATIONS you report as having cracked are undoubtedly some of the earlier ones produced by the Edison Laboratories and by a manufacturing technique that was discontinued several years ago. Cracking of the surface is not due to faulty material or defective workmanship, but is apparently caused by extremes of temperature or climate changes, possibly combined with age. You will be pleased to know that due to refinements introduced in manufacturing processes we have not heard of an instance where troubles of this character have developed with RE-CREATIONS of the present technique.

The question of surface friction to which you draw particular attention is one that has been and still is receiving close scrutiny and attention. While up to within a relatively short time we had not been able to make as much progress as had been anticipated, we believe if you will take occasion to compare the RE-

CREATIONS that have been going forward from the factory during the past few months with those heretofore issued, you will readily observe a very great improvement in this important detail.

You are perhaps not aware of the fact, but the principal ingredients used in the manufacture of RE-CREATIONS were obtained from abroad. The war closed these sources of supply to us and made necessary a vast amount of experimenting and the establishment of producing units in this country, which until quite recently precluded the standardization of the manufacturing technique. We however, believe that the past difficulties in this regard have been taken care of, and in connection with continuous improvement it will result in RE-CREATIONS with surfaces that will merit the approval of even the most discriminating.

. . . . .

[George Ruhlen
Tacoma, Washington
18 February 1921]

I have been an enthusiastic Edison Phonograph "Fan" ever since the Edison phonograph and records first appeared, beginning with the small brass horn cylinder machines and growing up with your progress until I now have one of your best $285.00 phonographs and a collection of some 200 records.

I am not a trained musician, never tried to sing correctly a single note and do not try to play any musical instrument of any kind, but am none the less fond of good music and for want of opportunities of hearing it have gone in for the phonograph. I have tried various makes but have after each trial always come back to the Edison because that, for some reason that I cannot explain nor describe in words, appear to me far superior in reproduction of the voice or instrument, and in expression. I began collecting discs while in Washington D.C. in 1912 and 1915 and brought them with me here and have been adding to my collection since. Many of my earlier disc records went "bad" after short use by cracking at the ends, warping and dishing and developing cracks on the surface, but your agents here have always been very liberal and exchanged those that had become entirely useless with records of the same grade although, unfortunately, I was not always able to receive in exchange the same record because it was out of stock or had been entirely taken from the catalogue. Records purchased within the last year or year and a half have held out better than those of

Excerpt from survey response by George Ruhlen

NAME OF TUNE	Have we recorded it?	Have you a RE-CREATION of it?	What is the number of the RE-CREATION?	WHY DO YOU LIKE THE TUNE?
Hear Me Norma— Instrumental Duet	Yes	Yes	80063	Excellent music and harmonious blending of the two instruments
Close to Thee— Vocal duet	Yes	Yes	50043	Good music— fine voices Fine sentiment of song
My Old Kentucky Home—Tho[ma]s Chalmers and Chorus	Yes	Yes	80321	Chalmers fine voice and clear enunciation
Evening Star— Vocal Solo Tho[ma]s Chalmers	Yes but not now on list	Yes	82031	Chalmers voice and good music; Do not understand why you have omitted this record
Spirto Gentil— Vocal Solo in Italian	Yes	Yes	83007	One of the finest records You ever made—Why did you drop it?

an earlier date and as far as I can observe those obtained within that time show as yet no sign of going "bad" except in some cases a slight warping or dishing in the center but not sufficient to interfere with proper action when being played.

I have found, however, with records purchased within the last two or three years, a very serious defect of which you are no doubt aware, namely the rasping or scratching noise that accompanies the production in the music. When this first came to my attention and I mentioned it to your agents they said that they acknowledged the defect but that they had been informed that measures were being taken to cure the defect and it would soon be overcome and records furnished hereafter would become free from it. But this defect has not yet been overcome, on the contrary it seems to be getting worse. Out of the ten new Edison records I obtained some weeks ago and put through a very careful test, I found only two that were so far free from this defect that I reluctantly concluded to keep them. Some of the others were so defective that it was a matter of surprise to me that the inspectors ever permitted them to leave the factory.

Is there any possible way in which this defect can be overcome and may we, your patrons, hope that it will soon be effectually cured? . . .

I will close by saying that it is my sincere belief that if Mr. Edison and his associates had never given to the world anything but his phonograph and its development into the perfect music producing device that it is, he would still be entitled to the gratitude of the millions of people whose pleasure, contentment and enjoyment of living he has added so much.

. . . . .

[Adolph F. Lonk[16]
Chicago, Illinois
no date]

The first four records I have owned at one time, but this was many years ago and tried to obtain same from your Chicago store on Wabash Ave but could not get them. There are many old records that I like better than many of the new ones.

I would certainly like to have a record of the "Inventors Chorus" which was composed especially for the inventors act in which Edison was one of the actors. I have many friends who would also like to get it if it were recorded.

When I sit next to the "Edison" and listen to some song it wakes up my

Excerpt from survey response by Adolph F. Lonk

NAME OF TUNE	Have we recorded it?	Have you a RE-CREATION of it?	What is the number of the RE-CREATION?	WHY DO YOU LIKE THE TUNE?
The Song of Songs	Yes	Owned it once many years ago but is broke now		
Mother	Yes	Yes		
My Sweet Adair	Yes	Yes		
In Monterey	Yes	Yes		
There's Someone More Lonesome Than You	Yes	Yes		

imagination just as it does all other people. If it is winter and a person listens to a spring song the person can almost believe that it is springtime, about the same as looking at a well played motion-picture. I invent inventions and improve on different things for a living and since I have the "Edison" I can invent more inventions while listening to a few records than I could in a month's time before I owned the "Edison." Somehow it seems to train one's imagination and without the "Edison" I believe I'd have to go back to my old job, "Jack of all Trades." In other words I would not sell my "Edison" for any amount of money, nor would I trade it for all other makes of machines combined.

I suppose you will find this explanation a little out of the ordinary, but at least it is the truth and have invented about sixty inventions for this very reason, but have only few patented and have sold some without a patent.

. . . . .

[W. C. Shott
New Philadelphia, Ohio
28 February 1921]
[No songs listed.]

I had intended to fill out this sheet per your request, but when you allow an agent to give concerts on Sunday to advertise your business, I protest, and will give no patronage to a concern that willfully attempts to break down the Christian Sunday, the only bulwark and safety of our nation. History, both sacred and profane, is sure proof that every nation that has disregarded the divine command to keep the Lord's day has perished, and no business concern can ignore the Christian Sunday and prosper. This community will not stand for such things, and your Sunday entertainment, instead of getting you business, will return a loss.

. . . . .

[Response to Mr. Shott from an unnamed Vice President of Edison, Inc., 15 March 1921:]

Dear Mr. Shott:
    Our dealers are their own masters and we would have no right to say to our dealer that he must not give concerts on Sunday. It is quite possible that he

would desist if we asked him to do so, but I am wondering whether the giving of concerts on Sunday is as bad a thing as you seem to think it. A good deal would depend on the kind of concert and the place where it was given.

Practically every great figure in religion has spoken of music as a divine gift. I never heard of the right kind of music doing any harm.

Your letter is the first information I have received concerning the giving of Sunday concerts by the Edison dealer in your city, but he is not the only one who gives Sunday concerts. I know of some dealers who are working with clergymen and their cooperation seems to be appreciated. I feel quite sure that this New Philadelphia dealer has no intention of desecrating the Sabbath, and, unless he is actually doing a mischief to the morals of your city, which is hardly conceivable, I hope you will not judge him too harshly.

Why don't you go to the dealer and talk to him? None of us is so bad that there is not some good in him, and, perhaps, none of is so good that he can afford to condemn out of hand those whose views differ from his own.

The Phonograph and Music Appreciation

11. Annie Pike Greenwood, "The Victor in the Rural School"
Journal of Education, 26 February 1914, 235

It has not been so very long since Southern Idaho was a free grazing ground for the big cattle barons. Then came the few settlers, and they also shared the privilege of allowing their cows, horses and hogs to roam at will. More settlers came, and the fences began to go up, and with the fences came bitter feuds, which, if they did not result in bloodshed, still prevented any social or religious life in the community.

Such was the state of things when I became the teacher of District 10, Milner, Idaho. The school, too, was in an unfortunate condition. Some idea of the indifference to its welfare may be gleaned from the fact that at the last election of a trustee only five persons were present, the two trustees and their wives, and the candidate for election.

The pupils could neither sing nor march, and the enthusiasm of youth found vent in most objectionable ways. It was in a mood of discouragement that I tore off the envelope of the Journal of Education. On the back of the Journal was the picture of a roomful of quiet, orderly children receiving instructions in [Richard Wagner's opera] "Parsifal" with the aid of a Victor Talking machine.

I decided to give an entertainment and work toward getting a Victor. This I did on Halloween night, and for the first time in the history of the valley, everyone, young and old, were gathered together under one roof, not to speak of the entire school of a nearby town, who were our invited guests. The mothers served sandwiches and individual pumpkin pies, and the schoolhouse was lighted by thirty-two jack-o'-lanterns with a scarecrow with a pumpkin head as the central figure, bearing a placard, "Please help me to help the school to get a phonograph."

Twenty dollars was promised that night. The children and I then joined forces to do the janitor work, for which we received $5.00 a month, which means a total of $45.00 per year. A box party[17] cleared the rest, so that on January 8 the Victor and ten dollars worth of records arrived.

We all gathered at the schoolhouse the following Sunday to hear them. It was a bitter day but those who could not ride, walked. The records were received with the greatest evidences of pleasure. I might select somewhat differently if choosing again, and yet we find them very satisfactory for our singing and marching and general enjoyment. Here is the list:

"Round the Village"—Folk game.
Semper Fidelis—Sousa's Band.
"High School Cadet March," by [John Philip] Sousa—Victor Band
(1) "The Jap Doll," (2) "The Gingerbread Man," (3) "The Woodpecker,"
    (4) "Robin Redbreast," "The Bobolink," by Mrs. Jessie L. Gaynor, sung
    by her daughters
"Birds of the Forest and Spring Voices," by Guido Gialdini.
"The Toymaker's Shop" ("Babes in Toyland" [by Victor Herbert]), Herbert's
    Orchestra.
"Wynken, Blynken, and Nod," sung by Evan Williams.
"Gently Falls the Dew of Eve," by [Giuseppe] Verdi.[18]
"Lift Thine Eyes Unto the Mountains," by [Felix] Mendelssohn.
"If With All Your Hearts," by [George Frideric] Handel.
"London Bridge is Falling Down"—Folk game.
"Sweet and Low."
"Round and Round the Mulberry Bush"—Folk game.

The direct result of the purchase of our Victor was the formation of an orchestra, the organization of a Literary Society, and a non-sectarian Sunday school which is to meet every Sunday at two o'clock.

We have only had our Victor a week, but have already used it to march by, to play games by, and to sing by. We are learning new songs from the records and the boys are trying to become excellent whistlers.

The Sunday school is planning to send for some records which will give us the old hymns and some good anthems. And already some of our mothers and fathers have asked if it will be all right to send for records which they especially like.

"Now it won't seem so bad to come to the old schoolhouse, will it?" said one little girl to me, after listening enchanted to the music.

The Victor is absolutely the first thing which has ever been bought for the school with money coming directly from the parents. It has caused the first interest ever shown in the school, and has already been worth to us many times what it cost in money and effort to get it. Besides, it is a handsome instrument, a credit to any schoolroom, and does not take up much space.

If ever a Victor was needed anywhere it is in the tiny, crowded, starved, ugly rural school. You would appreciate all it means if, on a dark and stormy day at recess or at noon, you could see the light in my pupils' eyes as they gather around the Victor to hear the records.

12. "Organize a Music Memory Contest"
Talking Machine Journal, March 1919, 8

Every dealer in talking machines wants the people of his locality to be interested in music. A plan which aims to develop their interest in music through a broader use of talking machines and records could not but be of value to him. That is just what a "Music Memory Contest" is, a way of teaching the people of a locality—especially the children—something about music, and using talking machine records largely to do it. When organized in a community it will inevitably result in a large increase in the sale of records. Any dealer with energy and willing to do some real work in organizing and directing can get one of these contests started in his locality and the result will be to the benefit of all.

The plan was devised by C. M. Tremaine, Director of the National Bureau for the Advancement of Music. It originated in his own experience with his children, a boy and girl who are fourteen and twelve. There had been a player piano in the home for a number of years, but the boy had shown himself seemingly tone deaf, and the girl had not any interest in the piano. One day the father, while playing at the piano, had the idea of a game, and he suggested that the children familiarize themselves with the list of good selections that was in the home, and then after a lapse of a certain time submit themselves to an examination on their power to recognize these selections and give the composers' names. From that moment the children took an active interest in music. The boy made a splendid record in the examination, finally taking up the study of the mandolin in order to play with an organization of his friends, and later began to pick out pieces on the keyboard of the piano.

In this way two unmusical children were made into music lovers, and the idea was quickly developed to apply the same process to an entire community, and a practical plan was worked out. In a Music Memory Contest the participants may be the children of one family, or neighborhood; the pupils of the upper grades of one or more schools; or, as is usually the case, all the school children of suitable age in a city or town. It becomes a competition in preparation for which those who are to participate are trained for a period of several weeks in hearing a selected list of 75 or 100 classics. Phonograph records offer, of course, the easiest way of giving this training. At the contest the competing children are required to identify by name and composer a certain number of the list of selections published at the beginning of the contest. Those who identify the largest number are given prizes.

The National Bureau for the Advancement of Music is always interested in assisting in every way the organization of such contests, and will give counsel and advice to any teacher planning to start one in his community. Where the contest is to cover the entire town, it is necessary to enlist the interest and co-operation of the school authorities, the supervisors of music, and one of the papers in the community.

Boards of Education and principals are recognizing the value of music in the mental development of children. The supervisor of music is probably the best equipped to take direct charge of the contest. He can himself or through the teachers arrange to have a few of the list of selected compositions played for the children each day by phonograph, either during the music period, during assembly, during the luncheon recess, or perhaps after school.

In order to keep the contest before the attention of the children, parents, and community in general it is essential to secure the cooperation of one of the best newspapers in the community. It is important that the conditions of the contest, together with the list of selected compositions, be published frequently.

The cooperation of the newspaper selected to receive the exclusive news of the contest can readily be secured by permitting that paper to announce the contest conducted under its auspices.

Parents of the competing children will naturally want to supplement the training for the contest received at school with drilling at home, and the children will be equally eager to familiarize themselves with the music at home. The contest numbers can be played at home on the phonograph or other musical instruments.

The usual procedure is for the music supervisor, or other person in charge of the contest, to appoint a committee of two or three prominent local musicians to select a list of seventy-five to one hundred selections of good music—the basis of the contest. The list should include standard compositions for piano, violin and voice. The usual working basis comprises one hundred selections of varied length.

The sum for the prizes, which will be an added incentive for the children, can be very small. A very satisfactory arrangement of prizes is as follows:

First prize—Check for sum varying from $5 to $25, according to the size of the city.

Second and Third Prizes—Checks for proportionate amounts.

The next ten to twenty highest (according to probable number of contestants) will be given the choice of a player piano roll or a book of sheet music up to the value of $1 each.

In order to make the money prizes a permanent evidence of having won the contest, it is suggested that arrangements be made to have the cancelled checks for the money returned to those in charge of the contest, to be framed together with a statement giving the facts and results of the contest.

The newspaper under whose auspices the contest is arranged will undoubtedly give one or more prizes. Citizens interested in promoting musical education might welcome the opportunity to offer the prizes for such an occasion. The National Bureau for the Advancement of Music will be willing to contribute one prize, providing sufficient local cooperation is obtained. A high-school auditorium is generally best suited to be the scene of the contest.

Seating Arrangements—In case the auditorium selected consists of a main floor and gallery, it is best to have the competing children seated on the main floor, and the parents and other interested members of the community seated in the gallery.

Card System—As each person enters the schoolhouse on the night of the contest he should be provided with suitable cards on which to record guesses (models for cards can readily be furnished by the National Bureau for the Advancement of Music). The contestants are to receive white cards, and the adults and those children not officially participating, who are desirous of testing their musical memories, should be given cards of a different color. The name and address of the contestant should be written on the card before being handed in to the committee of judges at the end of the contest.

Credits—One full credit should be given for each selection when both the name of the composition and composer are correctly identified; one half-credit is to be allowed for guessing the correct name of the composition without the composer; no credit is to be allowed for the name of the composer without the name of the composition. The highest score obtainable will thus total 20 counts.

Men, Women, and Phonographs

13. Victrola advertisement
Collier's, 4 October 1913, back cover[19]

The best friend of a hostess is the Victrola.

The hostess who has a Victrola never need worry about how the evening will "go." Is there an awkward moment after the guests leave the dinner table? A Victrola will "break the ice." Do the young people get tired of general conversation? A Victrola will furnish the latest dance music and set the feet to sliding. Does someone mention a melody from the latest opera? Let us try it on the Victrola. Always there is the Victrola—the treasure house of entertainment in reserve—never obtrusive but always ready. Is your home like this? It might be—so easily.

14. Aeolian-Vocalion advertisement
Vanity Fair, May 1916, 115

The Sweet, Old Song that Made Me a Musician

To my friends and associates and indeed to myself, I've appeared until recently, simply a plain, middle-aged, unemotional businessman.

And now I find that I'm a *musician*—must have been, in fact, all my life. Tho' I have no voice and never learned to *play* an instrument, I've been a *dumb* one.

How did I find this out? I'll tell you!

Last Tuesday night, my wife and I were at the Jones's. Jones had a new purchase—a phonograph—and he obviously wanted to play it for us. We stood him off until after the last rubber, and then he was no longer to be denied. He simply went and got a record and started the machine.

And then wife and I had the surprise of our lives. We never cared very much for phonographs. Wife called them "screechy." Personally, I'm prejudiced against musical machines.

But this phonograph was *different*. It wasn't screechy; it *wasn't a mere machine*.

"*Oh! Don't you remember sweet Alice, Ben Bolt?*"[20]

With the first notes I sat upright in my chair. How did any such musical tones get into a phonograph? A full-throated, rich, *human* voice was singing the old, familiar words. It was *beautiful*. The very melody seemed glorified by the inspiring tones that voiced it.

"Come over here and sing this yourself!" said Jones.

I went to him not to sing, but to see what the slender tube terminating in a handle, which he had drawn from that wonderful phonograph, could be. It looked interesting.

"Hold this in your hands!" said Jones. "Move the handle in to make the music louder; draw it out to make it softer." Then he started the record again.

At first I hardly dared to move the little device in my hands. Presently, however, I gained confidence. As the notes swelled forth and softly died away in answer to my will, I became bolder. I began to *feel* the music.

It was wonderful! Do you remember how in Du Maurier's famous story, the hypnotist—Svengali—used Trilby's glorious voice to express his feelings![21]

I was doing the same. I was using a splendid voice—I know not whose—*to sing with*. And as I sang the old, old song, and fairly trembled with the depth of emotion I was voicing, the fact that I was—must be—a natural musician dawned upon me. And with it came a glimpse of the glorious possibilities opened to me by this great new phonograph.

Violinist, singer, flutist, pianist, orchestra conductor—the whole musical genius of all the world—was *mine*, not to hear merely, but to use for the expression of *my own personality*.

15. Gladys L. Kimmel, "Having Different Types of Women Customers"

Talking Machine Journal, June 1920, 17, 74–75

If it is a woman's privilege to change her mind, the talking machine salesman will assure you he is firmly and thoroughly convinced of the fact. Experience has made him an expert in sizing up material: He knows the full value of the promising young couple of the family of one or two which comes in together. Or has he any reason to be in doubt when Mr. Man comes in unaccompanied? But, when the eternal feminine approaches him ALONE with no one to advise, suggest or remonstrate with her, he is utterly at a loss to know just what to expect.

This article has little bearing on the small-town dealer, where there is little competition and all local people are known to him. If Mrs. A.—comes in as a buyer or the most casual looker she rarely lacks for prompt and courteous treatment. He is in a position to know just who she is, and if there is a probability of converting her into a prospect for a musical instrument. But in the city store employing a large force, the situation is entirely different. They have absolutely no way of knowing the identity of their trade. People are constantly passing in and out and a sale is only counted as a real sale when the required amount of money has been dutifully collected. Of course, a live dealer will follow up prospects, but he does not depend or pin his faith in them. When a customer walks out unsold, he realized there are a hundred others waiting with promising inducements, so his one and biggest aim is to successfully close the transaction before his customer leaves the store.

Every year thousands of dollars worth of instruments are sold to women. But, to every three that are sold by each individual dealer, there is one lost for lack of the right kind of treatment, and the underlying cause is because the woman is so thoroughly misunderstood. There is every kind and type of woman buyer, but with a few exceptions they can be divided into three classes, namely the Advance Agent, the Purchasing Agent and the Real Buyer.

Every dealer in talking machines is familiar with the Advance Agent. The family having decided to purchase some make of musical instrument, has selected mother or some older sister to look over the different models, to get the prices. This type of customer is secretly disliked by the average sales force. In answer to your inquiry as to the kind of instrument she is contemplating purchasing, she is sure to answer, "Oh, I don't want to buy any today, I'm just looking around. We're going to decide later which one we really want." Mr. Salesman mentally begins to make unfavorable notes right then and there. He knows this type and he also knows she is telling the truth. Regardless of his best efforts, she positively will not make a selection without the approval of the whole family. No selling ability or diplomacy will induce her to have an instrument sent out on approval, and he figures he is wasting valuable time which might be used to better advantage.

But is it a loss of time? Absolutely not. It is true he cannot close the transaction at this time. Not to the extent of getting the money or making a delivery, but he can sell her the idea he has to offer. He can give her the attention which will bring her back the second time. Her general impression of the place is the message which she will unconsciously carry back to her family.

Instead of being turned to the care of a competent salesman, as a rule she is given to someone with far less ability. Mr. Dealer or Mr. Manager does not want his more efficient force "tied up" on this proposition. Because he is in no position to do otherwise the salesman makes this demonstration, but he begrudges the time, and though he may try to conceal the fact, the genuine spirit is lacking. This time which might have been made the most profitable in the world, is absolutely wasted is his general feeling.

If the merits of your particular line are so evident that she is impressed despite his indifference, he has made a profitable sale for some other dealer. The average woman will not return to where she did not feel comfortable the first time. She will look for some other merchant carrying the same line and buy from him.

The most important element in selling the Advance Agent is to make her your friend, the one thing which the salesman did not do. His demonstration may have been technically correct but he lacked the personality and magnetism to bring her back the second time.

A dealer will hire an outside man to follow up prospects, while this class of woman which has the most possibilities, is given little thought or consideration.

The second type, or Purchasing Agent, is far more welcome than the Advance Agent. This is the woman who is sent to your place of business with the explicit instructions to purchase an instrument of a certain make and price. Now, if there are a few deluded mortals who are under the impression that the woman who obeys her husband implicitly does not exist, in this day and age, they are badly mistaken. For every salesman has met the buyer who will return home regardless of the distance to inquire if she shall pay eighty dollars for a talking machine when she was told to pay only seventy-five.

The greatest danger with this particular type lies in "switching." Talk her into buying a more expensive model, and you are very apt to talk yourself out of a sale. She immediately becomes dissatisfied with the one she previously had in mind, but she will not risk the difference in price without consulting her husband. She returns home to talk it over and may have a complete change of heart. Of course she is apt to decide in your favor, but she is just as liable to conclude to look farther or to buy nothing at all. The golden rule for this type of customer is "Go easy." Never make any attempt to influence her into buying a different instrument until you have her name on the dotted line and the initial payment in your hand. Then, and only then, you may tactfully suggest the merits of a better model, and your willingness to make an exchange if she wishes to do so. If she seems interested in this proposition, you may risk one step farther. Tell her that it is absolutely immaterial to your firm which way the exchange is made. Perhaps she would like to have you send out the more expensive model first. But if she seems reluctant, above everything else, don't urge her. Ten minutes after she leaves your store she may regret the decision just because she is confused and wonders what they will say at home. Far better to use the extra time and small expense of an exchange late than have her delay or cancel the order. But if she is willing and you feel it is safe to follow up this method there is one thing to bear well in mind, "Go Slow and Easy" in making the sale but "work fast" afterwards. Get that instrument into the house before her husband returns home. Don't give him a chance to be under the impression that an exchange is going to be a lot of bother and red tape. Once the delivery is made the rest is comparatively easy. But you are risking a sale by giving them an evening to talk it over before the instrument is in their Home.

There are the evening papers with the inviting inducements that every other dealer has to offer. They come to the conclusion that perhaps they were a little hasty and it would be using better judgment to look farther before making a selection. The next morning you receive an early telephone call to hold the order.

Meanwhile your customer of yesterday becomes the Purchasing Agent at some other store today where they are just a little more clever than you. The instrument your competitor is selling is in their home before the day is over making an extra good impression that their service is superior to your own. So when the Purchasing Agent comes into your store be thankful for what the gods provide and make the most of your opportunity.

The Real Buyer is the woman who is open to conviction and who is not hindered either by sense of respect or obligation from following her own inclination. A woman of this type rarely buys a cheap instrument if she is financially able to purchase any other kind but like the Advance Agent and Purchasing Agent when all alone she needs extra consideration. As a rule she is buying in a line of which she is entirely unfamiliar, and she does not realize it until she is in the store facing the situation. The smiling individual who assures you that she came in for the express purpose of buying a musical instrument ten minutes later will defend herself against your most sincere efforts to sell her. The direct result of some fumbling on your part.

When a man is sent out to buy an article which puzzles him, he is more apt to buy wrong than not to buy at all. He has a delicacy about taking up the salesman's time with no results, but the woman familiar with department store shopping is not bothered by any such scruples. If she is perplexed, she instantly wants to "beat a retreat" and talk it over with someone. This comes from the salesman overestimating her understanding of woods, mechanism — things of which the average woman has no conception. Never talk motor to a woman unless you are coaxing for trouble. Her knowledge rarely runs in this direction. She instantly realizes her own limitations, and wonders after all if she acted wisely by coming in alone. If you are carrying a good, reliable make, your motor is the average and it isn't going to do any good trying to convince her of the fact.

But she will appreciate the beauty and tone quality of your instrument. These are your strong arguments. Don't try to convince her. Just try to please her. That is all the conviction she really demands of you. This doesn't mean making a hit or killing her with politeness, but it does mean observing the small things which a woman is very keen to notice.

16. Scrutator, "Where Are the Ladies?" [letter to the editor]
Gramophone, June 1925, 39

I am seriously perturbed, having been looking through the back numbers of our paper, to find an almost complete absence of the fair sex. Surely we have some fair readers in the fraternity, but if so, where are they? Have *they* no interest in the great affairs of state such as needle-track alignment, sound-boxes, gaskets, etc., etc.? How much brighter our pages would be if they contained some charming prattle from the fair sex. And I regret to say, sir [editor Compton Mackenzie], that you have done nothing to encourage them. Are you a woman-hater, or did you merely never think about them at all?

Are we a bachelor affair entirely, or are the sweet little things too shy, or what? Will some of them please tell us?

17. T.A.F., "Ladies and Gramophone" [letter to the editor]
Gramophone, August 1925, 147

The letter of "Scrutator" in your June issue, "Where Are the Ladies?" raises the question, why the ladies are almost universally opposed or at least indifferent to the finest gramophone music. In my long experience as a dealer in gramophones I have never met with a female gramophone enthusiast. In most instances when a lady is calling with her husband to purchase a machine her interest is in the instrument—as "an article of furniture" only. Its capabilities as a musical instrument are really of little interest to her. I find that the great majority of them simply do not understand *tone* at all, although they will frequently *pretend* that they do. They appear really to see no difference between the tone of a hundred-guinea machine and one costing 30s.[22] They will keep on talking incessantly when the most perfect records are being played, and one can see that they really do not understand the music at all and do not wish to. The only thing that will interest them slightly is dance music.

Anyone who has observed the ladies at any musical gathering where first-class music was being played must have noticed that almost invariably their interest was, more or less, assumed. It is the same, though to a much greater extent when listening to the gramophone. In their heart most of them simply hate it and are absurdly jealous of their husband's partiality for it. It is the same with wireless [radio]—after the novelty has worn off.

No, "Scrutator," ladies are *not* interested in any sound-boxes, needle-track alignment, or anything like that. They want to be *seen* and also to *see*. They don't want to listen. That will never interest them.

18. Gladys M. Collin, "Women and the Gramophone" [letter to the editor]
Gramophone, October 1925, 247

The recent attacks on the musical mentality of women in THE GRAMOPHONE, of which I am a constant reader, have aroused my indignation on their behalf, as I consider these reflections (when not merely flippant), both narrow-minded and untrue. Women *and* men may be divided into two distinct classes, lovers of the arts and those who are indifferent to them. I venture to assert, that there are at least as many women lovers of the gramophone and classical music as men. The fact that women enthusiasts do not write to *The Gramophone* is no proof that they do not exist, nor that women are indifferent, nay positively hostile, as Mr. [Compton] Mackenzie [editor of *The Gramophone*] asserts. It may be that the gramophone is not so widely patronized by women as it might be, but it must be remembered that cultured women have usually less money to spend on mental recreation than have most men. If gramophones and records were cheaper, the trade would doubtless benefit by increased feminine patronage.

I am in the habit of attending the International Celebrity Concerts in a neighbouring industrial centre, and have been struck by the preponderance of women, many of them poor, *all of them silent and attentive*, who have been drawn there simply to *listen* and certainly neither to *see* or to be *seen*.

I can only conclude that certain of your correspondents have been singularly unfortunate in the circle of women they have drawn about them.

19. Dorothy B. Fisher, "Women and the Phonograph" [letter to the editor]
Phonograph Monthly Review, October 1926, 30–31

Several months ago one of our English compatriots wrote a letter to the English magazine, *The Gramophone*, in which he undertook to say that women, due to their inherent desire to see and be seen, were not interested in music on the phonograph. That letter rankled me considerably at the time and I was glad to see that at least two English women took enough interest in this assertion to reply to his somewhat presumptuous statement.

The predominance of women over men at all our schools of music, in the galleries at concerts, recitals and the opera indicates anything but indifference to music. Having tried out every gallery in the city of Chicago, I should say that only a very urgent desire to hear would bring them there. But to get back to our interest in music on the phonograph, I sincerely hope that we shall soon hear on this subject from someone with a thorough musical education. My point of view is that of one whose musical education consisted of a few half-hearted piano lessons during vacations, whose musical experience in a western university consisted of two symphony concerts and one opera during four years. In short, should I have been asked to venture an opinion on anything musical at that time, my reply would scarcely have matched Zuleika Dobson's.[23]

With such a musical background, it would have been almost impossible to acquire enough musical experience or understanding to be able to really enjoy or have any appreciation of a [Johannes] Brahms Symphony or one of the operas of the Ring [by Richard Wagner] without the help of the phonograph which has provided the chance to study these things in a more leisurely and intimate way than would have been possible by attending concerts.

Just as I was beginning to realize that not until I had heard a symphony several times, which takes several years, did it begin to take on any meaning or form for me, which is the case I imagine with most people without a musically trained ear, I suddenly married a record collection—I mean collector.

Now I do not mean to imply that a desire for musical knowledge calls for such stringent steps as my own, but I do feel sure that there are many others whose musical training, like my own, is completely nil, but who have a desire for an understanding appreciation; whose intellectual curiosity about great music—and I hope our English friend will grant that it's possible for women to have such curiosity—will receive great satisfaction in becoming familiar with music through the medium of the phonograph.

I don't know how else a girl from Kansas would be conscious of the Siegfried motif from the Ring or that there is a great thrill to the last movement of the [Frédéric] Chopin B Minor Sonata or that [Claude] Debussy ever wrote a great quartette.

Music and the Great War

20. "Talking Machines Are 'Essentials'"
Talking Machine Journal, December 1917, 7, 50

As the process of girding our loins for the great conflict goes forward, and as the effect of our preparation goes deeper and deeper into the private lives of each one of us, it becomes increasingly evident that there must be a division of all things into two groups.

Just now there seems an inclination to consider music—all the host of industries that can be classed under that title—as one of the non-essentials. Reports are sent out of action taken already against musical industry, which indicates the governmental powers to be inclined to that opinion. At the very outset, before this attitude produces further discriminatory action, it should be protested against as unjust and falsely founded.

First of all, music is essential to a country in war because it has always been a part of war. No armies have ever gone to war without martial strains to inspire them. Soldiers must have music for their marching. There must be bands. And if band music, naturally there must be other music and other means of reproducing music, such as talking machines. You cannot draw a hard and fast line at bands, and proscribe the rest. Here is uncontrovertible logic to prove the necessity of music in wartime.

We have hundreds of training camps holding millions of soldiers. Every authority on military training declares that music is a miraculous camp disciplinarian. Nothing keeps the men out of mischief and kills idle hours so well, nothing gets the men together and cultivates the comrade spirit so effectively. Today talking machines by the thousands are in almost hourly use in the camps, and a stream of records is being poured toward the hundreds of thousands of the rookies, eager to hear them. There are thousands of pianos and player pianos enlisted in war work, with their stream of music rolls and sheet music of a varied character feeding them. There are also the company bands, and the little orchestras, to be thought of, and the thousands of instrumentalists who are all going to have more time than ever to devote to their music—and for these a good supply of printed music is necessary. Can the industry that is the source of this material and is looked upon to supply it be classed among the non-essentials?

Music is the food of patriotism. To have the national anthem played by a talking machine in every house before the family seated itself for the evening meal, would do more to hold patriotism at white heat than any one thing that could be devised. No one can estimate the importance of the thousands of patriotic songs issued in the days preceding the opening of the war, in preparing the spirit of the country for the great sacrifice. Today talking machines are repeating these songs in hundreds of thousands of households. Music is doing its "bit" and it is a great big bit, in getting the entire country whole-souledly behind the war in the right way and with the right spirit. This work should not be allowed to cease. It should not be hindered even in the slightest degree.

And music is a solace. No form of entertainment so cheers the drooping soul stricken by the grief of loss. Mothers have already scarred their hearts by giving up their boys to the draft. Families are bereft of fathers and brothers. Nothing can cheer the empty house so well as music—a piano or a talking machine can fill a big void and bring back courage like a miracle. Grief is an insidious enemy. We need all the music we can get in this country to keep up our courage. There will come days when the lists of the dead will crowd the front pages of our newspapers. It will be then we will be grateful for the talking machines and the pianos, for they will help us bear our sorrows and steel ourselves to accept the further sorrows and sacrifices that we will all know we must go through before the frightful work we have set out upon is rightly completed. There may be a few extra tons of coal required to produce these talking machines and pianos, a few extra pounds of steam required to get them delivered, a few extra freight cars needed to transport them, but, compared with the service rendered, what does that mean? It must not be forgotten that war is fought not only with the hand and with the stomach—it is fought with the heart.

Music is an essential in warfare because it contributes to the heart—courage and a blithe spirit to the heart of the soldier, and comfort and renewed resolve to the heart of the bereft. These are the principles upon which the decision must be made so that there will be no discrimination against music at this time on the ground of its being something that can be dispensed with during war.

It cannot be.

And passing from theory to facts, the testimony of other nations who have been at war for years enough to have tested the facts and proven the case, is universally to the effect that music is an essential—a demanded essential. In Great Britain talking-machine and piano concerns are being overwhelmed with orders. In Canada the music trades were never in so prosperous a condition. The conditions speak for themselves. The need brought the demand. It would be certainly unwise to discriminate—as a war measure—against what it has been proven is a people's need when at war.

21. Vivian Burnett, "When I Hear That Phonograph Play"

New York: M. Witmark and Sons, 1918

As I stand on watch while the evening falls,
Close to the firing line,
Through the dusk with a thrill the music calls,
It's a favorite tune of mine.
There's a phonograph a going near to me somewhere,
And my heart starts beating quicker as I note the air,
It's a piece my little girlie used to play to me back there.
Oh, was there ever a tune so fine?

REFRAIN
When I hear that phonograph play,
Oh that tune! Oh that tune!
The message comes from far away,
"Vict'ry soon!"
For the folks at home are back of me,
While I give my best for liberty:
"Soldier, fight! Day and night, with your might, for the right!"
Is what I hear that phonograph say, that phonograph say.

Now the record's changed and I hear again
A sweet familiar air,
There is comfort and help in the old-time strain,
And a power to soothe all care.
It's a quaint old-fashioned lullaby, my mother's song,

That has brought me strength and courage through my whole life long,
That has bid to be clean and true if I wished to be strong,
And when I fight, fight hard but fair!

REFRAIN

When I hear that phonograph play,
Oh that tune! Oh that tune!
The message comes from far away,
"Vict'ry soon!"
For the folks at home are back of me,
While I give my best for liberty:
"Soldier, fight! Day and night, with your might, for the right!"
Is what I hear that phonograph say, that phonograph say.

And again comes a dream like a melody,
Laden with mem'ries dear,
It is fragrant with all love means to me,
And it flashes a picture clear.
For I see the world's most precious girl sit down to sing,
Her happy song floats upward with a joyous ring,
'Tis the fav'rite of our courtship days when love to me was king,
It is the song of our Golden Year!

REFRAIN

When I hear that phonograph play,
Oh that tune! Oh that tune!
The message comes from far away,
"Vict'ry soon!"
For the folks at home are back of me,
While I give my best for liberty:
"Soldier, fight! Day and night, with your might, for the right!"
Is what I hear that phonograph say, that phonograph say.

22. "Phonographs on the Firing Line:
They Need Your 'Slacker' Records"

Independent, 19 October 1919, 126

Not one of the soldiers in the little group gathered round the phonograph but
has a decided opinion—and opinions vary. Voices call insistently for a "hot

jazz," others, frowned upon as sentimentalists, urge "Annie Laurie,"[24] still others demand "that rattling good march-thing."

The self-elected player of the machine, however, feels that his position entitles him to the deciding vote. He removes the well-worn disc at the final squawk and slips on his own particular favorite—perhaps the hot jazz, perhaps the rattling good march-thing, perhaps "Annie Laurie." The boys settle back contentedly. For after all, the selection is extremely limited and sooner or later every one will hear his favorite record, not once but many times.

For the one rain-or-shine, outdoors-or-in, twenty-four-hours-a-day, old reliable musicmaker for the soldiers has proved to be the often-scorned talking machine. The soldier cannot get enough of it. Any one who disliked the company phonograph might as well slur the company mascot. He would be equally popular. The man who can sing is in constant demand, fellows who can pluck a banjo or wail upon the mouth organ or bang the stout "Y"[25] piano are all useful in their own way. But a whole company can gather lazily round a single little squat music box and hear everything from opera to jazz band.

Yet, many as are its evident advantages, one drawback attaches to both machines and records—they will wear out or get broken. One phonograph now in use at the front has an amazing history of usefulness. It was bought by a company while they were at Camp Upton, New York, and its sponsor recently wrote home to a friend, "The old machine has been traveling ever since, as well as the boys, and it's still doing its bit. It has been hoisted in and out from dock to ship and out again, thrown into freight cars, from there to motor trucks, and has had the honor of being played in a monastery six hundred and nine years old; been thru shell fire, played in the open regardless of the weather, played with the same needle for weeks at a time, owing to the scarcity of needles, and played cracked records as well. The machine is camouflaged to give it a real warlike appearance, and if the boys are fortunate enough to return to the States, the machine will come back with us." The letter closes with an appeal for needles and records, both scarce when it was written and growing scarcer every day.

"Dancing on deck used to be regarded as a romantic occupation," writes a college man now on a submarine chaser, "but for a really hazardous sport give me that now, when we have no lights, no ladies for partners, and a space about as big as a pocket handkerchief to navigate in. The various stumbling blocks provided by the architect of the vessel add a touch of excitement, yet every chance we get we may be seen fox-trotting and kitchen-sinking to the accompaniment of our faithful 'Maggie,' as we affectionately call the wheezy little phonograph. 'Maggie' has only three songs in her repertoire and we do become rather weary of their sameness, but if any one is ungrateful enough to complain, we offer to throw her overboard and the killjoy immediately subsides. What we would do without 'Maggie' is too horrible to conjecture. She is helping win the war, all right."

Talking machines have penetrated even into the trenches, and if the various seagoing and warfaring "Maggies" could tell their tales, they would often be of heroic stuff. For in trench, dugout and shell-hole they have found a place to perch and grind out the rags, the stirring patriotic songs and the old-home tunes which the boys love — and which they actually need, as acutely almost as they need sleep, food, shelter.

Lieutenant Colonel Thomas Stanyan of the Salvation Army on his return from a special mission abroad reported that he had found Commandant Hughes of the Salvation Army in a dugout, playing a talking machine to six men who comprised the gun crew. The artillery opened fire, and the signal came to shell the enemy lines. As the men rushed out, several shouted back to Hughes to bring along the machine, so he followed after them, with it held tightly in his arms. While the men served, pointed and fired the gun, Hughes skirmished about till he found a tree stump with a fairly level top, where he placed the machine and proceeded to grind out popular airs in the midst of din and smoke. A gas shell broke up the concert and the gun crew's activity, but the doughty little phonograph was rescued and is still grinding out tunes behind the lines.

Hospitals, convalescent wards, Y.M.C.A. and K. of C.[26] huts abroad, hostess houses and canteens at home, all the different agencies which seek to make the tense, abnormal life of the soldier more comfortable and normal, find that a talking machine more than any single musical instrument solves the problem of keeping men amused at small cost and at wide variety of entertainment. Nor is their use entirely recreation. Foreigners who can speak no English, Americans who cannot "parley-voo," soldiers whose officers wish to drill them to music, are immensely served by this simple means. The record reproduces accent as well as phrasing perfectly. Many of the men are aurists rather than visualists — that is, learn better by the ear than by the eye. And when the lesson is accompanied by the comment of an experienced instructor and by the visual aids of blackboard and map, the men are very quick at grasping the new language and its conversational and military terms.

The very adaptability of the talking machine has made it hard, so far almost impossible, to keep up with the demands for machines, records and needles. The men have wanted it for work as well as play, and they have insisted upon their phonograph and its records following them actually into the thick of battle.

Small wonder that among the much-handled discs there is a high per cent of mortality. Yet, unless a record is really smashed to atoms, play it must, and the sensitive among the audience can cover their ears with their hands when the "sour note" or agonizing crack is reached.

So great has been the demand from both sides of the water, and so uneven has been both the supply and its distribution, that music-lovers who have had the providing of this form of enjoyment especially at heart have found it wise to organize a committee to direct the collection of surplus records and supervise their distribution so that no obscure training camp or small coast patrol vessel should be neglected. The idea of the "National Phonograph Records Recruiting Corps" originated with Mr. Vivian Burnett, himself a composer, who had informed himself thoroughly as to the need before launching his appeal for a systematic handling of the situation.[27] His presentation of the need was so convincing that an active national committee of more than fifty prominent musicians, singers and writers was formed, and has been attacking the problems of finding out what sort of records are most wanted, of collecting them, packing, shipping and distributing them so that each cantonment and ship receives a fair quota.

Performers and the Phonograph

In the Recording Studio

23. "How Talking Machine Orchestras Operate"
Violinist, September 1910, 38

The orchestra of sixteen pieces works all the year 'round for the talking-machine, and is made up of first-class musicians, receiving higher salaries than obtain in most of the great philharmonic orchestras. They would look natural enough if they sat around in civilized fashion, but they don't. They are perched on stools of varying height, some quite near to the ground and others stuck aloft on little platforms. This is because the carrying power of the instruments differs and has to be arranged for, so that the receiving horn will not get too much of any one thing.

The singer stands at a horn of his own, singing directly into it, so close that the voice sounds faint to those who sit at the back of the room. Sounds carry so well to the machine that everybody is warned not to whisper during the recording. Then the orchestra begins the opening chords.

All goes well for a time. The lovely melody makes one forget to watch the mechanics of the place.

Tap, tap, goes the baton of the leader against the stand, and the music stops. What was the matter? None of the listeners had heard anything wrong. The conductor explained that one of the violins had attacked a note too soon. The fault was so slight that not one person in even a well-trained audience of a thousand would have noticed it, but these tiny mistakes come out magnified many times in the record.

No concert or operatic performance is ever as perfect as a Victor record must be. Musicians are allowed on the stage an occasional infinitesimal error, but no matter how small it may be it would fairly shout from the talking-machine. It demands absolute perfection, and even the best of singers fail occasionally. Some fail frequently.

[Enrico] Caruso's voice and method are both so perfect that he holds the best record, but even he must some times repeat. Fortunately, it is not expensive if the error is caught at once. If the record has been cast before it is found it becomes an expensive matter, so the orchestra leader takes no chances.

24. Yvonne de Treville, "Making a Phonograph Record"

Musician, November 1916, 658

When I first sang for the phonograph several years ago, during my first engagement at the Imperial Opera of Petrograd, the company was not to be outdone in courtesy by the Imperial Intendant, General Teliakowski, who had sent the opera troupe to my hotel for rehearsals!

The phonograph company therefore sent the recording machine and operators to my suite in order not to "derange Mlle," as they said. The results, however, were so unsatisfactory to me that I not only insisted on having the records immediately destroyed, but felt very unwilling to undertake a second experiment.

However, having heard some remarkably lifelike tones coming from those weird little wooden birdhouses lately, I allowed myself to be persuaded to another trial.

"Trial" is, I think, a particularly appropriate word. For to sing the same song over seven or eight times, in front of a tin horn, with no audience except that tin horn and the operator who gently but firmly pushes you back and forth, is anything but inspiring! Of course, I was practically a novice, and no hint was given me as to the method of procedure conducive to best results, save the laconic remark, "Sing just as you would in public," which is insufficient and misleading.

So many persons have exclaimed eagerly, "Oh, do tell us how and what you did!" when they heard that I had yielded to the golden arguments of one of our prominent companies, that I decided to write it for the many rather than tell it, personally, to the few.

Fortunately, I carried away from the recording room many mental notes to be sorted out later! Most professionals prefer to sing after noon, and the longer after noon the better. So I stipulated for an appointment at three and arrived promptly and gaily, thinking that the ordeal would be over in an hour's time. To tell the truth, I had promised to take a cup of tea with some friends at half past four, but it was nearer seven when I gulped down that stale beverage, between the hurried narrative of my experience.

Well, to return to our "muttons," as the French say (which in this case are tin horns). I was led to the slaughter—no, to execution of my friend, Eva Dell'Acqua's *Chanson provencale* for a preliminary rehearsal with the orchestra, during which I pointed out the cuts and changes Eva had made for me. Of course, we had to run through it again to make sure it was all understood. That fact established, I was led behind a high cloth screen, where I had the company of a wooden chair, a tin horn projecting through the wall, and the aforementioned "Gentle Pusher."

During the scraping and tuning of the musical instruments I peeked around the edge of the screen and laughed aloud to see the first violinist seated astride of a little, low, rolling box, for all the world like the push cart of the beggar who has had his legs cut off and propels himself around Fifth Avenue, selling matches and shoe laces. It was explained to me that experience had taught the violinist to do for himself what the "Gentle Pusher" was doing for me, and he approached or rolled back from his particular tin horn as the pitch of the note made it available.

The 'cellist had a similar seat, but on a raised platform, and woe betide him should his enthusiasm carry him too far! He would certainly collide with the conductor and drive both their tin horns through the division wall. Other members of the orchestra did not occupy such elevated positions and were stationary, their music racks hung on wires pendant from the ceiling.

My curiosity satisfied in that direction. I turned to the opposite wing of the screen and, looking around that corner, saw the wall, from floor to ceiling, covered with various sizes and shapes of the ubiquitous tin horn. The size and shape vary according to the quality of the tone to be recorded, I was told.

The door leading to the next room, into which our receiving horns protruded through the wall, was covered with signs, "No Admittance," "Keep Out," etc., but, nothing daunted, I slipped through, to find directly under the small ends of the transmitting horns from the front room a machine that resembled a seismograph placed on top of a large pumpkin pie!

As I could not be on both sides of the wall at once, I was unable to watch the operations of this delicate series of tiny levers, disks, and cylinders while I sang from the first room.

At the close of the long, high trill with which I finish the *Chanson provencale*, hearing the continued light thrum of the recording machine, I exclaimed, "Why, if I had known there was more space on the cylinder I would have trilled longer," and perceived too late the horrified expression and admonishing gesture of silence of the "Gentle Pusher."

We all followed eagerly the operator who emerged from the "sanctum sanctorum" bearing aloft the pumpkin pie, like the Herald of Old King Cole in the nursery rhyme. After watching him place this cylinder on an ordinary phonograph, I experienced that peculiar sensation of hearing my own voice. If, at the end of the trill, I had not heard the words "Why, if I had known there was more space on the cylinder I would have trilled longer," followed by a horrified "S-s-h," I would not have been sure it was my own voice.

You doubtless hear your voice as others hear it, on the phonograph, but, presumably owing to the passage of the tone upward through the head it certainly sounds quite different to you coming from your own throat. Two operators bending over the phonograph, the orchestra leader, and the manager, each with a pencil and copy of the song in hand, jotted down effects as they kept up a running fire of comment! "She was too near the receiver." "The oboe should be stronger there!" "Bring out the flutes more!" "That A is too strong and the trill would have been more distinct if she had been farther from the horn!" etc.

I listened, speechless from excited interest and impatient to profit by what I had heard. A second, then a third time I returned to my screen for trial records until there was only one verse that needed a slight change. When I asked if they could not run through the same record (the aforementioned "pumpkin pie") the operator smiled at my ignorance and said:

"Why no, this cylinder has been ruined putting it under the needle while so soft." So back we went to my tin horn to repeat that particular passage.

At last the master records were to be made, and I trembled lest I should repeat some of the extreme dynamic shading which, while very effective in public, is disastrous on records. In order to concentrate my attention I closed my eyes, and although I could not, as in the case of the "trials," hear the three "master" records immediately after making them, I was glad, on my return in a fortnight, to hear they were the best of the eight-and-a-half repetitions of the *Chanson provencale* which I sang that afternoon.

25. Baby Dodds, *The Baby Dodds Story*

Revised edition. Baton Rouge: Louisiana State University Press, 1992
[On recording jazz in 1923 and 1927, pp. 69–76]

I've made a lot of recordings but the biggest kick I got out of any recording session was when the King Oliver band went out to Richmond, Indiana, to record for the Gennett Company.[28] It was in 1923 and it was my first recording experience and also the first for the rest of the band. It was something none of us had experienced and we were all very nervous. But Baby Dodds kept his nerves down in his usual way. I had a bottle and I went off and took a short intermission, and when I came back I was all set to go.

Joe Oliver got the contract through someone who had heard the band play at the Gardens[29] and Joe decided which tunes we should record. They were all numbers which we had worked out many times on the bandstand. We journeyed from Chicago to Richmond by train and we did all that recording in one day because none of us had quarters to sleep in Richmond. We went in the morning and came back at night. Of course everybody was on edge. We were all working hard and perspiration as big as a thumb dropped off us. Even Joe Oliver was nervous; Joe was no different from any of the rest. The only really smooth-working person there was Lil Armstrong. She was very unconcerned and much at ease.

On one number I was caught very unsettled. That was *Dippermouth Blues*. I was to play a solo and I forgot my part. But the band was very alert and Bill Johnson hollered, "Play that thing!" That was an on-the-spot substitution for the solo part which I forgot. And that shows how alert we were to one another in the Oliver band. The technician asked us if that was supposed to be there and we said no. However, he wanted to keep it in anyway and ever since then every outfit uses that same trick, all because I forgot my part.

On that recording date it was a small studio and we all had to be jammed together. The only ones who weren't right by the speaker [recording horn] were my brother John, Louis Armstrong and Dutrey. Oliver was close to the speaker. After we made the records they put them in the press right away and we heard a couple of them. It was quite a thrill to hear ourselves on wax for the first time. And in those days the records were actually processed in ovens. That's why they called them hot platters. Those records still sound to me very much like the Oliver band sounded when it played in the Lincoln Gardens.

Afterwards we recorded with Oliver's band in Chicago but that was the only trip we made to Richmond. And we had the same versatility in recording that we had when we played for dances. If anybody mentioned any novelty or anything which would improve the music we would try it. One time Joe asked Louis to bring the toy slide whistle he sometimes used in the Gardens to the recording studio. It was a novelty which helped make the band go over and Louis used it on our recording of "Sobbin' Blues." For the most part, though, I didn't do any special parts in the Oliver recordings. Only on the record of "Someday Sweetheart"[30] I had a little special bit. We recorded some of our very best numbers but the drumming didn't come out so well in the record of those days. It was wonderful that we got to put such things on wax as "Snake Rag," "Riverside Blues," and "Canal Street Blues."

After the Oliver band broke up I made a lot of recordings with the little outfits that John led. John used to contract with the Okeh Company and with Decca, which was then Brunswick. Quite a few of the numbers were written by members of the band. We recorded some of Lil Armstrong's music, and we used Natty Dominique's numbers pretty regularly. We also recorded quite a few of Jimmy Blythe's tunes. In fact John's band used to record for Blythe, who sometimes held the contract to make the records. Jimmy Blythe would demand to get John and the rest of his band. He held the contract for the records we made under the name of the Dixieland Thumpers. I only came in contact with Jimmy Blythe through those recording dates but found him a very quiet fellow, not the boisterous type at all. In appearance he was dark and short. And everything he did was always to the best of his ability. I didn't even know what outfits he played with but he played piano on the recording dates and when we used his numbers he would write out the parts and give each of us the part for our instruments.

For most of the sessions with John's outfit John used to get the contract. When we recorded for Brunswick the company would decide what numbers to record. We worked up numbers at rehearsal and then John and Jack Kapp, the person in charge of recording at Brunswick, would talk over what numbers we might put on records. Sometimes Kapp would change the numbers. Usually the other companies either gave us a list of the numbers they wanted or else took all that we had. But Brunswick was a bit more particular. Of course, they never told us how to play a number. John and the band worked that out. My brother used to take a watch and play so many choruses and ensemble or solo until the time ran out. We could never play as many choruses as we used in dances, and if there were solos they had to fit into the exact time, too. I've seen a time when we recorded a number once and were satisfied enough to let it go through without making it over. If John had any doubt about a record he would ask for the record to be played and if it didn't sound just right he would ask that the record be destroyed.

I had to make some records with John's outfit with washboard instead of drums. It was a novelty for John and for Natty Dominique but I never liked it. There wasn't anything to it, not even a tune. It was hard work, too. It worked me to death. I had never seen a washboard played but heard about it and got some sewing thimbles to put on my fingers. But still I could feel the vibration when my fingers got to the bottom of the thimbles. After making those recordings my hands used to hurt for half an hour or more afterwards.

Of course, I always felt that John's outfit sounded better in person than on the records we made. Hearing recordings is never just like seeing the musicians play. I could never understand how the record business made such a big hit because people that heard the music heard it plain without knowing the personnel. It makes quite a difference when you see the musicians and get to know them as people rather than just hear them on records.

But people wanted the records and we were glad to make them. We got paid well but it was tough work recording in the day and playing for dancing at night. We were on the go all the time. While we rehearsed the music in the recording studio we were not paid but when the technician held his hand up to signal that a master was made, that was your money. Each musician got thirty dollars a side. Sometimes we made records all week, and, of course, we played music every night, too. Working during the day didn't spare us at night. We had to go on the job and work just as hard. In the studios the air was tight and we worked hard to play through one horn or mike. When we came out we were tired. But we didn't have time to go home and eat, lie down and relax or sleep, we had to go right on and jump out of those sweaty clothes, and get into our dress clothes to go to work. Then many a time we had to report the next morning at eight o'clock for more recording.

In the spring of 1927 John and I made some recordings with Louis Armstrong's Hot Seven. With Louis's outfit we used to have rehearsals and anything that we had in mind for any particular number we would work out then. He would tell each of us when to take a solo or when not to, and who would come in at different times. We weren't a bunch of fellows to write down anything. That would have made it too mechanical. We would stop and talk it out more than anything else. If there was any writing involved, Lil would write down what the musicians were supposed to do. Of course we all had our ideas to give the band, and we would work them out at rehearsal. Later we rehearsed the number again in the recording studio. Whenever a fellow wanted to change something he would ask Louis for his opinion and if it was agreeable it was in. But Louis allowed each of us to take a lot of responsibility for those records. If I would even ask him a question about playing he'd say, "Ah, go ahead, you know what to do." That made us responsible and gave us plenty of leeway to use our own ideas. The only thing that Louis demanded was that we worked to do our best on the records.

Sometimes when recording with Louis I used the afterbeat cymbal to back him up. I used this on the record we made of "Willie the Weeper." It was my style of playing and I used it often for dancing. Some people today think that my drumming was heavy; it wasn't that at all, but rather it was because my technique was so sharp. Each time I hit the cymbal it was clear and distinct, but it wasn't that I was hitting it hard. I was careful to try to hit the cymbal or rims, or even the woodblock, just right, and the way I tried to drum required a good thinking brain and a sharp ear. And it was always necessary to keep a sense of humor, for God's sake, so that if something didn't sound right I could always change it or quickly insert something else in its place.

With Louis's recording outfit we used four beats to the measure. That was different from the older days in New Orleans when we always used two. King Oliver used two, also. And Louis used a tuba instead of a string bass. I had started playing with a bass viol [i.e., string or upright bass] and I always felt closer to it than to a tuba. It was no harder to drum with a tuba but it always made the group sound brassy to me. It seemed like it was a brass band or a street band. Jelly Roll Morton[31] also used a tuba on his records.

One time there was a little incident on a Louis recording session in connection with my drinking. It was a time when I had been drinking and forgot to report to the Brunswick studio. I had rehearsed for the session but when the time came to make the records John had a hard time finding me. Finally he located me at home and I hurried over to the studio. Jack Kapp and my brother got in a huddle and John told Kapp that I had been drinking so Kapp told me he didn't want anything like that in his studio. He was very strict about the musicians drinking while they recorded for him. And of course that pleased John, who never drank himself and always objected to my drinking. I had a bottle in my coat pocket and I tried to steal a drink while they weren't looking. I had the stopper out and was just about to take a drink when they started to play so I quickly hid the bottle behind the bass drum. But the bottle dropped and broke and they heard the noise and smelled the whiskey. All heads turned in my direction and I got a slight bawling out for that, but it didn't amount to very much.

26. Edwin McArthur, "Conducting for Record"

Listen, March 1941, 4–5

Whether it is providing piano accompaniments for [Edvard] Grieg or [Richard] Strauss Lieder on a not-too-new upright in a low-beamed Copenhagen attic, reached only by trudging up four spindly flights of stairs, or standing on the aluminum-tiered podium of the impressive Academy of Music in Philadelphia to wield the slender plastic wand that will guide a hundred master musicians through the mazes of a Wagnerian orchestration, the recording experience is one of the most grueling I know.

Things can go wrong in any musical activity, of course—a missed cue, a wrong note, a momentary stray from pitch. In the concert hall these may occasion a passing twinge, but in recording, on the other had, one is haunted always by the thought that the slightest slip-up will not only echo in the immediate listener's memory but will achieve actual physical immortality.

Yet the very tension one experiences in record-making often has the effect of stimulating one to greater effort, and very frequently the same selection, played by the same orchestra with the identical conductor and soloists, sounds incomparably better on discs than in the concert hall. This is the same psychological phenomenon that educators have observed when students in noisy classrooms work better than those in quiet ones—the additional effort summoned up to overcome the handicap increases the quality of the performance.

I personally witnessed an example of how this strain can lift great artists' achievements to even higher levels. It occurred out in San Francisco, where we were completing the recording of the colossal "Götterdämmerung" duet [of Richard Wagner] with [Kirsten] Flagstad and [Lauritz] Melchior. This is music that makes the most excruciating demands on its interpreters and now, transferring it to wax, all of us were under a doubly great nervous strain. So, when the last notes of the thrilling blending of those two incredible voices had faded, I let out an unconscious gasp of relief and a totally unpremeditated but very strong "Bravo!" After much painstaking retouching of the matrix, the Victor people have been able to eradicate the "Bravo," but a hint of the sigh still remains vividly audible to immortalize the experience.

Of course such tremendous music as this, or the "Tristan und Isolde" love duet in our first Victor album presents special difficulties for the recorder. For Wagner was one composer who never pulled his punches and when he wrote a crescendo it surged upward with the full resources of all the orchestra. In the open house or concert hall this is enormously effective, but on records, if you are not careful, a sudden loud passage may turn out altogether out of proportion to the dynamic pattern of the work and the dynamic capacity of the receiving instrument. However, skillful rearrangement of the orchestra's seating before the microphone will generally guard against this.

Tempi, as well as variations in volume, require special attention on the part of the recording conductor. A frequent complaint against orchestral records is that they seem slow and draggy. This is, in many cases, the result of failing to apprehend the subtle change in the approaches to music of the phonograph listener and the concert-hall or opera-house listener. When an exquisite gold curtain falls slowly before your eyes, or your attention is fastened on the conductor's hand poised in mid-air, a fraction of a minute passes unnoticed. Sitting before your phonograph, when you don't have these visual distractions, you find the same pause seems eternities long. For that reason, in making records there must be a conscious effort to minimize breaks and in general a subtle quickening of time and rhythm.

Just as the record listener must be compensated for failing to see the performer, the performer should be compensated for the lack of audience stimulation, and I have found this equally true in my recording work as piano accompanist and as orchestral conductor. Tension may give edge and polish, but relaxation lends it warmth and color. The place in which records are made may have a great deal to do with inducing an easy, fluent performance. For example, in the Philadelphia Academy of Music, where we recorded several Flagstad-Melchior Wagner albums, we worked in an atmosphere familiar to us all and closely associated with great music, and here we functioned more tranquilly than in any other recording place I can recall. Neither newness nor contrived mechanical perfection is a requisite for good results in recording environment, it seems. An attic room such as the one in Copenhagen in which I played accompaniments for some of Mme. Flagstad's first Lieder recordings, for example, or the Church in Camden [New Jersey] that Victor uses for many platter-making sessions, may provide a certain mellowness that brings out the best in the tone, in the same way that the aged wood of Cremona violins produced the best fiddle sounds.

Having worked both as pianist and as conductor in providing instrumental settings for great voices on records, I am frequently asked to describe the differences in my conception of the two approaches. I feel actually that there are more points of similarity than of difference. Certainly the understanding of the singer's situation gained through accompanying vocal stars at the piano is invaluable to the orchestral conductor directing a vocal recording, who must, in addition to conducting his orchestra, be responsible for drawing the orchestra and singer together at all times, for balancing the tone of the ensemble with that of the solo vocal instrument. One used to accompanying Lieder singing is, of course, quick to recognize those certain passages in which the mature singing artist must be given a certain freedom of expression. Moreover, he is not likely to lose sight of the vocal line in the welter of orchestration. In selections from the Wagner operas the conductor must be particularly careful not to obscure the vocal line, for, despite his elaborate orchestration, Wagner we know intended the vocal line to have prime importance always. In Bayreuth,[32] in fact, the orchestra, according to Wagner's own prescription, is covered from the audience's view so that the singing comes across with even greater directness than in other opera houses. When you recall too that Wagner not only composed his own texts, but even invented words when the existent language failed to convey exactly the right shade of meaning, you realize the emphasis the composer himself placed on the vocal score and the consequent responsibility of singer and conductor for recording it properly.

The Phonograph and Music Pedagogy

27. "The Effect of Mechanical Instruments upon Musical Education"
Etude 34 (July 1916), 483–84

The Following Questions Were Asked in This Symposium

1. Have you, in your own work, noted any progress upon the part of a pupil, directly attributable to music mechanically reproduced?
2. Do you know of any case where the musical interest in the study of any instrument has diminished owing to mechanically reproduced music?

3. Have your business interests ever suffered through the introduction of mechanically reproduced music in the homes of any of your pupils?

Rossiter W. Cole (Composer, Organist, Teacher):

From the standpoint of musical appreciation I can see a large preponderance of good results upon musical education accruing from the hearing of mechanically produced music, provided always that the music is of a sufficiently good quality, and in the long run this aspect of the problem will take care of itself, for, where there is an abundance of good music available in this form, even the most confirmed ragtimers will sooner or later reach up after it. There can be no doubt that the ability to reproduce successfully by mechanical means the individual interpretations of great artists has been of tremendous value in bringing these artists into personal touch with many thousands of intelligent lovers of music who otherwise would have been denied this privilege. I think no thorough teacher of music need fear the rivalry of any of these mechanical instruments. On the contrary, I have known of instances where they have brought about a very wholesome stimulation of interest in music study through the opportunities offered in the home for the pupils either to play or to hear played worthy compositions that were far beyond them technically and with which they had no other means of acquaintance. Anything that stimulates greater love for good music ultimately increases the desire for music study. But no matter how perfectly these mechanical instruments may approximate the performance of the artist-musician, they will never supersede him nor quench the desire of any person with music in his soul to equip himself as far as possible for self-expression through performance of some kind.

J. Warren Andrews (Organist, Composer, Teacher):

For some unexplained reason the mechanical player [i.e., player piano] has never interested me. While it is wonderful in its perfection, there is a coldness about its performance which fails to arouse enthusiasm. I have also failed to note any special artistic progress resultant upon its use.

With the sound reproducing machine [i.e., phonograph], especially with its recent improvements, great things may be expected; an advance in higher artistic appreciation must take place with its most common use, although, if musical taste tends in the wrong direction, more harm than good may result. There is, however, a tendency in most dispositions to hear the great things because they bear the stamp of approval of those versed in the art.

I have not noticed any diminution of interest in music students on account of these mechanical helps, for helps they certainly may become. On the contrary, musical zest and ambition seem to be stimulated thereby. According to my observation I do not think students, considering the general average, are as serious or as studious as they were a few years ago; nor do they continue their studies for so large a portion of each year as formerly. I do not believe this is due to any mechanical devices, but rather to the pleasure-seeking age. Then it was unceasing work if one would win. It is now rather exceptional to find the rigid determination to succeed that once actuated the students. Those who possess this usually have marked success. It might be well to state in this connection that the methods of teaching of today are *far* in advance of those of even twenty-five years ago. It then took longer to accomplish what is now done in a shorter space of time. We have learned better methods; how to think, concentrate and discriminate.

I do not think up to the present time, my business interests have suffered in any degree through the prevalence of these mechanical contrivances. I must plead guilty to the personal enjoyment of some things I do not have to work for, though I believe the joy of work is one of the greatest boons we have to be thankful for.

John J. Hattstaedt (Conservatory Director):

I laid the three questions you present in your letter before the principal members of our faculty and find a decided variance in their written answers. Judging from their experience and my own, I would give the following opinions:

Question 1. Various students have been benefited in their work by the use of the better class on mechanical instruments.

Question 2. In families owning player-pianos, students sometimes have lost their interest and stopped lessons.

Question 3. The American Conservatory has not suffered through the epidemic of producing music by mechanical means.

Personally I have no use for the player piano, and deem it more of a detriment than an advantage. The finer instruments of the sound-reproducing kind perform a real service and cannot but raise the general musical understanding and taste.

LeRoy B. Campbell (Conservatory Director, Teacher, and Author):

Human nature is predisposed to expressions, and mechanical instruments seem to have no deterrent influence upon this God-given disposition. On the contrary, these instruments furnish more and more impressions throughout the length and breadth of the land, and since every impression has its expression, there naturally comes much more into the general concept mass to express than before these instruments made their advent into our musical life. True, there are many unworthy records, but every dealer tells me that the course of his customers' tastes, as a rule, runs like this: The first few months after he buys a machine he uses ragtime and popular songs, the next period he tends toward the Italian and French opera, and ends up after a year with trading in most of his former records for the best arias and masterpieces by the great artists.

This inherent desire to express something ourselves is seen in the child—no matter what father does, Willie may enjoy seeing or hearing him do it for a time, but it always end up that Willie insists, "Let me do it." That same desire fosters our disposition toward the mechanical musical instrument; we enjoy listening to it for a time, but soon human nature asserts itself and *we* want to do it.

To illustrate, just last week a young man across the street from our school who runs a store filled with player pianos and who has in his stock nearly every piece (and, by the way, he has already arrived at the stage where nothing but the best music satisfies him) in mechanical literature, hearing many of them day after day, expressed an earnest desire to learn to play himself, if only to be able to play simple pieces of the [Jules] Massenet *Elegy* type. Simply one of the many coming under my own personal observation who, following the natural tendency, wishes to express something himself.

The mechanical instrument, as my experience proves, has been a stimulus to music study both as a factor in interesting more students, as well as often being a great help to the student in giving him good ideas on some masterpiece which he may be studying.

J. Lawrence Erb (Composer, Author, Teacher):

The invention of mechanically reproducing musical instruments can be likened in importance only to the invention of printing from movable type. As an educational asset it is of the very highest rank. In ten years or more of rather intimate acquaintance with mechanical instruments of one sort or another, during most of which time I have used them in my teaching, I have found not a single instance where they have been other than a benefit to the students. After all, even the most industrious and gifted human being is very much limited in his ability to learn and perform music. There are besides the limitations of natural endowment to aid to the handicap of only eight hours of work in the day. So that from the standpoint of widening the musical horizon alone, all such agencies are of the greatest value and have proven so in many cases. For instance, the dreary drudgery of learning to play the piano has been lightened in many cases and a new impetus given to students by the use of player rolls, which presented the finished product in such form as to remove the universal and hackneyed complaint, "But I don't like this piece," a complaint which arises in the vast majority of cases from the fact that the student is so busy disentangling notes and fingers that there is not the faintest conception of the musical beauty of the composition, and by the time that the mechanical difficulties have been mastered, all the freshness and spontaneity have been lost, with the result that though he may be able to play the notes, his mind is no longer interested in the composition. While in certain cases I have recommended the purchase of a player piano or a sound reproducing machine instead of taking lessons where there was no slightest evidence of either talent or inclination to study, yet the total effect of mechanical players has been to increase interest in music and to stimulate a desire to make music on one's own account. I suspect the proportion of the ungifted and uninterested who will study music will be lessened through the talking machine and the piano-player, but I can see no other result than that those who have musical inclinations will find these instruments simply aids to developing their musical ability. Interpretation, clearness of execution, and many other details which are lost in the maze of hieroglyphics on the printed page may be and are made manifest to the student through the mechanical players. The proportion of mediocre public performances ought to diminish with the increase of these instruments, and that will be a blessing. I do not see how they can ever diminish to any appreciable extent the number of those who want to make music in their own way, just as I have not observed any falling off in the number of candidates for the stage with the increasing ability to read and the cheapness and accessibility of literature. I think the two cases are entirely parallel.

John Orth (Teacher and Composer):
A most interesting question indeed. In the first place, then, what is all this talk about "canned" music? Don't you like canned peaches, pears, etc.? Well, then, what's the matter? Why isn't one kind of *can* just as good as another? If not, why not? I pause for a reply.

I have heard a good many foolish things said about "canned music" by people who wouldn't know a fine performance of a significant composition of any kind or for any instrument when they heard it. I believe in sense, horse sense, common sense, which isn't nearly as *common* as it ought to be, and I hope will be some day. Let us then look at these mechanical musical devices in a common-sense way. Strange, isn't it; but most people, especially the fond parent, would rather hear his daughter, or someone else's daughter, sit down and rumble, tumble, fumble, jumble through [Felix] Mendelssohn's *Spring Song*, a [Frédéric] Chopin waltz, or the *Sonata Pathétique* [of Beethoven] than to hear it done by an unseen performer on a much higher plane as regards all the fundamentals of interpretation, such as rhythm, tempo, nuances, and especially right notes which seem to play a very unimportant part in the mind of the average listener. All you have to do for most of those people is to sit down, hang onto the pedal, make a big swash and rumpus and the deed is done, as far as they are concerned.

I know of a little nine-year-old girl who went to call on her uncle with her parents on Thanksgiving Day. She soon spied a piano-player of the highest class in one corner of the room. She was told she might select and play any roll she wished. She selected the *Moonlight Sonata* [by Beethoven]. She was much interested and worked over it quite a while. After she had finished, her uncle said to her, "You like that piece?" "Oh, yes, I think it's the nicest piece I ever heard." "Is that so. Well now you see you won't have to learn that piece; you can come here and play it anytime; you won't need your hands at all." "Oh, but I just want to learn to play it *myself* and I want my teacher to give it to me just as soon as she thinks I am ready for it."

You see, this kind of a little girl would receive real inspiration for higher effort by this means.

A Talking Machine in Every Music Room

What is a person to do who wishes to hear one of many compositions like [George Frideric] Handel's *Hallelujah Chorus*, [Franz] Schubert's *Unfinished Symphony*, [Felix] Mendelssohn's Violin Concerto, and a [Johannes] Brahms, [Franz] Liszt or [Ludwig van] Beethoven concerto for the piano? How is he to satisfy this craving? Why would he not instinctively reach out for some device which would meet this desire? A man might have in his family someone who played the piano let us say, or violin, or 'cello, or who could sing, but what about symphony or oratorio? It looks to me that the day is likely to come when no music room, especially those away from musical centers, will be considered quite complete without a mechanical musical apparatus of some kind. Just think of being able to call upon [the violinist Fritz] Kreisler, [the opera singer Ernestine] Schumann-Heink, [the pianists Vladimir] De Pachmann and [Ignacy Jan]

Paderewski at a moment's notice to appear and play or sing anything one might like to hear, besides having at command a full orchestra or chorus for symphony or oratorio!

Don't you see what an advantage it is if children can grow up in an atmosphere of real music artistically performed? Wouldn't they learn to appreciate and love the real thing instead of being swamped in the superficial and meretricious?

Musical Turtles

How about the musical turtles who crawl over the keys, whose technique is bounded on the north, south, east and west by Handel's *Largo* and two or three pieces like that. Will they give up when they meet a mechanical device and see what it can do? I doubt it. I think they will stick just the same, although I find it difficult to figure out the basis for their persistence and patience.

The fact is the more I look into these mechanical instruments the more surprised I am at what they have already accomplished and the more enthusiastic I feel in regard to their possibilities in advancing the musical life of the future.

Frederic W. Root (Teacher and Author):

From the slight indications I have had of the influence of mechanically produced music upon my pupils in singing, I incline to the opinion that the influence has been favorable on the whole.

Reproductions of the singing of distinguished artists stimulate a desire to learn the music which they sing and give a model for its rendition. The objections to this, which sometimes become manifest, are that pupils are led to attempt that which in grade or method of phrasing are inappropriate for them.

This, however, is easily regulated by the teacher, who in other respects realizes the aid received from the pupil's interest in the reproduction. But it is only in repertoire work that mechanical music affects the situation appreciably.

The training of singers is so largely in voice-building and musicianship, work in which these artistic reproductions do not compete with the teacher, that the business of voice teaching is not likely to be interfered with.

Another view of the subject is suggested by the remark sometimes made by a pupil who has listened to a masterly performance: "I could never do like that; I might as well give it up."

However, such remarks are rarely if ever an announcement of genuine intention; they usually prelude a determination to work all the harder.

I have known of no instances in which the business of teaching was affected in this way. In the field of instrumental work the case may be different; but to the voice teacher's business I regard the "discs" as aids rather than opponents.

Hans Schneider (Noted Teacher and Lecturer):
The question whether the mechanical players and other such instruments are a blessing or a drawback to music depends a good deal upon how one looks upon "Music." If the musical faculty in man is developed only for the purpose to provide a living for the music teacher, then those instruments are surely a drawback to this profession, for in time the profession of music-teaching would be reduced to a very small size, but if the musical faculty is given to man to make him enjoy "music" and derive all the benefits therefrom, then these instruments are a blessing and the surest and quickest way to realize this ideal.

The enjoyment of music is one with acquaintance of its literature, and you will agree with me that ninety percent of all music students never get to the point where real "musical literature" begins. To them music as an art will forever remain a book with seven seals, if all the art of music they can consume must come through their own efforts. And the above is not alone true of amateurs, but also of music teachers, the majority of whom have not any too extensive acquaintance with literature.

I consider the mechanical player as one of the greatest aids to the music student. I know from my own home that my daughter has received more real music benefit from her "records" than from her music studies, and while she is but a very limited player, I consider her musical appreciation quite highly developed. I use records frequently in classes of our school and shall make extensive use of mechanical players as soon as I am able to work out a plan, which probably will be done next summer.

The mechanical player does for music what the oil print has done for painting and the printing years ago for literature, and I look forward to the time when music, real music, will be taught in schools and colleges in place of the present instruction, which may be practically called a waste of time and which does not get the students anywhere near real music.

Music means the thoughts of our great classic and modern composers, and to become acquainted with only a small part of it, by way of studying its technique first, would take two lifetimes, and a short cut therefore is not alone most welcome but absolutely necessary. Yet the absorbing of musical literature in a mechanical way does not necessarily do away with one's own personal effort, as the enjoyment from this activity is of an entirely different character than that of pure appreciation of good music.

Everett E. Truette (Organist and Teacher):

Replying to your queries relative to the effect of mechanical instruments upon music education, I will say that in my personal teaching (organ, piano, harmony, theory and counterpoint) I have not observed any progress attributable to the use of the mechanical machine. However, I have known of several vocal pupils of other teachers who have been materially benefited by repeatedly listening to the records of the great singers.

My personal business interests have never suffered, to my knowledge, from the introduction of the mechanical machines. I have known of several pupils who were making slow progress in the study of the piano, who gave up the study when they secured a mechanical machine, as it enabled them to enjoy correct performances of music which they could never be able to execute.

F. W. Wodell (Teacher and Author):

The player piano has no direct relation to my work as a teacher of singing.

The hearing of pieces—vocal records—on sound-reproducing machines of a high order has in certain cases stimulated a desire for vocal study, and in others a determination to persevere to further attainment in vocal technique and interpretation.

The writer is now specializing in the use of the sound-reproducing machine in his studio as a means of giving pupils an opportunity to "hear themselves as others hear them," to a considerable extent. He has established a system whereby records are made by students at regular intervals, of both exercises and pieces, and reproduced for critical hearing and comparison by the pupil. It is well known that in many cases it is extremely difficult to convince pupils of certain faults; as, for instance, of the existence of a "tremolo"[33] or disposition to sing "sharp" on certain pitches. Here is where the record is of a certain value in the studio. It is of especial service also in showing the pupil his lack of power to sustain tone firmly and evenly and to sing with the true "legato," avoiding occasional "explosions" on a pitch or a syllable.

While it is true that the talking machine as a means of reproducing the singing voice has limitations, and that there is a certain skill to be acquired in its use, these do not detract to any important degree from its value for the purposes mentioned.

28. Oscar Saenger, *The Oscar Saenger Course in Vocal Training: A Complete Course of Vocal Study for the Tenor Voice on Victor Records*

Camden, N.J.: Victor Talking Machine Company, 1916, 9, 10, 12, 13

We frequently hear that there is no longer such singing as the old masters knew and taught, but such statements need not be taken seriously. We have no means of knowing what the old masters taught, nor how they sang. We can only take the word of musical historians for the achievements and skill of such singers and teachers as [Nicola] Porpora, [Guiseppe] Persiani, [Maria] Malibran, [Carlotta] Grisi and many others who have become names only, for those of the present day. Then, too, we know musical opinion in those days was in the hands of a very few, as compared with the present time.

In this day of startling creations, such as we meet on every hand, none is more remarkable than the reproduction of the human voice by the Victrola.

Following the revolution in musical conditions brought about by the Victrola, it was to be expected that other developments might follow which would profoundly affect the musical art of the Nation.

As an organization devoted to the propaganda of music and its better understanding, we feel the same keen interest in the artistic development of young Americans as we have felt in the making of the world's best music available to all. The time has come when vocal study can be placed within the reach of every aspiring young singer, no matter where he or she may live.

In order that such instruction should be unquestionably the best, we entered into the exclusive arrangement with Oscar Saenger, of New York, to create a special course in vocal training. Our reason for doing so was that Mr. Saenger is recognized internationally as one of the greatest authorities and one of the *most successful* teachers of the present day.

In thus giving to the world this privilege of studying with Oscar Saenger at home, we also afford certain possibilities which the student may enjoy in no other way. The period of study is unlimited. Day after day the student may go over the same lesson and hear again and again those little details that a teacher gives during a single lesson at stated intervals only, but which may be overlooked subsequently, as the instruction proceeds. These lessons will be at hand for continual reference at any and all times.

Teachers, especially those who have devoted themselves to work in the smaller cities, far from contact with the wider musical activities, will find this

Saenger Course a valuable adjunct to studio work, for it will give them correct examples to serve as illustrations of their own instructions. If the pupil has a living illustration accompanying the teacher's words, the subject immediately becomes more intelligible and he comprehends clearly that which the words alone would have merely *suggested*. We confidently expect that teachers generally will be quick to realize the many opportunities afforded by these records.

In the records of the Oscar Saenger Course, a note of music, a phrase or a scale, is sung by the artist chosen to furnish an example. This is done with piano accompaniment. The artist's voice then stops but the accompaniment continues, and the student then sings the same notes in the same way as they were sung by the artist.

The Oscar Saenger Course in Vocalization has been prepared for soprano, mezzo-soprano, tenor, baritone, and bass. There is a separate set of ten double-faced records for each of the above voices with full instruction which is imparted both by means of the records and by this manual.

The Phonograph and the Composer

The Composer in the Machine Age

29. Henry Cowell, "Music of and for the Records"
Modern Music 8, March–April 1931, 32–34

What has mechanical recording done for modern music? And further can a special music be satisfactorily written for records as such?

Records available for player pianos, organs, or gramophones do not cover the field of modern music with any degree of accuracy. They are turned out by commercial companies with the natural object of financial profit and are therefore to a great extent of cheap, salable music. Since, however, there are some people who enjoy and buy music of a better type a number of "classical" records have also been issued. The purchasers of classical music have been as a whole more interested in who plays than in what is played, so one finds that the recording companies make a great advertising point of the fame of the interpreters. Between the different concerns, almost the entire field of well-known performers is covered and until quite recently the artists were allowed to play practically anything, provided it was innocuous and pleasurable. The result was that certain time-honored gumdrops were duplicated innumerably by different artists for different companies while some of the world's greatest music went unrecorded. At first no attempt was made to form a record library of the most important musical works. The situation is gradually changing, and some of the companies are covering the ground of the famous classics. Today by combining the American and European productions one finds a good proportion of the best music of the eighteenth and nineteenth centuries recorded, although the player piano rolls are far behind the discs in number.

The recording of modern music has just begun. There is no attempt to cover the field, but when a modern work becomes sufficiently popular to ensure a record's paying for itself, it is apt to be found on some of the lists. One feels also that some modern works have been included by chance because certain performers or organizations insisted on playing them. At present one cannot form a library of the most important modern works but may obtain some of them when they happen to be popular as well as significant. [Igor] Stravinsky's *Sacre* [*Le Sacre du Printemps*, or *The Rite of Spring*], for instance, is duplicated several times, but no composition by [Arnold] Schoenberg can be obtained anywhere. None of his works have ever been recorded except for *Verklärte Nacht*, Opus 4, and even this is now out of stock. Often when well-known modern composers are included, only their early and unrepresentative works are found. Certain foreign companies have published a fair number, for instance, the Odeon and Polydor Gramophone Companies, and the Pleyel Player Piano Company. American concerns have done little, and the player piano companies practically nothing. Although it is no more costly than it is to print, about a thousand times as many modern works are published.

Far more interesting than a survey of the few fine records of modern music, is a consideration of the possibilities of writing music especially for a recorded form, music which deliberately utilizes some of the advantages gained by removing the personality of performers from the performance.

A handful of modern composers have written for records, mostly for keyboard player rolls. [Ottorino] Respighi makes use of a disc of birdcalls in one of his orchestral works [*Pines of Rome*]. He used this device, however, not because he was interested in composing for the peculiar tone-quality of the record, but probably because he desired authentic birdcalls. Yet there are possibilities in the phonograph record which would be hard to duplicate. It produces new tone qualities which might be used in composition. A record of a violin tone is not exactly the same as the real violin; a new and beautiful tone-quality results. Many variations in tone can be artificially produced by different placements of the microphone in recording. Balance of tone in recording a composition of several complex strands can only be obtained if there is a separate microphone for each of the instruments played together.

Stravinsky and many of his followers have written for player piano rolls music which might be played by hand, but which they desired to divorce from the possibility of misconstruction or "interpretation" by performers. By using rolls the composer makes sure that the tempo, notes and duration of notes are right. [George] Antheil used several supposedly synchronized pianos in his *Ballet Mécanique* probably for this reason, for the music is nothing that cannot be played by hand. [Paul] Hindemith, [Ernst] Toch and others have written for mechanical organ but despite their claims it does not appear that they wrote things impossible to play on an unmechanical organ. Hindemith's *Triadic Ballet* produced in Donaueschingen[34] in 1926 is one of the more elaborate attempts made in this field.

The composer who goes about writing for mechanical instruments in the most penetrating fashion is Nicolai Lopatnikoff. He has experimented in works for all kinds of recordings, such as mechanical orchestras, organs, violins, and pianos. He writes things which can only be played mechanically, making the mechanism necessary to the composition. He has player piano passages that are impossibly fast, and combinations impractical for the hands of players, no matter how many should take part in the performance. Lopatnikoff also plans to make phonograph records of various factory and street noises, synchronizing and amplifying them as a percussion background for music written for keyboard recordings.

The field of composition for phonograph records and player rolls is wide and offers many prospects, but the workers have been few and too little has been done to try to summarize the results. Those making attempts in this direction have been hampered because the majority of music-lovers misunderstand their efforts.

One excellent line of possible development, which so far as I know has not yet been attempted, would be to work with subtle rhythms. To hear a harmony of several different rhythms played together is fascinating, and gives a curious esthetic pleasure unobtainable from any other source. Such rhythms are played by primitives at times, but our musicians find them almost if not entirely impossible to perform well. Why not hear music from player piano rolls on which have been punched holes giving the ratios of rhythms of the most exquisite subtlety?

30. Igor Stravinsky, *An Autobiography*
New York: Simon and Schuster, 1936. Reprint, New York: W. W. Norton, 1962, 150–54

About this time [late 1928] I signed a contract for several years with the great Columbia Gramophone Company, for which I was to exclusively record my work both as a pianist and conductor, year by year. This work greatly interested me, for me, far better than with piano rolls, I was able to express all my intentions with real exactitude.

Consequently, these records, very successful from a technical point of view, have the importance of documents which can serve as guides to all executants of my music. Unfortunately, very few conductors avail themselves of them. Some do not even inquire whether such records exist. Doubtless their dignity prevents others from consulting them, especially since if once they knew the record they could not with a clear conscience conduct as they liked. Is it not amazing that in our times, when a sure means is accessible to all, has been found of learning exactly how the author demands his work to be executed, there should still be those who will not take any notice of such means, but persist in inserting concoctions of their own vintage?

Unfortunately, therefore, the rendering recorded by the author fails to achieve its most important object—that of safeguarding his work by establishing the manner in which it ought to be played. This is all the more regrettable since it is not a question of a haphazard gramophone record of just any performance. Far from that, the very purpose of the work on these records is the elimination of all chance elements by selecting from among the different records those which are most successful. It is obvious that even in the very best recordings one may come across certain defects such as crackling, a rough surface, excessive or insufficient resonance. But these defects, which, for that matter, can be more or less corrected by the gramophone and the choice of the needle, do not in the least affect the essential thing, without which it would be impossible to form any idea of a composition—I refer to the pace of the movements and their relationship to one another.

When one thinks of the complexities of making such records, of all the difficulties it presents, of all the accidents to which it is exposed, the constant nervous strain caused by the knowledge that one is continuously at the mercy of some stroke of bad luck, some extraneous noise by reason of which it may all have to be done over again, how can one help being embittered by the thought that the fruit of so much labor will be so little used, even as a document, by the very persons who should be most interested?

One cannot even pretend that the easygoing fashion in which "interpreters" treat their contemporaries is because they feel that their contemporaries have not sufficient reputation to matter. The old masters, the classics, are subject to just the same treatment notwithstanding all their authority. It is enough to cite Beethoven and to take as an illustration his Eighth Symphony, which bears the composer's own precise metronomic markings. But are they heeded? There are as many different renderings as there are conductors! "Have you heard *my* Fifth, *my* Eighth?"—that is a phrase that has become quite usual in the mouths of these gentlemen, and their mentality could not be better exemplified.

But, no matter how disappointing the work is when regarded from this point of view, I do not for a moment regret the time and effort spent on it. It gives me the satisfaction of knowing that everyone who listens to my records hears my music free from any distortion of my thought, at least in its essential elements. Moreover, the work did a great deal to develop my technique as a conductor. The frequent repetition of a fragment or even of an entire piece, the sustained effort not to allow the slightest detail to escape attention, as may happen for lack of time at any ordinary rehearsal, the necessity of observing absolute precision of movement as strictly determined by the timing—all this is a hard school in which a musician obtains very valuable training and learns much that is extremely useful.

In the domain of music the importance and influence of its dissemination by mechanical means, such as the record and the radio, make them worthy of the closest investigation. The facilities that they offer to composers and executants alike for reaching great numbers of listeners, and the opportunities that they give to those listeners of acquainting themselves with works they have not heard, are obviously indisputable advantages. But one must not overlook the fact that such advantages are attended by serious danger. In Johann Sebastian Bach's day it was necessary for him to walk ten miles to a neighboring town to hear [Dietrich] Buxtehude play his own works. Today, anyone, living no matter where, has only to turn a knob or put on a record to hear what he likes. Indeed, it is in just this incredible facility, this lack of any effort, that the evil of this so-called progress lies. For in music, more than in any other branch of art, understanding is given only to those who make an active effort. Passive receptivity is not enough. To listen to certain combinations of sounds and automatically become accustomed to them does not necessarily imply that they have been heard and understood. For one can listen without hearing, just as one can look without seeing. The absence of active effort and the liking acquired for this facility make for laziness. The radio has got rid of the necessity which existed in Bach's day for getting out of one's armchair. Nor are listeners any longer impelled to play themselves, or to spend time on learning an instrument in order to acquire a knowledge of musical literature. The wireless and gramophone do all of that. And thus the active faculties of listeners, without which one cannot assimilate music, gradually become atrophied from lack of use. This creeping paralysis entails very serious consequences. Oversaturated with sounds, *blasé* even before combinations of the utmost variety, listeners fall into a kind of torpor which deprives them of all power of discrimination and makes them indifferent to the quality of the pieces presented. It is more than likely that such irrational overfeeding will make them lose all appetite and relish for music. There will, of course, always be exceptions, individuals who will know how to select from the mass those things that appeal to them. But for the majority of listeners there is every reason to fear that, far from developing a love and understanding of music, the modern methods of dissemination will have a diametrically opposite effect—that is to say, the production of indifference, inability to understand, to appreciate, or to undergo any worthy reaction.

In addition, there is the musical deception arising from the substitution for actual playing of a reproduction, whether on film or by wireless transmission from a distance. It is the same difference as that between the *ersatz* and the authentic. The danger lies in the very fact that there is always a far greater consumption of the *ersatz*, which, it must be remembered, is far from being identical with its model. The continuous habit of listening to changed and sometimes distorted, timbres spoils the ear, so that it gradually loses all capacity for enjoying natural musical sounds.

All these considerations may seem unexpected in coming from one who has worked so much, and is still working, in this field. I think I have sufficiently stressed the instructional value that I unreservedly ascribe to this means of musical reproduction; but that does not prevent me from seeing its negative sides, and I anxiously ask myself whether they are sufficiently outweighed by the positive advantages to enable one to face them with impunity.

The Phonograph as a Compositional Tool

31. Carol-Bérard, "Recorded Noises— Tomorrow's Instrumentation"

Modern Music 6 (January–February 1929), 26–29

Is the destiny of new music confined to the exploitation of counterpoint? Or to a linking together of chords according to different techniques, boldly taking any liberty and carrying dissonant and rhythmic combinations to a frenzied climax? Or does it lie in the gradual increase of the present-day orchestra's apparatus, which will bring new members to the already sufficiently large families of strings, woodwinds, brasses, and instruments of percussion?

[Igor] Stravinsky and [Arnold] Schönberg [Schoenberg], to mention only two influential musicians among contemporary innovators, are fundamentally not so far from Bach, Beethoven, Mozart, or Wagner. They speak different dialects of the same language or rather of the same kind of language. Their methods, as audacious as they once may have seemed, differ little if at all—in one respect at least—from those of the classicists and romanticists; paper is needed to inscribe their thoughts and instruments must be in the hands of performers to transmit these thoughts to the audience.

Are the instrumental achievements of the notorious Italian *bruitistes*[35] the authentic milestones of a new music? These noisemakers are in all probability spiritual descendants of the Czech, Blaha, who, in the nineteenth century, invented a quite intricate machine operated by a bellows. Not only could it reproduce the tones of instruments like the fife, the flute or the trumpet, but it created new sounds imitating the noise of the wind, the tempest, and, on occasion, proved to be a veritable thunder-box. The Italian noisemakers, launched in 1911 by the fiery manifesto of Balila Pratella and a precisely conceived proclamation on the *The Art of Noises* by the painter [Luigi] Russolo, have made no advances since their debut.

Russolo, who had quite an imaginative idea of the direction music might take, wrote as follows: "Life in antiquity was silence. Noise was born in the nineteenth century with the invention of the machine. Today noise reigns supreme over human feeling." Further on he says: "Every act of our life is accompanied by noise. Noise is familiar; it has the power to recall us to life. Tone, on the contrary, is strange to life, always musical, a thing apart, occasional; it has become to our ear what a too well known face is to our eye. Noise, jutting out in confused and irregular fashion, never completely reveals itself; it holds innumerable surprises. By collecting and coordinating all noises we will enrich mankind with a wealth of new treasure."

To introduce and defend their idea, the noisemakers found a fervid apostle, completely convinced, enthusiastic and eloquent, in [F. T.] Marinetti. The name will always be associated with the period when mankind, viewing the splendid flight of the machine, felt the need to create a new esthetics. Marinetti is one of those who have given form to the spirit of our time. A belligerent and passionate advocate of futurism, he set himself rigorously to destroy the past before building his new structures. As we look back today we cannot but wonder at this deeply felt need to heap up verbal ruins in order to create something new. Though I may prefer the Eiffel Tower to the Tour Saint Jacques, some day I may wish to linger in the shadow of the old building and delight myself with the phantoms of another age.

The noisemakers were dedicated to the purpose of the music of the future, but their realization fell far short of the goal. For all the hummers, the exploders, the thunderers, the whistlers, the rustlers, the gurglers, the crashers, the shrillers, and the sniffers of the "futurist" orchestra obey the same laws of execution as the common violins, violoncellos, flutes, oboes, and other instruments in the traditional orchestra. No matter how new the acoustic effects they create, they are always in need of performers.

Other producers of sound have succeeded the noisemakers. Not only do we have the peculiar instruments of the jazz-band, but various new devices for the electrical production of music, notably those of Professor [Leon] Thérémin, the Russian, and of Frenchmen, [Armand] Givelet, [Maurice] Martenot, and René Bertrand, the engineer who has given us the dynaphones. (The orchestra of radio-electric dynaphones seems destined to play an important role in music today. Arthur Honegger has just used it successfully in *Roses en Métal*.)

. . . . .

Music must evolve in spirit and in expression. But before discussing its future, let us agree on some definition of music. Let us take the most commonly accepted meaning, namely, that this is the art of associating sounds in a manner agreeable to the ear. Then let us turn to noise, which, I believe, holds the secret of the future.

How far removed from music is noise? Where is the line of demarcation? Is this not indeed, just a question of the time and the individual? Before certain masterpieces were recognized as such—the *Ninth Symphony* [Ludwig van Beethoven], *L'Après-Midi d'un Faune* [Claude Debussy], *Le Sacre du Printemps*

[Igor Stravinsky], or *Pacific 231* [Arthur Honegger]—how many heard in them only noise? It is largely a matter of what one is accustomed to hear. I have met a music-seller to whom Debussy's *La Mer* represented nothing but a trolley with bad brakes.

What has differentiated noise from music is that the orchestra makes no use of it except as the incidental effect of expressive dissonance or of great intensity of sound produced by the usual instruments. If we take a definite noise, capture and associate it with other noises according to a definite design, an act of composition is performed and a work of art is authentically created.

Why, and I have been asking this for fifteen years, are phonograph records not taken of noises such as those of a city at work, at play, even asleep? Of forests, whose utterance varies according to the trees—a grove of pines in the Mediterranean mistral has a murmur unlike the rustle of poplars in a breeze from the Loire—? Of the tumult of the crowds, a factory in action, a moving train, a railway terminal, engines, showers, cries, rumblings?

If noises were registered, they could be grouped, associated and carefully combined as are the timbres of various instruments in the routine orchestra, although with a different technique.

We could then create symphonies of noise that would be grateful to the ear. There are plenty of symphonies today which are anything but agreeable, while there are at large and unregistered, a myriad of delightful sounds—the voices of the waves and trees, the moving cry of a sailing vessel's rigging, an airplane gliding down, the nocturnal choruses of frogs around a pool.

Once registered, naturally no significance other than that of sound can attach to the individual noises. They will cease to be the creaking of a bus axle, the rumbling of a cauldron, the roaring of a cataract. They will have become merely noise factors, as saxophones, clarinets, violas or oboes are factors of musical sound.

A new field will open up for an art not imitative but truly creative, intriguing and difficult. To the sonorous material already at the artist's command a wealth of unforeseen riches will be added.

And what security recorded noises will hold for the composer of the future. No longer at the mercy of interpreters, he may first listen to the sounds he wishes to combine, choosing what he wants from numberless possibilities at his disposal. Noises captured on separate records may finally be gathered as a symphonic ensemble on a single disk. A work may be heard at any time exactly in the form of its creation, as a picture presents itself always just as the artist has made it. The exact, the definitive work will ever be at hand, for the time approaches when the recording and reproducing apparatus will be perfect; it is nearly here now. Then the composer will have a laboratory and not a study.

The future of music lies in the conquest, the subjugation and the organization of noise. A new spirit will be served by a new material. That, for a time at least, will free us from the bondage of reminiscence.

32. Igor Stravinsky, "Meine Stellung zur Schallplatte"
Kultur und Schallplatte 1 (March 1930), 65
[translated from the German by Mark Katz]

It is necessary for each of us working artists of long practice to collect those experiences, for which work before the recording microphone is a vital necessity. The artist will be rigorously examined, mistakes will be mercilessly emphasized. Only the so-called "Microphone-Experience" lets the practical-minded take these factors into account and face them accordingly.

Recognizing the great importance of the disc, I have dedicated myself to the study of recording and support the view that the reproduction of a musical work through the talking machine should have a specially phonographic character, and that one must not be content with a dead sound-photography in which the real plasticity [of the music] is lacking. With this in mind I have become well accustomed to making recordings with Columbia.

It would be of the greatest interest to create music specifically for the phonograph, a music whose true image—its original sound—could only be preserved through mechanical reproduction. This would well be the ultimate goal for the phonographic composers of the future.

Phonograph Debates

Con

33. John Philip Sousa, "The Menace of Mechanical Music"
Appleton's, 1906, 278–84

Sweeping across the country with the speed of a transient fashion in slang or Panama hats, political war cries or popular novels, comes now the mechanical device to sing for us a song or play for us a piano, in substitute for human skill, intelligence, and soul. Only by harking back to the day of the roller skate or the bicycle craze, when sports of admitted utility ran to extravagance and virtual madness, can we find a parallel to the way in which these ingenious instruments have invaded every community in the land. And if we turn from this comparison in pure mechanics to another which may fairly claim a similar proportion of music in its soul, we may observe the English sparrow, which, introduced and welcomed in all innocence, lost no time in multiplying itself to the dignity of a pest, to the destruction of numberless native song birds, and the invariable regret of those who did not stop to think in time.

On a matter upon which I feel so deeply, and which I consider so far-reaching, I am quite willing to be reckoned an alarmist, admittedly swayed in part by personal interest, as well as by the impending harm to American musical art. I foresee a marked deterioration in American music and musical taste, an interruption in the musical development of the country, and a host of other injuries to music in its artistic manifestations, by virtue—or rather by vice—of the multiplication of the various music-reproducing machines. When I add to this that I myself and every other popular composer are victims of a serious infringement on our clear moral rights in our own work, I but offer a second reason why the facts and conditions should be made clear to everyone, alike in the interest of musical art and of fair play.

It cannot be denied that the owners and inventors have shown wonderful aggressiveness and ingenuity in developing and exploiting these remarkable devices. Their mechanism has been steadily and marvelously improved, and they have come into very extensive use. And it must be admitted that where families lack time or inclination to acquire musical technique, and to hear public performances, the best of these machines supply a certain amount of satisfaction and pleasure.

But heretofore, the whole course of music, from its first day to this, has been along the line of making it the expression of soul states; in other words, of pouring into it soul. Wagner, representing the climax of this movement, declared again and again, "I will not write even one measure of music that is not thoroughly sincere."

From the days when the mathematical and mechanical were paramount in music, the struggle has been bitter and incessant for the sway of the emotional and the soulful. And now, in this the twentieth century, come these talking and playing machines, and offer again to reduce the expression of music to a mathematical system of megaphones, wheels, cogs, disks, cylinders, and all manner of revolving things, which are as like real art as the marble statue of Eve is like her beautiful, living, breathing daughters.

Away back in the fifteenth and sixteenth centuries rebellion had its start against musical automatics, [Giovanni Pierluigi da] Palestrina proving in his compositions, that music is life, not mathematics; and [Martin] Luther showing, in his sublime hymns for congregational use and in his adaptations of secular melody for the church, that music could be made the pouring out of the souls of the many in one grand, eternal song. From the days of these pioneers, all great workers in the musical vineyard have given their best powers to the development of fruit, ever finer and more luscious, and in the doing have brought their art near and nearer to the emotional life of man.

The nightingale's song is delightful because the nightingale herself gives it forth. The boy with a penny whistle and glass of water may give an excellent imitation, but let him persist, he is sent to bed as a nuisance. Thunder inspires awe in its connection with nature, but two lusty bass drummers can drive you mad by what might be called a fair reproduction of Jove's[36] prerogative. I doubt if a dramatist could be inspired to write a tragedy by witnessing the mournful development and dénouement of "Punch and Judy";[37] or an actress improve her delineation of heroic character by hearing the sobs of a Parisian doll. Was [the biologist R. L.] Garner led to study language and manners of the orangutan and his kin by watching the antics of a monkey-on-a-stick?

It is the living, breathing example alone that is valuable to the student and can set into motion his creative and performing abilities. The ingenuity of a phonograph's mechanism may incite the inventive genius to its improvement, but I could not imagine that a performance by it would ever inspire embryotic Mendelssohns, Beethovens, Mozarts, and Wagners to the acquirement of technical skill, or to the grasp of human possibilities in the art.

[Louis] Elson, in his "History of American Music," says: "The true beginnings of American music—seeds that finally grew into a harvest of native composition—must be sought in a field almost as uncompromising as that of the Indian music itself—the rigid, narrow, and often commonplace psalm-singing of New England."[38]

Step by step through the centuries, working in an atmosphere almost wholly monopolized by commercial pursuit, America has advanced art to such a degree that today she is the Mecca toward which journey the artists of all nations. Musical enterprises are given financial support here as nowhere else in the universe, while our appreciation of music is bounded only by our geographical limits.

This wide love for the art springs from the singing school, secular or sacred; from the village band, and from the study of those instruments that are nearest the people. There are more pianos, violins, guitars, mandolins, and banjos among the working classes of America than in all the rest of the world, and the presence of these instruments in the homes has given employment to enormous numbers of teachers who have patiently taught the children and inculcated a love for music throughout the various communities.

Right here is the menace in machine-made music! The first rift in the lute has appeared. The cheaper of these instruments of the home are no longer being purchased as formerly, and all because the automatic music devices are usurping their places.

And what is the result? The child becomes indifferent to practice, for when music can be heard in the homes without the labor of study and close application, and without the slow process of acquiring a technique, it will be simply a question of time when the amateur disappears entirely, and with him a host of vocal and instrumental teachers, who will be without field or calling.

Great Britain is experiencing this decline in domestic music and the English press is discussing it seriously in its editorials. A recent writer in the London Spectator dwells at considerable length upon the prevailing condition, and points to the novel as a sign of the times. The present-day fashionable writer of society fiction, he declares, does not find it necessary to reinforce his heroine with vocal accomplishment, "as in the good old days." He ascribes the passing of home performance, both vocal and instrumental, to the newborn love of athletics among the maids of Albion,[39] together with the introduction of the phonograph as a mechanical substitute for amateur performances.

He believes that the exclamation of the little boy who rushed into his mother's room with the appeal: "O mamma, come into the drawing room; there is a man in there playing the piano with his hands," is far less extravagant than many similar excursions into the domain of humorous and human prophecy. He states from observation, that music has been steadily declining in Great Britain as a factor in domestic life, and that the introduction of machine-made music into the household is largely helping to assist in the change.

While a craze for athletics may have something to do with the indifference of the amateur performer in Great Britain, I do not believe it is much of a factor in this country. It is quite true that American girls have followed the athletic trend of the nation for a long while; at the same time they have made much headway in music, thanks to studious application. But let the mechanical music-maker be generally introduced into the homes; hour for hour these same girls will listen to the machine's performance and, sure as can be, lose finally all interest in technical study.

Under such conditions the tide of amateurism cannot but recede, until there will be left only the mechanical device and the professional executant. Singing will no longer be a fine accomplishment; vocal exercises, so important a factor in the curriculum of physical culture, will be out of vogue!

Then what of the national throat? Will it not weaken? What of the national chest? Will it not shrink?

When a mother can turn on the phonograph with the same ease that she applies to the electric light, will she croon her baby to slumber with sweet lullabies, or will the infant be put to sleep by machinery?

Children are naturally imitative, and if, in their infancy, they hear only phonographs, will they not sing, if they sing at all, in imitation and finally become simply human phonographs—without soul or expression? Congregational singing will suffer also, which, though crude at times, at least improves the respiration of many a weary sinner and softens the voices of those who live amid tumult and noise.

The host of mechanical reproducing machines, in their mad desire to supply music for all occasions, are offering to supplant the illustrator in the class room, the dance orchestra, the home and public singers and players, and so on. Evidently they believe no field too large for their incursions, no claim too extravagant. But the further they can justify those claims, the more noxious the whole system becomes.

Just so far as a spirit of emulation once inspired proud parent or aspiring daughter to send for the music teacher when the neighbor child across the way began to take lessons, the emulation is turning to the purchase of a rival piano player in each house, and the hope of developing the local musical personality is eliminated.

The country-dance orchestra of violin, guitar and melodeon had to rest at times, and the resultant interruption afforded the opportunity for general sociability and rest among the entire company. Now a tireless mechanism can keep everlastingly at it, and much of what made the dance a wholesome recreation is eliminated.

The country band with its energetic renditions, its loyal support by local merchants, its benefit concerts, band wagon, gay uniforms, state tournaments, and the attendant pride and gaiety, is apparently doomed to vanish in the general assault on personality in music.

There was a time when the pine woods of the north were sacred to summer simplicity, when around the camp fire at night the stories were told and the songs were sung with a charm all their own. But even now the invasion of the north has begun, and the ingenious purveyor of canned music is urging the sportsman, on his way to the silent places with gun and rod, tent and canoe, to take with him some disks, cranks, and cogs to sing to him as he sits by the firelight, a thought as unhappy and incongruous as canned salmon by a trout brook.

In the prospective scheme of mechanical music, we shall see man and maiden in a light canoe under the summer moon upon an Adirondack lake with a gramophone caroling love songs from amidships. The Spanish cavalier must abandon his guitar and serenade his beloved with a phonograph under his arm.

Shall we not expect that when the nation once more sounds its call to arms and the gallant regiment marches forth, there will be no majestic drum major, no serried ranks of sonorous trombones, no glittering array of brass, no rolling of drums? In their stead will be a huge phonograph, mounted on a 100 H. P. [horsepower] automobile, grinding out "The Girl I left Behind Me," "Dixie," and "The Stars and Stripes Forever."[40]

How the soldiers' bosoms will swell at the thought that they are being led into the strife by a machine! And when in camp at night, they are gathered about the cheery fire, it will not be:

Give us a song, the soldier cried.

It will not be:

They sang of love, and not of fame,
Forgot was Britain's glory;
Each heart recalled a different name,
But all sang "Annie Laurie."[41]

But it will be:

Whir—whir—whir—Song by the Bungtown Quartet: "Your Name is Dennis."

Shades of Alexander, of Washington, of Napoleon, of Wellington, of Grant, and of the other immortal heroes! Never again will the soldier hear the defiant call of the bugle to battle, and the historic lines must be changed to:

"Gentlemen of the French guards, turn on your phonographs first."

And the future d'Auteroches will reply:

"Sir, we never turn on our phonographs first; please to turn yours first."[42]

It is at the fireside that we look for virtue and patriotism; for songs that stir the blood and fire the zeal; for songs of home, of mother, and of love, that touch the heart and brighten the eye. Music teaches all that is beautiful in this world. Let us not hamper it with a machine that tells the story day by day, without variation, without soul, barren of the joy, the passion, the ardor that is the inheritance of man alone.

And now a word on a detail of personal interest which has a right to be heard because it voices a claim for fair play, far-reaching in its effects beyond the personal profit of one or many individuals. I venture to say that it will come as an entire surprise to almost every reader to learn that the composers of the music now produced so widely by the mechanical players of every sort draw no profit from it whatever. Composers are entirely unprotected by the copyright laws of the United States as at present written on the statute books and interpreted by the courts. The composer of the most popular waltz or march of the year must see it seized, reproduced at will on wax cylinder, brass disk, or strip of perforated paper, multiplied indefinitely, and sold at large profit all over the country, without a penny of remuneration to himself for the use of this original product of his brain.

It is this fact that is the immediate occasion of the present article, for the whole subject has become acute by reason of certain proposed legislation in Congress at Washington.[43] The two phases of the subject—fair play to music and fair play to musicians—are so naturally connected that I have not hesitated to cover the legal and the artistic sides of the question in a single discussion.

A new copyright bill was introduced in Congress at the last session, a joint committee met on June 6th, to hear arguments on the bill as presented, and the following paragraph was cause for lively discussion on the part of the various talking-machine interests and composers represented:

Paragraph (G) of Section I, which provides "that the copyright secured by this Act shall include the sole and exclusive right to make, sell, distribute, or let for hire any device, contrivance, or appliance especially adapted in any manner whatsoever to reproduce to the ear the whole or any material part of any work published and copyrighted after this Act shall have gone into effect, or by means of any such device or appliance publicly to reproduce to the ear the whole or any material part of such work."

I was among those present, and became particularly keen on the efforts of opposing interests to impress upon the committee by specious argument and fallacious interpretation that the composer of music had no rights under the

Constitution that they were bound to respect; and that remedial legislation was wholly out of the question until the Constitution had first been amended.

One gentleman went the length of declaring that he would never have worked out his reproducing apparatus, had he not felt confident that the Constitution gave him the right to appropriate the brightest efforts of the American composer, and he voiced the belief that any act giving the composer ownership in his own property would be most unconstitutional.

Asked if he claimed the right to take one of my compositions and use it in connection with his mechanical device without compensation to myself, his unselfish reply was: "Under the Constitution and all the laws of the land, I say Yes, decidedly!"

Asked if he was not protected in his patents, his answer was promptly in the affirmative, but he seemed wholly unable to grasp the proposition that a composer should ask for similar protection on his creative work.

Asked finally if he desired the Constitution amended, he replied magnanimously: "No, sir, I want the Constitution to stand as it is."

Of course it must not be overlooked that in the United States Circuit Court of Appeals a case has just been decided adversely to the composer's rights in the profits accruing from the use of his compositions on the talking and playing machines, but this case awaits final adjudication, on appeal, in the United States Supreme Court. Judges Lacombe, Coxe, and Townsend rendered a decision as follows:

"We are of the opinion that a perforated paper roll, such as is manufactured by defendant, is not a copy of complainant's staff notation, for the following reasons:

"It is not a copy in fact; it is not designed to be read or actually used in reading music as the original staff notation is; and the claim that it may be read, which is practically disproved by the great preponderance of evidence, even if true, would establish merely a theory or possibility of use, as distinguished from an actual use. The argument that because the roll is a notation or record of the music, it is, therefore, a copy, would apply to the disk of the phonograph or the barrel of the organ, which, it must be admitted, are not copies of the sheet music. The perforations in the rolls are not a varied form of symbols substituted for the symbols used by the author. They are mere adjuncts of a valve mechanism in a machine. In fact, the machine, or musical playing device, is the thing which appropriates the author's property and publishes it by producing the musical sounds, thus conveying the author's composition to the public."

May I ask, does this machine appropriate the author's composition without human assistance? Is the machine a free agent? Does it go about to seek whom it may devour? And if, as quoted above, the machine "publishes it," is not the owner of the machine responsible for its acts?

Is a copyright simply represented by a sheet of music? Is there no more to it than the silent notation? The little black spots on the five lines and spaces, the measured bars, are merely the record of birth and existence of a musical thought. These marks are something beyond the mere shape, the color, the length of the pages. They are only one form of recording the coming into the world of a newly fashioned work, which, by the right of authorship, inherent and constitutional, belongs to him who conceived it. They are no more the living theme which they record than the description of a beautiful woman is the woman herself.

Should the day come that the courts will give me the absolute power of controlling my compositions, which I feel is now mine under the Constitution, then I am not so sure that my name will appear as often as at present in the catalogues of the talking and playing machines. Evidently Judge Abinger, of the English bar, believes in the doctrine of substance, for he says: "The most unlettered in music can distinguish one song from another; and the mere adaptation of the air, either by changing it to a dance, or by transferring it from one instrument to another, does not, even to common apprehension, alter the original subject. The ear tells you that it is the same. The original air requires the aid of a genius for its construction; but a mere mechanic in music can make the adaptation or accompaniment. Substantially the piracy is where the appropriated music, though adapted to a different purpose from that of the original, may still be recognized by the ear."

Again the English court says: "The composition of a new air or melody is entitled to protection; and the appropriation of the whole, or of any substantial part of it, without the license of the author, is a piracy, and the adaptation of it, either by changing it to a dance, or by transferring it from one instrument to another, if the ear detects the same air, in the same arrangement, will not relieve it from the penalty."

The section of the Constitution on which my whole legal contention is based provides: "The Congress shall have power to secure for limited time to authors and inventors the exclusive right to their respective writings and discoveries."

And my claim is, that the words "exclusive" and "writings," particularly the latter, are so broad in their meaning that they cover every point raised by existing copyright laws, even to the unauthorized use of musical compositions by mechanical-reproducing apparatuses, and all this because these two words deal, not alone with the letter, but with the spirit as well.

But let the ambiguities in the text of law be what they may; let there be of legal quips and quirks as many as you please, for the life of me I am puzzled to know why the powerful corporations controlling these playing and talking machines are so totally blind to the moral and ethical questions involved. Could anything be more blamable, as a matter of principle, than to take an artist's composition, reproduce it a thousandfold on their machines, and deny him all participation in the large financial returns, by hiding back of the diaphanous pretense that in the guise of a disk or roll, his composition is not his property?

Do they not realize that if the accredited composers, who have come into vogue by reason of merit and labor, are refused a just reward for their efforts, a condition is almost sure to arise where all incentive to further creative work is lacking, and compositions will no longer flow from their pens; or where they will be compelled to refrain from publishing their compositions at all, and control them in manuscript? What, then, of the playing and talking machines?

34. Portland (Oregon) City Council, "An Ordinance Regulating the Use of Phonographs, Graphophones and Like Instruments within Certain Districts"
Minutes of the Portland City Council 26, 14 August 1907, 499

The committee on Health and Police to whom was referred Ordinance entitled "An Ordinance regulating the use of Phonographs, Graphophones[44] and like instruments within certain districts" presented a report recommending that section 1 be amended so as to read as follows:

"Section 1: That it shall be unlawful within the limits of the City of Portland for any person to operate or cause to be operated any automatic or electric piano, phonograph, graphophone or any instrument of like character between the hours of ten o'clock P. M. and seven o'clock A. M. or to operate or cause to be operated any automatic or electric piano, phonograph, graphophone or any instrument of like character at any time during the day or night within two blocks of any place where the public assembles, or at any time during the day or night within any building any portion of which is occupied as a hotel, or at any time during the day or night in any place whatsoever within two blocks of a hotel excepting the same be operated within closed doors."

By unanimous consent the report of the committee was adopted.

Portland (Oregon) City Council

Minutes of the Portland City Council, 27 November 1907, 70

The Committee on Health and Police to whom was referred the use of phono-graphs, graphophones etc., presented a report recommending "that said ordi-nance do not pass."

By unanimous consent the report of the committee was adopted.

35. Joseph N. Weber, "Canned Music—Is It Taking the Romance from Our Lives?"

Musician, November 1930, 7–8

Unless music is restored to life, romance will to a great extent perish. We are living in a highly organized mechanical age. Its clamor and rattle and cacophony are not conducive to fostering romance which is so necessary to alleviate the humdrum of daily life. Our young people work all day in offices where type-writers click incessantly, where telephones jangle, and in plants where in ma-chines whirr, in surroundings where mechanical iceboxes buzz, and where me-chanical music is played by the hour.

There is often even a tinny flavor to their meals, for the canned diet is grow-ing ever more popular in kitchenettes not built for cooking man-sized meals. The can-opener hangs prominently on a hook, like a symbol of the age in which the arts are forgotten.

. . . . .

Formerly, people not only enjoyed good music in their homes, but they found it in the theater, where splendid orchestras took them out of the prosaic atmo-sphere of every-day life and put them in the mood for weaving dreams. Talented musicians gave forth their own dreams in harmonious and rhythmic sound. But today a machine supplants the musician. The artist and his genius and his career have been tossed in the discard. It is estimated that salaries paid theater musi-cians have been cut nearly $25,000,000 a year, since one-half of the musicians formerly employed in theaters lost their jobs.

Defenders of the canned variety of music will argue that it, too, can arouse the emotions, but this is fallacious. Living music and living music only has the power to stir the soul of a listener. Where is the person who has not at one time or another been moved by the warm quality of a living singer's voice pouring his heart out in a serenade? Who is there who can honestly say that he has not experienced a genuine feeling of compassion when listening to [Enrico] Caruso sing [Ruggero Leoncavallo's opera] "I Pagliacci"?

Who wants wholesale mechanical music in place of the real live art? People are becoming satiated with mechanics. They want surcease from it, and at least out to get it in the realm of music and through romance. Today romance has almost passed out of existence along with living music. Romance must have a background, a setting. If living music is to be also gone, a mechanical substitute cannot take its place.

. . . . .

All of us lose culturally by this mechanization of a great art, and in this respect we face decadence. Continentals, who have a well-developed aesthetic sense, object violently to mechanical music in the theater, and they are amazed at what they think is the indifference of Americans to their loss.

American symphony orchestras are threatened by this widespread epidemic of canned music. Symphony orchestras depend to a certain extent on theater orchestras for their personnel, and if the latter are permanently put out of existence, they will be unable to obtain recruits. Our symphony orchestras are national institutions, and their passing would spell a terrible loss to this country. Our leading orchestras cannot be surpassed anywhere in the world. Extinction of these world-famous orchestras would be a tragedy, but this is what they face if mechanical music continues to prevail. Professional musicians are responsible for the art of music; if their services are no longer required, there will be no incentive for them to cultivate their talent. Musical genius will be a thing of the past.

It takes long years of patience, inspiration, ambition to pursue a musical career. Our youth will spurn the hard road to achievement in the musical field if it continues to see musical machines take the place of talented musicians. Why strive to reach a goal which will eventually be denied them? And, as a result, will America be dependent on foreign talent for the future personnel of its celebrated orchestras?

I have just read a report that five hundred French musicians were thrown out of work the other day as a result of the introduction of the talking picture apparatus in the cinema theaters where they had held jobs. This invasion by the machine will surely find opposition in France, for the French temperament is not keyed to the harsh, unmusical tempo of a mechanical arrangement which attempts to dispense music. The French have a true sense of harmony, and I am awaiting with interest further reports of the manner in which they will organize and rebel against the loss of their cherished live music.

It is somehow axiomatic that when we lose our delicate tastes of discrimination in one field, we lose them in others. When our feeling of appreciation in the musical field deteriorates, we lose also our sensitiveness to the perfections of other arts. Our bond with all the arts grows weaker when we permit one to die.

. . . . .

However, there are a few bright rays on the dark horizon of our culture. I have observed recently that people are tiring of dead music in the theater. They are weary of the soul-less quality of the machine. I have seen people walk out on musical features. That is why the comedy talking picture is more popular today than the one featuring musical numbers.

Neurologists and psychologists have come out with statements regarding the dangers of noise and mechanical devices that people are beginning to realize that their nervous systems are paying the penalty for our so-called "progress" in this mechanical age. Living in close proximity to one another in big apartment buildings in all our large cities, where the neighbors' radios destroy their sleep and tranquility, they want to escape from the mechanical pest during their hours of relaxation. They don't want to pay at the theater for the very nuisance which they are trying to escape by getting out of their apartment homes in the evening.

Everyone is tiring of the theme song, which runs monotonously like a never-ending thread through the patchwork of a score. And scores these days are made up after the fashion that a quilt is made, one piece of silk here, another strip ripped from a silk dress in this corner.

Canned music scores are made up of borrowed bits, a shred from a master's gem here, a bit of another there, and so on, with nothing a hundred percent original anywhere in evidence. The original scores in canned music which are played on synchronized machines do not number half a dozen.

We can easily detect the slapdash, hurried methods of the manufacturer of musical scores today. They lack the dignity, the soul-moving, the measured beauty of scores of other days—those which have proved to be enduring. The abrupt jumps from cheap jazz to the classics irritates the sensitive ear of the true music lover.

. . . . .

When the element of surprise and unexpectedness is removed from anything it ceases to be of interest. Life to all of us is a Pandora's box. We want to be surprised. When one listens to a living artist sing or play an instrument, anything might happen. A singer, on one certain night, might sing an aria in an altogether unforgettable way. An obscure artist might, in one evening, achieve the heights. Or a pianist or a violinist might, unexpectedly, one day play as he had never before, play in such a glorious fashion that he would bring the whole house to its feet with excited cries of "Bravo! Bravo!"

Thus every concert, every opera or operetta, every theater performance, every musical entertainment of any kind in which living music has a place, may prove to be an epoch-making occasion. A music lover, holding a ticket of admission, thrills with anticipation as he enters the place of entertainment.

But not so today! The records have been made months ago; they have been tried out; they have passed the board of censors. Why it is like eating a stale cake, from which hundreds of others have already nibbled. There is no use having the taste or appreciation of a connoisseur when connoisseurship is rendered sterile.

Is it any wonder that we all feel a nostalgia for the old days when the arts were not looked upon as little stepsisters, particularly the art of music? Certainly I, for one, am not surprised that millions of Americans have put themselves on record as demanding the revival of living music, the kind that will vitalize us, and quicken our stagnant blood, which now runs cold to the mechanical kind.

Pro

36. Paul H. Cromelin, "'The Menace of Mechanical Music': Some of the Replies Evoked by Mr. Sousa's Article"
Appleton's, 1906, 639–40

I have read with much interest an article under this title, in the September APPLETON'S, written by my distinguished friend, John Philip Sousa. Having been closely identified with the development of the talking machine, I was curious to learn how many and which of our cherished institutions were menaced by the great and growing use of these mechanical reproducers of music; and after having read the catalogue set forth in the above entitled article, I confess to having breathed a sigh of relief.

But before taking up the details, I cannot refrain from calling to mind that the mechanical reproducer of musical and other sounds has received, in the article referred to, precisely the same greeting that has been accorded to the other really great products of mechanical genius. There are not lacking, in such cases, those who see in the device some peril to the community, and who seek to excite opposition to it; though usually, if the opposition be probed, a selfish motive may be found. One of the distinguished instances was the cotton gin, which was regarded as so serious a "menace" to those who earned a livelihood by separating cotton fiber from its seed that the inventor was stoned by the infuriated representatives of the "menaced" industry. Now, the annual output of about ten million bales of cotton is the answer to that historic wail of unfounded apprehension.

There are those still living who can recall the outcry against the sewing machine, and the predictions that it would deprive the sewing girl of her scanty wage. But notwithstanding these predictions, plausible as they appeared to be, there are today a score of sewing women earning, and with comparative facility, good wages by the aid of the mechanical device, where there was then one securing a pittance by plying her needle.

But after all, what *are* the existing institutions which are menaced by the talking machines and automatic piano players?

First it is complained that the expression or rendition of music suffers, with a threat of deterioration of the public taste and appreciation in music.

To this assertion, a general denial can be confidently entered. No one who reflects upon the matter for a single moment will deny that the average rendition of music by the amateurs in the homes of our land is far, far below that of the mechanical reproducer of today. It is just because these devices bring into our homes renditions of superior quality, to which the vast majority of our people are total strangers, that they are meeting with such universal acceptation.

But there is much more than this. The average amateur is generally limited to *one* instrument, and his or her proficiency admits only of the indifferent rendition of a small number of compositions, usually of elementary character and mediocre quality. The graphophone, on the contrary, brings into the home the widest range of musical renditions, vocal and instrumental, solo and concerted, rendered, it may be, by the greatest living artists. So far, therefore, from the musical taste and appreciation of the public being menaced from this cause, it is safe to say that nothing has yet been devised by the wit of man so calculated to promote these qualities.

But let us hasten to the next of our menaced institutions. Our author assures us that the onward march of mechanical music will cause the girls of our nation to desist from the effort to make mediocre piano players of themselves, and will also diminish the use of the banjo, mandolin, and guitar. Assuming for a moment the correctness of this statement, which of our readers, upon hearing it, will not cheer onward the march of the mechanical music maker, and wish that it may soon accomplish its wholesome mission? What a fearful waste of time and what needless suffering have been caused by futile but persevering attempts to make all our Mary Janes "learn the piano." And to think that now a mighty reforming agency has appeared, which will abolish from our houses and flats the horrors of scales and exercises, and will confine these tedious performances to the musical colleges, or to those who really possess the gift of musical expression!

But I deny that the progress of the mechanical music maker will diminish individual application to the art of musical rendition. On the contrary, one important result of the present-day musical sound records is to excite an interest in music in millions of homes which otherwise have absolutely no access to really artistic musical renditions, or even access to renditions of any sort of great musical compositions. To those gifted by nature with a singing voice the opportunity of listening repeatedly to the phrasing and expression of great artists is of incalculable benefit. Already the high-class musical sound records have produced great educational results, affording to gifted persons in remote places and of slender means the extraordinary advantage of singing lessons from the greatest living artists, and a career of great utility is opened in this direction.

The idea that any person having the natural ability and desire to sing, will permit a mechanical device to do his singing for him is laughably absurd. On the contrary, the mechanical reproduction of songs by correct methods will only stimulate him to sing the more and enable him to sing the better.

Music and musical tone production has differed in the past from all other forms of art in that the pleasure which it afforded was but of a momentary and passing existence. We love the pictures and paintings in our homes and in the great galleries, and delight in feasting our eyes upon the masterpieces which noted sculptors have produced. There is a certain sense of possession and security in the knowledge that, if we care to, we may cross to Dresden and linger as long as we will in silent contemplation, not to say awe approaching adoration, before Raphael's Sistine Madonna. A few steps into another room, and once again [Heinrich] Hoffmann's wondrous masterpiece, Christ in the Temple, is ours to remain with and to behold in sweet meditation.

But oh! the memory of that night when Jean de Reske sang at the Metropolitan. Beautiful and sweet and blessed memory, but only a thing of memory now; and the recollections of the nightingale tones of Jenny Lind's remarkable voice! Ah, but a recollection now; a thing of the dead, dead past, gone, gone forever.

But the talking machine will change all this, and future generations will rejoice and be able to enjoy forever the music of the great artists of today. [Francesco] Tamagno is gone, but the voice of the great Italian tenor remains and brings pleasure and instruction to thousands of homes. Our well-beloved [actor] Joe Jefferson is no longer with us, but we have a precious legacy in Rip [Van Winkle]'s quaint and pathetic meeting with his daughter "Meenie," after twenty years' sleep. The matchless and incomparable triple-tongue cornet tones of Jules Levy remain to delight and please us, although all that was mortal of the great artist lies buried in a country churchyard.

Can we pay too great a tribute to the genius in the invention which makes it possible to bottle up this wine of music and song inexhaustible, and should we not offer up our thanks for "The Blessing of Mechanical Music"?

37. Anne Shaw Faulkner, "Phonographs and Player Instruments"
National Music Monthly, August 1917, 27–29

It was twenty-odd years ago that I first began my work as a lecturer and writer on musical subjects. The phonograph was only an uncanny toy, the player piano was a separate instrument, which was wheeled up before a piano and the roll was only 58 notes long. The phonograph was not taken seriously, but musicians looked askance at the player piano. With some of the younger piano teachers, panic reigned; where were they to get pupils if people actually took these things into their homes and played good music upon them? Would anyone want to learn to play the piano if they could make music so easily and with so little effort?

Some musicians, who really saw possibilities in the instrument, decided it was safer to encourage their use as a plaything, and they assumed an easy tolerance of them that is amusing in the light of present-day developments. There are many, who by their attitude toward player pianos, actually have done much to encourage the ragtime habit in the American home.

But fortunately there have always been a few of the truly great who have realized the importance of the self-playing instrument. I remember being present when the late William H. Sherwood was shown a very fine new type of player piano. It was considered quite an achievement to get him to listen to the instrument at all, and a small group of onlookers assembled. The Beethoven Sonata "Appassionata" was played; after it was over Mr. Sherwood turned to the demonstrator with these words: "You have there my friend, all of the technique that it has taken us pianists many hard long years to obtain, but you have not yet musicianship; that you will have to acquire by really learning the music, by hearing it so often that you will come to know it as well as the pianist, who has had to memorize it. And to really play that instrument well you must get that musicianship." It made a great impression on me, this statement from that famous pianist, for it was self-evident that the instrument did have the technique, yet the performance was mechanical and far from being musical. Yet even then I realized that the real musical feeling could and would come after repeated hearing and that with each hearing the performer would find that he was becoming better able to bring out the true beauties of the composer. I remember how in my enthusiasm I once stated to a few well-known musicians that the time would come when musicians would consider player pianos their best friends, how they laughed at me! But my prophecy has been more than justified by the place in education which mechanical instruments have made for themselves, for as everyone knows, they are now part of the equipment of practically all the schools and colleges in this country. It is no longer necessary for me to defend mechanical music. It is today recognized by musician and layman alike as being the most vital force in the upbuilding of America's musical knowledge.

Musically, America is most deficient in its musical listeners. We have felt for so many decades that the right to be recognized as having a part in music depends upon ability to sing or to play upon some instrument, that it has been hard to readjust ourselves to the truth of our need which is for a group of listeners far more than for performers. Such a group of listeners is constantly growing and its growth is due largely to the influence and development of mechanical instruments.

An interesting example of this is to be found in both the case of [the tenor] John McCormack and [the violinist] Fritz Kreisler, two of the most popular artists before the public today. Mr. McCormack has always chosen for the main part of his program the old ballads, yet his concerts became much more popular after his records of these songs were given to the public. The increasing sale of his records, which is said to be well over the million mark each year, shows from whence come the vast audiences which assemble for every McCormack recital. With Mr. Kreisler the case is a little more surprising, for the great violinist had never made any concession to public taste by playing familiar compositions. His audiences have been chiefly developed through the aid of his records, and it is safe to assume that he attracts at least five times as many auditors to his recitals than he did five years ago.

From the layman, I hear most often the expression, "You know I really love music, although I am not musical." It is always hard for me to explain that if one loves to listen to good music, one *is* musical. It usually requires no little argument to make the point clear, for the American public has built up a strong barricade between music and other things in life. We seem to think that music is something to approach, either with tears and sighs, or with the technical equipment which will justify its analytical dismemberment. For many years we have drawn such a definite boundary line between "popular" and "classical" music that we have forgotten that definition of the great [conductor] Theodore Thomas, that "popular music is only familiar music." We have spoken of "light" and "heavy" music, whatever that may mean, and we have felt that only the technically trained musician had either the privilege or the right to discuss music at all. If we did speak of music it was usually to moan meaninglessly about its beauties. The American business man has been almost ashamed to acknowledge that he cared for music, and his reasons for going to concerts and the opera usually were stated to be the necessity of providing an escort for the feminine members of the family, who felt they ought to be seen there.

This was the condition of the general public in America not longer than twenty years ago. But a great change has come, broadening the musical horizon of our land; people have found that music can easily be a part of their home life and that familiarity with the great musical compositions means a growing enthusiasm for the best in music. Before the days of the inexpensive photograph, a very few people knew the greatest architecture, sculpture and paintings of the world. Today every schoolchild is so surrounded by great art in the home and school that it has become a vital part of his daily life. The same thing is true regarding the use of mechanical musical instruments. People are realizing the importance of owning an instrument that can produce music, even if it is not played by a technically trained performer. But alas! many of them are stopping with the purchase of the instrument. Few realize that after all, even if one does own the instrument, it is just as necessary and important to train one's ear to listen to it as it is to train one's voice to sing or one's fingers to play. It is just in this one great point that the first mistake regarding mechanical music is made.

The instrument or voice student has to learn to use his ears, and as his technique develops his musical perceptions are quickened. But the owner of a player piano or phonograph persists in the absurd belief that the instrument is going to do it all for him, and that he actually has no part in the proceedings at all. The instrument becomes the fad of the moment, which is forgotten for long intervals and is brought out only to entertain or amaze the neighbors.

One class of owners of mechanical musical instruments count their records or their rolls entirely as to their cost and the great fame of the artist who made them. Another class of people use their instruments solely as a means to provide music for the dance or to perpetuate the vaudeville entertainments of the period. But there is a constantly increasing public who are coming to realize that a real knowledge of music can be developed by the true listener, and they have proven this so often to themselves, in their own homes, by means of their own instruments, that they no longer allow anyone to question the fact. They have learned by their own experience that each time they have heard great music they have discovered new beauties.

When one realizes that in twenty years the phonograph, with its old-time terrible whirr and wheeze, has become an instrument which produces not only the true message of the composer but that one can also distinguish the artist's own peculiar individuality as one listens to a good record, one wonders what the next twenty years will bring! The player piano has now become the most important part of piano manufacture, and the rolls, which were first made only by means of mathematical deductions, are now actually recorded for us by the greatest artists of the day, so that we may hear and learn to know the interpretations of all the greatest pianists, just as we have learned on our phonographs to distinguish between the voices of the world's greatest singers.

I predict that within the next twenty years the musical illiteracy of America will have been so reduced that it will be considered just as much of a disgrace not to know the greatest works in music as it is to be deficient in the greatest works of literature. I believe that there will not be a home in the land that does not realize the importance of music. I believe that the small boy of the future will be proud to acknowledge that he is taking music lessons, that he will be happy in his practice hours because he will know that music counts for something. I believe that at least three quarters of the youth of this country will be studying the technique of some instrument. I believe that musical education will be considered of such importance in our general educational scheme that all schools and colleges will give full credit for music study. I believe that before the next generation the American School of composers will hold equal rank with the greatest schools of the past. I believe that long before twenty years have passed America will be considered the most musical nation on the earth. And because I believe these things will come to our country because of the vital importance of mechanical music, I am taking charge of this department in this new magazine, hoping to make of it an aid—indeed, a most important part—in this development which is surely coming to America.

This department, as planned, will publish articles and discussion on music and musicians; the problems and plans of constructive musical education, particularly as they may relate themselves to the advancement of mechanically reproduced music. We are anxious for contributions on these topics and for assistance from those of readers who have discovered the possibilities of the phonograph and the player piano. We ask for correspondence, questions, ideas or suggestions. Will you not cooperate with us?

PART II. CINEMA

. . . .

CINEMA

Introduction   Tony Grajeda

The emergence of the cinema in the 1890s coincided with a tumultuous era of social and cultural modernity. This period was marked by the widespread industrialization of mass production, a massive wave of immigration to the United States (mostly from eastern and southern Europe), ongoing turbulence from rapid urbanization, and the increasing mechanization of daily life across much of Europe and North America. More specifically, cinema contributed to the larger development of commercialized mass culture throughout this era, in which numerous forms of entertainment and public amusements attracted large audiences by generating new modes of experience around mediated and technological sensations and spectacles.

The audiences for early cinema, not unlike those drawn to other forms of industrialized mass culture, were largely composed of urban, working-class, and immigrant groups, although the "moving-picture craze" made its way to small towns and rural communities as well.[1] The first decade of the twentieth century became known as the nickelodeon period (since admission to the shows would cost as little as a nickel), when motion pictures (still limited to mostly one-reel shorts) were often exhibited in makeshift storefront spaces. By early in the second decade, with the popularity of moviegoing increasing every year, nickelodeons as the primary exhibition space for showing films gave way to theaters dedicated to screening motion pictures regularly, with more luxurious "picture palaces" cropping up in cities large and small. As the films began to expand in length and achieve a more sophisticated narrative development in these years, so too were audiences expanding. The nascent film industry and film exhibitors were increasingly successful in attracting more middle-class patrons, the so-called better classes, with a family trade appealing especially to women and children.[2]

Although we may now, a full century later, have a fairly firm grasp of these early audiences in terms of class and ethnicity, much less is known with regard to their gender and racial makeup. Recently, work by a handful of scholars has uncovered the degree to which nickelodeons and early movie theaters provided an alternative public sphere for women,[3] and one study of Chicago's African American community in the silent era has finally given us a rich portrait of the audiences and movie theaters of the city's Black Metropolis. Mary Carbine's work here would be of special interest to readers of this anthology: she focuses on the vital role that music played in South Side movie theaters, often sites of black musical performance by what were sometimes called "Race orchestras." According to Carbine, "Jazz performed during the exhibition of films offered black spectators a lively demonstration of ethnic difference and invention, quite separate from the entertainment on the screen."[4]

Given such emerging work on "race orchestras" and the growing body of scholarship on sound and music in this period more generally, it is important to recognize the extent to which the "silent" cinema was never truly silent, notwithstanding the persistent myth that this silence was suddenly shattered by the "talkies" in 1926 and 1927. A close examination from film scholars over the past two to three decades has revealed a much more detailed account of the theatrical and performative aspects of early cinema, such as the live voiceover narration of film lecturers and the voices of actors behind the screen delivering lines roughly in sync with the images. Further research has revealed the wide array of mechanical sound systems that proliferated after 1910, as well as numerous attempts to combine the phonograph with projected images ("phonograph movies" and the practice of illustrated song, discussed further below). And a fair amount of work has been dedicated to recovering the historical evidence of both the steady presence of music (piano players, small ensembles) and the "extra-musical" dimensions produced by sound effects personnel (often the musicians themselves, more or less improvising).

Moreover, a modest amount of attention has been given recently to the ambient sound of the cinema itself—that is, sounds of theatrical spaces, including the "noise" of the audience. Such nascent research on early film spectatorship and the heterogeneous conditions of exhibition has allowed us not only to wonder what came of the raucous patrons of film's vaudeville days (traditional historical accounts insist that those unruly patrons would eventually be muffled, as would most audible elements), but also to listen more closely to the development in the second decade of the century of a classical narrative cinema once said to be accompanied only by the "underscoring" of orchestral interludes.

Even though the introduction of "the talkies" appears to be unexpected and thus altogether dramatic, at least to the casual observer, there were in fact numerous experiments with sound-image synchronization in the years following the First World War and in the 1920s as well. Lee de Forest's Phonofilm system of the early 1920s, for example, is probably the most widely recognized such attempt at synchronization (even if it never found sufficient financial backing to have much of an impact on the industry). Furthermore, one scholar's landmark study on the gradual—rather than sudden—transitional period reveals the less familiar efforts across this decade at "combining moving images and broadcast sound," such as "radio talking pictures," Radiophone, and Radio Film, all of which helped create "a climate of acceptance" for the eventual realization of synchronized sound cinema.[5]

Seeking to fill in some of the gaps of both classic and current scholarship on the cinema's first three decades, this anthology speaks to such silence by including historical texts and responses that still tried to give a "voice" to what the filmmaker René Clair once called "the silent land of pure images."[6]

The recent scholarship on the sounds of "silent" cinema corresponds to a parallel and at times overlapping body of work by film historians paying greater attention than ever before to the reception of films by audiences. Such attention marks a notable shift in focus from text to context, which is to say from the specific text of a film and its academic interpretation to the larger context of public reception and social and cultural experience.[7] In keeping with this orientation on reception studies, and of course central to the overriding purpose of the present anthology, I have selected historical documents from the late nineteenth century to the early 1930s with an eye and ear toward the users of new technologies around music and film (technicians, musicians, conductors) as well as the audiences of viewers, listeners, and fans of audiovisual media within an increasingly commodified public sphere. The discourses from this period of modernity on the emerging technologically based commercial amusements and mass culture of screen and sound entertainments such as the cinema and the phonograph often disclose how participants and practitioners were heavily invested in their audiences—whether real or imagined. What resonates across many of these documents, then, is a palpable concern (if not preoccupation) with attracting, holding, and building an audience, as expressed in one such account from 1910 on the lingering practice of illustrated song performances, with the author here discussing how a singer, in particular one of limited ability, could still be "a drawing card" to a theater: "He hasn't a wonderful voice, but it is good and has a mellow, plaintive sweetness. You imagine he is sincerely singing to the girl he loves, as though no audience were present, and nearly every girl in front has an idea that he is singing directly to her. His words ring true, and when he tells how much he loves his lady friend, the audience believes every word of it. They can't help it" (item 45). If the actual, empirical audience for such moments has for the most part been lost to history, the ways in which those audiences were addressed and conceived at the time can still be heard in the traces of the historical documents that have survived. Consequently, it is left to us to reconstruct those audiences and their likely responses in order to complete the circuit of the production and consumption of sound and music through early audio technologies.

In what follows, I briefly touch upon the concept of intermediality, a theoretical notion developed by early film and media scholars as a way of exploring the relational aspects between cinema and other media within a roughly coextensive time period. As a conceptual framework for bridging between and among media, intermediality has particular relevance to the present anthology, and it will be useful to readers in listening for points of contact and overlap with other media technologies, especially radio and phonography. From there I discuss the various sounds of "silent" cinema, emphasizing the many musical practices associated with emerging and evolving screen cultures, with reference to some of the historical documents in part II.

To many students and scholars alike, it might be surprising a century later to realize that as the film historian Rick Altman contends, "the technology today confidently called cinema was for over a decade considered quite differently by its contemporaries." From its emergence in the mid-1890s to at least twenty years later, "projected moving images," according to Altman, "were subjected to multiple contradictory definitions and treatments."[8] This moment when "cinema" was still in formation—when its future did not yet appear predetermined—has been mostly lost in the traditional histories of cinema, but it is worth noting that at one time there was a good deal of speculation over the very nature of the technology, and a good deal of confusion over what it actually was. Not unlike what occurred around early phonography (and to some extent early radio as well), this uncertainty over cinema's identity is worth bearing in mind while poring over the historical documents gathered in this collection.

This formative period in which cinema suffered an identity crisis is perhaps best illustrated by the different terms used in the very titles of various journals and publications pertaining to the emergent practice: *moving pictures, photo-*

play, picture play, cinematograph, motion pictures. Referring to photography, theater, performance, and new technology, these different appellations suggest, as Richard Abel and Rick Altman write, "early cinema's configuration as an unusually complex hybrid medium." Consequently, scholars of early cinema have developed the concept of intermediality to better apprehend this complexity, a notion that "has to be understood as referring to relations both between cinema and other cultural practices and within cinema itself, particularly defined in terms of exhibition."[9] While the former model of intermediality views cinema in relation to a range of media practices such as phonography, radio, and other sound technologies (apropos the present anthology), the latter model exceeds the film-based focus of previous historical accounts by instead emphasizing the conditions of exhibition. Such conditions, as this discussion demonstrates, encompass in particular a wide array of sounds, musical practices, and audio technologies of production and reproduction.

Thus, as noted, it is now widely accepted that what had once been called the silent cinema was never truly silent. As one early cinema scholar insists, "It was quite exceptional, in the silent period, for a film to be projected in complete silence." Indeed, "the filmic spectacle" of early cinema "was nearly always an *audio*-visual one like (for example) circus or theatre."[10]

To begin with, we need to consider the role of the film lecturer, until recently a fairly unexamined figure who, in presenting this new form of screen entertainment, often provided a kind of running commentary to early moving pictures—a live voiceover narration that would serve to direct audience attention and apprehension of the event. The not-uncommon presence of the film lecturer suggests the extent to which this new cultural form of storytelling and visual representation required a certain amount of guidance—one had to be trained to "read" film. Such cultural work was likely more than a mere supplement to reception for early audiences, which typically included large numbers of immigrants who undoubtedly were new to the English language itself, and thus did not necessarily benefit from the increasing use of titles—the visible text that otherwise provided narrative legibility and comprehension (see for example Van C. Lee, "The Value of a Lecture," item 46, and the accompanying letters, item 47). Descending from and for a while coexisting with magic lantern and stereopticon shows, early film exhibition practices in the 1890s directed by traveling showmen and lecturers persisted into the nickelodeon period, when film still shared a stage with other attractions in a vaudeville format.[11] And as part of a more theatrical performance, from around 1908 to the early years of the following decade, "films were often supplemented by carefully rehearsed actors speaking lines in sync with the image," writes one film historian, who calls this practice the "human-voice-behind-the-screen" (see item 48).[12]

Apart from this quite frequent role of the voice, the presence of music was of course the foremost reason that the silent cinema was anything but silent. As is relatively well known, large orchestras were a major draw in the picture palaces of the 1920s, but live music accompanied film screenings right from the beginning (as many of the historical documents in part III indicate). The most common musical ingredient was provided by piano players, yet it was not unusual to find a small ensemble of musicians (often from the music hall tradition), as well as sound effects personnel, accompanying films in most exhibition spaces.[13]

Live musical performances that supplemented and no doubt shaped the image were in turn supplemented (or in some cases displaced altogether) by a variety of attempts to combine the phonograph with projected images. The illustrated song, for example, was one such novelty of screen and sound entertainment at the turn of the century, "billed," according to one scholar, "as part of Edison's [among others] ongoing efforts to synchronize sound and image" (see items 43, 44, and 45). Such "Picture Songs" produced by the Edison company as *The Astor Tramp* and *Love and War* (both 1899) were organized around and through phonograph recordings, an arrangement that to some degree reversed the weight of narrative responsibility: the images here appear to have supplemented the stories told primarily through song.[14] And the practice of illustrated song as "the Latest Novelty of the Stage" seems to have paved the way for the many "phonograph movies" produced in the not-quite-silent era, especially in Europe. In Germany, for example, Oskar Messter, utilizing a synchronized sound projector called the Biophon, had produced by one account some fifteen hundred short sound films by 1913.[15]

Although exact (mechanized) synchronization of sound and image would not emerge until the Vitaphone sound-on-disc (1926) and the Movietone sound-on-film (1927) formats, it should not be forgotten that a variety of sound systems proliferated before the arrival of the talkies, including Edison's Kinetophone (1895, reintroduced in 1913), Léon Gaumont's Chronophone (1902, reintroduced in 1913 with "an improved synchronizing mechanism"), and E. E. Norton's Cameraphone (1908), among many others (see items 41 and 42). As one film historian emphasizes, "Cameraphone, Chronophone, Cinephone and dozens of other competing systems were not only invented in this period; during the end of the century's first decade they were installed in hundreds of theaters across Europe and from coast to coast in the United States."[16]

While several of the documents collected here attest to the technological mediation of sound and music in relation to the screen well before the achievements of 1926 and 1927, most of the documents illustrate the prominent role that "live" music played during the first three decades of moving-image culture. What may be surprising to many of us today, given the long tradition in film culture of treating music as merely supplemental to the image, is to discover that it was not unusual at the time for music to be placed on an equal plane with the image, as one commentator in 1910 argues:

> The demand for good music is such that it is now as much of a rivalry between exhibitors to brag of their good orchestra as it is of bragging of the quality of their pictures. In other words, the managers are now taking as much interest in the music as in the projection of the pictures, and the great demand for extra musical accessories, like the Deagan electric bells, xylophones, chimes, automatic orchestras, pipe-organs, etc., shows that, in the very near future, moving picture theaters will be real concert halls and that the public will go to the shows not only for the sake of seeing pictures but to hear good music. (item 53)

From the performative accompaniment of pianists, small ensembles, and organists to the larger orchestras and matters of conducting and scoring to the motion pictures, what is at stake for all concerned is figuring out the proper relationship between music and screen, between what is heard and what is seen. Thus many of the following documents are overtly instructive in design, directly addressing the full spectrum of organists or pianists—from budding to accomplished—or even orchestra conductors or musical directors, with such instructions clearly aiming for establishing appropriate or, in the parlance of the day, "suitable" musical accompaniment (see all the items under the heading "Playing to the Pictures," as well as most of those under "Conducting and Scoring to the Movies").

A columnist for the *American Organist*, for example, writing in 1918, speaks approvingly of a theater manager who insisted "that the play was the thing, and the music was subsidiary and contributory, and that it should never at any time draw attention away from the picture" (item 60). Yet we also read a contrary suggestion to invert that ratio by another writer who asks, "Why not reverse the process and build a picture around some great piece of music?" (item 63). Although the eventual Hollywood filmmaking practice of habitually and structurally subordinating sound and music to the image can trace its roots to this formative period, there is also competing evidence for a counter-tradition, one in which the aural dimension appeared invaluable rather than just supplemental to the visual field. What can be gathered nonetheless from these historical accounts is that the intermediality between sound/music and image/screen was not fixed or predetermined but rather unstable and conditional, a series of relations in the process of being negotiated by practitioners, musicians, technicians, and other parties. What these documents also attest is how such intermediality nearly always lent an ear toward actual audiences and the imagined or potential auditor-spectator.

Finally, what the discourse from this period further demonstrates is that along with the deliberate training of musicians, composers, personnel, and so on in the guidance of "suitable" music for motion picture presentations, there was also an equally vigorous attempt at training moviegoing audiences to listen to and appreciate "picture music." Corresponding to similar discursive practices accruing to the phonograph and radio, the documents under the heading "Taste, Culture, and Educating the Public" exemplify the earnest efforts by cultural guardians of the day to legislate taste publics and to patrol the hierarchical division of high culture and low or mass culture. As some of the commentators represented here ask: Can the general public be properly educated into "good" music? Should the cinema try to raise musical standards, or will it be content to give a mass audience what it already seems to want? And, with the introduction of the talkies, will "canned music" overwhelm if not destroy the genuine article? All this and more was bandied about and debated at the time, and a surprising number of these time-worn issues still resonate into the present.

Audiences for early cinema were primarily made up of working-class patrons. (Industrialized)

CINEMA

Readings Compiled by Tony Grajeda

Technologies of Sight and Sound
....

38. "The Kineto-Phonograph"
Electrical World, 16 June 1894, 799–801

Thomas A. Edison conceived the idea of the simultaneous record and reproduction of sound and motion in 1887, the idea naturally being suggested by that familiar toy, the zoetrope. The work of the inventor and his assistants has borne fruit in the kinetograph and kinetoscope, which are now making claims upon public attention, and which, whatever may prove to be their practical value, will stand as striking illustrations of human ingenuity and patience. That Mr. Edison himself believes in the future possibilities of this device is evidenced by the following recently published statement: "I believe that in coming years, by my own work and that of Dickson, Muybridge, Marie and others who will doubtless enter the field, that grand opera can be given at the Metropolitan Opera House at New York without any material change from the original, and with artists and musicians long since dead."[1]

The principle of the kinetograph—the recording—and the kinetoscope—the reproducing—instrument is doubtless generally understood. A series of photographs of the object or objects which it is desired to reproduce are taken with a rapidity of between forty and fifty views per second. These photographs are then developed and by means of the kinetoscope are either projected upon a screen or exposed directly to the eye at the same rate of motion. As the interval between the exposure of the successive photographs is too short to be appreciated by the human eye, the motions of the subject appear continuous to the observer. It is apparent that this invention lies largely in the realm of photography and, as in the phonograph, electricity plays a subsidiary part.

The kinetograph reaches its highest sphere of usefulness in conjunction with the phonograph, by which it is intended to reproduce every word and movement of the subject in their proper relation. For the combined instrument, the name "kineto—phonograph" has appropriately been suggested. While the kineto-phonograph has not been brought to a sufficiently practical form for public exhibition, as has the kinetoscope, the experiments in the inventor's laboratory have been so successful that it is regarded only as a question of time, by those engaged in the work, when the apparatus will be perfected.

The credit for the development of the kinetograph and kinetoscope belongs, after the inventor himself, to Mr. W. K. L. Dickson, whose wide experience in photography and familiarity with the application of electricity have rendered him an invaluable assistant to Mr. Edison. In the June number of the "Century," Antonia and W. K. L. Dickson trace the history and development of the invention and point out some of the many difficulties which beset the path of the experimenter along these lines.

The first experiments were made with a cylindrical shell, the same size as the ordinary phonograph cylinder, upon which minute photographs were placed. The two cylinders were placed on a shaft side by side, and the photographic and phonographic impressions taken as nearly at the same time as possible. Photography at such a high rate of speed was a new art and the first results were not especially promising. The Daguerre, albumen and other similar known processes failed, and an attempt was made to use cylinders coated with the Maddox gelatine bromide of silver emulsion, but the difficulty here was that when the minute photographs were enlarged they were unduly coarse.

The next move was to try larger impressions, which were swiftly rotated upon the edge of a wheel or disc, supplied with a number of pins, which projected under the centre of each picture. These pins successively broke the primary circuit of an induction coil, to the secondary of which was connected a Geissler tube.[2] The tube was lighted at the exact moment the picture passed before it. The results were very encouraging. Experiments were then made with celluloid films placed on drums something like the old tinfoil phonograph. The pictures were taken spirally, the sheet of celluloid removed and developed and then placed on a hollow drum, inside of which was a Geissler tube connected to an induction coil. Brass pins on the exterior of the cylinder broke the circuit at the proper moment and each picture was in turn illuminated. A highly sensitized strip of celluloid half an inch wide was then tried, but the width was soon increased to an inch and a half. The photographs were but an inch in width, but the extra width was perforated and a locking device employed to hold the film steady during the infinitesimal time—about the one-fiftieth part of a second— during which the shutter opened and a photograph was taken. Then in about 1–460th part of a second the film is jerked forward and again held at rest and another photograph taken. This system allows an exposure of one-hundredth part of a second for each picture, which is sufficient for excellent work.

The speed of this photographic work is certainly astonishing. Forty-six impressions are taken each second, which is 2,760 a minute and 165,600 an hour; or, as Mr. Dickson has graphically put it, "were the spasmodic motions added up by themselves, exclusive of arrest, on the same principle that a train record is computed independent of stoppages, the incredible speed of twenty-six miles an hour would be shown."

After securing the negative, the next step is to secure a positive strip of film. When this is prepared it is ready to be placed in the kinetoscope or photo-kinetoscope. When a phonographic record has been taken simultaneously with such a strip, the two are started together by a simple device and kept together throughout the reproduction, a single electric motor operating both. One of the greatest difficulties met with by the experimenters was the nicety of adjustment required to simultaneously record and reproduce the sound and motion.

In taking the photographs, either sunlight or artificial light is employed; in the latter case four parabolic magnesium lamps or twenty arc lamps, provided with highly actinic carbons, supplied with powerful reflectors, are used. A special building has been constructed for photographic purposes, interior and exterior views of which are herewith given. It swings on a central pivot, so as to obtain any desired light. A stage is arranged inside and provision made for very sharp contrasts of light and shade.

The only form of this apparatus yet placed on public exhibition is a nickel-in-the-slot form of the kinetoscope. Several of these machines may be seen in one of the accompanying views, which shows the interior of an exhibition room on Broadway, New York City. They consist of a cabinet containing an electric motor and accumulator cells for operating the mechanism which moves the film. The film is in the form of an endless band, fifty feet in length, which is passed through the field of a perpendicular magnifying glass. The impressions pass before the eye at the rate of forty-six per second by means of a rotating slotted disc, the slot of which exposes a picture at each revolution and separates the fractional gradations of pose.

Portions of two different kinetoscopic bands are here reproduced showing several sections of the films. Close examination will show the almost imperceptible change between one view and the next.

As to the future of this most ingenious and interesting bit of mechanism, time only will demonstrate whether it is to be a mere scientific toy or an invention of real practical value.

39. "The Perfection of the Phono-Cinematograph" [editorial]
Moving Picture World, 14 September 1907, 435

The combination of the phonograph and the cinematograph has at last become a thoroughly practical success. One for the picture and the other for words or sounds, they instantly seize and afterwards reproduce at will living scenes, enabling interesting and useful records to be preserved of a period, an industry, or an art.

If, separately, the phonograph and the cinematograph record interesting events, it is evident that their combination in one apparatus, producing at the same time a living scene and voices of all kinds which accompany it, with rigorous exactitude, presents a far greater interest.

Perfect synchronism between the phonograph and the cinematograph is indispensable. All illusion would disappear if, for example, the voice continued to sound when the mouth of the image had already closed and was not moving. Originally the synchronism was only obtained by the skill of the operator in turning the crank handle of the cinematograph more or less quickly while following the sounds emitted by the phonograph. The phonograph, operated by a special electrical motor, governs synchronously the motor of the cinematograph, whatever may be the speed adopted for the whole apparatus. Two motors operated by the same continuous current are connected together by means of wires. It is necessary also to be able to establish this synchronism in case the point of the phonograph leaves the furrow and jumps into a neighboring furrow. This is obtained by the interposition, between the motor and the mechanism of the cinematograph, of a deferential apparatus, operated by a small special motor. This is started by the operator only in case of such an accident. A commutator is employed to cause this mechanism to start in the necessary direction, either forwards or backwards. The taking of negatives is made generally, for the sake of facility, in two operations. Records are made first of the words or the music, then the two apparatus are united, and while the subject re-enacts the scene, accompanying it by his own voice, the cinematograph records the actions. Sometimes also the two apparatus record simultaneously the actions and the sounds, but it is naturally necessary to have very skillful operators to operate thus at some distance from the subjects. The makers of phono-cinematographs have private theaters furnished specially for taking records. The lighting is obtained from two powerful batteries and arc lamps.

The brief description which we have just given of the ingenious apparatus which absorbs the varied resources of mechanism, photography, acoustics, and electricity, shows the great amount of minute work which underlies a phono-cinematograph scene, and the great expense which it entails. No doubt this recent industry, which is being perfected from day to day, promises success and a development similar to photography. Its role of usefulness will no doubt also become as important as its role of pleasure, and no doubt we shall soon see new applications in this direction.

40. Advertisement for Picturephone, "Singing and Talking Moving Pictures"
Moving Picture World, 11 January 1908, 31

(see figure overleaf)

41. "The Singing and Talking Picture— What Is Its Future?" [editorial]
Moving Picture World, 7 May 1910, 727–28

The passing of the Cameraphone Company closed an interesting and important chapter in the history of the moving picture. Two years ago it seemed, chiefly by the agency of this company, as if we were on the eve of the realization of an old dream of the inventor, that is, the combination of the phonograph with the moving photograph. In other words, of offering to the public what is known as the singing and talking picture. But with the disappearance of the Camera-phone Company from the field, we seem to be suffering a setback in the realization of this dream.

On the other hand, the line of practical work is by no means extinct. In the first place, there is the Gaumont Chronophone, which is popular with audiences in the United States. We heard and favorably commented upon this beautiful piece of apparatus about a year ago. Yet curious to tell, it does not seem to have made its way into the moving picture theater of New York City, and we do not hear so much of it in the country as we should like to. Then there is the Cinephone, which has been the subject, to say the least of it, of a somewhat varied, if not romantic, career in this country since its introduction here a year ago. Fourthly, there is a solitary moving picture house in New York City which gives a display of the singing picture known as the Fotophone. We allude to the Eden Musee, on Twenty-third Street.

Matters then stand today pretty well where they stood twelve months ago. Perhaps on the whole they are more encouraging now than then, because of the added experience which American and other inventors have acquired. It is not our present object to inquire as to why the Cameraphone failed. It seemed to be an excellent scheme for combining phonographic effects with those of the moving picture, yet it is the barest truth to say that it was not a public success. We saw and heard the system under conditions which inclined us to think that there was a great future for it. Apparently, however, it was before its time and has gone the way of many conceptions that are too previous.

From what we hear, public interest in the matter is by no means dead, so that the field before Messrs. Gaumont and the Cinephone and the Fotophone is as large as ever. In our opinion the singing and talking moving picture is bound sooner or later to become a permanent feature of the moving picture theater. The immediate object of this article is to place on record the fact that public interest in the matter is not dead, and to advise the reader to keep himself on the *qui vive* with regard to probable early developments of these singing and talking pictures. Seen and heard under the best possible conditions these subjects are so real, so lifelike, and so attractive, that we never falter in our opinion that the inventive mind will overcome the practical difficulties that are at present in the way, and so pave the ground for the commercial and artistic success of the combined phonograph and photograph.

Reference to the subject would be incomplete without mentioning the fact that it is generally understood the Edison Company is at work in perfecting a synchronizing system for vocalized moving pictures. We do not know how far the company has progressed in their experiments, but it may reasonably be assumed that in due course they will put a satisfactory system on the market.

This adds, then, a fourth possibility in the field. Since we started to write this little article we have heard further from Messrs. Gaumont on the subject, and they tell us that their Chronophone, under their recently inaugurated system of educating exhibitors and operators, is acquiring increased popularity. They are booking one-week shows in one theater in every town of New England, and, judging from the demand, they may have to send out other demonstrators. Several exhibitors have written us in glowing terms of the success of the talking picture and its drawing power on the week they had it. The New Bedford (Mass.) "Times" gives the Nickel Theater of that town a good boost on the excellence of the Harry Lauder pictures and the clearness of his songs on the Chronophone.[3]

Answering our own question, then, which forms the subtitle of this article, we would say that the future of the singing and talking photograph is at this moment fuller of promise than ever it was.

42. "Talking 'Movies'"
Outlook, 8 March 1913, 517

Just as moving-picture actors had succeeded in resuscitating the art of pantomime, comes word that the ban of silence has been lifted from their flickering lips. This edict of freedom has been long foreshadowed by various tentative efforts to link the phonograph and the kinetoscope. It remained, however, for the Frankenstein of both these machines to break his creatures to double harness. Though Mr. Edison's new kinetophone involves no principles unfamiliar to the general public, the combination of old ideas seems as startling as it is successful. Briefly stated, he has devised a recording phonograph as delicate as the human ear. In the past, phonographs, however sturdy their voices, have been decidedly deaf. They have declined to take in anything that was not spoken or played for their especial benefit, directly into their capacious trumpets. With such instruments, those who have previously striven to make the "movies" speak have been forced to take their pictures first and then to create an independent voice-record to fit that film. The difficulty of such a method can be readily imagined. With this new phonograph all such makeshift systems are abolished. The machine is placed anywhere within ear-shot and out of range of the camera's lens, and picture-taking and record-making proceed simultaneously. Of course such a process involves the invention of governing mechanism whereby the speed of film and disk can be simultaneously controlled. This also Mr. Edison has accomplished. The first public exhibition of the kinetophone was given Monday, the 17th of February, in four New York vaudeville theaters. Two "films" (there is yet no inclusive term for films and phonograph records) were shown and heard. In the first a man discusses with many oratorical flourishes of voice and limb the history and future of the invention and then illustrates the possibilities of the kinetophone by breaking plates, blowing horns and whistles, and by the introduction of a singer, a pianist, a violinist, and a barking dog. The second "film" presented to the audience was a minstrel troupe in full cry. The value of the kinetophone is too obvious to be emphasized or discussed. What would we not give for such a record of the Gettysburg Address!

Sounds of the Cinema
Illustrated Song Slides; The Role of the Voice (lecturers, actors); Incidental Musics, Special Effects, Ballyhoo, and Noise of the Audience

....

43. Chas. K. Harris,[4] "Illustrating Song Slides"
Moving Picture World, 9 March 1907, 5–6

The art of illustrating songs with the stereopticon is now one of the features at all vaudeville performances; in fact, it has become one of the standard attractions. To illustrate a song properly often entails a large expenditure of money. The most beautiful illustrated song pictures are those having natural backgrounds. It is not always possible to secure such pictures, and backgrounds have to be painted and prepared with scenic effects. After all the arrangements for the scenery have been made, there comes the hardest and most perplexing part of illustrating a song—procuring the subjects to pose in the pictures. They are generally secured by advertising, and often several hundred applicants will be turned away before suitable models are secured. If the song calls for a beautiful child with golden hair, 95 percent of the applicants (brought always by their parents) will be black-haired, freckle-faced, snub-nosed youngsters. The same rule applies to adults. In every case, however, where the work is well done, beautiful children, pretty women, and handsome men must be secured for some songs, while old men and women, representing types from the beggar to the millionaire, must be found for others. Everything, whether pathetic, sad or comical, must seem real and perfectly natural. Interiors must also be furnished for the occasion, special costumes must be made or hired, and often the models must be taken long distances to secure harmonious surroundings. All these things cost large amounts of money and often before the negatives for from fifteen to twenty-five slides have been secured the expense has amounted up to hundreds of dollars. In the case where large numbers of negroes posed in a cakewalk for a new song which I have illustrated, entitled "Linda, Can't You Love Your Joe," it was necessary to send photographers as far as Alabama and Tennessee, there to remain until the real Southern negro was rounded up and asked to pose for a picture. At least sixty subjects were used in this one set, and their services cost money. The cost of this set of slides has exceeded one thousand dollars [about $23,480 today]. This gives an idea what it costs to illustrate a song properly.

Often the most expert of song illustrators sometimes fall into error and incorporate ridiculous incongruities in their pictures. I have noticed a certain song, by a well-known publisher of this city, where he has a wedding party dressed in costumes of the eighteenth century issuing from a church of the very latest packing-box style of architecture, yet if he had taken the exterior scene of the church four or five blocks away from where he took the photograph, he would have found an old Dutch church whose picturesque exterior would have been in absolute harmony with its subjects. There are many song illustrators who do not take the trouble to make their pictures harmonize with the sentiment of the songs. They never go to the trouble or expense of posing a song; most all of them, in fact, know little about the art of photography. They illustrate their songs by passing off upon the public a hodge-podge of old engravings which they have picked up in the old print shops and picture stores. A great many of these song illustrators are found mostly in this city, and Philadelphia also has its share. Some of these cheap slide-makers are pirates in a small way. As soon as some reputable slide-maker brings out a new set of song slides they manage to secure a set, and after washing the paint from the picture until the slide is left plain, they proceed, at the cost of a few cents, to copy by the "contact process" the work which has cost hundreds of dollars. They then proceed to flood the market with wretched imitations of the original slides at less than one-half the price. Even copyrights on pictures do not deter them from stealing, as they have nothing to lose and to prosecute them under the present copyright law would only be throwing money away. But the new copyright law changes all that and makes it a misdemeanor for any print or picture containing the word "copyrighted" to be used by any person or persons whatsoever without the consent of the owner of the copyright.

Singers as well as managers are now alive to the fact that a poor set of slides will do them more harm than good and managers of theaters are quick to recognize a first-class set of slides, as they must cater to ladies and children, and it is to their interest to see that their patrons get the best the market affords.

My new song entitled "The Best Thing in Life" (which is being illustrated by A. L. Simpson of this city) will revolutionize the slide industry. This set contains twenty-eight slides; in fact, is a drama in three *acts*. The song takes you from a club room crowded with club members in full evening dress, to Broadway, Fifth Avenue, Madison Square, and to the principal points of interest in the city of New York. It was also necessary to secure a snowstorm scene for this set of slides, which was taken at night several weeks ago, corner of Forty-second Street and Broadway, during the great snowstorm, and is an exact reproduction of same, which will no doubt create a sensation when thrown upon a canvas.

At the present time I have a staff of photographers in Florida, where they are now posing my latest Southern pastoral song, which will also no doubt be appreciated by both the singers and managers of America.

To illustrate how hard it is to sometimes secure a scene or a certain subject, I have sent photographers to San Antonio, Texas, to get the "real thing," which was a cowpuncher and his cabin for a song entitled "The Star and the Flower." It would have been easy enough to get some stage setting in some photograph studio and get some person to represent the cowboy, but I preferred to send where I could get the real thing. In another scene a herd of cattle grazing was necessary. To secure same, photographers were sent into Wyoming Territory, and there secured the finest slide ever thrown upon a canvas, which always receives a great round of applause. For my child song, "Hello, Central, Give Me Heaven," it was desirable to photograph the interior of a metropolitan telephone exchange. The officers in charge of the centrals are by no means anxious to have their switchboards photographed, and do not cater to curious visitors; but, as I was on friendly terms with the director of the Chicago Telephone Company, by his courtesy a camera was allowed to be introduced in the operators' exchange one Sunday morning and the necessary pictures were secured. Sometimes it is necessary to take an entire theatrical company to certain parts of the city, paying them their regular price, to pose for a series of illustrations on a farm or in any vicinity where the scene is cast. A great many of my personal friends often assist in posing, but I have found it more satisfactory to engage or accept the kindness of actors and actresses, as they understand the art of posing much better.

Publishers should take a personal interest in their slides; the slide manufactures would then be more careful. As it is, some of the publishers take a new song and hand it to an illustrator, with the instructions to go out and make a set of slides for same. They forget all about it until they see the slides flashed in some theater, and are then horribly disgusted and disappointed. They have only themselves to blame. If they would have given a little time to the illustrator to see that he got his work in harmony with the song, they would get much better results. Each and every slide posed for any of my songs is under my personal supervision. A great many times one hundred and fifty negatives are taken of one set of scenes to secure sixteen slides. No set of slides is ever placed on the market unless O.K.'d by myself. Once they are there I am satisfied that the public, the managers and the singers have what they paid for.

44. Chas. K. Harris, "Song Slide Review: 'The Best Thing in Life'"

Moving Picture World, 16 March 1907, 30

1. *Title.*
2. *In a well-known club.* Shows interior of club room, with a group of five gentlemen, in the attitude of listening, one of them recounting a story
3. *One young fellow* of the same group asking a question with upraised arm, to emphasize its importance.
4. *Some passed through adventures.* A saloon interior, with its usual sordid surroundings; a drunken quarrel over a girl, resulting in the shooting of one. (A picture true to life.)
5. *There are many here have sweethearts.* Quite a contrast from the last picture. A woodland scene, peaceful and calm, with sluggish brook running through; two figures, a lad helping a lass over the stepping stones of the brook.
6. *Come now, won't you tell us, General?* This question is being asked of a Civil War veteran, who is persuaded to take the floor, and in the recounting of doughty deeds exclaims:
7. *The best thing in life is glory*, fighting for home and its flag; winding up with the admonition,
8. *So never let it drag*—a picture showing lady with flag trailing on the greensward, with background of trees.
9. *You listen and hear crowds cheering.* Regiments of Uncle Sam's soldiers returning from the war, marching through the streets, with the crowd of onlookers cheering them on their way.
10. *'Tis then that your heart's blood's beating*, brings us back again to the club

room, where the General's story has roused the enthusiasm of his fellows, and they stand, waving their handkerchiefs in their excitement.

11. *The dear General, he had spoken,* and they are shown applauding the sentiments he had expressed so well.

12. *They in fancy all could see him,* as he held the flag in his left hand, standing at guard, defending it even at the risk of his life, with a background of the setting sun in a blood-red glow.

13. *Then spoke a young financier,* brings us once more back to the club room, showing a millionaire extolling gold by saying.

14. *The best thing in life is gold, boys,* holding aloft before the eyes of his companions evidences of wealth, with the assertion that it aids those in poverty

15. *And gives you pleasures, too.* Showing a night scene at the great exhibition at St. Louis, with the buildings lit up with myriads of electric lights, boasting.

16. *You live like a king in his palace.* A fine interior view, with every luxury shown in its surroundings; beautiful lady seated in cozy chair, husband standing, both in earnest conversation, as though no troubles assail.

17. *The world's at your feet.* Same interior, with man looking out on the world below bathed in moonlight and the houses lit up.

18. *Then they all sat there in silence.* Changes again to the clubhouse, where the group sit in reverie, pondering over the statements made.

19. *A crash upon the table* was caused by the eldest of the group, a gray-haired old gentleman, seemingly well-preserved in spite of his years, making assertion, most empathetic, that

20. *'Tis the love of wife or sweetheart.* Shows rustic garden seat, on which are a young couple; man has arm around neck of girl, who is smiling in response to his words, which sound pleasing to her ears; her left arm encircles a dog on her lap; the background of evergreens adds to the effect.

21. *The best thing in life is love, boys.* Brings a nursery interior to our view, wherein is depicted mother and child.

22. *A mother's love ne'er was equaled.* Gives a bedroom scene, with child saying prayers, kneeling in her cot, with mother listening.

23. *Your sweetheart, your home or your baby.* Takes us to a family at tea.

24. *So take all your gold and your glory.* Introduces us to a garden scene, where December and May are making love, with the god Cupid shooting arrow, showing that both old and young must succumb to his arts.

25. *Chorus.*

This set is well arranged and staged, the models are appropriate to the scenes, the photographing and coloring all that can be desired, and reflects highly upon the artist, A. L. Simpson.

45. H. F. Hoffman, "The Singer and the Song"

Moving Picture World, 4 June 1910, 935

We learn each week through various publications that the public taste for good moving pictures is improving. It is quite a settled fact that those who pay their admission at the picture houses are no longer pleased with the old-time chase, the slapstick comedy, or the knock-down-and-drag-out melodrama. The demand is for something better and they now insist upon good acting, proper staging and a better regard for the eternal fitness of things. They want a picture play that does not insult their intelligence. They are done with crime for crime's sake, and horseplay is quickly distinguished from clean, quiet comedy. All this is as it should be, and we are glad to observe that the public's wants are being duly catered to. But what about the singer and the song?

We still have in our midst that time honored chestnut, the "illustrated song." Nothing seems to have been done to improve this branch of the exhibition business. Probably the managers have an idea that because an audience endures some of these horrible outbursts that they like it, and therefore it should be continued without change.

Disposing of the song itself; there is something to be said on both sides of the question. The song publishers have done well to meet the demand for frequent changes. It is not possible to turn out three song hits a week. Perhaps no one realizes that any better than the publishers themselves, but still the songs are called for and instead of quality we get quantity. Unlike a film, a good song may be repeated every six weeks while its popularity lasts, and it is a pretty safe rule that an old song that is good is better than a new song that is bad.

The slide makers have done their part best of all. Most of our slides come from the hands of a few firms that are eminently capable of their task, who have really outdone the moving picture men in selecting scenes of natural beauty, and who were the first to put art into their product. In moving pictures "the play's the thing," but with songs, the song is half the thing, and the singer is the other half.

The singer being half the song, half of the singer is the voice, the other half being the way the voice is used. It is with the singer that the great fault lies in illustrated songs. Properly done the picture song is a splendid adjunct to the moving pictures, but why murder it when it can be made such a pleasing number? There are lots of illustrated singers with good voices but very few know how to use them, and what is worse, there are fewer managers who know good singing when they hear it. Only a few know just what to listen for when they try out a singer. The majority of exhibitors think that all they have to do is to find someone with a husky set of pipes and they have a real singer. If they can only get a person who can stand up and make enough noise to crack the walls, they think they have what the people want.

I dropped in at a Broadway picture theater not long ago, and there I saw the best of pictures and some acts far above the ordinary run of moving picture vaudeville. It was a house that could afford the best of everything, but there the illustrated song was as bad as the worst you ever heard. It was a female singer, the song was fairly catchy and the slides were pretty, but oh, what a voice! It haunts me even now. The voice was clear enough and she sang in time and tune, but the hardness of it and the noise of it was like unto one of those compressed air riveting guns that they use in riveting the framework of a steel building. She sang of love, but there was about as much love in her voice as there is in the roar of an elevated train. When she cut loose on her top note of love I thought my ears would split and my head began to ache.

Had it not been for the printing on the chorus slide, I should never have known she was singing of love. She might as well have been singing in Chinese for all I understood her pronunciation, and then to top it off she resorted to that moth eaten gag of demanding the audience to join with her in the chorus. Ye gods, will there ever come a singer who will have the good sense to cut that out? The idea is as old as the hills, but it is still kept up as though it were first thought of only yesterday. The audience never sings, only once in a great while when a song is very, very catchy and very, very popular, and then they do so without being forced to it. As a rule they refuse to be a party to the crime.

There are two kinds of illustrated singers. The one with the good voice and no expression; the other with the poor voice but plenty of feeling. I knew a singer once, I know him yet in fact, who had no voice at all. The noise he made was a throaty falsetto. You would think that someone was choking him to death and he was calling for help; a gurgle, or a gargle, but he always got by. He was full of feeling and the sentiment of the song fairly oozed out of every plainly spoken word. The sadness or tenderness of a song were handled with the sadness or tenderness of a true born actor, and coming to his finish (high class songs were his specialty), he would pause a full moment, take a good breath and come out strong and bold, with an emphatic, dramatic shake of his head, sustaining it long while he padded out on the piano with many chords and wonderful modulations that continued some moments after he had done singing. The effect was electrical, sending a thrill through his audience that always ended in a roar of applause. He had no voice but he certainly could handle a song.

Not far from the theater I have spoken of is another of the same kind. At this latter theater the illustrated song is a feature and the singer is a drawing card. They pay him $75 [about $1,760 today] a week and he draws several times that amount of money to the theater. He hasn't a wonderful voice, but it is good and has a mellow, plaintive sweetness. You imagine he is sincerely singing to the girl he loves, as though no audience were present, and nearly every girl in front has an idea that he is singing directly to her. His words ring true, and when he tells how much he loves his lady friend, the audience believes every word of it. They can't help it. He digs in and brings all there is in a song right out of it.

With comedy songs this singer never fails to catch the spirit of them; he is a good-natured fellow and the fun is never lost. Whenever he takes a day off the patrons, on their way out, want to know why he isn't there, and go away feeling that they have been buncoed out of a certain part of their admission fee. It pays to have a man like that around. No matter if you pay him a hundred a week, he will bring it back to you with interest. You may get a passable singer for $25 [about $590 today], one whom the patrons will endure patiently, but seldom will you get one at that figure who will have any power to increase the receipts.

Let the manager imagine for the moment that he himself is possessed of an excellent voice and a power of attracting by the sweetness of his song. Do you think you would put in eight hours a day, Sundays included, for a measly $25 per? Ask yourself that fair question and answer it fairly. No indeed; you could easily command that amount singing twice on Sundays in a church choir and have the rest of the week to yourself. You are willing to pay well for a feature vaudeville act but you prefer to let the illustrated song remain a chestnut and a bore. You refuse to bolster up that weak spot in your program and turn it into a feature. As applied to films and acts you believe in the twentieth century axiom that "you can't get something for nothing," but it applies none the less to the singer and the song.

46. Van C. Lee, "The Value of a Lecture"

Moving Picture World, 8 February 1908, 93

The following paragraph appeared in a recent issue of a theatrical magazine: "Many moving picture theaters are adding a lecturer to their theater. The explanation of the pictures by an efficient talker adds much to their realism."

It is indeed surprising that the managers are just awakening to the fact that a lecture adds much to the realism of a moving picture.

We might ask: "Of what interest is a picture at all if it is not understood?" And it may correctly be stated that the story of not more than one out of every fifty feature films is properly understood by the audience to whom it is shown unless it is adequately described.

In former articles, I have repeatedly urged, perhaps I should say suggested, that the managers of picture theaters demand of their renters a class of pictures which draw the crowds. The present-day subjects of drama, melodrama and tragedies, etc., are not a drawing card.

The demand of the public is now for the picture machine to bring to them its immense *possibilities*. Show to the patrons what they cannot see or realize in any other way except by attending these theaters.

Only a limited number can enjoy the advantage of having unlimited means with which to fully enjoy the pleasure of traveling, while unlimited is the vast majority who would like to see and realize what other parts of the world are like, if the opportunity was only theirs.

But it is theirs, and the picture machine is the instrument which makes it such, and which only a miraculous invention can ever put out of existence. *Unlimited* are the possibilities of this machine, and it can bring before the public what they cannot possibly see otherwise.

The majority will still go to the theater to see the stage enactments, but the stage cannot show what the picture machine is capable of producing.

Let the picture theater, therefore, keep in its place; not show what is being shown every day on the stage, but entertain its patrons with pictures which will hold their interest from the time they enter until they leave. But also, let them *understand* what they see; let them fully comprehend the meaning of every link of the film as it is being shown, and this can only be accomplished by the aid of a lecture.

Look, for instance, at Lyman H. Howe and other traveling moving picture exhibitors of note. Did you ever stop to think and wonder why it is that they can fill a large hall at high prices, right in cities and towns crowded with picture theaters, while these same theaters are almost begging for patrons at five cents admission?

There is only one answer. They show the *kind* of pictures people want to see, and those assembled are satisfied because they fully understand the subjects they are looking at.

Think of such subjects as "A Trip Through Switzerland," "Daniel Boone," or even "The Passion Play," being thrown upon the screen with not one word of explanation. Might just as well imagine that the public was invited to pay their nickels to see merely an "invention" *via* a machine that can throw upon a sheet pictures which can actually move with life-like motion, as certainly the majority would not, any further than that, understand what they see.

Some time ago, in a theater in which I was employed, the subject of one of the pictures was "Napoleon Bonaparte." Getting the printed description a few days in advance, I studied it out, changed it around to where I thought it would best suit the picture, and during the three nights it was shown described the life and history of Bonaparte as it was being portrayed upon the screen. And my lecture was quite lengthy, starting with an introduction preceding the exposure of the first scene and continuing throughout the length of the entire film.

On the second night, the management had invited the entire high school to attend in a body, free. The superintendent of the schools took kindly to the proposition, and I might add that it did more by way of an advertisement than anything else that might have been resorted to.

The next day the superintendent paid a visit to the management and he stated that the lecture, combined with the pictures, accomplished more by way of impressing upon the minds of his students the important phases in the life and history of Bonaparte than the best books on the subject the library contained. The same may be said of a lecture combined with any moving picture.

Managers will do well to give it a trial. Note the difference in the interests shown by the audience. Watch, for example, some well-known peanut fiend, and notice how quick he forgets his peanuts as he watches the pictures with an interest never before shown.

47. E. Esther Owen and W. M. Rhoads, "The Value of a Lecture with the Show" [letters to the editor in reply to Lee's article]

Moving Picture World, 22 February 1908

Augusta, Ga., February 15, 1908.

Editor, *The Moving Picture World*:

Dear Sir:—Permit me to say how pleased I was to read Mr. Lee's article in your issue of February 8, on "The Value of a Lecture." For some time I have been trying to convince the picture show managers here of the desirability, nay, necessity, of such an addition to their attractions. In most instances, while admitting the value in an artistic way of such a combination, they contend that while the public is willing to accept the pictures without the lectures, stories, dramas or poems, they (the managers) would be foolish to increase their expenses by the addition of the lecture. Yet the business here is beginning to languish. Various expedients are being tried to bolster it up, cheap vaudeville and drama, chiefly.

One reason, perhaps, for the non-use of the lecture or story is that all managers do not take your paper, in which they can find the story of the films, and supply houses do not send printed descriptions with the films; another reason is that qualified lecturers and readers are scarce. Lastly, because it is more or less of an innovation. But doubtless the first reason is the true one. The managers seem to think the public will not pay more than ten cents no matter what they put on and do not seem to realize that people grow weary of what they do not understand.

It is a pity that so many of the managers of the moving picture shows look at the business only from the commercial side and not from the artistic and educational. It is a business that can be made a tremendous force for good if rightly used, but if not it will soon run its course like other "fads" and become a thing of the past.

I am glad that you are putting things in the right light, and hope that your efforts will meet the success they deserve.

Mr. B. R. Mitchell, of Augusta, called my attention to Mr. Lee's article on the subject and I then showed it to several local managers.

Wishing you every success, I am,

Yours truly,

E. ESTHER OWEN.

. . . . .

Newton, Ia., February 12, 1908.
Editor, *Moving Picture World*:

Dear Sir:—I have been quite interested in reading your article in last issue of Moving Picture World wherein Van C. Lee suggests that the moving picture theater add a lecturer to the theater. Many a time I have watched a new film subject projected on the screen and thought to myself: If I only knew what this or that part of the picture meant, then I could get very much more enjoyment out of the entertainment. But how would it be possible for the theater manager to explain the film subjects unless the film manufacturer furnishes a printed description of each picture when they are sent out? I think that half of the time the theater manager himself does not understand the picture as it is projected on the canvas. If some film manufacturer would make every one of his film subjects explain themselves as they pass through the machine he would soon have all the business he could attend to. If instead of having a few words of explanation on his film about every 100 feet, as most of them do, they would have these explanations come in at every 20 or 30 feet (or at every place on film wherein an explanation was necessary), then the theater manager would have no use for a lecturer.

On page 94 of last issue of *Moving Picture World*, an article regarding "Electric Light in Lantern," please advise me as to why we should use a hard carbon below (one that does not burn up as fast as a soft one), when, in fact, the lower carbon would last longer than the upper one, even if they were both soft carbons?

Respectfully,
W. M. Rhoads.

48. Sydney Wire, "How Talking Pictures Are Made; Scarcity of Picture Actors"

Moving Picture World, 22 August 1908, 137

Since the advent of the moving picture as an amusement feature no phase of the industry has ever become so popular as the talking picture.

Various devices of a phonographic nature have been placed upon the market, and some of them have been in a large measure successful, but they have all, more or less, been characterized by the unnatural and discordant mechanical grate so usual with most forms of talking machine.

The most successful idea in the talking picture field is the plan recently introduced by Will H. Stevens, of New York City, and which consists of a small cast of versatile actors who speak the lines which are apropos to the various characters from behind the screen, and who imitate the different sounds descriptive of the varied situations in the picture.

The above system was termed "Humanovo" and was a phenomenal success from the start. Many different companies were sent out, each with one or more reels of film, and in most cases playing week stands. The Humanovo, like all successful undertakings, soon had its imitators, and up to the present moment there are at least a dozen different concerns engaged in the promotion of moving talking pictures.

The putting out of this new form of talking picture, is by no means as simple as one might at first imagine, and it requires a thoroughly competent and long-experienced stage director to select suitable people and to rehearse the varied subjects. Many inexperienced and incompetent people have naturally drifted into the business, but their efforts are always immediately recognizable by the marked insipidity and amateurishness of their productions. In the staging of the talking picture there are many important details to consider, and the smallest detail is ofttimes the most important. It is, of course, imperative, that the author of the dialogue for the different parts be a writer of ability, with an all-round experience of foreign travel and a good knowledge of human nature. He must also be of an imaginative nature and quick of eye, as the overlooking of some small situation is sometimes apt to spoil the entire story. The writer must now be assisted by a rapid and able stenographer who can take down the lines as fast as the composer speaks them off. In the framing up of the impromptu dialogue for the talking picture, the reel is usually run off a few times to enable the producer to become familiar with his subject.

The lines and business are then crudely recorded in shorthand and are afterwards typed and modified, and the characters are sorted out to suit the different talkers. The actors are then rehearsed, and after a few suggestions and alterations, the company is ready for the road.

In the selection of actors some judgment must be used, and care must be taken to secure, when possible, people properly fitted for the work. They should be possessed of good voices, above all things, as in talking behind a picture screen much depends upon the carrying power of the voice, as a feeble voice is unable to penetrate through the sheet and is soon lost in the echoes of the fly-loft. The talking picture actor should be a good all-around player and an artist, capable of extemporizing when occasion demands. In the rehearsing of talking pictures attention should be paid to mechanical effects, as thereupon depends much of the success of the picture. It is the better policy to allow the talkers themselves to work their own effects, as they are the most familiar with the subject, and will get better results than by relying upon the different house employees, who are often neglectful and careless, and are often absent when the cue for effects arrives.

Now that the regular season is at hand it will perhaps be a matter of some difficulty to obtain capable people for the now popular talking picture, as most actors and actresses are either already on the road or are rehearsing for some legitimate production. The talking picture producer is unable to pay large salaries, and amateurs and dramatic students are being largely utilized. Much of the success of the talking film depends upon the competency of the talkers, and it is to be deplored that good professional people are so scarce. When the talking picture man is able to pay higher prices for talent, the pictures will be materially improved; as it is, many companies are doing excellent work, and there is a demand for this kind of attraction all over the country.

The Humanovo pictures were put out during the light season and some excellent talent was secured, the people being recruited from the ranks of the many thespians who were at that time idling and who were glad to take advantage of the opportunity it presented to earn a few dollars during the light season. The work was easy, as it does not necessitate any changes of costume or facial makeup. For this reason, and in spite of the small remuneration, many of the people have stayed in the work, but with the springing up of so many new producing concerns, and with the increased demand for picture actors, it seems as though the demand will more than counterbalance the supply, and will necessitate the employing of many who are hardly proficient enough for the work, which will be the cause of many weak and unsatisfactory productions.

The talking picture is in demand today, and is sure to have a big run during the coming season, and it is more than probable that most every picture theater that can afford the extra expense, will make it a feature until something newer and more suitable turns up to replace it.

49. W. Stephen Bush, "The Human Voice as a Factor in the Moving Picture Show"
Moving Picture World, 23 January 1909, 86

Most of our knowledge and a good deal of our pleasure and entertainment is imparted to us by eye and ear. All public amusements appeal to the eye and ear alone. It is indeed impossible to move mankind through the drama, to instruct it with knowledge, without the aid of both these senses, and as a rule no entertainment or amusement is complete or truly pleasing without these channels to the soul combined. There are, of course, exceptions. It is possible to enjoy music without seeing the musicians (sometimes this is the only way of enjoying it), and a man may listen to the solemn and inspiring strains of an organ without looking to see whence the sound is coming. Likewise a pantomime may be enjoyed without a sound of any kind. As a rule, however, the burden of absorption soon becomes too heavy and tiresome for the one sense alone; the eye demands to be satisfied as well as the ear, and the ear becomes eager to share its burden with the eye.

In some vague and wandering way this fact was felt from the very beginning of the moving picture, and numerous have been the attempts to supply sound, and especially the sound of the human voice. Our poor and patient English tongue has been subjected to cruel and unusual punishment in an effort to find names for both the inarticulate and the articulate sound in the moving picture show. At one time a craze for effects infected the electric theaters and instruments were devised to imitate common sounds. There was little success and much failure, and there is to this day, and there always will be. Then came "cameraphones," "synchronizers" and "talking pictures," produced by men and women hiding behind the screen and endeavoring to "make the pictures talk." Not one of these devices has solved the problem: What is the proper function of the human voice in the moving picture show? The trouble in all cases was the inability to produce a perfect illusion. Illusion is pleasing only when it is without a flaw. The ventriloquist with his dummies upon his knee pleases and amuses the audience with his illusion, though of course everybody knows that the sounds and voices are produced by himself and that the dummies are nothing but painted pieces of wood and rags. As soon as the illusion is broken the thing becomes tiresome in the extreme. Even, however, where the illusion is perfect, a little of it goes a good ways. It is very much the same with all the vaunted devices, summed up in the fitting name of "talking pictures." In the first place, the illusion is hardly ever perfect, and even where it is nearly perfect it cannot hold the attention long, for the whole business is unnatural, and nothing that is unnatural will ever last long, though persistent and reckless puffing may give some of these contrivances a fleeting vogue.

The effort to make the human voice count in the moving picture show has not, however, been confined to the "talking pictures." The more common way is the so-called illustrated song. No doubt there are many very fine illustrated songs, and there are actually some good and clever singers, strange as this must sound to the average visitor of the moving picture theater. There is, however, a recurring sameness, a sad monotony about the moving picture song and singer, which begins to afflict people more and more and which makes even the exhibitor tired, a thing not easy to accomplish. It needs no long argument to show that the illustrated song does not supply the proper function of the human voice in the moving picture show.

It may be that the voice best suited to the moving picture is the voice that runs with the picture, not with the individual figures in a silly attempt to imitate their very words, but the voice that runs with the story, that explains the figures and the plot and that brings out by its sound and its language the beauties that appear but darkly or not at all until the ear helps the eye. Take any dramatic or historic picture; in fact, almost any picture, barring the magic and comic subjects. Stand among the audience and what do you observe? As the story progresses, and even at its very beginning, those gifted with a little imagination and the power of speech will begin to comment, to talk more or less excitedly and try to explain and tell their friends and neighbors. This current of mental electricity will run up and down, wild, irregular, uncontrollable. The gifted lecturer will gather up and harness this current of expressed thought. He has seen the picture before, and convincing his audience from the very start that he has the subject well in hand, all these errant sparks will fly toward him, the buzz and idle comment will cease, and he finds himself without an effort the spokesman for the particular crowd of human beings that make up his audience. What all feel and but a few attempt to express even imperfectly, the lecturer, if he is worthy of the name, will tell with ease and grace in words that come to him as naturally as iron obeys the law which draws it to the magnet. All at once the human voice has found its proper mission; the darkened house and the dumb show cease to be a strain to the overworked eye, and as the ear shares the burden the amusement becomes doubly attractive and the period of exhaustion or disgust is deferred. No longer any need on the part of the audience to make loud guesses and supply the voice themselves; the entertainment is complete and the patron feels that he has seen a different kind of moving picture.

This is felt and appreciated by the well-known Parisian art critic, Cellatier, who in a recent issue of the "Temps" speaks of the picture, "The Assassination of the Duke of Guise" [1908], and who after praising the acting and staging of the piece goes on to say: ". . . But after I had sat there a while and looked at the pictures I felt a great longing to hear the human voice. If this sort of entertainment is ever to stop being a toy and is to become a permanent institution in the amusement world it needs the assistance in some shape or other of the human voice."

50. James Clancy, "The Human Voice as a Factor in the Moving Picture Show"
Moving Picture World, 30 January 1909, 115

The writer of the article, "The Human Voice as a Factor in Moving Picture," in the last issue of the *Moving Picture World*, brought out some useful facts, but leaves himself open to slight criticism, in regard to talking pictures produced by people behind a drop. He states in his article that the illusion cannot be made perfect. He is right to a certain extent, but if judgment is used in selecting the reels to be used as talking picture, a great deal of difficulty can be overcome. Certain reels which are very good for a lecture (a point I will take up later in my article) will not be suitable for talking pictures. If details and effects are to be brought out in talking pictures, the actors and actresses must use judgment in regard to placing the voices of the character in speaking from the center of the drop. The line should be read directly behind the character that he or she is impersonating. This will apply either to the right or the left of the center. At all times, in talking from behind a drop, try to keep as near to where the character is standing as possible. All letters and titles, before scenes, should be taken out, so that the story will not be told before the actors and actresses have read their lines, as this will have a tendency to kill the dramatic climax. The operator must also be drilled carefully and thoroughly in regard to the running speed of films, of struggles, horses galloping, battle scenes, which must be run very fast, while scenes in offices and homes must be run at a certain speed to bring out the desired effect of the character, and to give the necessary illusion. But many will ask, How can this be brought about? The answer is in rehearsing and drilling the people, not alone by explanation, but by having everyone act the character thoroughly, as if he were appearing on the stage, without being hidden by the drop. As an example, take a woman in tears. She should go through the same action that she would if it were happening to her in real life, using the handkerchief and hands and all gestures that accompany it. Struggles should be gone through in the same manner. To make the effect more complete, the breaking of a glass or the shooting of a revolver or a gun, or slapping the hand on a table to bring out a convincing point in an argument should always be done by the person speaking the line. A great deal of thought and consideration must be given when selecting a company. I have found that people with stock or repertoire experience, that are bright and can think, usually make the best talking picture actors and actresses, as they study the script much quicker than the others, and sometimes they have lines which are much better than the ones which you provide for them. Still, I do not advocate or advise rehearsing the people too much, as they lose a certain amount of interest in the subject, and as we all know they are compelled to do anywhere from four to ten shows daily, it is a hard matter to keep them interested, and if they lose the interest they lose the effect which you are after. Talking pictures can and will receive applause from the audience for speeches and climaxes, the same as a traveling theatrical company, providing the proper spirit is put in the work. Applause will also be given to characters when they are shown on the drop, like the late President Abraham Lincoln or General Grant, or any other well-known character. The only fault that I have found with this is that the actors do not impersonate the characters with the dignity and bearing called for. They all seem to think that they should shout to be heard through the drop, which is wrong, as we all know the voice will carry much better when spoken in an ordinary tone. The actors and actresses back of drop must watch every minute, so that they will not be talking when characters are not seen before their entrance or after exit. No doubt a great many will wonder what subjects are best adapted for talking pictures. This will depend a great deal upon the clientele to which you are playing. War pictures are always sure-fire hits. Melodramatic ones are always very good, providing they are not too sensational. Plays like "East Lynne," "Camille" and "The Two Orphans"[5] can be made to stand out with proper attention to the minor details. It is advisable in plays of this nature to follow as near as possible the original script. Any subject of a historical nature must be one that your audience is familiar with, or else it will not be a success. Comedy reels are also good, providing that you can keep up swift action. The talking pictures are only in their infancy, and they will grow and get better, and the people are going to like them more every day, providing judgment is used in these suggestions. An audience will sit and listen to good grammar and proper pronunciation, and stories with some logic, but they will not stand for fake lines and people back of the drop talking about something that they do not understand. If the artists will put their heart and soul into their work they will make this part of the moving picture line as much a success for themselves as for the manager. In regard to lecturing upon reels, it will always be a success, providing it is handled in the proper manner and the lecturer uses judgment in his language. If he will use plain, everyday English, and not words which he does not know the meaning of himself, and that the audience will not be compelled to have a dictionary beside them to find out what he is talking about, he will find that they will give him their undivided attention. If the lecturer will go right on with his lecture and not stop until he has finished, he will find the applause of the audience will show him that they are satisfied with his efforts. As I stated early in this article, talking pictures are only in their infancy. The lecturer also is only in his infancy. I think the time is not far off when three and four-act dramatic productions will be produced in moving pictures by persons behind the drop. People themselves will get away from the idea that they are getting buncoed by five and ten-cent theaters, but are receiving more for their money than in any other branch of the amusement line. The recreation which they thereby receive will make them regular patrons of the moving picture theaters.

51. "Trade Notes," "When 'Music' Is a Nuisance"
Moving Picture World, 28 December 1907, 702

A peculiar phase of the nickel theater is on trial, literally as well as figuratively, in quiet Philadelphia. The cheap "shows," in addition to other objectionable features, have introduced "outside music" by phonographs and small bands. As Market Street, one of the best business thoroughfares of Philadelphia, is blessed with an abundance of the 5-cent theaters, the result of the energetically applied innovation will easily be imagined. A local contemporary speaks of the music discoursed by the competing instruments and bands as "a horrid din" that reminded the traveled citizen of Cairo and the average man of the midways or pikes or trails of the world's fairs.

Gentle suasion was first resorted to in the hope of inducing the owners of the picture shows to dispense with the musical forms of street advertising. It failed sadly. Police admonition came next, but for some unexplained reason that, too, proved ineffective. Finally the businessmen of Market Street applied for an injunction to restrain the employment of bands and instruments and the making of "outside music" for the purpose of attracting patronage to the cheap establishments.

This measure raised delicate questions of law and art. Unnecessary noise has, to be sure, been held as a nuisance, but is music unnecessary noise? And if the answer be that a lot depends on the "music," who is to determine when harmony passes into discord? Again, if the employment of barkers is lawful in advertising legitimate business, why is the use of bands or phonographs unlawful?

The court, however, was equal to the difficult task. The injunction was granted, but the noise versus music issue was evaded. The opinion contained some dicta about "constant and incessant playing" becoming intolerable, even maddening, where an occasional performance might be pleasurable, but these were only incidental observations. The order stopping the outside music was based on the fact that it had resulted, according to the evidence, in the blocking of the street, the interference with the business of adjoining stores, obstruction of entrances and views of artistically arranged shop windows, and injury to trade at least as entitled to protection as the moving picture entertainments.

This is hard sense rather than art criticism, but it will answer.–*Chicago Record-Herald.*

52. "Sound Effects: Good, Bad, and Indifferent" [editorial]
Moving Picture World, 2 October 1909, 441–42

Is it best to undertake to reproduce the sounds to go with the pictures or not? Probably this question has presented itself more than once to managers, and probably it is no nearer a solution satisfactory to all parties than it was at the beginning. One will reach one conclusion, and one will reach another, reasoning from exactly the same data, and it would be a wise man indeed who would dare say positively that either was right.

It would seem, however, that one feature of the attempted imitations would appeal to every manager with irresistible force. The imitations should be fairly accurate or they shouldn't be attempted. Inaccuracy is worse than nothing. It creates wrong impressions and often it wrongly interprets the pictures. They must correspond or else they should be let alone.

One example will, perhaps, suffice to show what is meant. In almost all theaters some attempt is made to imitate the hoofbeats of running horses, but the noises are exactly the same whether the horse is running over hard or soft earth. The quick, sharp ring of a hoofbeat on a hard road is quite different from the hoofbeat on a sandy road or on grass ground, yet in practically all theaters they are made the same. Perhaps it is impossible to make a change. Maybe the instruments used do not admit of it. If they do not it would be wiser to omit the one which is not true. The impression is false and the picture is spoiled for those who are at all critical in their observations, and more and more the audiences are becoming critical. More care should be exercised in this particular if the noises are used at all.

Another of the same general observations can be made about automobiles and locomotives. In a good proportion of theaters the noises supposed to imitate these two are substantially the same, yet everybody knows they are different and the imitation should be different to correspond or else be omitted. The clang of the trolley car's warning bell sounds more like a cow bell, and so one might go on enumerating the different noises which fail to copy the original. There are many more that do not than there are that do.

One exhibitor has made a special study of this phase of motion picture shows, and has achieved a high degree of perfection. Reference is here made to Lyman H. Howe. His sounds imitate and to the mind of a great many who see his pictures they add to the attraction of the entertainment. Others do not care particularly, and wouldn't mind if they were omitted entirely. Many others would be better pleased if they were omitted. They prefer that the silent drama shall be truly silent.

Playing to the Pictures

Performative Accompaniment

53. Clarence E. Sinn, "Music for the Picture"
Moving Picture World, 23 April 1910, 593–94

Introductory
It is gratifying to see how the broadminded exhibitors, those who aim to show the pictures to the best advantage, are fast taking to the idea that good and appropriate music does not only enhance the beauty of the picture but gives it life. From every town we hear that such and such a theater has discharged the music killer, the man or woman at a low salary who believed that any old ragtime music was good enough for motion pictures, to engage more experienced musicians. It is surprising to note how many theaters are improving the sound effects while many of them are adding a violinist; in fact, many other instrument players. The demand for good music is such that it is now as much of a rivalry between exhibitors to brag of their good orchestra as it is of bragging of the quality of their pictures. In other words, the managers are now taking as much interest in the music as in the projection of the pictures, and the great demand for extra musical accessories, like the Deagan electric bells, xylophones,

chimes, automatic orchestras, pipe-organs, etc., shows that, in the very near future, moving picture theaters will be real concert halls and that the public will go to the shows not only for the sake of seeing pictures but to hear good music.

A full orchestra costs less than two cheap vaudeville acts and is more profitable to the exhibitor. Good music captivates and pleases, while cheap vaudeville acts give a very unfavorable reputation to a moving picture theater.

Realizing, therefore, the importance of the music, we make no apology for introducing this new department to *World* readers. We believe that Mr. Sinn will find a hearty response to his suggestions and invite every exhibitor and orchestra leader to write him for particular information or offer suggestions, addressing same to Music Department, *Moving Picture World*, Drawer 727, Chicago, Ill.

J.M.B.

. . . . .

MUSIC FOR THE PICTURE
By Clarence E. Sinn, THE "CUE MUSIC MAN"

First Article

Much has been said in criticism of the music accompanying moving pictures, but so far as I have noticed few practical suggestions have been offered which would put the novice on the right road to "working up" his pictures musically. I am daily in receipt of inquiries whose general purport is: "What shall I play — where shall I play it — and why?" It is the purpose of these articles to try and give a few hints along these lines which the writer hopes may stimulate interest among his fellow-workers in this great field, and invite questions which will be answered so far as lies in his power.

The moving picture is almost infinite in its variety of subjects, but for the present we may divide them roughly into three classes: scenic, industrial, and dramatic — the last including all pictures in which the characters enact a story. The moving picture drama (or photoplay) is simply a play in pantomime, and the accompanying music is essentially the same as that of a play given on the stage. There is this distinction, however. In the drama proper, music is only introduced at intervals to heighten the effect of certain scenes, while in pantomime it is continuous, or nearly so. The reason is apparent. The drama depends upon both speech and action to convey its story: the eye and ear of the auditor are in sympathy; we see the action and hear the words. This sympathy of eye and ear must exist else there is no sustained interest—no intelligent appreciation of the story. To hold this double interest the stage manager employs as accessories, lights, scenery, music—always keeping in view this sympathy between the eye and ear.

Pantomime depends solely upon the action to convey its story, and appeals to the eye alone. Now the ear demands gratification as well as the eye, and, to this end, music is employed, but whenever possible it should be consistent with the story and not merely a concert program on the side.

Certain forms of music are accepted as suitable accompaniments for certain situations; as soft and plaintive for pathetic scenes, stormy and turbulent for the violent ones, etc. All the emotions have some sort of musical analogy and if these are correctly applied the dramatic effect is heightened and the interest of the auditor is intensified. If, on the other hand, the music be incongruous, the attention is diverted and the interest is lessened. Bear in mind that the picture is the show—that is what the audience is paying for—and any accessory (musical or otherwise) should carry out and amplify the impression intended by the producer.

A picture was shown some time ago containing a scene wherein Pharaoh's daughter discovers the infant Moses in the bulrushes. The pianist played "Oh, You Kid." He got a laugh which is probably what he wanted, but at what a sacrifice. The whole picture was dignified and serious, and the music should have sustained that character throughout.

It is the general character of the picture which you must observe. Taken altogether, what is the predominant feature? Is it pathetic, mysterious, tragical or comical? Work up to this general effect whatever it is. The producer takes great pains to convey certain impressions and preserve a certain atmosphere, and it is his due that these unities be preserved so the audience may receive his story in the same spirit in which it is told. To begin with, you should have a good library, which in these days of cheap music is not difficult. A few marches and waltzes, though these are indispensable, are not sufficient. Long andantes [slow selections] such as "Traumerei," "Flower Song," "Angel's Serenade" and the like are useful. The intermezzo, valse lento, and gavottes make convenient "fill-ins" where the scene is neutral yet the general character of the picture is subdued or pathetic. Religious music, national airs (of different countries), Oriental music and dances are frequently called for. Popular songs are useful, especially in sentimental pictures and comedies. The titles of these, if well known, frequently carry out the suggestion of the picture, but care should be taken that the music is also in keeping with the scene. Don't try to get a laugh when none was intended, as it only cheapens your work and hurts the picture. Your library should also include some melodramatic music, such as mysterious, agitato [agitated], "Hurrys" for combats, storms, fire scenes, etc. These are in constant demand.

Overtures, medleys, popular selections, etc., have their place also, but as a general rule it is not wise to use them in dramatic pictures, as the chances are a lively movement will come at a time when you should be playing a slow one, and vice versa. I suspect this is at the bottom of a great many criticisms that have appeared lately. Some of the scenic and most of the industrial pictures as a rule do not require special music—there's a good place for your concert music. Once in a long time you will get a picture that runs in a dead level—no high lights or deep shadows—very difficult to shade musically, as nothing in particular happens. An overture or selection is probably as good as anything else, but be careful.

Some intensely dramatic pictures are tuned to one pitch, yet are full of suggestions as to the musical setting. "Auld Robin Gray" is a recent and easy example. We open the picture with the song "Auld Robin Gray" once through, the same as if we were taking up the curtain on the stage. As it would be monotonous to repeat the song over and over throughout the picture, we relieve it occasionally; "My Highland Laddie" in the first scene, [Francesco Paolo] Tosti's "Good-bye" at the parting scene—always filling in with the titular song. I heard the [Felix Mendelssohn's] "Wedding March" played for the wedding scene; while this might be criticized, it accented the scene and did not detract from the general effect. After that "Auld Robin Gray" until the end with all the expression possible.

In the next article we will take up this matter of incidental music more in detail.

C. E. SINN.

(To be continued).

54. Louis Reeves Harrison, "Jackass Music"

Moving Picture World, 21 January 1911, 124–25

SKETCHES BY H. F. HOFFMAN

Civilization is not a crab, but theatrical managers walk sideways if not backwards when they allow their musicians to play the wrong accompaniment to the right composition whether of song or picture. O, what a noise when the lights are turned low and Lily Limpwrist takes her place at the usual instrument of tor-

JACKASS MUSIC
BY
LOUIS REEVES HARRISON
SKETCHES BY H.F.HOFFMAN

ture! With a self-conscious smirk she gives a poke to her back switch, dabs her side teasers with both patties, rolls up her sleeves and tears off "That Yiddisher Rag." She bestows a clam smile on the box-of-candy young man in the first row, but the presentation on the screen fails to divert her "I-seen-you" glances any more than if it was the point of a joke.

The chorus-girl who attempts to pose as a prima-donna with little more equipment than a tuft of bleached hair, a pair of high-heeled slippers and a cigarette voice can be tolerated, we often endure the howling and screeching of a Tommy trying to sing "Come into the Garden Maud," but when Lily Limpwrist assails our unprotected organs of hearing with her loony repertoire it seems a shame to throw away ten cents on such a performance, to say nothing of the time wasted. We sit patiently through the act of an imported star, who commends to our attention the interesting intelligence "Me Rag, moy Bess used-ter droive em cryzy at the Croiterion," we submit to the inanities of the chin-whiskered, pillow-paunched Dutch comedian, who says: "Vot it is, is it? Ask me,"

LILLY LIMPWRIST

and we even tolerate the Irish comedian, shaved yesterday, who looks like an undertaker out-of-a-job when he wails in a holdover voice: "Where thuh dear-ol Sha-hamrock gurrows," but there is a limit.

Lily is all right at home, when her mother importunes her to "play something and don't wait to be teased," or still better as a summer-eve girl on a Coney-Island boat, but no man will ever marry a girl who plays a dance while the pictured man is in a death struggle; she would probably be *at* one when the real one was in trouble. The girl of sympathy will play music in accord with the pictured story, the girl of ambition will try to improve the quality of her work, the girl of sense will try to improve the quality of the performance, draw patronage instead of driving it away, benefit the management, and show to others who are looking for pianists that she is not a fat-wit but a woman of ideas and good taste.

The performance of Lily Limpwrist is a poetic dream compared to the diabolical dipso-mania of Freddy Fuzzlehead and Percy Peashaker when they cut loose between the "vodeveal" [vaudeville] acts. Gee! *Non compos mentis* and *le diable au corps* for theirs and a free pass to Matteawan [state hospital in New York] for what they have done to kill the box-office receipts at moving-picture shows. Percy is really a wonder. When there is water in the picture it goes to Percy's cerebrum. If there is a lake shown on the screen, no matter if it is a mile away, calm or stormy, he shakes his box of peas so that we may know that it is principally made of water. Realism becomes intense when a vessel appears and Percy blows a whistle "Oo-Oo" to enforce the fact that it is a steamer and not a full-rigged ship. "Bow-wow" indicates that we are looking at a dog and not a door-mat, "Honk-honk" gives one a thrilling remembrance of crossing Broadway after the theatre with fifty cow-boy taxis in full pursuit, and he is a master of such startling effects as clapping two blocks of wood together when an old nag candidate for the glue factory trots along a country road. But Percy's star act, the one that gets a laugh, is his imitation of a baby crying, no matter whether the one on the screen is nursing or merely dying. Percy is a comparatively new type of the egomaniac, but whether we must humor him or put him in a padded cell must be left to the alienists.

If you were to ask a large proportion of the audience what should be done to Freddy Fuzzlehead they would vote to shoot him, but I am in favor of slow torture, making the punishment fit the crime, put him in a room where there is another of his kind playing with the piano and let him die a lingering death.

Ten thousand dollars [about $234,750 today] a day is spent to amuse people with moving pictures, good, bad, and indifferent, but all are bad or indifferent when Fuzzlehead does his long-eared stunt. Ten millions of people pay their nickels and dimes to see the moving pictures, and these shock-headed klepto-pianoacs steal their pleasure away in order to practice the accompaniment for the song-and-dance comedians, those who come on the stage and say "I will now sing you a little ballad entitled 'Show you are a clod-hopper by keeping time with your feet.'" The same comedian who gets no applause from the long-suffering audience and asks if they are hand-cuffed, or says to the piano man, *sotto voce*, "Did y'ever s-see suchalotta dubs?" The hall-room lobster on the stage is "great" to Fuzzle-head, the boob action exactly suits the boob at the piano, the moving pictures are rot, he could do better himself if he had time, but he would say the same thing if he was shown the treasures of the Louvre or the Palace of Lux-embourg. Ten thousand dollars a day is spent to *produce* the moving pictures, and it would

PATHOS

be impossible to say how much more to keep going the ten thousand motion-picture theatres throughout the country. These pictures are not all masterpieces, many of them are very crude, but the whole art is in a primitive state, is con-stantly improving, and the exhibitions are kept alive by their production. People go every day to see the pictures, once in a while for the variety entertainment, and it is not only asinine but un-businesslike to lower the grade of musical ac-companiment when the lights are turned down. Inappropriate music may "do" for an unintelligent part of the audience, but what is the use of driving away the intelligent portion? All other parts of the theatrical working force move in har-mony, like the wheels of a clock, but these fatheads against the stage apron are like the clock alarm that goes off when you don't need it and never when you do. Attention of managers to the comfort of patrons would help matters some, and little higher salaries would help a great deal to get suitable music. Better music means better patronage and more of it, and superior patronage means a demand for superior photoplays. Suitable music is an essential. If the drummer cannot be taught to subordinate his morbid craving for attention to the gen-eral effect, cut him out altogether and pay more for a pianist who can impro-vise softly during scenes of pathos or utilize operatic selections for the dramatic effects.

Bangity-bang-bang. Bing-bang-bang!

Desperate Desmond has got Claude Eclaire in a tight place, but no matter, the "rag" is on, "hit it up."

Bangity-bang-bang! Bing-bang-bang!

There is a tender-hearted mother dying in the little play, the world around her is subdued and silent, her face is pale, her frame attenuated, her respiration is heavy with sighs of sorrow and unsatisfied desire to have her children properly cared for. Tears are falling like her life illusions, she is overcome with her double burden of pain and sorrow, her eyes, inflamed by the fever of unattained hopes, turn beseechingly to the infinite power above, a last faint sigh, the eyes close forever:

Bangity-bang-bang! Bing-bang-bang!

55. Wm. H. McCracken, "'Jackass Music'" [letter to the editor]
Moving Picture World, 28 January 1911, 176

Dear Sirs—I have just seen the article on "Jackass Music," by Louis Reeves Harrison, in the issue of January 21, 1911, and I am sure Mr. Harrison has not exaggerated his views as far as music in moving picture houses is concerned. For I, also, have heard some jackass music, as he describes it and wonder how on earth managers can expect anyone to come into their theaters, and sit down, and listen to such unappropriate music, as I was obliged to listen to while there. The week commencing January 2, 1911, I had business in Allentown, Pa., and on the evening of the same day, with another traveling man, I went to see some picture plays. The first house we entered was a small one, in which there was only a piano to furnish music, and I will say the music at that house was quite fair. The young girl presiding, played music in harmony with the picture, in fact, it suited the pictures quite well, and she kept the piano going from the time the picture started until it was ended, when she took a short rest, or until the next picture was shown on the screen, when she again started to play, which is more than I can say for the larger house, to which we went afterward and where we found they had a six-piece orchestra. But oh! such torture as we were obliged to suffer while in that place was indescribable. The orchestra was there all right, but very little music was rendered, for they never started to play to a picture until it was almost over, and when the end of the picture appeared they shut off the music abruptly, not even waiting to get to the end of a line, and worse still, we noticed that when a comic picture was on the screen, they did not play at all, not a sound of music during the entire reel, instead of that, they got up and scattered through the audience. When the next picture appeared, which was dramatic, entitled "The Refuge," the musicians reappeared and by the time this picture was almost, or more than half over, the leader of the orchestra had at last found some music, which, no doubt, she thought was appropriate for this particular picture (judging from the length of time it took her to find it), imagine our surprise and disgust, when they struck up the strain of "John Took Me Home to See His Mother," when the scene appeared in which the drunkard's child was dying, and the poor mother, beside herself with grief, is left to fight the battle against the world without the only treasure that had given her strength to go forward. Then, they switched off to the strain of "Meet Me Tonight in Dreamland," and it seemed as if the pianist was trying to race with the rest of the orchestra. Finally, we could stand the torture no longer, so we left the theater in disgust, vowing we would never enter it again, to be made to endure such torture—for torture it certainly was to be obliged to sit and look at pictures to which there was no music. One might as well listen to a singer unaccompanied by music as to look at pictures without music, for it would detract all the beauty from the song and singer, same as it did from the pictures which would otherwise have been good.

—WM. H. MCCRACKEN.

56. Mrs. Buttery, "'Jackass Music'" [letter to the editor]
Moving Picture World, 4 February 1911, 258

Allentown, Pa., Jan 23, 1911.
Editors, *Moving Picture World*.

Sirs—I would like to say a word or two in answer to the letter entitled, "Jackass Music" which appeared in your paper, the *Moving Picture World*, January 28, 1911.

The person who wrote that article is entirely in error as regards the music which he says he heard played in the largest picture theater in Allentown, Pa. I am the leader of that orchestra, and in justice to myself and the other musicians, I must contradict his statement.

Firstly, he says that I do not start the music until the picture is nearly over, and that I end abruptly when the picture is through, not even ending the strain; both of which are absolutely untrue. I, as a professional pianist, would not be guilty of such gross carelessness, and as to not playing the comic pictures, that is the rule of the house, as those pictures have a better effect without music. As to his remarks about the length of time in finding suitable music, the picture he referred to was a sad one, entitled "The Refuge"; the house was dark, the music plaintive, and the only conclusion I can come to, is that he must have fallen asleep, and woke up in time to see the end of the picture.

The selection in which the song occurs, "John Took Me Home to See His Mother," was played for a Thanhouser [film company] comedy, called "Looking Forward," and "Meet Me Tonight in Dreamland," was played along with "You Taught Me How to Love, You Now Teach Me How to Forget," for a Reliance picture, called "A Woman's Way" [1908], which was not shown on the day mentioned, which proves the traveling man must have been in the theater more than once.

When a man writes an article to a popular and reliable paper, he should take lessons before posing as a critic. He has unwittingly paid me a compliment, when he praised the young lady who played the piano at the small picture house which he says he went to. I would like him to know through your valuable paper, that the lady piano players at the two picture houses were my pupils, and were taught the business by me.

—MRS. BUTTERY.

57. W. Stephen Bush, "Music and Sound Effects for Dante's Inferno"

Moving Picture World, 27 January 1912, 283–84

MUSIC

It may seem unnecessary to those who never had to combat the Powers of Human Stupidity to say that in the proper presentation of the Milano Films version of Dante's "Inferno" music plays a great part, second in importance to that of the lecture alone. After you have witnessed a performance of that great production with either "faked" or shockingly unsuitable music, you feel as if it were a solemn duty to prevent any further desecration by offering a few simple suggestions.

Wherever possible an orchestra of six or eight pieces should accompany the pictures. In the absence of such an orchestra there should be at least two instruments, a piano and a good organ (one not over fifty years of age). It is folly to employ cheap men to play organ and piano. The methods of conducting a gent's furnishing store will not apply here. The organ's place is behind the screen; the piano had best be placed in the orchestra.

The musical program should be opened with the piano (in the absence of the orchestra), and almost any short overture will answer the purpose. Part of the *William Tell* overture [by Gioacchino Rossini] is especially recommended, because it is generally at hand and the musicians are more or less familiar with it. There are, of course, many pieces more suitable than this, but the ordinary orchestra seems paralyzed at the mere mention of [Richard] Wagner or [Franz] Liszt, and extraordinary orchestras are negligible quantities. After this overture follows the brief introductory of the lecturer and at its conclusion comes the next distinct number on the musical program, the "Garibaldi Hymn," which may be found in any of the ordinary collections of national anthems. This air is believed to be suitable for several reasons. It has plenty of fire and spirit, is in keeping with the initial titles in the original Italian and, last but not least, is sure to please the Italian part of your audience, which is generally large. Italians come to see the Inferno because they revere the genius of their immortal countryman, Dante Alighieri, who wrote the Inferno. The strains of the Garibaldi Hymn should be continued until the first scene of the Inferno proper appears, showing Dante lost in the gloomy forest, when the music gives way to the lecture.

The next distinct musical number in the performance comes with the scenes following the meeting of Virgil and Dante at the mountain's foot. This number is best rendered by the orchestra or the piano in front. Its character should be weird and mysterious; in a full orchestra the violin should dominate the situation. Let this music be continued without any interruption whatever up to the end of the title announcing the arrival of Charon on the shores of the River Acheron. It may be said here in passing that the music should always be busy while the titles are on the screen. There can, of course, be neither lecture nor effects while the titles are running, and to have complete silence makes a dead and disagreeable pause in the performance. The rest of the first reel has no distinct musical number.

If your first reel ends with the scene showing the great spirits of the ancient days on "the green enamel of the plain," finish with the strains of the "Evening Star" from [Wagner's] Tannhäuser. It is best to have your first reel end with this scene, such an ending being both natural and logical; the audience is led up, as it were, to the brink of the real Inferno. The proper atmosphere has been created.

The spectators, though they have not so far witnessed any of the more tragic scenes, are, with psychological skill, prepared for what is to come in the next reel. It goes without saying that here, too, we should be entirely guided by the spirit of Dante. It is part of such a program to pay attention to the order and sequence of the various cantos of the poem.

The Music for the Second Reel
About a minute before the second reel is begun the organ behind the screen should get into action. The first scene of this reel shows Minos, the infernal judge, and his dreaded tribunal. By starting the proper music just about one minute before the house is darkened, you resume your sway over the spectators' feelings. The most suitable music for this purpose is the playing of the Gregorian measure of the stirring and impressive hymn, "Dies irae, dies illa" [from the requiem mass]. The words and music of this ancient hymn will be found in any good-sized complete Catholic hymnal, which can be bought for about fifty cents. The very simplicity of the Gregorian measure makes it so powerful. It is very easily played and ought to offer no difficulty to an organist of fair, average ability. Now this hymn should be in full swing when the first scene of the second reel appears on the curtain. The music should stop promptly with the end of the title following this scene and the next musical number should be rendered by the piano. The music then should be something of a character to suggest "the stormy blast of hell," and such music is to be continued to the ending of the title announcing the spirits "injuring each other with bags of gold." There is no more distinct and special music until the announcement of Virgil's and Dante's passage across the foul waters of the Stygian swamp. Here let the organ resume the strains of the "Dies irae" up to the title ending with the words "assistance of an angel" when both music and effects give way to the lecture. When the lecturer has finished here, effects and music may be resumed, both diminishing, to end of this scene, which concludes the second reel.

Reel Three
The music for this reel may be taken from the same source as the "Dies irae." I suggest that the organ play in rotation, or with variations, "Miserere," "In Exitu Israel," and "De Profundis." All these hymns may be easily found in the hymnal mentioned above; all are in the simple but sublime Gregorian measure, and all of them are easy for a fairly competent musician, pianist or organist.

The Last Two Reels

Music of the character just indicated, all to be played on the organ, will be found most suitable in the fourth and fifth reel. In the fifth reel, during the scenes showing Ugolino and his offspring in the Tower at Pisa, music of a more secular character, to be played on the piano, may be found suitable and effective; for example, the well-known air from [Pietro] Mascagni's "Cavalleria Rusticana." During the passage of the poets over the fields of ice the music should be mysterious rather than ecclesiastical in character, and the piano will be found to be better adapted for these scenes than the organ.

There remains one fine distinct musical number, which should begin at the middle of the second last scene of the fifth and last reel. When Virgil and Dante appear in this scene let the organ begin the "Gloria in Excelsis" from [Wolfgang Amadeus] Mozart's Twelfth Mass and continue this to the very end of the performance. It gives a triumphant and satisfactory ending, doubly welcome to an audience that has just witnessed so much of terror and tragedy. Let the organist do his best here, play forte and with plenty of expression. Whenever the music ends simultaneously with the disappearance of the silhouetted forms of Dante and Virgil, its wonderful fitness will be felt and appreciated by every audience, composed in the main of human beings.

SOUND EFFECTS

There are few pictures more capable of improvement through the introduction of suitable sound effects than the Milano production of Dante's Inferno, and there is none more easily and thoroughly spoiled through violent, unnatural and misplaced effects. In preparing a series of good sound effects for this feature, we must follow the example of the makers of the film, who, in turn, have followed with almost literal exactness the text of the cantos that have been filmed. Unless we consult the all-pervading genius of the great poet we are very likely to make the effects silly and offensive.

To begin with, we must reject the theory that an extraordinary noise outfit is needed in order to secure the best sound effects. Nothing could be more absurd than this idea, which seemed to guide one or two ignorant and incompetent individuals who, being utterly unable to understand a line of the poem, sought to drown their stupidity in a lot of unnecessary noises. The simplest outfit, such as is kept in all theaters, is amply sufficient. It is not the quantity, but the quality of effects which counts. At the psychological moment the most delicate and subdued effect will produce an impression on an audience which all the rioting of the average effect-man cannot hope to create. Nothing more is needed than a wind-machine, a bass drum, a thundersheet, rain, cocoanut shells, a horn, a chain, and a piece of iron or steel. The secret of working the sound effects successfully lies in the manner and method in which these simple tools are used. The guiding principle is to follow as closely as possible the letter or, at least, the spirit of Dante.

But Three Effects Needed in the First Reel

An intelligent "effect-man" will husband his resources and not fire away all his ammunition in the first few scenes. The attempt to imitate noises which panthers, lions and wolves are supposed to make generally mars the otherwise beautiful second scene of the first reel. Either all the sounds will have to be imitated or none at all. It is stupid to have the panther growl and then have the lion "with head aloft and hunger-mad" stand there as if he had lost his roar through catching a cold, and the wolf follow in profound silence. The spectators are far more interested to know the meaning of the presence of these animals, as explained by a competent lecturer, than in having some one behind the scenes give a weird exhibition of what he thinks these animals might do just before feeding time.

In the next scene, where Beatrice ascends into heaven, it is the height of absurdity to make a noise like the wind on a stormy day around the Flatiron Building.[6] The ascent is that of a spirit, noiseless and swift. The first good effect in the reel comes after the title, "The Gate of Hell," where the robes of Virgil and Dante are seen to flutter in the wind, which comes up from the bluish, vapory depths below. Stop when the wind stops on the screen. Properly rendered, this is a fine effect, as it is the first and comes upon the audience with a proper introduction by the wind.

The next effect comes in the scene where the poets enter the gloom which greets them after they leave the rock with the fateful inscription: "Now was the day departing and the air imbrowned with shadows," etc. A clap of thunder just one second after the appearance of the poets in the imbrowned shadows, with a low rumble following, is effective; in the picture Dante is seen to turn around as if startled, and it appears as if the thunder had struck upon his ears.

There is nothing in the letter of the canto which would make these effects necessary, but the spirit of the whole description well justifies the effects, and the average spectator who knows nothing about the poem will understand the horror at the thunder much more readily than the recoiling "from some false resemblance in the twilight gloom." The third effect is a quick clap of thunder to accompany the lightning when Dante faints on the strand of Acheron.

The Second Reel Is Best Helped by Effects

In many respects the second reel is perhaps the strongest, and it certainly is the one containing the most dramatic moments. A splendid effect may be worked in the second scene of this reel, "where the carnal sinners are condemned, in whom reason by lust is swayed." Dante describes the "stormy blast of hell" to be irregular and fitful. "As starlings on their wings are borne abroad, so bears the tyrannous gust those evil souls." His meaning becomes even plainer a few lines further on, where Francesca tells him her story, "while e'er the wind, as now, is mute." It appears then that Dante meant us to think of this wind as coming in gusts and fits with very short intermissions. Watch the picture closely and you will see that the filmmakers have carried out this idea most faithfully; the bodies move in groups, some resting for a moment, others in the main current of the hellish blast. Translated into instructions for the effect-man, this means that the wind-machine should be worked in fits and gusts, rising, diminishing to almost nothing and slowly rising again. With a proper rehearsal, following the motion of the groups, this effect is one of the strongest in the entire production.

Closely upon the Francesca da Rimini scene follow two scenes where simple rain effects skillfully and intelligently worked illustrate the picture wonderfully well. "Large hail, discolored water, sleety flaw through the dun midnight air, streamed down amain." It is, however, in the three scenes showing the passage of the poets through the foul waters of the Styx that the effects may be rendered overpowering. Here again we follow the spirit rather than the letter of Dante, for the poet, in his encyclopedic way, completes the description of the journey across the slimy pool in less than a hundred words. He says nothing of thunder or lightning. Both thunder and lightning may, however, well be introduced in harmony with the general spirit of the two cantos here filmed.

As soon as the title announcing Phlegas has been flashed on the screen there should be distant thunder, which may be best imitated by having the bass drum worked in the furthest background of the stage, as far away from the screen as possible, though, of course, straight back of it. The effect is then suspended during the showing of the "Philip Argenti" title, to be resumed with increased force when the title disappears, and worked to its height when the replying signals of Dis, i.e., the fires of Dis, the evil city, appear.

The drum should then be close behind the curtain and may be aided by the thunder sheet, and the effects should be continued fortissimo to the next succeeding title. After the appearance of the angel toward the close of the last scene of the second reel, finish the picture with rumblings of thunder, dying away with the picture.

Little Room for Effects in the Last Three Reels

Except when the puffing of flames and vapors seem to make it appropriate, there should be little thunder in the third reel, and that little of a subdued character. It is well here to resist the temptation to an anticlimax to the splendid finish of the end of the second reel. The scene showing Capaneus in the third reel allows of some vehement thunder and lightning. There are effects with a chain and piece of iron that may be worked in the scene showing the torture and death of Piero-delle Vigne (Peter of Vigna). These effects, however, should be well studied and rehearsed, or else entirely omitted. There is, however, one magnificent effect that may be introduced immediately after Dante and Virgil have left the bridge from which they gazed down upon the lepers and before they enter the circle of the giants. Says the poet: ". . . I heard a horn sounded so loud, the peal it rang had made the thunder feeble." The moment the title announcing the giants is flashed on the screen the horn ought to be sounded, and the blowing continued until Nimrod appears with the horns about his body. Properly worked this is a most appropriate effect. There remains but the Ugolino incident in the last reel. Here the galloping of a horse, first approaching and then dying away, may be imitated to good advantage, as well as the sound a key sharply thrown against the stones on the ground is supposed to make. This not only adds to the realism, but takes away some of the horror of the subsequent scenes. The idea of one effect-man to show the stumbling of Virgil's foot in the next to the last scene of the fifth reel by creating a noise like a riot on a bowling alley or at a wake is characteristic of the intelligence, or rather the lack of it, which moves some of these noise-makers; a sensible person will of course avoid it.

Effects Subordinate to Music and Lecturer

It should always be borne in mind that the pictures are to be chiefly illustrated by music and lecture, and effects are of value only when they fit in with the general harmony of things. Neither music nor lecture should ever suffer on account of effects. The idea that Dante's Inferno depends for its success on the amount of noise made behind the screen is a popular one with those whose intelligence carries them no further, but it must always appear ridiculous to the general public, who possess an instinctive feeling of what is becoming, and whose taste, we grieve to say, is frequently much better and cleaner than that of the men who seek to entertain them.

58. L. Szeminanyi, "Playing to Pictures"

Strad, February 1921, 327

A little Information for Violinists and other Musicians who contemplate entering the "Picture Profession."

How many of the people who constitute the average picture house audience ever give a thought to the amount of work which falls to the lot of the orchestra director?

Of course there are picture houses which boast a pianist of the coal-breaking variety, or at best, a very third rate combination of musicians which the management term "an orchestra," but of these I will not speak, as there is no attempt on the part of these "artists" to study either pictures or music. Moreover, it is the existence in picture houses of such untrained and incompetent people which justifies the contempt which many people have for musicians who play in cinemas.

I am dealing in this article with trained musicians, many of whom have studied their instruments in well-known colleges both in England and on the Continent, and who, being endowed by nature with ambition and organizing ability, become directors of cinema orchestras. Now the head of such an orchestra has much to do of which the public knows nothing, and it may interest the average picture-goer, and especially the many amateur string players and students who have at most only a very vague idea of "playing to pictures," to know something of what goes on behind the orchestra rail.

The enterprising musical director has two ideals: (1) really to fit the pictures; (2) to play the best music possible.

There are several methods of fitting pictures; the usual one is to play, let us say, half-a-dozen bars of one melody to a particular episode in the picture; then, suddenly to snap off and begin something else for the next incident, and so on. Now, my own particular theory is—and I speak from experience—that you can use the *whole* of many good works without any slicing of passages, and yet fit the various incidents appropriately. My method is to find out the exact time certain works take to perform—for instance, the Adagio [slow movement] from [Ludwig van] Beethoven's Sonata Pathetique, [Claude] Debussy's L'Enfant Prodigue Suite, etc. Then make a note in pencil of the exact time taken, on the first violin part. So that when you have to fit, say, a dramatic incident, you ascertain the exact length of time it occupies on the screen, and pick a suitable number which takes a corresponding time to perform, and so on throughout the entire picture.

Of course this means that the picture must always go through the machine at the same rate, but that can generally be managed by having a word with the operator.

I know that this method of fitting pictures entails a considerable amount of labour, but it is the only way, if we wish to present uncurtailed to the public the works of great composers. And this leads me to another point. It is possible to play much of the best music in kinemas. There is a wide selection of orchestral arrangements of big works to suit combinations of any size, from three upwards. The French arranger, Tavan, has done much for the kinema in this respect, his arrangements of operas, the lesser known as well as the more familiar, having enabled many small orchestras to play selections from operas which would otherwise have been impossible from original scores. Also the Alder arrangements for trio are very effective adaptations of the modern composers.

There is always the question of a library of music. This is usually personally selected by the musical director, who is responsible for it, and whose work it is to catalogue, cover and label the music, to say nothing of keeping it tidy and in good condition.

Apropos of picture fitting; an incident came within my own experience which is absolutely true. A pianist (very good, but without the slightest sense of humour) was playing to a film of the "educational" sort, depicting the habits of beetles and other crawling things. The musical setting chosen to accompany the film was "Abide with Me" — with variations!!

So, budding picture players, it behooves you when you enter the kinema business to keep well before you the fact that a sense of humour is one of your most priceless assets! For if it does nothing else, it will at least keep you from making public invitations to fleas and other six legged things to take up their abode with you!

59. A Cinema Musician, "Atmosphere"
Strad, March 1926, 17

When a producer wrote in his advertisement concerning a very famous film that suitable music was halfway towards the financial success of the picture in any cinema, the majority of managers merely said, "Certainly, certainly the film must be fitted well," and then thought little or no more about that word suitable. There were, however, a few wise managers who, when booking the picture, had requested that the music, which had been specially selected and compiled, should accompany it. The result of a week's running was that the wise men shook hands all round, and that the others said "A remarkable film, but"—something wrong, the weather, competition, the orchestra, but certainly not themselves. The truth is they failed to understand the real meaning of that word "suitable."

To them, and to many cinema musicians besides, suitable music meant music that fitted well. They understood the producer's advertisement to mean that the picture was so changeable in its action that unless great care was exercised it was very possible to continue a dirge into a wedding or a "simple love episode" into a leap for life. In a word suitable music, and in fact all cinema music, was and is to them purely programme music.[7] The successful managers, and some few musical directors, know that though it is true musical accompaniment to films will always to a great extent be program music, yet it is the judicious choice of that music that makes all the difference, because nowadays a film needs atmosphere which no amount of very accurate fitting can give unless it be *suitable* music.

Atmosphere is as essential in a moving picture as it is on the artist's canvas. The most accurate drawing or most perfect perspective leaves the spectator cold unless there is that something in the picture that draws him into it and makes him feel that there is life in it, makes him almost feel the rush of the wind or hear the roar of the sea, or taste the salt in the air that is dense with flying spray. So with the film.

Anyone who has sat through the performance of a complete film to which there has not been a single bar of musical accompaniment, will readily admit how absolutely dead the whole play seems. Even the most "furioso" parts seem unable to make one oblivious of one's surroundings. Add music of any description, and there is a distinct improvement, though often one is conscious of an emotional pull in one direction by the music and a distinctly opposing pull by the action on the screen. Cause the music to fit in emotion and something of rhythm, and one can become quite absorbed in the play, but add to the perfect fitting *suitable* music and one becomes steeped in the whole atmosphere of the play, seems almost to live in the scenes portrayed, and takes away a vivid impression of the whole play that is never quite forgotten. Add even one more feature, and that is a theme (or two) which accompanies a principal character or the meeting of the two principals, and the audience can take away something tangible, which whenever they hear or hum immediately makes them say "That does remind me of so-and-so." As for example, the [Ludwig van] Beethoven Minuet in G, the principal theme in "Scaramouche" [1923].

As somewhat extreme examples of films requiring very definite atmosphere,

"Monsieur Beaucaire" [1924] and "The Thief of Bagdad" [1924] might well be mentioned. The former, without any very intricate or thrilling plot, but full of the stately grace and ceremony typical of the way of court and society prior to the French Revolution, requires all manner of minuets, old-fashioned gavottes and stately rhythms to recall the atmosphere of those days of powdered wigs, ceremonial dances, and gallant gentlemen. It was even possible to play a modern foxtrot as a principal theme by playing it in slow 4/4 ballad time. On the whole, the atmosphere of "Monsieur Beaucaire" was fairly easy to obtain. On the other hand, "The Thief of Bagdad" was a film which required the most extravagant music to accompany it. Winged horses, flying carpets, deep-sea monsters, magic crystals, these, and all the other wonders of the Arabian Nights, seemed to have no parallel in music. But it was curious to note how the most extreme of modern music came to the rescue and provided the right atmosphere of one of the oldest of fairy tales. Naturally, much oriental music was combined with it, and well fitted, the film was a success.

There are, of course, innumerable nondescript films which are just one jumble of sorrow, murder, and mockery, that it is almost unfortunate that music should have to accompany it, but even these the public will swallow if they are helped down with plenty of popular dance music and a well-chosen theme.

The atmosphere of such films is much like that enveloping slum and society life of today, and it is any popular tune which is in the air that gives the films some life.

The ever-popular "Peter Pan" [1924] is as pleasant a film as an orchestra could wish to accompany. Full of children's frolic, with humorous, happy and sentimental themes for the crocodile, Peter Pan and Wendy, Captain Hook and Tinker Bell, it is a film where "you just think wonderful thoughts and you can fly." That is the atmosphere the orchestra must produce.

The Organist of the Picture Palace

60. Ernest M. Skinner, "Cinema Music"
American Organist, August 1918, 417–18, 421

MOVIE MUSIC is of two kinds, Dual and Absolute.

The Dual serves as a stimulant to conversation and as an accompaniment to the picture. The Absolute puts the picture out of business.

Some time ago, on a business trip to the Pacific Coast, I met the wisest man in the moving picture business. I think his name was Kerlein. He was running a picture house in Berkeley, California, with a seating capacity of about fifteen hundred. The pictures were fine and he specialized on the music, which for the purpose was the best organ music I have ever heard at a Movie.

His idea was that the play was the thing, and the music was subsidiary and contributory, and that it should never at any time draw attention away from the picture. He had an organ of not over four or five abbreviated stops, the same being linked up to a piano. The organ was of local build and not much of an organ, a mild diapason [the quintessential organ tone], a dulciana [a diminutive diapason], and two or three medium-toned ranks of ordinary type. The affair was played by a duplicate music roll mechanism. When one was playing, the music roll could be changed in the other. A simple movement would stop one roll and start the other, which took care of quick changes in the picture. Never under any circumstances was there any ragtime or a loud sound from the organ.

I had an opportunity to look over the library of music, and there I found [Ludwig van] Beethoven, [Wolfgang Amadeus] Mozart, [Richard] Wagner, [George Frideric] Handel, [Frédéric] Chopin, [Johannes] Brahms, [Edvard] Grieg. The audience were silent and intent on the picture. The music furnished just enough atmosphere to vitalize the picture and hypnotize the audience. I, at that time, learned the true function of music at a Movie.

I more recently had another experience at a Movie in California. I heard of a new and wonderful organ costing Twenty-five or Fifty Thousand Dollars that had just been put in. Of course, I knew that meant at least Seven or Eight Thousand, allowing the usual Movie discount, so I went into this theatre with my friend Struble and heard the monster.

Here again was atmosphere. The organist faced a rainbow of many colored devices known by various names; Flop Keys will do as well as any other. The tones of this organ were voiced as loud as possible. The first that struck my ear was a wood flute of vast proportions and it was subject to a tremolo of terrific effectiveness, accompanied by one of those bean blower strings on a fifteen-inch wind so stridently voiced that they tasted like copper, the kind you hear in the merry-go-round affair that makes you think the pipes must be screwed into the wind chest to keep them from blowing out. The whole sound a riot of immodest vulgarity that was an absolute shock to the sense and that made it impossible to fix your attention on the picture.

This organ had traps.

Once upon a time a man said to himself: I will make an organ imitate an orchestra; so he studied the orchestra, but all he could see was the traps, so he made organs having a few stops and many traps. This organ was built after this plan. It had ding-dongs, sleigh bells, xylophones, and an epiglottis or something that sounded like that, and a pneuria that buzzed, and a tuba on many inches of wind and the effect of the full organ was most original. It put the picture entirely out of business. The whole thing was most carefully designed to create an appetite for vulgarity. I did not hear one single musical note at this performance or the slightest indication of the influence of good taste. The organs of the above type are the logical outcome of three elements obtaining in their manufacture, i. e.,—

FIRST: An entire ignorance of all the traditions of organ building.

SECOND: An entire absence of good musical taste.

THIRD: A purpose that recognizes novelty as the one desirable requisite.

As far as my sensibilities are concerned, organs of this type are an abomination.

With regard to the more usual condition, it seems to be taken for granted by the Movie organist that the organ is at least half the show. But, oh! will some one tell me why all Movie organists lean so heavily on the sub-couplers? I have never yet heard a Movie organ that didn't growl most of the time. Why will organists use a 16-inch reed on the manuals with a sub-coupler, making a 32-inch on the manuals, and a general effect one octave lower than the pedals? And why, especially in New York City, are the Movie organists so fond of a large, large flute, and a thin, thin reed in combination with a seasick tremolo [a regular repetition of a musical figure], for melting melodies and extemporaneous maunderings that are like a bologna sausage, you can cut them off anywhere without marring their symmetry!

And now comes the comedy where the Movie Virtuoso really cuts loose. Note the avalanche of chromatic scales—ascending and descending, appassionata [passionate]. The sustained chords in the left hand, marcato [accented], with a pedal point [sustained tone] on the trombone. It baffles description and the picture.

How many times have I heard a familiar composition played with a casual fidelity in the right hand and an absolute disregard of the original harmonization in the left, because of a trifling modulation or two that happened to lie outside the repertoire of banjo chords at the command of the artist.

Of all the arts, Music is most vital and the most abused. Why do musicians make it so cheap and wretched when it may just as well be made beautiful? I find many reasons for the poor quality of Movie music.

FIRST: The Movie manager has a low idea of music and of the public taste.

SECOND: The Movie manager will spend half a million on his building and beautify it in every way, and then buy the very cheapest organ that can be found.

THIRD: Manager and organist have a badly mistaken idea of the function of music with regard to its contribution to the picture. I have seen pictures of wonderful scenery and had my ears insulted with vile sounds at one and the same time.

This recalls the many times I have seen films of waterfalls or tumbling surf and received a perfect impression of it, to have it knocked completely by some idiot working a wind machine behind the screen. Any sound that draws attention from the picture is a tactical and psychological error. It is impossible to take in the movement of a full organ or any loud sound at the same time without dividing the attention.

If the attention is divided it leaves the picture and confusion results. I have on many occasions been driven away from a perfectly good picture because the organist played the full organ ALL THE TIME. I have heard many bitter complaints of the Movie organ music.

An instance of ideal picture music occurred at the Strand Theater, New York, in the orchestral accompaniment to Tom Sawyer—never a Forte [loud passage] at any point, and all beautifully adapted to the subject. Organists will learn much of the true function of the picture accompaniment by taking careful note of the orchestral music incidental to the pictures in the best picture houses in the Times Square district, New York City.

But let me whisper it. Never extemporize if you can help it, and if you must, cut it short. There's a reason. Too much Movie music is in the extemporaneous form consisting of a repertoire of three chords in the left, and chromatic runs in the right hand, and an occasional pedal note in some unrelated key. The injunction not to let your right hand know what your left hand does should not apply to the Movie Organist in his professional capacity.

Cut out the full organ while the picture is in progress. Try the classics on some soft stops. If opportunity comes your way persuade the manager to get a small organ but a good one, having rather more charm and less noise in its tone; omit the traps. Avoid the present movie idiom; it is very bad and characteristic, revert to first principles and respect the instrument, to say nothing of the picture.

No story was ever told that cannot be better told in music, than which no more wonderful example will be found than in Rosette's poem, the Blessed

Damoiselle, and told in music by [Claude] Debussy. Some scenery is too grand and stupendous to be reconstructed by the written word, yet we all know that it is no greater or more stupendous than certain music which may well describe it.

The importance of good music is not sufficiently appreciated. The picture show is an opportunity of vast proportions for the employment in a large way of good taste and good music. Why, then, has practically the whole fraternity, apparently with a common impulse, set up the most abominable din that ever debauched the public taste? I suppose it was by arrangement with the genius of ragtime.

The Art of Music in respect to the picture is defined by its effect on the picture. Its part in the art should be limited to the exact point where it contributes most to the picture without drawing attention from it in the slightest degree.

The Movie organist has great opportunity for the display of musicianship, for the use of a great variety of vital music, for the association of a particular action with a musical idea that is closely related to it, for deftness in modulation both by note and color suitable to change of scene or action in the picture, and, most important of all, for making the organ vitalize the picture, being at all times subsidiary, suggestive, never obtrusive or distracting.

61. J. van Cleft Cooper, "Creation of Atmosphere"

American Organist, June 1922, 240–42

This is a subject about which a volume might easily be written and still leave much unsaid. In a short article such as this the most that can be done is to offer a few suggestions and leave the working out of the matter to the individual organist. Each organist has his own problems and must solve them in his own way. I shall try to show how some of these problems have been met and solved in the hope that it may be of assistance to some of the rest of us.

First, let it be understood that what the organist does is not to create but to reflect atmosphere—if such a term is permissible. There are pictures with no more atmosphere about them than there is on the moon. With these the organist has a thankless task and I have still to hear of the successful creation of atmosphere for a single one of them. Others fairly exude atmosphere and when the organist is favored by the fates with such a one, all there is to do is to allow the moods of the picture to reflect themselves in the music.

This whole matter of atmosphere is largely one of psychology. If the situations in the picture are logical and the characters react to them in a manner approximating at least that in which similar characters would react to similar situations in real life, the picture will have a psychological basis which will render it convincing. Add to this good photography and the result will be atmosphere. It is a pleasure to play such a film whether it be a comedy or a tragedy.

Music may reflect the moods of a picture either in a general way or by following specific actions occurring in the film. In the first case the tone of the scene must determine the character of the music to be used — whether stately, quiet and serene, melancholy, or sprightly. A fine example of this sort of atmosphere occurred in "Deception" when [Edward] Elgar's "Coronation March" was used during the coronation procession of Queen Anne. Hardened as we theater organists become, I never played that scene throughout the four weeks' run of the film at the Rivoli without feeling a sense of exhilaration with an occasional tingle up and down the spinal column. Another fine bit was the scene in "The Miracle Man" [1919] where the little cripple boy threw away his crutches and ran into the arms of the old Miracle Man while the organ played a majestic and triumphant motive. And even "In the Gloaming" and "Marching through Georgia" took on atmosphere when used with Lionel Barrymore's "The Copperhead" [1918].

And that brings up a beautiful point to note about gaining musical atmosphere, which is this: whatever the screen calls for that we must play, whether it be "Old Hundred" or "Turkey in the Straw." Even the most threadbare melodies become atmospheric if a convincing scene on the screen demands them. Not long ago in "Just around the Corner" [1921] during the scene where the mother was dying, the old gospel hymn, "Shall We Gather at the River," played softly and sympathetically, caused an epidemic of sniffles and clearing of throats throughout the house whenever it occurred. Such a combination of a convincing scene and its appropriate — one might almost say its inevitable music is irresistible.

I well remember the place in "The Birth of a Nation"[8] where the Little Colonel came back to his home which had been ruined by the war and the orchestra insisted on playing "Home, Sweet Home." "If only that confounded music would stop for just a minute," I thought, as I felt the catch in my throat and the smart in my eyes, "I could stand the pathos of the scene itself." But with the combination — well, I was not the only one to wipe a tear from my cheek. A fine instance of musical atmosphere.

Scenics offer excellent opportunity for the organist particularly the beautiful scenes of nature such as the Post-Scenics show. They are full of atmosphere and can be accompanied with the best there is in music. That old war horse, the

ANDANTINO in D flat by [Edwin Henry] Lemare is the type of music we need here. Or the PRELUDE TO THE DELUGE by [Camille] Saint-Saëns. Any organist has in his library plenty of such quiet melodious music and should be under no difficulty to accompany a scenic with the proper atmosphere.

Sometimes a film is stronger if allowed to run without any music whatever. It may be necessary to educate your house manager up to this bit of heresy in case he is a relative of the producer who, when he saw the bassoon was not playing in a passage scored for strings alone, protested, saying he was paying for a bassoon player and he wanted him to play. So if your manager insists on getting his money's worth out of you, you may be put to it to show him that you are giving him more for the "weekly insult" in your pay envelope by not playing during certain scenes than you could possibly do by trying to trail along with some sort of music. Most managers have the fixed idea that if the organ is not droning out an accompaniment to the license number granted by the N. Y. Board of Censors the organist is lying down on the job. However, in the [Hugo] Riesenfeld scores these periods of silence are not infrequent. And they are always effective, whether in a feature, a news review, a scenic, or a comedy. Only one must use judgment, if one has any, in selecting the spot to run "dry." In "Across the Continent" [1922] the scene where Wallace Reid's father, Theo. Roberts, has news that his car has been wrecked, and slowly gets up and pulls the marker out of the map, is most effective without music. A flood disaster, a wrecked "Roma," a funeral, may be allowed to pass in silence with good effect in the weekly. Such spots are more rare in comedies but they do occur. And I remember one Post-Scenic which was very effective this way.

The scene was a quiet meadow landscape, with the hush of evening over it and clouds floating lazily aloft. Just such a scene as you yourself have often dreamed over. Across the middle distance ran a passenger train. You saw but did not hear it. The music died away so imperceptibly that you did not notice when it stopped. Then floating in from the distance you heard the locomotive's whistle. And presently the music began again very softly and finished in entire harmony with the picture. Very effective, you said. The whistle, of course, was done on the organ with an augmented triad, say C–E–G sharp, on a soft flute in the way an engine whistles for a crossing. You don't know how an engine whistles for a crossing? Well then, you are not a theater organist.

This device of imitating specific sounds, meanwhile stopping all other music, is very useful and often invaluable to the organist in depicting atmosphere. In "The Sea Wolf" [1920] there was a scene in which a ferry was crossing from Oakland to San Francisco on a very foggy morning. The fog was so dense that objects a boat's length away were completely swallowed up. Several different "whistles" were set up—a low C on the open diapason [the quintessential organ tone], and augmented triad on a big flute, a higher pitch on a clarinet and a soft reed, and the audience heard only the boats signaling each other. As two boats that were in collision were drawing nearer to each other the swell shades were opened and the approach of the steamer indicated. Then a fortissimo crashed at the collision followed by the resulting hurry. The effect was much stronger than if there had been music of whatever type throughout the scene. Sometimes a clock striking at a dramatic moment, with no music, adds to the atmosphere, even though there may be considerable action: Or the tolling of a funeral bell as in the film when Thomas Meighan escapes from Sing-Sing [prison] just in time to see his mother's body carried from his home. During the excited action immediately following his escape the repeated blowing of the prison whistle was much more effective than any hurry could have been. The ringing of the heavy bell in the "Bronze Bell," was another case in point.

Occasionally a deliberate clash of tone will indicate a clash of emotions and add atmosphere to scene. In the "Spreading Dawn" [1917] with Jane Cowl the heroine was having her final supper out of doors with her lover who had enlisted in the Civil War, while the organ played "FAREWELL MY OWN TRUE LOVE." Suddenly came a cut-in of a bugler followed by a return to the lovers. A wonderful chance! The organist continued the song without interruption but on the shot of the bugler added the bugle call "Assembly" with a strong reed stop on another manual and in an entirely foreign key. The shock of the clashing pitch, tone color, and rhythm in the music tallied with the shock to the emotions depicted on the screen and the effect was electrical. The bugle shot was repeated, giving the organist another chance to prove to the manager that he meant it that way the first time.

Examples might be multiplied. Every organist can doubtless recall situations to which the forgoing observations will apply. The creation of musical atmosphere requires first of all a convincing situation on the screen. Without this the organist's task is hopeless. But given such a situation, let the organist add imagination, a reasonable amount of organ technic, an understanding of the resources of his instrument, and finally let him have the courage of his convictions, and he will find that he can create atmosphere in his music which will be appreciated by even the most unmusical among his audiences.

Conducting and Scoring to the Movies

62. "How Music Is Made to Fit the Films"
Literary Digest, 26 January 1918, 58

Setting the "movies" to music, or, more correctly speaking, setting music to the "movies" is an art in itself. When one witnesses some especially thrilling photo-play the music and the action on the screen usually synchronize so perfectly that the spectator is scarcely conscious of the accompanying music until it ceases. Moving-picture promoters in Cleveland have made a special study of this musical feature. The Spitalny brothers — there are three of them — conduct the orchestras at three of the photo-play theaters, where the music is made to fit the film, and the Cleve-land Plain Dealer *declares*:

It is a trick and an art, this arranging a musical setting for a photo-play — a trick to record the memorandum as the film flashes past, an art to arrange the orchestration, synchronize it, and, finally, offer it with an orchestra.

The general scheme of arranging and directing corresponds in all cases. Some, perhaps, are a trifle more elaborate in working out their detail. But the general plan is identical.

This is the way it is done:

When a new film is booked for an engagement the print to be used is sent on a week ahead for a private screening. This may occur in a private projection-room, in the theater proper before the performance time, or in the studio of some film exchange. In any instance, it is at the private screening the work of the musical director begins. It is there he lays the foundation for his next week's score.

The picture is projected at the same speed at which it will be shown to the public. As the scenes flash across the screen, the director jots down his notes as to varying incidents and characters. Three or four of the leading characters are selected as vital to the action. Varying themes may be given them, character themes, in fact; or the basic principle of the play may be themed, theme of idea.

Elaborate notes are made as to the varying scenes, with memoranda whether the action is fast or deliberate, long or short, and what characters participate in them. This is the working model, as it were, the skeleton, upon which the direc-tor fastens his themes and builds up a musical composition to fit the perfor-mance.

Then comes the real task — the arranging of the score.

The average feature of the program presented today runs from five to ten reels, with an average of 1,000 feet of film to a reel. The six- and seven-reel feature is employed as frequently as any. The total of musical numbers selected in making up the score for such an offering may number from eighty to one hundred different compositions, irrespective of repetitions; the number is never less than from forty to fifty.

When these arrangements are completed, the music selected, the themes worked out, the cuttings indicated, and the rough version of the setting is ready, then comes the second showing of the film, which is reviewed by the director and the pianist. Then, says The Plain Dealer:

The music is made to fit. Some bits may be found to be too long; some may run too briefly; all this is noted, tried, rearranged, and, finally, when the session is ended, the score has been synchronized to a nicety. The musical arrangement is reviewed. The part for each of the various instruments is made to correspond with the master score. Then, when this is done, all is ready for the dress rehearsal, at which not only orchestra and operators, but stagehands, electricians, and others may be present.

Hyman Spitalny takes a wide view of the responsibilities of the musical director of a photo-play, for, he says:

He is a conductor, in fact, not only of the music but of all other departments. The director's desk at the Stillman is equipped with telephone connections to all parts of the house, a series of buzzers for signaling, and a speedometer, which assist materially in synchronizing during the actual performance.

When the time of a performance arrives the stage buzzer is signaled for lights out. The orchestra starts. The operator is signaled, the film is projected on the black curtain, the curtain is signaled and withdrawn, and the projection curtain displayed. All these signals are sent from the director's desk.

Here at the Stillman we employ a speedometer for synchronizing. One of these is on my desk; another is attached to the machine in the projection-room, while still another is installed in the manager's office, that he may check the running time if he desires. This machine has a double index-sheet, on which the footage per minute is indicated, and, at the same time, the minutes per thousand feet. Usually we run about 1,000 feet to sixteen minutes. Of course, actual projecting time may vary a bit, due to one reason or another, and we may find, in the midst of a scene, that it is necessary to change the tempo of the film in order to preserve the musical setting. I signal by the buzzer, and the speed of projection is changed to suit the occasion.

And it is thus that time, effort, and many dollars are expended on that part of

the picture-play which really appeals only to the subconsciousness of the spectator.
The Spitalnys are the pioneer photoplay musicians in Cleveland. They have as-
sembled a musical library containing completed orchestrations valued at $15,000
[about $209,000 today]. The Plain Dealer *says:*

In the setting to "The Woman God Forgot" [1917], Geraldine Farrar's[9] spectacle of the Aztec days, $700 [about $9,745 today] worth of music was used,
while the numbers employed in [actress Alla] Nazimova's "War-Brides" [1916]
approximated the same.

63. Doron K. Antrim, "Possibilities of Movie Music— Present and Future"

Metronome, 15 February 1926, 20, 75

The musical interpreter of motion pictures, whether he is a lone pianist, a pipe
organist, or director of a hundred-piece orchestra, is playing an increasingly important part in the development of the film drama. He may increase the effectiveness of a picture to a considerable extent, or he may diminish it by filling in
the required time with any haphazard selection of music that comes to hand.
He may become a potent factor in his community of elevating the standard of
music appreciation among the movie habitués—and the movie populace is a
large and representative one in this country. He may accomplish these ends
if he sees the possibilities in his position; in short, the field is one calling for a
high order of musicianship, attested by the fact that very capable musicians are
turning their attention to it.

The "silent drama" will, in all probability, remain silent, notwithstanding
much experimentation and rumors of "talking pictures," which would indicate
that movies and music would remain inseparable for some time to come. The
public prefers to be entertained in a way that requires little or no expenditure
of mental effort. In fact, a movie show presents one of the most restful kinds of
entertainment. The theater is in semi-darkness, a tale of love and intrigue is un-
wound on the silver screen, to the accompaniment of music. There is no straining to catch spoken words; one just looks and listens to music.

The music of the pictures has developed appreciably along with the film. At
first, it was seen that the film alone was not sufficient to make a complete entertainment. Music was added at that time simply to break a rather oppressive
silence. It has continued up until the present time as the logical accompaniment
of motion pictures and it may some day reach the plane of an art. It has not

achieved that stage yet, however, but it is tending in that direction, and musical directors of motion picture theaters may do much to hasten the time.

In the first place, the energetic film musician will make an attempt to offer a fresh and varied program of good music, he will try to educate his audience musically by playing some of the best things occasionally, and he will seek out new music. Getting into a rut with the music and playing the same things over and over is a besetting sin of a large number of music directors. Orchestras especially get a standard overture worked up and continue playing it the rest of their lives. I used to take in a picture show occasionally out where I lived. The orchestra consisted of five pieces and organ. This ensemble had finally mastered the intricacies of [Franz von Suppé's] "Poet and Peasant." Now this number is a good old warhorse in its way, although it has seen palmier days. But the orchestra in question played it as an overture and made a steady diet of it every other show. About the sixth time I heard this piece, I would have welcomed an opportunity to accompany its funeral cortege to a final resting place.

Another instance of working a piece to shreds is to be found in the same orchestra's playing of [Franz] Schubert's "Erlking." The piece is a capital one for any musician's repertoire, but this orchestra plays excerpts from it whenever there is depicted a storm at sea or on land, war scenes of all descriptions, all kinds and varieties of the chase, etc., *ad infinitum*. There are instances in film presentation where the "Erlking" would enhance the dramatic action but it soon becomes cheap and inappropriate when applied persistently to any and all dramatic situations. So one of the important requirements of the successful musical director is to seek out and to use new music.

The opening overture presents a good opportunity for playing new music. Here the music *per se* shines all by itself and the audience can give undivided attention to it. The leading theaters are presenting new and high-grade music on their programs. Of course, they have the facilities, the trained musicians and the film program is usually of a week's duration, thus allowing a complete change of music every week. Those who are confronted with a more frequent change of program have a harder musical problem to solve. However, the constant addition of new numbers of the better sort will aid materially.

The director who gives considerable attention to suitable music for news pictorials will soon find this to be one of the best parts of the show.

The feature picture offers the greatest difficulty for proper musical depiction. Here again the director will find it expedient to have a large and comprehensive library of music to draw upon. I know of one man who keeps a rather complete filing system, the key to which is found in a little book. Here are listed about all the phases and gradations of emotion experienced by human beings. There are first such broad heads as joy, grief, anger, fight, tragedy, mystery, sadness, love, etc. Under the general title of joy, for instance, are more subtle expressions as exaltation, jubilation, festivities, sports, simple mirth, hilariousness, prankishness, etc. This man has catalogued every piece of music and he has a very large collection, which is constantly being added to, according to a wide variety of situations. One of the advantages of the system is that the music appropriate to a certain picture can be quickly classified and found, which is almost a necessity with film musicians.

There is no lack of music for musical directors; in fact, the literature of worthwhile music is very extensive. One of the most fertile sources of supply is to be found in the operas. There is music here that provides excellent accompaniment material. Opera music was primarily written as a medium for expressing dramatic action and for that reason is well adapted for film purposes. One who delves deeply among the famous operas will find himself well rewarded.

Then again, folk songs offer a prolific source of supply. The folk melodies of Scotland, England, Ireland, France, Spain, Sweden, Russia, and our own Negro and Indian melodies provide great music that will go well with many film scenes. Especially with the growing number of pictures that are taken in foreign countries, folk music of the country depicted will prove capital fare.

Atmospheric or music of nature is splendid for certain film purposes and such composers as [Claude] Debussy, [Edvard] Grieg, [Arnold] Schoenberg, [Edward] MacDowell, and others offer abundant material.

For the lighter type of music, there is always an ample supply and is no doubt essential to a well-balanced program. Numbers from the current musical shows and the hits of the season provide the spice of the musical fare.

As stated previously, the trend of moving picture music is in the direction of an art, although it may have some distance to travel before it arrives at that stage. The ideal condition would consist in having the music to a picture especially composed by some capable composer. This has been done on several past occasions and more pictures are made today with supposedly original music to accompany their action. When such eminent composers as Deems Taylor, Chas. W. Cadman, Hugo Felix and others turn their attention to the field, something may be expected. One of the difficulties today is that it is well nigh impossible for even an able and skilled composer to think up music for an entire production during the time at his disposal. Pictures are rushed through usually with such rapidity and offered to a rapacious public so hastily that anyone but a genius of the highest order would be unable to accomplish the feat of providing an original musical score. Even if the composer travels along with the company during the filming of the story (as is done quite often) and tries to imbibe atmosphere, color and inspiration, he will be unable to write fast enough unless he is satisfied with the kind of stuff the song fakirs manufacture to the lyrics of a misguided public. There are indications at present pointing to the production of fewer and better pictures and when this movement gets in full swing there will be unlimited possibilities in the field for serious composers.

There are a number of opportunities at present, however, in the smaller pictures of one or two reels that are scenic in nature. There are some beautiful colored pictures now being shown as well as some exquisite scenics depicting Nature in its various moods. Such films offer splendid possibilities for the welding of musical art to the pictorial. Organists who are able to improvise have an undeniable advantage in playing for such pictures, or in fact any picture.

Then again, why not reverse the process and build a picture around some great piece of music? In this instance, we already have the music and it would but remain for some synchronizer to devise scenes suggested by the music, with particular reference to Nature pictorials. It would seem that some worthwhile results could be obtained by following such a plan.

But there remains for the present-day director, who would make the musical program distinctive, to cultivate a large and comprehensive library and to prevent his numbers from becoming hackneyed. He can accomplish much in the way of education by introducing music of the highest type on his programs.

64. Victor Wagner, "Scoring a Motion Picture"

Transactions of the Society of Motion Picture Engineers,
September 1926, 40–43

It takes years to accumulate a fund of musical knowledge before one is able to synchronize the music with the picture. A musician who through ignorance or whim chooses music which burlesques a serious scene commits an offense, he destroys the science and art of musical presentation of motion pictures. One has to have at his command a musical library of a thousand different numbers and a sensitive feeling for their different moods to be able to classify the numbers properly. The well-known operatic melodies are not very useful, as they fit only the scene for which they were written and which scene the public visualizes on hearing the music. It is therefore important to consider the key in which each number is written to make a smooth musical bridge from one selection to another. In selecting the most appropriate music, one has to be careful not to anticipate the development of character so as not to stamp immediately the man with the cigarette as a villain; or, when a particularly beautiful girl enters, not to draw too hastily the third line of the triangle. Again, if one sees a man walk into a room wearing a derby and having a cigar in his mouth, one does not play mysterious music at once, because he may not be a detective after all. Not only is a knowledge of high-class music necessary but also a knowledge of most of the popular and national music with their characteristics of practically all the civilized and uncivilized nations.

There is one task laid on the music director who arranges a musical program of accompaniment for motion pictures which is seldom appreciated. This is the task of making music supply in a measure the spoken word—the missing dialogue—the play on the speaking stage—where this is not provided in action and in subtitles. The musical adapter has thirty, forty, or more scenes instead of a series of three or four acts. This I mention, because it must be remembered that no scene of any great length will maintain the same emotional key throughout. In the spoken play, there is a constant shift of emotional appeal as the incidents of the scene progress. But in the motion picture the play breaks up, not into acts, but into scenes, and scenes so arranged that a much closer sympathy of emotional suggestion may be obtained scene by scene, than is possible act by act. Thus it is that musical accord with the poetry of action and mood can be made scenically unified, and can really produce a more concise and closely correlated emotional suggestion than any other form of union of music and action. Now, I have said that it is one business of the adapter to make the musical accompaniment supply the motion picture with an important part of what the speaking stage gets from dialogue. I mean that while the picture vividly gives to the eye the story, the characterization can suggest constantly a mood to make the spectator mentally sympathetic. It follows that one preparation which the musical director must make is careful study of the picture, sufficient to bring to him definite and vivid impressions and emotions derived from it; he must himself feel the need of the music which he will later select and arrange.

The appropriateness of selection of motion picture accompaniment depends largely on this preparation. Scenically, the motion picture is a great inspiration; no speaking stage can in completeness, in gorgeous realities, and in generous detail approach the scenic richness of the motion picture. So, the musical director is always under the inspiration of an art kindred to his own. And so adept are good motion picture actors and actresses becoming, that careful observation of their pictured pantomime is all the inspiration needed for an impression that readily suggests music best suited to express it. It is therefore the study of the musical director of the picture with special regard to opportunity to make the music aid in its emotional suggestion of something truly felt and appreciated that counts most for the success of his work.

We speak of accompanying motion pictures with music. Now the accompaniment of song, the expression by means of music of a beautiful idea or of a dramatic idea is a province of art; if the song or the idea or scene or story has strong element of beauty, the art of accompaniment becomes really a king to the poetic art. The poet takes ideas and thoughts and gives them beautiful word forms; the accompanist, given this sort of material to inspire him, can add beauty to his work. Now, turning to motion pictures, the arrangement of a musical accompaniment for pictures in which there is definite mood, a central idea, a real emotional element that is consistent, makes a congenial task for a musician, and in the majority the arranger does find pictures inspirational; he does find opportunity for a musical accompaniment that is really expressive of the appeal which the picture makes.

But there are kinds of motion pictures which present difficulties. Take, for instance, the detective story picture, the adventure story, or the farce comedy. In each story the interest centers in the plot. There may be excitement of emotion in looking at the picture, but the emotion is not in the picture itself. Here the difficult thing is not so much to know what to play as what not to play. Music that strikes any hearer as incongruous will do much to spoil that picture for him. Then, too, the action is rapid, and this causes the change in mood of the onlooker and hearer to be abrupt—too abrupt to be successfully followed in music. The point made is that it is awkward and impracticable to accord intimately with the incidents of such pictures. For instance, picture a scene in which two men are struggling in a cellar while a dance is going on above them. I suppose for realism we should have a dance orchestra off-stage playing dance music steadily while the regular orchestra plays dramatic music according in mood with the fight. This is an extreme illustration perhaps but one which the motion picture adapter will recognize as within his experience.

The film play is a form of art and is analogous to the ballet in that it necessitates, for its adequate presentation, the synchronization of action with music. Thus, in its right development, we find a new art form in music, the possibilities of which are practically limitless. In film play we see one art-form which is dependent upon another—music—for its completion, and it is still incomplete and imperfect for presentation to the public without its musical counterpart accompanying it, just as is the case in the ballet, where dance and action are synchronized with music to ensure a perfect whole. The time has come when the motion picture theater orchestra is receiving universal recognition as an organization of artists who are working to achieve and maintain a high standard in a distinct art. Many times the question has been brought to me, "How do you synchronize the music with the pictures?" When we come to the screening room to work on our next pictures, the most important part from the very start is to make a title sheet, which lists the first few words of each main and subtitle and indicates the beginning of each new reel. These titles are used as milestones in the music score as well as descriptive cues. A piano part or a full orchestral score of each orchestration is filed on shelves in the screening room, classified according to mood, nationality, etc. We have one hundred thirty-five such classifications all the way from "Airplane Music" to "Funeral Music" and from "Wedding Music" to "Happiness Music." The next important move is to find the music best suited to the action and mood of the picture without allowing the music to dominate the play, in which event it would distract the attention of the onlooker from the picture to the music. It is mostly sensitiveness of the adapter which enables him to balance the action on the screen with the music in the orchestra pit. Of especial assistance is the up-to-date motion picture machine which allows the film to run in either direction. If the music which has been selected does not fit the scene, the film may be reversed without taking it from the machine, and another selection tried.

Scoring a good picture is just as fascinating as composing. When a picture is scored, one has the satisfaction of knowing that he will have at least twenty-one orchestral performances the first week which is more than a well-known composer of fame can ever expect. It may be interesting to know that no music is furnished with the film. Our library consists of about 15,000 different selections with separate parts for each instrument of our large orchestra. The original orchestration cannot always be used exactly as bought from the publisher. In order to make it of the proper length for a scene, endings or modulations are written which must be technically correct. Many times when we are unable to find a suitable selection, we cover the action with music which is originated in our department for this particular scene. In selecting a music theme for a leading character, the principal aim is not only to be consistent with the atmosphere or period but to portray and intensify characteristics through music. One morning last week, when we were screening our next week's picture, a young singer entered the screening room just as we had reached a touching scene of Stella Dallas [1925]. In the dark silence of the room, interrupted only by the buzz of the projection machine, the singer sat down at the piano and sang a tender melody. The effect was spontaneous; each of us realized what new intensity had been given by the song to the fine acting on the screen.

65. Josephine Vila, "Hugo Riesenfeld Tells How He Scores a Film"

Musical Courier, 17 February 1927, 48

*Has Arranged Musical Accompaniment for Covered Wagon, Ten Command-
ments, Beau Geste, Old Ironsides, and Other Great Pictures—Now Working on
Scores for Rough Riders, to Be Released Soon, and Also The Wedding March and
King of Kings, New Paramount Films*

"Do you know the origin?" asked the writer of Hugo Riesenfeld, who had just said that Hot Time in the Old Town Tonight would be one of the themes in his new score for the next Paramount picture, Rough Riders.

"Yes," Mr. Riesenfeld replied, "Hot Time in the Old Town Tonight used to be sung at camp meetings, I have found—"

"I was told by Theodore Mitchell, who knew the composer, that it was writ-ten before the Spanish-American war by Joe Hayden, of the vaudeville team of Hayden and Heatherton, and sung by them on what was then called the variety stage. It had a little success those days and Hayden sold his rights to a publisher for about a hundred dollars, never realizing that, with the out-break of the war, that song would be adopted by the Rough Riders for their particular one."

"That may also be true," agreed the composer-conductor, "but I happen to know that it was sung at camp meetings. I can even quote the old words."

"How do you go about arranging your scores?"

"Well," he went on, "I resort mainly for themes to the songs of the period of the particular film for which I am arranging the score. For instance, with the Rough Riders, I have taken Hot Time in the Old Town Tonight, Break the News to Mother, Good-Bye Dolly Gray, and The Blue and The Gray, as themes. Some of these, to be sure, were old before the war, but the others sprang into popu-larity during it. In order to be exact about my musical scores or arrangements, I do considerable research. You have seen my library?" he questioned. "Well, I have all kinds of literature and music which I consult when necessary. I also have a man who does little else but go to the public library and copy material from books which are not available outside."

"Do you see the film first, or what?" the writer asked.

"I should see the finished film, of course," he replied, "but sometimes that is impossible. It may require me to stay too long on the coast, so I am shown the uncut film of, perhaps, 25,000 feet, which is eventually cut down to seven or eight thousand feet. In the big films I try as far as possible to synchronize the music and action without making it choppy. In former days only the general mood was expressed. I am in favor of synchronizing only for the important happenings and for emphasis of the humor. I do not synchronize the entire picture for to do so it loses the melodic line. It becomes choppy and is not an ideal film accompaniment.

"It is much the same as with operas. Those who preserve the melodic line through all the dramatic action are the surviving operas. We call arias the melodic line. People may talk and belittle it, but the fact is ever present that all the great composers of opera, like [Richard] Wagner, used the long, broad, resting melodic line. In [Wagner's opera] Die Meistersinger, we find the arias distributed throughout, no matter how great the dramatic climaxes are; also in [Wagner's opera] Tristan and Isolde. Take, on the other hand, the most successful of the modern writers of opera, [Giacomo] Puccini! You again have lovely arias here and there, for which people anxiously wait. I believe that is why the many hundreds of operas perish and pass into oblivion. They lack that so necessary melodic line and are too synchronized.

"I believe therefore that the successful composers of motion picture scores must have not only a good knowledge of literature of all periods, but must also know opera. In operas you find always some scene similar to one on the screen. When arranging a certain score, I usually divide the film into sections according to moods. For instance, sentimental, pastoral, dramatic, heavy, dramatic, ominous, or—even everyday life. Then I have hundreds of compositions representative of the pastoral, the dramatic, etc. My course is to go through these and eliminate. My leading themes come in between these miscellaneous selections and may be as elaborate or as simple as the action requires. Once, perhaps, they are heroic; again sentimental, then allegro—all sorts of variations of the same theme. Do you see?"

"But this writing for Paramount feature films must take a great deal of your time?" the writer queried.

"All of it," he said quickly. "It is tremendous work and keeps one occupied all the time with the coming new pictures. I am at present finishing the score for Rough Riders, and I am also working on one for The Wedding March [1928] and King of Kings [1927], the film depicting the last three months of the life of Christ on earth.

"For the King of Kings score, I have employed beautiful hymns and Gregorian chants for some of the themes. You remember Liszt used the Gregorian in his St. Elizabeth . . ."

"Mr. Riesenfeld," interrupted the writer, "while we are on the subject of your scores, what others have you done in the past besides The Covered Wagon [1923]?"

"Let's see! The Miracle Man [1919], Ten Commandments [1923], Covered Wagon, Hunch-Back of Notre Dame [1923], Beau Geste [1926], Old Ironsides [1926], The Volga Boatman [1926], and yes—one of the best, in my opinion, that I have ever written, which was somewhat lost because the film did not meet with acclaim and that was Beggar on Horseback [1925]. That score was called by musicians a forerunner of the now prevailing jazz opera. It was, if you saw the film or play, a satire, and the music was in similar vein."

Remembering Mr. Riesenfeld's pioneer work in educating the motion picture audiences to an appreciation of better music, which he did so successfully during his association with the Rialto and Rivoli theaters, the writer asked him if he expected to return to the theater in such a capacity at any time in the near future. After a slight hesitation, Mr. Riesenfeld replied that he could not say just at this time, but would, perhaps, have some interesting announcement to make later on. This brings to mind the fact that Mr. Riesenfeld was one of the pioneers in bringing better music to the masses. In addition to programming the classics on the weekly programs at the motion picture houses, he and his orchestra gave Sunday concerts and also delightful ones for the children.

When the writer remarked that Josiah Zuro, a life-long friend and one who was associated with him at these theaters for some years, is at present giving a similar series of free Sunday Symphonic concerts at the Hampton Theater, with much success he commented with enthusiasm:

"Yes, Zuro is doing a great work. You see I had the Rialto theater behind me in my enterprise, but Zuro is doing that work all alone and depends only on contributions for the general expenses, giving his own services, as well as that of his orchestra, gratis. I call that a feat of accomplishment."

Taste, Culture, and Educating the Public

66. Frank A. Edson, "A Word about Suitable and Unsuitable Music in Moving Picture Productions"

Metronome, March 1918, 44

The casual observer, who enjoys a good moving picture and who, at the same time, is affected by the musical accompaniment, frequently finds much food for thought as to the attitude of the general public toward the questionable connection between the screen picture and the orchestra's musical description.

There can be no question as to the sincerity of some of the larger producers in their endeavors to supply suitable and artistic musical accompaniments to their output. Some spend considerable time and money in providing original scores, while the greater majority have elaborate musical settings compiled from every conceivable source. But while this works out admirably in larger houses with a good orchestra and plenty of time for preparation, the smaller houses with inadequate musical combinations and no time for preparation as a rule can give hardly any attention to a proper musical accompaniment, whether provided by the original producer or not. It might be added that the excellent musical cue sheets issued by producers, arrangers, and publishers for a large majority of our more important screen productions, have helped immensely toward a better understanding of what would be effective in a musical way, giving an opportunity to leaders to prepare ahead of time and helping in innumerable ways to meet the demands of the picture. But this excellent assistance is not taken advantage of nearly as much as it should be, even in our larger centers. Quite to the contrary, we find many theaters with imposing entrances, foyers and magnificent interiors which employ so-called orchestras, which are almost as primitive in makeup and ability as during the bygone days of the piano and bass drum and cymbals period.

Sometimes when a movies admirer feels glum and is in need of a good laugh it might prove beneficial if he visit some of these picture theaters, providing he can see the humorous side of some of the musical accompaniments offered. As an example, the writer strayed into such a house not long ago. It was on one of the principal downtown thoroughfares; the entrance was brilliantly illuminated and special announcements of a Charlie Chaplin and another important dramatic feature adorned the outside of the place. Inside of the swinging doors the spectator's attention was immediately arrested by the sounds of the orchestra which, in this particular place, consisted of a piano, presided over by an iron-handed young lady, two violin players and a cellist. Under ordinary conditions considerable effect can be gotten from such a combination, particularly if the players would know their business and have sufficient sense to select the right kind of arrangements. All that would be necessary would be to provide themselves with some of those admirable arrangements for piano solo and obbligato violin and 'cello, such as Charles J. Roberts has made famous, and they could furnish a musical accompaniment, worthy of the name, for any picture.[10]

But to come back to the above performance, the Charlie Chaplin picture was accompanied by every conceivable shoo-fly march, and it seemed that every publisher who had ever given away complimentary copies of music had been remembered in the musical setting to Charlie's antics. But the surprise came with the dramatic picture, the main action of which revolved around Wall Street, speculators and financial operations in general. Hardly had the picture started with its announcement of cast, etc., when the orchestra commenced with the first tutti [full orchestra] of [Charles Auguste] de Bériot's well-known Seventh Violin Concerto, and to the amazement of the writer of these lines, one of the two violinists—evidently "the leader"—played the three movements of this work from start to finish. One is justified in asking how in the name of common sense such a thing is possible and how a New York manager would pay a musician who had so deplorable an idea of the fitness of things. But after all it goes to show what kind of sins are perpetrated in these theaters and what the managers and audiences will put up with. In a way it was really funny to look at stirring scenes in Wall Street, love scenes, scenes of quarrels, serious pictures, all passing along to the tune of de Bériot's sweet and inoffensive melodies scratched and torn to tatters by a player who probably imagined he was supplying appropriate music to the picture and giving an artistic (?) treat besides.

At any rate, people who take it upon themselves to accept an engagement at moving picture theaters ought to be able to do two things well. To begin with, they should know how to play an instrument (preferably the violin) exceedingly well; and, secondly, they should have the tact and instinct to select appropriate, suitable music for a picture and the necessary musicianly ability to arrange it for the exact purpose for which they want to use it. The cue sheets, already mentioned, which can be had for the asking nowadays, provide an excellent help for leaders who are really in earnest about supplying suitable music, and even if not interested to such an extent, no end of appropriate dramatic, descriptive and characteristic music can be obtained from our music publishers, who are issuing every conceivable kind of material for this very purpose.

The lesson to be learnt from such an occurrence as the above seems a very simple but at the same time a very important one. It proves that correct methods in doing things, and capable understanding for essential needs in connection with the musical end of the moving picture industry, need looking after, possibly more carefully than anything else. The idea that "any old thing" will go with a picture is still too prevalent, and something should really be provided for those admirers of the screen who know the difference between a pathetic and a barroom scene, and who have a right to expect suitable descriptive music. But the one who should take the lesson most seriously to heart and endeavor to profit by it is the leader; for he is the one upon whom falls the responsibility of either helping the picture or making it ridiculous. With this statement, of course, the writer has in mind that part of an audience which really listens to the music and which considers it an important adjunct of the picture. Little by little the moving picture producers are improving their output with more artistic perfection; no detail of scenery, action or ensemble is overlooked, no expense spared to create illusions of the most magnificent or unheard-of kind, and still some of these remarkable and effective productions are placed on exhibition with practically no suggestions or plans for the music, which is to form an important part of the presentation. The time seems at hand when a decided step should be taken toward improvement of such conditions. In a way it matters little whether the music for a production is provided by a lone and lonesome pianist, or by a combination of three to ten players, or by an orchestra of fifty. The real and vital things to consider are *the quality and fitness of the music* which is played. In the eyes of an intelligent, musical onlooker it is just as ridiculous and out-of-place to play a clap-trap musical number for some affecting, serious scene as it would be to have the producer prepare for us a magnificent ball room scene in a millionaire's mansion and have the hostess appear in a skimpy, ill-fitting and cheap-looking evening dress.

Music carries a message all its own, and whether people agree or not about its illustrative qualities there is no denying the fact that it is the most powerful and potent aid to the spoken drama, and consequently a doubly powerful one to the silent, screen drama. It furnishes a background such as no other means can provide, and can be made to emphasize every possible mood, situation and character in almost as precise and fitting a manner as the spoken word. But the provision of such music demands a mind which is able to discriminate between various kinds of music, just as one must be able to differentiate between the various kinds of people which enliven a scene or a situation.

Managers of moving picture theaters ought to consider one thing in particular. In the old-time days of the dramatic stage each house had its particular clientele, which came to see the dramatic offerings and for which a certain kind of music, either good or poor, was provided. Nobody expected to see a high-class or ennobling production in a Bowery or vaudeville theater, and no preparations were necessary for such productions. But with the moving picture industry conditions have been fundamentally altered, and one is just as likely to meet with a splendid dramatic, historic or humorous production in a dingy, cheap theater as in a pretentious Broadway house; and now that such a thing has come to pass, the cheaper theaters attract a very large percentage of people who, while not so well-to-do, are musical, and while fully competent to appreciate a good music program, are also capable of criticizing a poor one. It is in these theaters that the ennobling, developing powers of music in connection with moving pictures counts for most, and it is here that every effort ought to be made to bring about genuine improvement.

67. "Choosing Picture Music That Pleases the Patrons: An Interview with Edward L. Hyman"

Metronome, 1 February 1926, 55, 70

Big theaters are, as a rule, lacking in that air of intimacy so much to be desired by audiences. There are many showmen who would probably tell you that this is because of the size of the theater and not due to the method of operating the house. Be that as it may, the fact cannot be denied that the Brooklyn Mark Strand Theatre, a playhouse seating about three thousand people and with standing room for five hundred more inside the doors, has that intimate atmosphere which tends to make the performance more enjoyable to the patron. Those who have been curious enough to delve into this mystery have discovered that Edward L. Hyman, who has presided over the destinies of the theater for the past six and a half years, since it was opened, is responsible for the successful solution of this problem. Hyman has discovered ways and means to put before his public shows which they thoroughly enjoy—shows which exude a contagious air of friendliness, resulting in the "theater intime."

It is reasonable to believe that this feat is not accomplished through photoplays alone. However, it is accomplished through musical presentations which Hyman considers fifty percent or more of his program. These musical performances are originated, planned, and mapped out in Mr. Hyman's office and are staged and lighted by him.

Those who know Hyman personally realize that he has no ambition greater than to give the public the most remarkable show he can get together for it. Being a lover of music himself, and understanding music in all its phases, makes the task more pleasant to him than it would probably be to the average show-man. Hyman has that happy faculty of being able to choose music which his public understands and thoroughly enjoys. After choosing it he is able to put it before his audience in the best possible way. In the first place, the Brooklyn Mark Strand Theatre is fully equipped with every conceivable device for the proper presentation of musical and stage numbers. It has been said that Hyman has added to his equipment constantly since the day he took charge of the theater, at which time its stock of lights and effects was as low as the proverbial one pickle with which Heinz started. Today it is the pride of the Brooklyn Mark Strand Theater that no other theater surpasses it in point of equipment. Only during the past two weeks has Hyman enlarged his presentation stage, installed new and elaborate settings and added more lighting facilities.

When asked to prepare a series of articles for this publication, Mr. Hyman chose to start with an explanation of his method of choosing music. In this respect, he said: "After all, it is a comparatively simple matter to please the public in the matter of music. As the magician said, it is all in knowing how. I congratulate myself that I have been very successful during the past six years at this theatre in building up a loyal clientele through the performances which we give. I have no doubt at all that music and its presentation accounts for fifty per cent or more of our regular business. My method of selecting music for presentation is to pick those selections and melodies best known to the public. It has been my experience, not only here but in Buffalo and Denver, that the average patron does not receive warmly a selection which he does not know. Thus we always avoid trying to educate the people as to what they should hear, but instead give them the things that they know best. There is practically no end to vocal and instrumental selections which are known to every man, woman and child. These range all the way from the light numbers to grand opera. When it is necessary to repeat one which was done formerly we always strive to dress it in a new setting and stage it so differently that its attractiveness for the public is just as strong as it was before. On the other hand, I have found that it is better not to have the orchestra play the best-known selections for the motion picture. In scoring the photoplay we have found it wise to use selections which fit the tempo and mood of the picture but which do not draw the patron's mind away from the picture, as a well-known number would be bound to do. Take for example 'Roses of Picardy,' which is excellent as a stage number but if played by the orchestra in the score for the photoplay would be almost sure to draw the attention from the screen to the song, thereby spoiling the illusion created by the picture.

"For the latest popular melodies, we solve the problem by using them in revues, revuettes and pantomimic offerings. Our motto is 'popular diversified musical programs' and to live up to this it is necessary that each of our musical programs contain a wide array of subjects. Thus it is that the patron will often find an overture of light nature, a ballet of heavier material, a presentation of standard selections and a scene or two from opera on the same performance. This is done to satisfy all musical tastes and artistic desires, so that we may bring our people back week after week instead of having them come some particular week when there would probably be something on the program to their liking. This policy of diversified musical programs is the reason why we never have any weeks with only one kind of music, such as 'Jazz Week.' Instead we choose from each category and blend them all into a show as nearly perfect as we can make them."

68. Dr. Sigmund Spaeth,[11] "Why Music Is Becoming the Important Element in Picture Presentation"

Metronome, 15 March 1926, 21, 25

If within the next fifty years America can pat itself on the back as a really musical nation, a situation which seems at present a distinct possibility, the chief recipient of congratulations will be, not the deliberate propagandists and pedagogues, not the concert-givers and lecturers, nor even the wonderfully beneficent phonograph and player piano. The first prize may be awarded to the lowly moving picture. For it is through the motion picture theater that young America is today acquiring its most solid and practical education in music.

Part of this education is consciously applied and imbibed, as when the orchestra or the organ plays a definite piece for itself alone, announcing its name on the program, perhaps with an explanatory note attached, and trusting for success in the inherent appeal of the composition plus the impracticability of immediate escape. But by far the greater part takes place unconsciously, by way of the musical accompaniment to the pictures themselves, and it is here that the permanent results are accomplished.

Music whose title would produce either inarticulate reverence or bored indifference if conventionally introduced, carries an intelligible message to ears insidiously opened through the parallel absorption of the eyes. What first sounds pleasing with the help of visible beauties attains through gradual familiarity a distinction of its own, and its acceptance is assured before the handicap of title, history or tradition can assert itself. Many a movie fan, confronted with the undeniable fact that he has just been listening with every evidence of pleasure to an excerpt from the "highbrow classics," answers defiantly, "Well, I like it just the same," and from that moment becomes a music-lover worth ten of those who never express an opinion until they have made sure that it is the conventionally correct one.

It is difficult to think of moving pictures without music, and from the earliest days of twitching and spotty films the followers of Saint Vitus have been accustomed to the accompaniment of at least a piano for their devotions. Primitive movie music ran parallel to primitive melodrama. For melodrama is properly the declamation of words to a musical accompaniment, and every stock melodramatic effect of the stage had its recognized and inevitable musical tag. Upon such custom was built the fame of "Hearts and Flowers," "Silver Threads among the Gold" and the "Hoochee-Coochee."

When motion pictures reached the stage of definite plots and wholly imaginary scenes (and they were not always thus) the melodrama of the legitimate stage was transferred bodily to the screen, and its traditional music went with it. The stealthy step of a burglar was glorified with as definite a rhythmic series of suppressed explosions as the fall of a comedian enjoyed in fuller measure from the undiluted bass drum. Love, Home, Mother, Virtue, and all the other estimable abstractions had their motifs as clearly assigned to them as did the heroes and heroines of Wagner himself.

Those were the days in which a skilled pianist would risk the improvisation of an entire film accompaniment at sight, a feat which few movie musicians would care to undertake nowadays, in the face of far higher standards of interpretation and greater complexity of plot and action. It could be done most readily, of course, by making use of familiar titles rather than obviously expressive music, the nature of whose meaning could not be mistaken. The names of popular songs sometimes convey the idea.

Patriotic pictures, and those of special historic occasions were of course easy to accompany musically, and still are. As song titles became more and more descriptive, more slangily expressive of one limited but definite thought, the movie musician acquired enough material to fit a phrase to every situation, every implied word or emotion on the screen.

Conditions have changed, however, since those delightfully empirical days. The movie music of the present is not only carefully prepared in advance, but has ceased almost entirely to depend for its effect upon a presupposed familiarity with stock titles. It represents in general a sincere attempt to express mood and atmosphere, rather than definite words or descriptions, and it therefore invokes a far higher art of interpretation, upon a more delicate eclectic sense, and eventually, on the part of the audience, a more intelligent and finely responsive appreciation. This is true, no matter whether the music is supplied by a full orchestra or a lone pianist or organist. It applies to slapstick comedy as well as to tragedy, or the imposing spectacles of modern technic.

The well-trained musical director of the new temple of the motion picture is too wise to be misled by either titles or traditions. He has discovered by experience and careful experimenting just what the normal human reaction is likely to be to certain combinations of melody and harmony, and he is not worried over the possibility of competition between [Ludwig van] Beethoven and Irving Berlin, nor by the fear that a symphonic Adagio [slow movement] may fail to create the mood of tranquility that he knows to be inherent in its strains. It is an endlessly absorbing task, this of selecting, fitting, arranging and composing the music to the modern films, and some of the best musical instincts and equipments in America are being entirely devoted to this one end. No wonder that the chronic movie enthusiast is involuntarily turning into a musical amateur of the most discriminating type.

The chances are that he has unconsciously listened to all the gems of opera and touched the high spots of orchestral, pianistic and vocal literature as well, while holding down a self-rising seat and watching every detail of the silent drama of photography. Mary Pickford[12] may have flitted across the screen, musically supported by the melodious simplicities of Beethoven, [Felix] Mendelssohn and [Franz] Schubert; Charlie Chaplin himself can throw his pies as accurately, even though the classic humor of the [Rossini opera] "Barber of Seville," a [Franz Joseph] Haydn trio, or [Giuseppe] Verdi's "Falstaff" inspire his versatile arm.

When "Les Misérables" [1925] was turned into an epoch-making film, the music of [Edvard] Grieg contributed most of the atmosphere of pathos, particularly those two perfect little mood-pictures known as "Heart Wounds" and "The Last Spring." [Franz] Liszt's "Les Preludes" and "Liebestraum" have the musical foundation for many a dramatic upheaval of the emotions on the screen, and practically all of his Hungarian Rhapsodies have served to express some phase of human conflict. [Johann Sebastian] Bach, [Johannes] Brahms, [Richard] Wagner, [Claude] Debussy and even [Igor] Stravinsky have given of their treasures to enrich the expressive resources of the modern motion picture.

With the steady advance in artistic photography, the screening of "grand opera" in general must be considered a development of the very near future. Already we have had [Georges Bizet's] "Carmen," [Jules Massenet's] "Thaïs," [Richard Wagner's] "Siegfried" and [Giacomo Puccini's] "La Boheme." The film possibilities of [Ruggero Leoncavallo's] "Pagliacci," [Puccini's] "Madame Butterfly," [and] "Tosca" and [Gustave Charpentier's] "Louise" cannot long be overlooked. As for Wagner, many of his stupendous dramas might actually be made more impressive on the screen than on the operatic stage. One can image a highly realistic "Valkyrie," "Rheingold" or "Goetterdämmerung" in celluloid, without the necessity of seeing physically distorted gods and heroes, or of listening to explosive voices of the guttural Teutonic type, with a great orchestra and magnificent scenery supplying an inspirational interpretation that no operatic conventions could possibly equal.

It has already been suggested, and with reason, that some sort of motion pictures could well be utilized for those portions of [Wagner's] "Parsifal" that demand extraordinary scenic effects, but are actually devoid of singing.

Will the motion picture eventually offer a field for composers more fertile than that of opera or absolute music, and can the great musicians of the world be expected in future to develop seriously a form of art whose significance is not yet universally appreciated? It seems more than probable. The operatic composer has always been hampered by the necessity of writing within the limits of the human voice, and of keeping his orchestra subdued whenever important words had to be projected over the footlights (not that this made much difference to the perpetrators of operatic enunciation). The creator of symphonies and chamber music has perpetually faced the handicap of having to express abstract ideas without the concrete help of words, colors or forms to make them inevitably clear to his audience. With the motion picture all such barriers are automatically removed. The composer may write as high or as low, as loud or as complexly as he pleases. He may put skyscrapers and railroad stations and the Stock Exchange into his music, with the knowledge that the pictorial accompaniment will make his meaning clear.

69. Josephine Vila, "Opera Singer Gets Thrill out of Screen Debut"

Musical Courier, 20 January 1927, 40

Andrés de Segurola to Appear Soon With Gloria Swanson[13] in [The Love of] Sunya [1927] — Will Continue Screen Work — Offer of Fifty Weeks — Believes It Is Just as Necessary to Keep in Physical Condition Now as When on Metropolitan Opera Stage.

When Gloria Swanson's new picture, Sunya, is released some time next month (there is talk of its opening Roxy's new theater, although as yet nothing definite has been decided upon), it will mark the screen debut of two singers, one of whom we know very well. Andrés de Segurola, for twelve years a leading basso at the Metropolitan Opera Company, was sought out the other day for the purpose of finding out what his reactions were after completing his first film. Through him it was also learned that the young lover in Sunya is played by John Bolles, who formerly sang the lead in Kitty's Kisses, a musical comedy that had a short run here not so long ago, and who was also a pupil of Oscar Seagle. Mr. de Segurola assured the writer that is was Mr. Bolles's screen debut too, so that now there are two artists entering the silent drama for the first time and each distinguished in his profession.

"Now that you have cut your first tooth in the movies, Seggy, will you delve further into the mysteries of the silver screen?" the writer asked.

"To be sure," he replied with alacrity, "my dear, I have already had an offer for fifty weeks at a very wonderful salary, but I first want to see how my initial picture turns out. Yes, I shall continue my screen career!"

"I knew you would; your enthusiasm told the tale. But what impressed you most about this new kind of work?"

"That's just the point," he interrupted; "I found the technic — or in the language of the pictures, the mechanics — absolutely different from acting on either the operatic or dramatic stage. I know now that artists of the screen are merely slaves of the angles of the lights and of the reduced space in which they are obliged to move about for a correct focus. What interests me, however, is that one has to have the power of commanding or awakening in himself any kind of an emotion or sensation at quick notice — like that!" and he snapped his fingers in rapid succession.

"It's not easy either!" ventured the listener.

"No, because you must be much more sincere before the camera than any actor is while facing his public in reality, because the camera registers—and registers very cruelly—any semblance of affectation or insincerity. If you don't feel the right emotion then the camera shows it. It might seem impossible, yet it's true. The camera reveals any tiredness or dissipation on the face of its actors.

"For example," and he smiled, "one night I went to a very delightful party which kept me from bed until five in the morning, but at nine I had to be at the Cosmopolitan Studios, dressed and made up for my set. I must confess, however, that I was a very stupid actor that morning. My mind and my nerves did not respond quickly to my desires. I was so disgusted with myself that I swore then and there that in the future I would behave for the screen as well as I did when I was singing on the stage of the Metropolitan Opera House."

Of Gloria Swanson the former basso was warm in his praises. "I found Miss Swanson a born, and a very great, actress. And to work with her was a tremendous help and inspiration. There were a couple of scenes in which she acted so realistically that she had us all crying. Yes, truly! I do not exaggerate one bit. One, I remember, was when she was talking over the telephone to her father, a banker, who tells her they are in bankruptcy. Gloria Swanson's emotion at that phone," he emphasized, "was so great and her tears so natural that those about her in the scene were much affected."

"But you told me in your last interview," said the writer, that "when scenes were being 'shot' an orchestra played so as to act on the emotions."

"Yes, perfectly true," he answered, "and all the twelve weeks Sunya was being made the former orchestra of the Russian Eagle was engaged for that purpose. By the way, Sunya is the new name for the film based on the Eyes of Youth. It is a Serbian name and means Illusion."

"What do you consider was the most valuable thing you got from your movie experience?"

"Well," he continued after only a hesitation of a fraction of a second, "do you know there comes a time in everyone's life when we thank God (there are some people who don't pray to Him but like to hear about Him, he added slyly), because we have found a new kick in life—a new form of love! My motion picture experience, in short, has simply 'pepped' me up again!"—which is saying a good deal, coming as it does from a man who was a leading artist of the Metropolitan for twelve consecutive years, also singing in the important opera houses of Europe, an impresario on both sides of the ocean, in addition to being a great traveler who has met kings and rulers of all sorts, and who is now successfully conducting his third consecutive series of Artistic Mornings at the Hotel Plaza in New York. Yet this man, Andrés de Segurola, gets a "kick" out of being a "debutant" in motion pictures.

70. L. K. Sidney, "What Modern Music Has Done to the Motion Picture Theaters"
Metronome, January 1928, 26

I suppose every long-haired teacher and pupil and followers of [Richard] Wagner, [Franz] Liszt, [Ludwig van] Beethoven, etc., etc., will rise up in wrath and prepare to slay me when I make the following statement in regard to the trend of music in the motion picture theater.

A few years ago I would never have dared to make this statement and perhaps in the near distant future I will retract every word I am uttering, but, until that time, here goes. Priding myself on being an observer of the likes and dislikes of theater-going audiences, I will be glad to retract this statement when that happens, but for the present, also being a firm believer in trying to serve the public with what they seem to desire, I must issue the following thought. Who would have dreamt that the popular form of music would chase the classics out of all picture theaters insofar as feature orchestral numbers are concerned? No one, but unfortunately or fortunately, that is exactly what has happened.

It is hard to believe but nevertheless true. Have you on your recent visit to any high class motion picture theater observed the slow, draggy feeling that seems to hit the atmosphere when the big symphonic orchestra tackles the strains of [Karl Goldmark's opera] Queen of Sheba, [Ruggero Leoncavallo's opera] Pagliacci or [Pyotr Ilych Tchaikovsky's] Marche Slave? No? Well, next time you visit one of these tremendous theaters see if that isn't so!

It is probably done in fine musicianly style, but, it becomes tiresome and draggy and asks a long waiting audience a good deal to sit thru a number of this type — and expect them to enjoy it. Just glance around at your next-door neighbors and see how many of them are paying attention to the musicians and what they are doing. For at least ten minutes you hear a mumble of conversation and finally the orchestra outplays their talk and beats them into submission, winning the battle against conversation only because the audience has run out of breath and conversation. Then the orchestra with a majestic fanfare and blare of brass climaxes itself into a big ovation, not in appreciation of the splendid artistic phrasing or musical technical work, but because they are glad it is over.

On the other hand, visit a theater and note a production overture in which the tenor in clown costume sings the Pagliacci number. Then, perhaps, the scene fades into a tremendous ballet of striking design and color. The dramatic soprano sings an aria from Faust. After this you will have learned why the motion picture theater audiences appreciate it. They do so first, because of its color; secondly, because of its magnitude and sight.

But, there are not any too many numbers of this type. The straight overture in motion picture theaters is a thing of the past, particularly where there is a small orchestra. Insofar as the large theaters like the Capitol are concerned, this does not apply, because here is the world's most wonderful orchestra and director. David Mendoza, in my opinion, is the finest director of an orchestra of that size in this country. He fortunately possesses a great faculty for knowing the public's likes and his magnetic personality seems to win his audience with his artistic gestures while handling his baton.

But, take a peep into the smaller theater, where you will find an orchestra of ten or twelve men struggling with the classics. Here it is all wrong, and acts as a terrible damper for the rest of the show to follow.

The stage band with its jazz instrumentation has served a splendid purpose in bringing to the theater audiences who patronize motion pictures a fine conception of rhythm and popular music. The public can't keep its feet still and when you accomplish that you have placed them in a happy frame of mind.

The public attending theaters or any amusement place love to hear the music they know and I can assure you from observation that they know more about popular music than they do about the classics. There are many reasons for this. First, I might instance the quick popularity these numbers attain via the radio; then, the records; then the singing of these numbers by the famous variety artists.

Take a song like "Tonight You Belong to Me." There isn't any reason to select that as an example, but I daresay the public has heard that song played less than they have Pagliacci. Yet how many average theater-going persons can hum Pagliacci through with the exception of "Ri di Pagliacci," as compared to the popular song mentioned above.

Surely everyone will agree that Leoncavallo's number has been played for years and years on every concert and operatic stage, vaudeville theater, and phonograph; yet, while still popular to a great degree it will never be known in completeness by the theatergoer as has "Tonight You Belong To Me," "Only a Sun Shower," "Blue Heaven," and "Broken Hearted."

Why? That is simple! Popular music has a simple melody built for popular appeal; the other one is difficult for the ordinary person to remember. In picking Pagliacci, I might also include numbers like [the overture from Richard Wagner's opera] Rienzi, [the tenor aria from Karl Goldmark's opera] Queen of Sheba and a host of others. Citing more numbers would simply make my argument more sound.

Mind you, personally, I would rather have my orchestra play fine, high-class artistic music. Personally, I would rather hear it myself. But what is one to do when one is an humble theater manager and when one attempts the education of the public with high-class numbers, the only result is to have the audience speak to each other about what they are going to buy for Christmas, or, "When does the baseball season open?" and "Where are we going to spend our next vacation?" Mayhap in a few months hence it will all change and we will again have back those melodies that have been handed down for years. Mayhap not!

It is hard to believe that the tradition of good music is lost in modern theaters but next time you hear a fine overture bear my thought in mind.

Popular vs. Classic Music

L. K. Sidney is the executive in charge of the De Luxe chain of motion picture theaters on the Loew Circuit. He is responsible for the entertainment which is provided in these houses, and since they have been very successful under his guidance, what he says about the form of music found most successful in such theaters may be taken as authoritative.

Is Mr. Sidney's experience typical of the whole country? Have others who are responsible for motion picture entertainment had the same experience as he has? Will popular music force standard and classic music out of the motion picture theaters?

The Metronome believes that this question is of paramount importance to the music publisher, the composer, the motion picture theater owner and the musician. It would like to have the views of its readers on this subject so as to present the question in full. Don't hesitate to express your thoughts on this subject. Your name will be held in confidence if you so wish it. Send all communications to Editor, The Metronome, 62 Cooper Square, New York City.

Responding to the Talkies

71. An Interview with Joseph N. Weber, "Will Machine-Made Music Displace Real Music in Our Theaters?"

Metronome, September 1928, 50, 102

No industrial development within recent years has caused the amount of perplexity and concern as has the introduction of the talking movies and the synchronization of the human voice and music with motion pictures. The public don't know what to make of this newest development in the picture industry, the theater owner has visions of cutting down the expense of production but not the price of admission, the theater musician foresees his job in a precarious position and himself displaced by a machine. And the movie actors and actresses—they are also very much up in the air. For so many years they have been seen and not heard, beautiful but dumb, that the idea of mustering up a voice in addition to the other requirements is causing considerable consternation in the ranks. Then international complications arise. English-speaking films will be useless in France and Germany and vice versa. It will be necessary to have films spoken in a dozen languages to be available for the world market. What will Pola Negri[14] and others like her do who can speak English only in a limited way and that almost indistinguishable? How will cuts be made in the speaky film? However, these are problems for the masterminds of Hollywood to solve.

What concerns the American musician is just how far will the substitution of canned music displace the genuine article. This is a question of vital importance to the musician and to the art of music and THE METRONOME sought out the one man which it considered best qualified to consider such a question, Joseph N. Weber, President of the American Federation of Musicians.

"We should view this question," said Mr. Weber, "in its broad aspect, not solely in the light of what it will mean to the American musician but what it will mean to the American nation, to the development of music in this country. The idea briefly is that machine music is threatening to displace the human element. There have been innumerable instances in the past of labor saving machines displacing the human element who opposed them strenuously. But these were machines to save labor and their advent contributed to human progress. But does machine music contribute to progress? Let us see. A musician in the first place is not a laborer as the term is commonly understood, but is rather an artist, because he follows music which is an art. A personality and a soul are therefore required to make music. A machine has no soul nor personality and never will have. Accordingly you do not get real music on a machine, only a reproduction of the genuine.

"The question arises as to what the cultural value of all this may be. Surely, if machine-made music or singing displaces the presence of the artist in hundreds, nay, thousands of instances, the incentive for any individual to perfect himself, so necessary for progress in all art, is minimized, and music will no longer have the cultural value which it formerly possessed. Any art is dependent upon the number of its enthusiastic executants, and if their activities in the main are replaced by machine productions, then in time their number will be greatly reduced, and as a result, we will find the minimizing of the very field from which they are drawn, and so we will have a restriction in the art itself, and consequent reduction of its cultural value.

"Twenty-five years ago America found it necessary to import most of its musical talent. There was hardly a native player in any of our symphony orchestras. But what a vast improvement has been made in the meantime and now the native musician has come into his own. Talent develops where there is incentive and the motion picture theaters have offered a big incentive to the musician. But if all our theater music is to be canned and ground out by a few people stationed in a laboratory, there will be little incentive for individual musical development and all the talent we have in this country will have restricted outlet for its expression. Consequently music will become an industry and will die out as an art and that would be a calamity. However I do not look for any such condition to come about as long as people consider music as an art and the human element necessary for its expression. We have just made a nation wide survey of the situation with a view to offering a solution to the problem about which many local unions are asking us for advice. I should like to lay before readers of THE METRONOME the results of this survey.

"One conclusion our survey of the situation has brought to us is this: Developments, attained and promised, contain no provision for giving the public more for its money, or for decreasing the cost of entertainment to the public, and that is why we are convinced that the final adjustment will not greatly injure the cause of music. The public will demand the best and personal appearances of musical and other performers far outclass mechanical offerings.

"Fourteen thousand theaters in the country contain a seating capacity of 15,000,000, it is estimated. Fifty percent of these seats are in the 4,000 larger houses. Three hundred of these larger theaters are now wired for synchronization. Within the next year the number wired will reach 1,000. Hundreds of other houses have ordered wiring but will be unable to get the service in a year. At the same time talkie exploitation is throwing the silent drama into a deep shade. Hundreds of exhibitors are running about in circles wondering what to do. Synchronization equipment is expensive, and talking pictures are more expensive still. A real talking movie, which as a silent picture would rent to a certain theater at $250 [about $3,075 today], now costs $1,000 [about $12,300 today]. A talking short, worth, silent $50 [about $615 today], is held at $350 [about $4,300 today]. Extra exploitation and increased operating costs are not entirely offset by dispensing with musicians and the mechanizing of the performance makes necessary a greatly increased gross return. However problematical that increase may appear, many exhibitors are dashing in, fearing overreaching by competitors.

"Attempts to use sound pictures as a substitute for music are largely due to the desperation of the exhibitor to retrieve some of these costs. We do not believe he will find it feasible to do this retrieving at the price of debasing music because that will mean box office losses at a time when the contrary is indicated.

"Realistic sound effects have been variously attempted since the beginning of cinema entertainment. Years ago actors stood behind screens and supplied talk. Clever ones mystified audiences, but the plan failed to develop. Drummers also became versatile at providing sound effects, thought necessary to carry the illusion.

"Time demonstrated, however, that the silent picture carried its own illusion pretty adequately, and that music, in sympathy with the spirit of the action portrayed, was more effective than chattering coconut shells for hoof-beats or shaking metal sheets for thunder. The charm of the music was glamorous rather than realistic, and the stage has always known that there is a point beyond which realism must not go in dramatics lest the emotional appeal be reduced. The value of music in that connection is seen in the reluctance of producers to have pictures reviewed by critics in 'cold' projection rooms without music.

"As to canned music ever substituting adequately for the real performance, we are not alarmed. The ballyhoo about picture scores performed by great 100-piece symphony orchestras is misleading and cannot endure.

"Just why mechanical music never attains the charm of real music is a problem for the higher critics and scientists, but I think most persons will agree that it never does. The average listener complains that it is 'too perfect.' The real reason, of course, is a lost quality, which may well be called 'the soul of music.'

"We are not confronted here by a competition between art forms. The conflict is between the exhibitor's desire to economize and the requirement of high-grade entertainment. We are confident that in the long run the latter factor, which reckons with the human element in entertainment, will control.

"Personally I think that introducing the spoken word into the silent drama destroys much of its charm. The motion picture has had a remarkable development during the twenty-five years it has been in the making. It has established itself as a legitimate art in pantomime. Music has been the language of the films and music and pictures have merged most satisfactorily and shown possibilities of developing into a real art form just as opera has merged drama and music. I would regret to see this development retarded at this stage of the game by the introduction of talking movies which are not a distinctive art form in themselves but a canned version of the stage. However I do not think talking movies will displace the other. There is a quiet restfulness about the silent drama accompanied by music with no straining of the attention to catch spoken lines which I don't think the public will be anxious to relinquish. The public will be interested in it as a novelty only, not as a permanent thing.

"However, we professional musicians are not solely interested in maintaining a just material standard for the members of our profession, but, in the furtherance of the art of music as well, and, inasmuch as both are threatened by the attempt to universalize the dispensing of canned music, we would fall short of our duty if we would fail to protest and advise the public, that not only we, ourselves, but likewise, they would be imposed upon were this policy to proceed unchallenged. Let us enlighten the public and let them decide."

72. Warren Nolan, "Talking Pictures and the Public"

Transactions of the Society of Motion Picture Engineers, 1929, 131–34

The old road has been electrified and it is not, paradoxically, as easy to travel as it was when steam was the rule. With the dawn really coming up like thunder and with ham and eggs sizzling on the Transvox screen of the Roxy, the press agent has his troubles. He is asked,—and the answer must be ready,—"Was that really Rin-Tin-Tin that barked?" He coins names like "talkies," "audible cinema," and "non-sinks," and he does not always pick the term that is most descriptive. He must decide whether to publicize the fact that those swords didn't clash in the reconstructed palace of Louis but that Hugo Riesenfeld's musicians tapped some teacups with spoons inside the Trinity Baptist Church in Camden, N.J. He must take the blame for making audiences conscious of mechanical contrivances while they are seeing and hearing productions that aim to achieve an emotional effect; it is undoubtedly true that in the magnificent job of publicizing sound devices publicity departments went beyond the life lines and planted the whirling discs and the tiny sound tracks in the mind's eye of every moviegoer.

Our English cousins took the infant to the font and sprinkled the title "audible cinema" on the lusty one. That's a contradiction in terms. It has been pointed out by Faure, Grierson, Reinhardt,[15] Chaplin and others who have taken the motion picture seriously as an individual art form that the term "cinema" is visual in its connotations, that the essence of cinema is visual expression of drama in photographed movement, to the exclusion of the spoken word. Cinema made audible is not, then, cinema at all. We shall have to coin some phrase that may be passed on to the public as accurately descriptive of the new form. As press agents accept facts as they are and do not idealistically create Utopias, I consider the present all-talking production schedules of all major film companies as a certain indication that we shall have but one form within two years: the legitimate recreation of actuality, the simulation of a reflection of life, this to result from fusion of sight and sound. I think that "Alibi" [1929] and "Broadway Melody" [1929] in which people talk when they would talk and not whenever it seems necessary to demonstrate the wonder of science, come closest to the new form. There will be visual action, and there must be visual action because still life won't hold anybody's attention for two hours unless that person is so highly cultivated that he can view photographed beauty, a single scene, for hours. That, literally, is the art gallery's contribution. "Talking pictures" is probably the best term yet devised, because the illusion achieved is one of a reflection that emits sounds that are electrical echoes of human speech.

There has been, for one year, and there will be, for at least two years more, certain difficulties in publicizing sound. As for production, I don't think that technical tricks should be told about sound any more than they are now revealed in the case of photography. Of course it is an age of exposes, an age in which aviators and explorers sign contracts to tell the readers of *The New York Times* how they did it even before they take off to do it, in which *The American Mercury's* influence on other magazines is so apparent in the "debunking" contents of all publications, even our fan magazines that formerly fed their readers the stuff from which pipe dreams are made. But the film, even the talking picture, depends for achievement of its effects on illusion. That illusion ought to be maintained out of consideration for the audience. This is difficult, from the publicity man's standpoint, because our better newspapers have gone scientific so completely that two technical terms will land a story on page one in place of the widows-and-orphans yarn of the pre-war days. I am trying to tell the Society of Motion Picture Engineers that the individual achievements of its members, when they endanger the illusion of a darkened theater, should not be publicized. It is like listening to [Vladimir] de Pachmann playing [Frédéric] Chopin and thinking all the while of the Baldwin or Steinway publicity about the quality of the wood and the arrangement of the keyboard. Mechanics are an auxiliary, an aid to an emotional effect.

Every publicity man knows that the best publicity an actor can have is his own performance on the screen, for that is direct, personal in its projection to the mind of the audience, and it causes praise to be talked by admirers. The gentlemen in charge of projection of sound pictures—to say nothing of those who record them—have been constituted individual showmen by this new form of presentation. They have been given power, and they have been given responsibility. Timing and tone are in their hands, and artists on the screen and audiences in the seats are at their mercy. One or two distinctly lamentable demonstrations of carelessness at most inopportune times seem to show that rehearsals such as stage producers employ are not attempted with talking pictures. With the performance its own best press agent and with the public judging that performance, it becomes important that motion picture engineers develop appreciation of the significance of publicity. The public only gets an impression, it never penetrates to causes.

The public retains some skepticism about talking pictures because it has always been a Thomas as far as show business is concerned and because there has been inferentially misleading information handed to it in several isolated instances that have undermined the general confidence. The term "Sound Picture" has caused tremendous confusion; it should be displaced by a line, "With Synchronized Musical Score." The kickback is on the gentlemen who misled by inference, for Patrons feel Barnum is charging them a dime to see the egress once more and they resent it. Publicity and advertising on all pictures should state exactly and explicitly how much dialog there is in a picture. The term "Part-Talking" is used in the trade but I have not seen it used to the public. "With Sound" is like a tail stuck on a paper donkey; the traps player in Camden clicks the hoof beats just like a drummer in the theater's pits. Publicity should be educational in its effect, and press agents are professors in the sense that they spread knowledge of a particular subject to many people. I don't know any editors who have learned to accept the teachings as gospel, but nothing will be done to remove editorial prejudice against press agents if there is incorrect information or inferentially misleading information distributed about the talking in pictures.

When the late Rudolph Valentino[16] was dying, it was part of my job to appease the demands of the press. This meant the boys had to be told why they couldn't carry their cameras into sick rooms and take pictures of all dying patients, that doctors had to be predisposed to recognize the over-anxiety on the part of the reporters and to give them bulletins, and so on. Well, I learned one day that Valentino had virtually no chance of surviving. That night I was asleep and the telephone rang, out at my home. It was nearly three o'clock in the morning. A tabloid's managing editor was on the phone, and he made no apology for waking up the press agent nor for the insult in his question.

"Say," he asked, "we got a hunch this Valentino ain't sick at all. We hear it's all a gag, just a publicity stunt. What about it?"

It so happens that Valentino died about nine hours later. I offer the incident as evidence of the skepticism in the minds of some editors, and the necessity for bending over backwards in passing out the truth about Rin-Tin-Tin and other actors, and about the contents of talking pictures. This publicity, I repeat, will be necessary for another year or so. Then the sound-and-sight medium will have taken definite form, it will have been christened, and the vaccination by the Victrola needle will undoubtedly make the Infanta of America's industries immune to all the ills that flesh is heir to.

Discussion

MR. RICHARDSON: At one point, Mr. Nolan, in speaking of the new synchronization device said that the operator would throw it out to prove how wonderful science is. I want to say to Mr. Nolan that as long as writers and others talk about machine operators that is what is likely to happen. Motion picture projectionists, however, don't do things that way!

MR. NOLAN: I don't know the name of the gentleman, but he embarrasses me by a lack of a sense of humor (laughter). I could say a great deal about some projectionists who caused us a great deal of embarrassment one evening.

73. "What the Fans Think," *Picture Play*: "Talkie Gets a Guffaw," March 1929; "Voice Censor Suggested," March 1929; "Another Fan Deserts!" April 1929; "*Real* Singers Would Go Over," February 1932; "Carrying English to England," February 1932; "Adores Yankee Talk," November 1932; "Our Rural Accents," November 1932

Talkie Gets a Guffaw

At this moment, while everyone is taking an interest in talking pictures, I want to write a few words about them. "Wings" was shown in our town, with sound effects. The drone of the airplanes was so beautifully produced that it seemed they were flying inside the theater. Therefore, I am for the sound effects. But spare us, for Heaven's sake, from the talking movie in its *present* form. At the International Film Exhibition, which was held at The Hague, I attended a demonstration of the Vitaphone. First, a cellist appeared on the screen and started to play. The sound was clear and natural, but when a person appeared on the screen and started to speak, the audience burst out laughing, for the voice seemed to come from everywhere—from his ears, from his nose, his hands, but not from his mouth. We hear too much of the mechanism; but I think when the apparatus has been improved considerably, talking pictures will take an important place in the film industry.

—H. Leonhart, Tolstraat 138, Amsterdam, Holland.

Voice Censor Suggested

If we take away the glamour of the screen, and really look at some of the great stars closely, don't you think they're rather disappointing? Perhaps you've heard Adolphe Menjou speak? Oh, where is the polished, cynical dilettante, with the soft voice and slight French accent? Certainly it isn't to be found in the "vurry pleased to meet you" that bursts on one's astounded ears.

Can you truthfully say that May McAvoy's voice enhances her charm? But we do have compensations. Marion Davies has a most fascinating little stammer in her speech that makes it doubly attractive, and Dolores del Rio has the slight foreign accent that we expect from her.

But if talkies are to be thrust upon us, let some sane judge decide whether a star's voice is suitable before we hear a harsh, nasal horror that completely destroys our ideal.

It might interest fans in America to know that Clive Brook is one of the greatest draws in London now, and in him there is at least one actor to whose initial talkie we can look forward without trepidation.

—Richard L. Norton, 22 Grosvenor Rd. London, S.W. 1, England.

Another Fan Deserts!

If the movies intend to continue with this Movietone and Vitaphone business, they are going to have to stagger along without the patronage of this fan. I can stand a lot of punishment but when it comes to talking pictures I have to draw the line.

Why this thing was started is a mystery to me, and just when the films were showing such a decided turn for the better, too! "Sunrise," which I had waited for, and expected so much of, was entirely spoiled for me by the blatant racket of the Movietone; and now I learn that von Stroheim's picture "The Wedding March" is also accompanied by this noisy effect. And Emil's "The Patriot." Gosh, it's enough to bring tears to the eyes of one who has always been an ardent fan and booster of the movies. But, as Fanny the Fan stated, I'll have hereafter to spend my evenings with my books—the films are a thing of the past with me, so long as they continue in their present noisy state.

—Joan Perula, San Francisco, California.

Real Singers Would Go Over

There appears to be a controversy raging as to whether singing films are wanted or not. I think this all depends on the type of singing. If it is a Buddy Rogers, a Nancy Carroll, or a Janet Gaynor singing film, by all means no, but if we are privileged to hear Lawrence Tibbett's magnificent voice, the producers need have no fear that musical films are on the wane.

When I saw "New Moon" there was prolonged applause—proof positive that the audience was carried away by the beauty of the singing.

I see that Lawrence Tibbett, in "The Cuban Love Song," is to be an American marine—Heaven forbid! Such a voice as his belongs to cultured and romantic backgrounds, not to the rough atmosphere that inevitably permeates films dealing with soldiers.

Why doesn't he insist on making "Robin Hood," as was at first intended? Also, why not have a screen version of "The King's Henchman," the opera in which he appeared with such success in New York?

—Ruby Deere, 234 Munster Road, Fulham, S.W. 6, London, England.

Carrying English to England

As an interested reader of "What the Fans Think," I should like to tell our American cousins what I think of their films, and please take my letter as an average Englishman's views, that is, the picture-going multitude—about 99.9 percent. I must say that American films hold sway over here for the simple reason that they are good. Sometimes we produce a good talkie, but the average British film is terrible. They seem to delight in showing the world that an Englishman must either speak "higgerantly" or "so very refanedly." Now, thank Heaven, the American films show the English how to speak their own language. True, you have some examples of real Englishmen over there—Clive Brook, Ronald Colman, and others.

I am sure if you see certain British films, you will forgive our producers, for they know not what they do, or rather, what harm they do.

We have enjoyed those magnificent productions such as "Hell's Angels" [1930], "The Dawn Patrol" [1930], "Min and Bill" [1930], "The Big House" [1930], and "Romance" [1930]. No matter what type of spectacle, from cow-punching to comedy, from backstage to blood and sand, I can honestly say, if it's American, I sit back and enjoy it.

Maybe I should have been born an American. I must be honest, though, and I say again we want your talkies. Take it from me, the American accent is cultured enough for us. Don't mind those certain few who condemn your accent. What they find wrong in it, goodness only knows. All I hope is that in the near future the young will aspirate their "aitches" as nicely as the Yankees.

—Leonard John Cushen, 508 Downham Way, Bromley, Kent, England.

Adores Yankee Talk

In the August Picture Play Karen Hollis seemed to be on the warpath with Miriam Hopkins and a few others. I don't know how some people feel about it, but to me just picking on people to fill up space is a bad way to spend valuable time. She was raving about Miss Hopkins's refusal to see reporters. Well, that's her business and not Miss Hollis's.

To make matters worse, she put in a little dirty dig, saying, "I wonder if Miss Hopkins considers it an intrusion on her privacy if we go to see her pictures?"

Well, my dear Miss Hollis, since sarcasm seems to be your language, I'll reply that I'd rather intrude on Miriam's pictures than miss them, because they are always worth the trouble.

Last, but not least, I think the accent discussion is so silly that I get dizzy just reading about it. I'm about as Southern as they come and I just adore hearing

Yankees talk. I've entertained plenty of them with my drawl, so let's all make up and be friends.

—Dinah Trenton, Birmingham, Alabama.

Our Rural Accents

While the conflict of accents is raging among the fans, permit me to make a few comments.

Why is the contention between the Northern and Southern accents only? There is no complaint about any other accent. The Swedish, the French, the English accents are all adorable. It is the so-called Northern and Southern accents which get on the nerves.

In reality the difference of accent is wrongly interpreted on both sides. What some Southerners classify as the Northern accent is simply the provincial type of speech with its intensified R's. Likewise, the Northerner's conception of the Southern accent is the brogue of the rural population with its eliminated R's. The difference is between the two rural types of speech only.

The speech of the educated upper class of both sections differs but little. The drawl or the vivacity is characteristic of temperament and is not a matter of geography.

Anyway, who cares for accents? The fans want good acting, good stories, good enunciation, and above all, genuineness.

—Ines de Blanc, 213 West St. Peter, New Iberia, Louisiana.

PART III. RADIO

· · · · · · · · · · · · ·

RADIO

Introduction   Timothy D. Taylor

However humble or quaint it may appear today, radio inaugurated major changes in American culture when it first came to prominence in the 1920s: the reconfiguration of public and private; the consolidation of the star system; the use of advertising to fund new communications systems; and more. The overall effect on everyday life was unprecedented. What once could be found only outside the home now entered on its own: news, music, information, advertising. The veteran entertainer George Burns wrote about radio's impact many years later.

> The only problem was that just as we were becoming stars, vaudeville was dying. No one could pin the rap on us, though. Everybody believes it was the movies that killed vaudeville. That's not true. Movies, vaudeville, burlesque, the local stock companies—all survived together.
>
> Then radio came in. For the first time people didn't have to leave their homes to be entertained. The performers came into their house. Gracie and I knew that vaudeville was finished when theaters began advertising that their shows would be halted for fifteen minutes so that the audience could listen to "Amos & Andy" [a popular radio program beginning in 1928]. And when the "Amos & Andy" program came on, the vaudeville would stop, they would bring a radio onstage, and the audience would sit there watching radio.
>
> It's impossible to explain the impact that radio had on the world to anyone who didn't live through that time. Before radio, people had to wait for the newspaper to learn what was happening in the world. Before radio, the only way to see a performer was to see a performer. And maybe most important, before radio there was no such thing as a commercial.

Radio made everybody who owned one a theater manager. They could listen to whatever they wanted to.[1]

Given how central the radio was in reshaping American life in the decades before the Second World War, it is striking how little scholarship there has been on the subject. There is still no scholarly history of broadcast advertising, for example.[2] In part, radio has been overshadowed by the dominance of television and the prestige of film after the Second World War. And with regard to music reproduction, scholars have always assumed that the phonograph (and later the cassette tape, compact disc, and mp3, among others) was more important. Recently, however, numerous publications have appeared that are helping radio scholarship catch up to that of other media.[3]

This collection, while primarily concerned with users and their perspectives, nonetheless includes material that speaks to the development of radio as a technology. It is clear from the earliest articles represented here that the distribution of sound into one's home was an idea that grew out of an existing technology, the telephone (items 74–76). Indeed, the early history of radio is closely intertwined with that of the telephone. This is mainly because the older device allowed people to conceptualize the transmission of sound and music over long distances.

Like so many technologies, radio began as a hobby for men and boys, with military applications part of the early picture: some of the first hobbyists had worked with radio during their service in the First World War.[4] For early enthusiasts, radio was about technical questions more than programming, and one of the main fascinations was for listening over long distances, trying to pull in stations from as far away as possible, which these early listeners found thrilling. Hobbyists verified and kept track of their long-distance listening triumphs by collecting QSL cards (see figure 6, and also item 87 for a description of the allure of long-distance listening). In Q code, the code of amateur radio operators, QSL means "I acknowledge receipt," and a QSL card was proof that a person had heard a station's broadcast. A listener would write a QSL postcard to a distant station in which he included technical and program details of a recent broadcast; then the listener would receive in response a QSL postcard from the other station verifying that the transmissions were heard in both directions.

People who weren't hobbyists and who wanted to hear the radio could go to a radio parlor and listen for a nickel (item 78). These "nickel-in-the-slot" radios followed earlier devices such as the nickel-in-the-slot player piano and phonograph. These machines helped introduce new technologies to a broad audience.

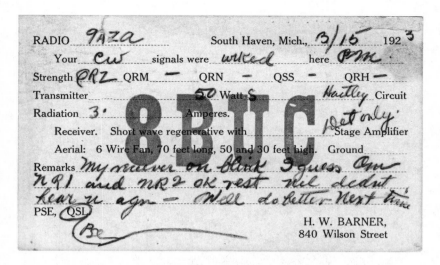

RADIO _9AZA_   South Haven, Mich., _3/15_   192_3_

   Your _Cw_ signals were _wlked_ here _Om_.

Strength _PRZ_ QRM _—_ QRN _—_ QSS _—_ QRH _—_

Transmitter _50_ Watt S _Hartley_ Circuit

Radiation _3·_ Amperes. _Det only·_

  Receiver. Short wave regenerative with _/_ Stage Amplifier

  Aerial: 6 Wire Fan, 70 feet long, 50 and 30 feet high. Ground

Remarks _My receiver on blink I guess Om nR1 and nR2 ok rest nil dedn't hear u agn — Well do better Next time_

PSE, QSL

_Be_

                                      H. W. BARNER,
                                   840 Wilson Street

Figure 6. QSL card, 1923 from H. W. Barner of station 8BUC with various data about the transmission of station 9AZA. Collection of Timothy D. Taylor.

By about 1920, interest in radio exceeded the small circle of hobbyists and tinkerers. This was evident from the broadcast covering the returns of the presidential election between James Cox and Warren G. Harding, which generated great interest.[5] In 1921 the broadcast of the prizefight between Jack Dempsey and Georges Carpentier was one of the most anticipated of the day, making clear that radio was finding users beyond hard-core hobbyists. That same year saw the creation of twenty-eight new stations; by 1922, Susan J. Douglas writes, "the floodgates were opened."[6] Frederick Lewis Allen writes that although radio broadcasting had been publicly available since 1920, it wasn't until the spring of 1922 that radio sales took off.[7] It was a veritable craze, amounting to $60 million in sales that year, climbing higher afterward. The craze registered in American culture in many ways, some silly, some creative, some serious.

The frenzy of interest in radio did not mean that people simply purchased radios and began listening. Even after the radio became popular, one still had to purchase components and assemble them into a working set. The apparatus was later housed in a wooden cabinet to appease those who found wires and batteries in public spaces of the house to be ugly (see figure 7). Even with this development, radio was still a new technology integrating itself into everyday life. The articles in this part show the many ways in which radio ceased being merely a technological novelty and became something that people used regularly for pleasure, information, and more. The owners of a radio would even hold "radio

FREED-EISEMANN

THE RADIO OF AMERICA'S FINEST HOMES

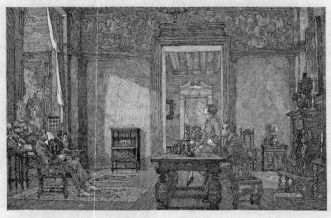

In radio, too, *Social Prestige* has been established

ONE AUTOMOBILE—*one* piano —*one* organ—stand in the public mind as the summit of excellence and *social recognition*. Now, among radios, *one* has reached the same eminence. That Radio is the FREED-EISEMANN. It was selected by the United States Navy for use on the President's yacht, the Mayflower. Today, the blue book of FREED-EISEMANN users is the "Who's Who" of each community.

The amazing advances made in the new FREED-EISEMANN sets have still further intensified FREED-EISEMANN leader-

ship. Think of it! These sets offer: Complete metal shielding from outside interference; single control; steel chassis construction for permanence; cabinets of unapproached

Model C-40* (Illustrated above) Six tube shielded single control set. Price (less loud speaker unit) $150.00. Table model of same set $85.

Model 50* (Illustrated below.) Six tube double control shielded set. Price $75.00. *Licensed under a group of Latour Patents.

craftsmanship. All sets can be run from alternating house current by the use of FREED-EISEMANN power units.

This year, the economies of vast production bring FREED-EISEMANN quality down to these surprisingly low prices:

TABLE MODELS BEGINNING AT $60

BEAUTIFUL CONSOLE SETS $95 *to* $650

Prices slightly higher in Canada and West of the Rockies. You may have a free demonstration in your own home and can arrange convenient terms if desired.

FREED-EISEMANN RADIO CORPORATION
Junius St. & Liberty Ave., Brooklyn, N.Y.

Figure 7. An advertisement for Freed-Eisemann radio consoles, 1926.
Collection of Timothy D. Taylor.

Figure 8. Radio party invitation, 1920s. Collection of Timothy D. Taylor.

parties" for friends and neighbors who didn't yet have one, the idea promoted by manufacturers who printed invitations for such an occasion (see figure 8).

Early broadcasts were a haphazard affair that frequently employed whatever happened to be available, with the results often inspiring awe, disdain, or a combination of both in listeners (items 77 and 81). Music was broadcast much of the time, since scores were already available; radio plays hardly existed yet. The easy availability of printed music did not mean that broadcasting music was simple. Performers, particularly singers—who were frequently unpaid or barely paid (see item 79)—had to learn what sounded good on the air and what did not, and, perhaps most challengingly, how to perform without a live audience (item 80). There were plenty of publications about radio singing technique, some of which are reproduced here (for example, item 115).

Radio hobbyists who became proselytizers for the medium extolled the virtues of the new technology in countless magazine articles, including articles about radios being installed in wheelchairs (item 83), hotels, baby carriages (item 84), buses (item 85), cable cars, and automobiles, and also how radios could even be used on camping trips.[8] Also in the mid-1920s, instruments were modified to enable them to broadcast directly. So there was the "pianorad," the "tromborad," a "new radio violin," with a pickup for amplification, a "giant-tone radio violin," and a pipe organ modified for broadcasting.[9] There was also a spate of weddings broadcast in the 1920s (item 89). And there were apparently

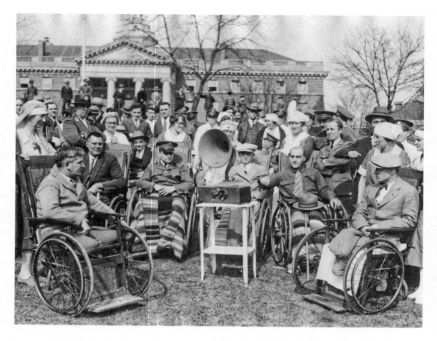

Figure 9. Convalescing soldiers listen on the radio to Roxy and His Gang on the lawn at Walter Reed Hospital, Washington, in 1927. Collection of Timothy D. Taylor. See item 82.

difficulties in the home concerning who got to listen to what and when (see item 86).

One of the most salient discourses about radio in the 1920s concerned healing; radio was said to be able to soothe and heal people (not to mention lulling cattle to sleep—item 88). Notwithstanding that it was *music* that was thought to have healing powers, this belief was buttressed by the novelty of radio, so that in many contemporary writings there was a good deal of slippage from the healing ability of music to the wonder of radio itself. For example, in 1922 a doctor in Brooklyn installed radios throughout his hospital for patients to listen to (item 91); around the same time, an ambulance in Arkansas was equipped with a radio (item 90). Even those whom radio couldn't heal could nonetheless be touched by it (see figure 9). Radio's cultural force was so potent when it was new that even the deaf reported that they could "hear" radio music (item 92).

Another major issue in the early days of radio concerned funding. Since musicians performed for little or no money, the "talent" (as it came to be called) on the air varied widely. As such, there was considerable controversy about how to

Dear Ipana Friend:

Thank you for expressing your appreciation of the Ipana Troubadours who take their name from Ipana Tooth Paste, a product that is as stimulating and delightful as the music they play for you over the Radio.

A sample tube of it is being sent you with our compliments. And if you like it, the regular large size tube can be bought in any drug store.

IPANA
TOOTH PASTE

THE IPANA TROUBADOURS

Direction: S. C. LANIN *(Center)*   *(Insert)* PHILLIPS CARLIN, WEAF *Announcer*

Figure 10. Ipana Troubadours postcard, 1920s. Collection of Timothy D. Taylor.

fund radio on a more permanent basis. An early scheme to solicit funds from listeners was unsuccessful (item 93). Commercial interests, including newly powerful advertising agencies, argued strenuously against European tax-based models; instead they favored funding through advertising. With the passage of the Communications Act of 1934, these interests won, though their victory was by no means inevitable.[10] The entry of advertising into broadcasting made the costs of "talent" and thus of putting on a program rise quickly (item 94); most programs were produced by advertising agencies for their sponsors, frequently reflected in the titles of the programs.

A problem for advertisers in this era was that unlike with print advertising, which could rely on the numbers of newspapers or magazines sold, radio advertisers had no idea who was listening. They therefore quickly devised ways of ascertaining their audience, giving away free samples or free photos of favorite radio performers, for example (see figure 10, depicting the Ipana Troubadours, the radio musicians of Ipana toothpaste).

Presenting quality musicians on the air was difficult at first, not only because of fiscal issues but also because of technical problems and because radio was not yet considered thoroughly legitimate for serious musical performances. Opera would prove to be the holy grail of radio broadcasting. When the Metropolitan Opera finally embarked on a series of regular broadcasts in 1931, it was front-page news in the *New York Times*.[11] But it had been a long time in coming. There had been resistance from Metropolitan Opera administrators and stars as well as the inevitable technical difficulties. In the meantime, the Chicago Grand Opera built a new studio that could be used for radio and began broadcasting operas in the 1921–22 season, much to the discomfiture of New Yorkers who felt that their city should be first in all things.

Since putting on a radio program was a complicated set of negotiations between sponsor, advertising agency, broadcaster, and listeners' desires (at least as perceived by advertisers and their agencies), I have included information about an early program that gives a sense of how all these different interests were served. *The Davey Tree Hour* was broadcast weekly in 1930 for twenty-six weeks. The program was produced in New York City by the J. Walter Thompson Company, the biggest advertising agency in the world at the time, and was broadcast over eighteen stations by the National Broadcasting Company, whose flagship station in New York City at the time was WEAF. The program consisted mainly of old favorite musical selections interspersed with poems and other paeans to trees. The company president, Martin L. Davey, offered short talks on the Davey approach to caring for trees. Included here are a script of the program (item 96, minus Davey's speech); excerpts of a staff meeting from the J. Walter Thompson Company discussing the program and its success (item 97; the cast of characters includes William Resor, son of Stanley Resor, the president of the company, and John U. Reber, the head of the radio department); a letter from Martin L. Davey to NBC on the benefits of radio advertising (item 98; such letters were common, used to entice future broadcast advertisers); an article by Davey about the program (item 99); and a fan letter (item 100).

Once radio began to become commonplace, early debates about music broadcasts intensified (see item 101); there were those who opposed music on the radio, fearing that it would inculcate a taste for less than optimal circumstances (item 102); others thought that music on the radio would enrich the lives of Americans (items 103 and 104). But the greater number of debates concerned what kind of music to broadcast. There were potent national discourses about uplifting the tastes of the nation (item 105); and there were therefore many debates between advertisers, sponsors, and broadcasters about what kind of music to broadcast, and endless surveys and discussions about what listeners wanted (item 106). There were strenuous debates about whether classical music — which, it was argued, would uplift national tastes — or jazz should predominate, because the two kinds of music marked important barriers in American culture: between educated and less educated, between middle and lower classes; and between whites and blacks. Many of the articles in this collection reflect these debates. That "classical" really referred in practice to light classics, and "jazz" referred in practice to highly arranged dance music without improvisation played mainly by whites, not African Americans, shows how ideological the division really was, for these two kinds of music are closer stylistically than their proponents would have admitted.

Yet it quickly became clear that what audiences wanted were programs that featured popular music of the day, usually called "jazz" in this period, which was frequently but not always dance music. Musicians who obtained regular work on such programs could become huge stars in a new medium that thrived on the presentation of stars to sell goods and bring in listeners.

Jazz, blues, or any other music by African Americans was largely absent from radio for quite some time after its advent in the 1920s. African American musical styles tended to be represented by white musicians, and it was the dance orchestra leader Paul Whiteman, not an African American musician, who was popularly known as the "King of Jazz."[12]

Early white radio musicians such as Samuel L. "Roxy" Rothafel could become big stars (item 82), and their stardom was exploited by advertising agencies to sell products, helping to establish the star system as we now know it.[13] This had a detrimental effect on the careers of many who were forced to change their stage names depending on the sponsorship of the program. Probably the most famous case is that of the singing duo of Billy Jones (1889–1940) and Ernest Hare (1883–1939), who gained fame as the Happiness Boys in the mid-1920s (on a program sponsored by the Happiness Candy Company), but who later worked as the Interwoven Pair (for Interwoven Socks; see figure 11). People changed their names as well; two singers for a Palmolive program became known as "Olive Palmer" (Virginia Rea) and "Paul Oliver" (Frank Munn; figure 12).[14]

Perhaps the biggest change wrought by radio that continues to affect listeners today concerns the transformation of intimacy, which George Burns hinted at in his memoir quoted above: people could hear live music at home without making it themselves, for early radio broadcasts were live. In part, this transformation was helped along by a new singing style ushered in by radio that came to be known as crooning, which wasn't simply a new style but served as a powerful signifier of the kind of intimate relationship that listeners could fantasize about with the singer, as Douglas writes.[15] Radio played an important role in reconfiguring the nature of the private, of intimate space—it was being integrated into individual lives, into individual private fantasies. As many authors have noted, radio was a crucial factor in blurring the distinction between public and private in America in the twentieth century.[16]

Crooning was the most salient and controversial of radio sounds that seemed

Figure 11. Billy Jones (left) and Ernest Hare, 1932. Collection of Timothy D. Taylor.

Figure 12. Olive Palmer and Paul Oliver with accompanist, 1930.
Collection of Timothy D. Taylor.

Figure 13. Vaughn De Leath. Collection of Timothy D. Taylor.

to cross the boundary between public and private (items 107–12). Crooning arose because other styles of singing—operatic, Broadway, and vaudeville—were too loud for radio equipment in the 1920s. A softer style of singing was necessary to preserve the equipment, and it was a woman, Vaughn De Leath (1894–1943), who pioneered this new style (see figure 13). But this new style was quickly picked up by male singers such as Whispering Jack Smith (1898–1950) and Gene Austin (1900–1972). Rudy Vallée (1901–1986) became the first hugely popular crooner, however, and he was also the first national mass media popular music star in America (see figure 14).[17]

Crooning didn't grow only out of a technical problem, but also out of changing conceptions of American masculinity. The older, virile notions of masculinity seemed anachronistic to some in the early twentieth century. And the explosion in the number of white-collar jobs in this era made it more difficult for men to conform to older notions of masculinity. Crooning was attacked for being effeminate and unmanly, and its fans were overwhelmingly thought to be women.

The striking feature about crooning was that even when broadcast or played back on phonograph records, it offered a greater sense of intimacy than live singing. Opera singers are specifically trained to sing loudly so that they can be

Figure 14. Rudy Vallée.
Collection of Timothy D.
Taylor.

heard, unamplified, in the back of the concert hall. Vaudeville and other popular singers cultivated singing styles that utilized a piercing, nasal singing style, or a mode of enunciating words, almost barking, that rendered them audible to people sitting in the cheap seats. Pre-radio singing styles, therefore, were manifestly "public"—meant to be heard by many listeners.

Crooning, on the other hand, had the effect of the singer singing to only one listener. Whereas the other styles mentioned above were clearly intended for listening in public spaces, with singers projecting as much as possible, crooning was just the opposite—it was as if the singer were singing only to the listener at home, through the miracle of radio. Few recordings of these early programs survive, but Vallée and other crooners in the 1920s and 1930s made commercial recordings that are still readily available. Today the style seems unremarkable given that most popular singers still use it. And yet the reason it would have seemed strange at the time is still accessible. Listening to Vallée sing songs such as "I'm Just a Vagabond Lover" from 1929, in which he doesn't simply croon but seems to be deliberately decreasing his volume, one is struck by the intimacy and directness of the style.[18]

Crooning thus introduced a paradox: while radio was proclaimed as uniting disparate Americans into a single culture, the singing style that radio ushered into existence helped to create and maintain an illusion that listeners' relationships to singers and other broadcasting individuals were unmediated and personal. Even when broadcast, crooning was a more personal mode of musical expression than what audiences could have heard live in the theater.

Crooning, combined with the intimacy that was thought to be intrinsic to radio because of its placement in the home, resulted in an unprecedented intrusion into people's domestic lives. The focal point of this intimacy, however, was not all listeners, but women. Singers such as Vallée became hugely popular with women, though he had many male fans as well. Crooning might have been the most intimate form of singing at the time, but radio itself was thought to be intimate, even though listeners well knew they were tuning in simultaneously with thousands or millions of others. The idea that the radio waves were entering almost directly into one's own head was powerful, as a poem by John Webster from 1922 suggests:

The Radioman's Love Song

I am high on the breast of the swelling sea,
And your voice comes from faraway home to me;
It comes clear and true from the weird above —
And you sing of love — you sing of love.
I start — I look! But you are not near!
I wonder — I ask: Is it you I hear?
Yes — 'tis you! — though your voice comes o'er leagues of sea —
For you sing to me — you sing to me![19]

Though, of course, the singer sings to anyone with a radio. A cartoon from early 1923 entitled "Perfectly Satisfied" depicts a young couple on a loveseat, his arm around her, each with their own headphones — separated, yet united by their connection to a radio. The dialogue reads, "Gee, Annabelle! Ain't it nice of them to broadcast 'That Ever Lovin' Pair' for our benefit. They know us, all right."[20] Sheet music covers that thematized radio also addressed this idea, such as "Broadcasting Station L-O-V-E" from 1924, the crooner's song going directly to the radio of the lonely woman at home (see figure 15).

Radio musicians' rise to stardom and wealth led many to pursue careers on the air, and how-to guides on the subject proliferated (item 113), as did queries to broadcasters from people seeking on-air employment (item 116). NBC and other broadcasters auditioned people and devised forms for applicants to fill out (item 114). Musicians counseled others on how to develop a "radio voice" to

Figure 15. "Broadcasting Station L-O-V-E," 1924. Sheet music cover.
Collection of Timothy D. Taylor.

turn an anxious listener into a performer (items 115 and 117). And people used whatever connections they had to get on the air. The NBC archives contain numerous letters from people seeking employment or attempting to pull strings, as well as internal memos about whether Mr. Important Person's niece with a nice voice should be put on the air. I have also included an account of what the production of a radio program was like (items 119 and 120), which by 1933 was a fairly well oiled machine.

The meteoric rise of the popularity of radio resulted in, among other things, a plethora of guides for listening to music. Many popular books were written to introduce the average listener to the glories of classical music; I include a short guide by a well-known music educator of the period (item 123). And I include two articles (items 121 and 122) about composing music for the radio: many composers realized that the way they had been trained to write—for the concert hall—would not always result in music appropriate for the radio.

Thus radio, which started as a gadget for hobbyists, quickly became a widespread medium. By foregrounding the historical moment after radio's invention but before its unquestioned acceptance in society, these articles and accompanying images show the myriad avenues that radio's proselytizers used to push it into people's everyday lives.

And once people found uses for radio in everyday life, from lullabies to weddings to hospitals, radio's social existence began to shape people's experiences of music and entertainment more generally. No longer did one have to leave the home to hear professional-quality live music, for the radio brought it into the home, transforming peoples' conceptions of public and private, as formerly public voices and sounds and modes of discourse were heard in private settings. With music and voices, radio connected people from distant places, even as those people maintained a notion that radio was speaking to them alone.

With all these innovations, all these alterations to social life, radio in the 1920s and 1930s came to symbolize, perhaps more than any other technology with the possible exception of the automobile, Americans' sense of themselves as modern people. And yet radio allowed Americans to maintain an older sense of unmediated relationships, as it seemed to speak to listeners directly. While radio may seem to be a humble technology today, in many real and important ways—bureaucratically, legally, and culturally—it paved the way for all communication technologies that followed.

RADIO

Readings   Compiled by Timothy D. Taylor

Radio as Dream, Radio as Technology
....

74. "Distributing Music over Telephone Lines"
Telephony, 18 December 1909, 699–701

Wilmington, Delaware, is enjoying a novel service through the telephone exchange. Phonograph music is supplied over the wires to those subscribers who
sign up for the service. Attached to the wall near the telephone is a box containing a special receiver, adapted to throw out a large volume of sound into the
room. A megaphone may be attached whenever service is to be given. The box
is attached to the line wires by a bridged tap from the line circuit. At the central
office, the lines of musical subscribers are tapped to a manual board attended
by an operator. A number of phonographs are available, and a representative
assortment of records kept on hand.

When plugged up to a phonograph the subscriber's line is automatically
made busy on the automatic switches with which the Wilmington exchange is
equipped. Several lines can be connected to the same machine at the same time,
if more than one happens to call for the same selection.

Each musical subscriber is supplied with a special directory giving names
and numbers of records, and the call number of the music department. When
it is desired to entertain a party of friends, the user calls the music department
and requests that a certain number be played. He releases and proceeds to fix
the megaphone in position. At the same time the music operator plugs up a free

phonograph to his line, slips on the record and starts the machine. At the conclusion of the piece the connection is pulled down, unless more performances have been requested.

The rate of charge for this service is very reasonable. It is three cents, for each ordinary piece, and seven cents for grand opera. The subscriber must guarantee $18 per year [about $418 today].

In most cases the actual amount of music used makes that revenue greater than the regular telephone rent.

The working of the system attracted much attention at the International convention in Chicago last week, where it was exhibited by the Tel-musici Company, which has its headquarters in the Hoen Bldg., Baltimore, Md. Mr. Geo. R. Webb is president of the company, and Mr. J. J. Comer the general manager, had a very fine working exhibit in the Auditorium Annex.

This proposition, which has taken some years of time and patient study to develop, appears to have at last been brought to the point where it can now be employed for practical purposes by telephone companies generally. The more important features of this proposition are briefly stated as follows:

At the central telephone office is kept a supply of phonographic records, embracing a complete line of all the latest productions.

By turning a switch, operators can throw any subscriber who may call for music over onto the music board which is divided in two sections—one for a general program, the other for special selections, the latter coming a little higher. A subscriber, who merely calls for "music," is thrown onto the general board, where the regular program for the week or month is furnished.

In addition to this, pay stations are installed in restaurants, cafés, hotels and other public places, where selections can be obtained by depositing a coin in the box.

At Wilmington, Del., where this proposition has been carefully developed, under the supervision of Webb and Comer, there are now 80 residence subscribers taking this musical service regularly, while something like 40 pay stations are installed. During the past year, there has been a gain in the patronage of the musical service, without the loss of a single subscriber.

The returns from residence stations run from fifteen to twenty cents per day [about $3.50-$4.50 today], while pay stations have averaged as high as $10 [about $232 today] in a week. On the whole, it has been estimated by its introducers that the service will pay local telephone companies from thirty to 35% on their investment.

In addition to the direct returns it is believed the musical feature tends strongly to popularize the service of those companies, which furnish it to their subscribers. For instance, in the various localities of the United States where there are competitive telephone companies, it is claimed that the company which provides its patrons with the Tel-musici feature will not only be the one which will have a good paying by-product, not enjoyed by the other company, but will have a very strong inducement to offer for securing new subscribers, as well as holding old ones.

It must not be imagined from the superficial description of this proposition herewith, that this service is merely a reproduction of phonographic records. The apparatus perfected by the Tel-musici Company not only greatly intensifies and enlarges the volume of sound of all phonographic records but eliminates the metallic, rasping and grating features which have heretofore constituted an objectionable feature of phonographic concerts. As a matter of fact, the music, as reproduced over telephone lines by means of the Tel-musici apparatus, possesses a sweetness and an almost-human quality not hitherto to be found in any kind of mechanical music.

Much of the success of the system is due to the unique and remarkable loud-speaking transmitter developed by Mr. Comer. Another feature of the Tel-musici service, which will be appreciated as a strong point in its favor, is the fact that the cost of the original installation is very low and that the special receiver and horn attached to it can be mounted in any room however remote from the telephone itself, thus enabling the subscriber to place it where it will be least conspicuous and in the way. It will also be appreciated that another point which appeals strongly to prospective subscribers is the fact that no initial expense is necessary on his part and that all he has to do in order to have the most entertaining of music, while at the same time without venturing out into cold or inclement weather, is to merely step to his telephone and notify the central office.

It is reported that the Tel-musici Company is preparing for a thorough campaign to introduce its system among the telephone companies of the United States and that it will very soon establish a Chicago agency to cooperate with its Eastern offices in the placing of its musical and other apparatus properly before the public.

75. "Radio Telephone Experiments"

Modern Electrics, May 1910, 63

A very interesting experiment was held on the afternoon of February 24th, by Dr. Lee de Forest in the transmission of music and operatic selections by wireless.[1] The operatic selections were sung by Mme. Mariette Mazarin, the new star of the Manhattan Opera Company, whose first American interpretation of [Richard Strauss's 1909 opera] *Elektra* occasioned much comment by the music-loving world.

This demonstration holds particular interest as it is the first successful one of its kind ever held and is one more step forward to prove that in the near future we will have "Wireless Music."

The transmitting station was located at the de Forest laboratory, near the Grand Central Station, N.Y. The operatic selections and music were clearly heard at the Metropolitan Life Building over a mile away and at the inventor's Newark, N.J. station, as well as by some hundred or more amateurs within a 20-mile range.

Among those present at the Metropolitan Life Building were the well-known inventor Prof. Hudson Maxim, John T. Murphy, the New York Tenement House Commissioner, and a number of singers of the Manhattan Opera Company.[2]

The first song Mme. Mazarin sang was the aria from [Georges Bizet's 1875 opera] *Carmen*. The listeners at the Metropolitan Life Building station, not being familiar with the notes as received from the wireless telephone, expressed great surprise at the clearness of the articulation. As is well known, an operatic selection is particularly hard to transmit by other medium than the natural sound striking distance, due to the extreme high and low notes reached by the singer's voice. This point, however, was not noticeable over the wireless telephone. Every intonation of the singer's voice was brought out clearly. The writers noticed the difference between the wire and wireless by first listening over the wire telephone and then over the wireless. Over the wire line the received notes were louder but the wireless brought out the vowel sounds with a "velvety" tone. For the benefit of those interested on the technical side it will be of interest to state that this difference is due to the distorting effect the wire line has to the telephonic voice current; the other, being the natural conducting medium, has no distorting effect on the wave, consequently we get the received tone in all its beauty.

The prima donna, when informed by the Metropolitan Station, the Newark Station, and a number of outlying ships, of the success of her first song responded with selections from *Elektra* to the great enjoyment of the distant listeners.

After the exhibition Mme. Mazarin and the audience became the guests of the Metropolitan Life Insurance Company and were shown the wonders of the building and allowed to view Manhattan from the tower, some 600 feet above Madison Square. Through the fog and distance could be seen the tower of the station from which the music was transmitted.

The new muffled spark system was explained to the audience by Mr. C. C. Heselton, the tower operator. He demonstrated the actual working utility by getting into immediate communication with Chicago, Washington, and Key West.

76. David Sarnoff, "Radio Music Box," memorandum to Edward J. Nally, vice-president and general manager, Marconi Wireless Telegraph Company of America, c. 1916–1920

In David Sarnoff, *Looking Ahead: The Papers of David Sarnoff*. New York: McGraw-Hill, 1968, 31–32[3]

I have in mind a plan of development which would make radio a "household utility" in the same sense as the piano or phonograph. The idea is to bring music into the house by wireless.

While this idea has been tried in the past by wires, it has been a failure because wires do not lend themselves to this scheme. With radio, however, it would seem to be entirely feasible. For example, a radiotelephone transmitter having a range of, say, 25 to 50 miles can be installed at a fixed point where instrumental or vocal music or both are produced. The problem of transmitting music has already been solved in principle and therefore all the receivers attuned to the transmitting wavelength should be capable of receiving such music. The receiver can be designed in the form of a simple "Radio Music Box" and arranged for several different wavelengths, which should be changeable with the throwing of a single switch or pressing of a single button.

The "Radio Music Box" can be supplied with amplifying tubes and a loudspeaking telephone, all of which can be neatly mounted in one box. The box can be placed on a table in the parlor or living room, the switch set accordingly, and the transmitted music received. There should be no difficulty in receiving music perfectly when transmitted with a radius of 25 to 50 miles. Within such a radius, there reside hundreds of thousands of families; and as all can simultaneously receive from a single transmitter, there would be no question of obtaining sufficiently loud signals to make the performance enjoyable. The power of the transmitter can be made 5 kilowatts, if necessary, to cover even a short radius of 25 to 50 miles, thereby giving extra-loud signals in the home if desired. The use of head telephones would be obviated by this method. The development of a small loop antenna to go with each "Radio Music Box" would likewise solve the antenna problem. . . .

The manufacture of the "Radio Music Box," including antenna, in large quantities would make possible their sale at a moderate figure of perhaps $75 per outfit [roughly $1,600 today]. The main revenue to be derived would be from the sale of "Radio Music Boxes," which, if manufactured in quantities of a hundred thousand or so, could yield a handsome profit when sold at the price mentioned above. Secondary sources of revenue would be from the sale of transmitters. . . .

The company would have to undertake the arrangements, I am sure, for music recitals, lectures, etc., which arrangements can be satisfactorily worked out. It is not possible to estimate the total amount of business obtainable with this plan until it has been developed and actually tried out, but there are about 15 million families in the United States alone, and if only 1 million, or 7 percent of the total families, thought well of the idea, it would at the figure mentioned, mean a gross business of about $75 million, which should yield considerable revenue [about $1.6 billion today].

Aside from the profit to be derived from this proposition, the possibilities for advertising for the company are tremendous, for its name would ultimately be brought into the household, and wireless would receive national and international attention.[4]

77. Bruce Bliven, "The Ether Will Now Oblige"
New Republic, 15 February 1922, 328–30[5]

The taxi driver at 181st Street wasn't at all sure he could find the place. It was a dark night, and the streets out that way were being fixed. We coaxed him to try, crossed the river on a high bridge, and slid up and down several dark lanes, before we reached the spot we were seeking, a long and narrow brick shed with one lighted doorway in the middle.

In at the doorway, down a long passage, up a flight of stairs into a room with that curious atmosphere of a place intended for daytime business and used instead at night. Desks and chairs; a huge phonograph horn coming out of the wall at one end at a height of six feet from the floor; and across the corner by it a large white marble switchboard standing out a little as a pier-glass [a large, high mirror] might be placed. The face of this board was cluttered with instruments—dials, handles, and, dominating the rest, several hooded electric lights in glass tubes, which reminded one visitor immediately—so much stronger is literature than life—of the ray and its vigilant slave in Mr. Kipling's [futuristic story] *With the Night Mail*.

A phonograph and some men completed the furnishings of the room. The phonograph, one of those ornate cabinet affairs, stood near the switchboard, and the men were clustered about it. They were properly dressed as businessmen, yet you saw at once, or imagined you did, that they belonged to that extraordinary group which dedicates itself to Machines and is never truly happy unless attired in overalls and a wad of cotton waste.

All ready for the demonstration? Right! One of the gentlemen steps forward and picks up a telephone which is connected with the switchboard (there are also several sets of telephone headdresses such as operators wear, lying on a neat little mahogany box with a black metal front into which their cords are plugged). A switch is pushed home on the whiteboard; remotely under our feet somewhere the sound of machinery in agitation is heard; the bright tubes of light are brighter and steadier; without so much as a "by your leave" our gentleman is speaking into his telephone. "Hellohellohellohellohello," he says in a voice just a little above an ordinary speaking tone. "This is station KLG. Stand by for a little music on the phony-graph."

He drops the telephone, and puts a record on the machine. We hear, very faintly as though it might be several doors down the street, the Sextette from [Gaetano Donizetti's 1835 opera] *Lucia*.[6]

"There are probably five or six thousand people hearing that record," says our gentleman, leaning gracefully against the instrument. "Might be twenty or twenty-five thousand; you never can tell. The amateurs all listen in about this time of evening."

It sounds incredible, yet it is undoubtedly so. In hundreds and hundreds of homes, all over New York City, New Jersey, Long Island and up through New York State, in apartments, suburban villas, farmhouses, the amateurs are sitting beside their boxes twirling the knobs on top, listening with the "headset" over their ears, while the Sextette wings its way through the ether in three hundred and sixty meter waves [frequency]. They listen, not because they love the music—which would sound much better played on the phonographs which doubtless stand silent in their own homes—but because they love the magic of the radio-telephone.

"Want to hear it?" says our own high priest of the mystery. Before we can murmur that we are already hearing it and don't much care for it, another of the group is at the mahogany chest, twisting knobs like Jimmy Valentine opening a safe.[7] From the huge phonograph horn above our heads comes a sudden shrill whistle which rises and falls, a terrific volume of noise battering at our ears, which is, no doubt, made by some far-off world as it flees shrieking in agony across the firmament.

Friend No. 2 continues his knob-twirling and in a moment this celestial caterwauling is shouldered aside, so to speak, by the Sextette, being sung in our very ears and evidently by giants a hundred feet tall and on the point of bursting all their blood vessels. It is much too loud; even the radio zealots perceive this, and they choke it down with the knobs until it sounds no noisier than Sousa's band does to Sousa.[8] Behind the music one still hears a wailing of winds lost somewhere in the universe and very unhappy about it. Still, science has conquered; the music is there, and more than recognizable. From the phonograph it has been tossed off into the limitless ether which it fills for hundreds of miles in every direction; the ethereal waves have been caught again by the antennae on our roof, brought down and hurled upon us from the horn.

Would we care to listen to the broadcasting going on from some other station? By all means; we are determined to make a night of it, even though it means hearing the Sextette eleven times. Perhaps we would like to use headpieces as most of the amateurs do, instead of the more sophisticated horn? The receivers are adjusted to our ears; the knobs are twirled again. The genius of the place explains, as a noise like the crackle of frying fat grows louder in our ears or dies away.

That noise we hear is the static electricity in the air; much worse than usual tonight. It's one of the big problems confronting radio-telephony. The other is how to prevent "owning the air." When stations are working at a wavelength (in the ether) of three hundred meters, nobody else can operate in their part of the world at a rate anywhere near that, either up or down the scale. This means that only a few stations can talk simultaneously in the same territory. Some experts think the answer will be found eventually in transmitting through water or earth, with even more powerful amplifiers than are in use today, to pick up the weak waves and translate them into such an uproar as we have already been hearing.

He is interrupted by the sound of another phonograph coming rather faintly through the telephone receivers. "That's Trenton broadcasting station," we are told. "People listening to him for three hundred miles—perhaps five hundred—in all directions." But great Heavens! It is Caruso in [Ruggiero Leoncavallo's 1892 opera] *I Pagliacci*!—Caruso dead and buried these many months, yet singing to us and perhaps twenty thousand others, down out of the ether on this cold winter's night, all by way of a phonograph and a few feet of wire in Newark, a few feet of wire and a telephone in New York.[9] Oh, Signor Cagliostro, how your jaw would drop at this!

Caruso ends, magnificently as always, and is followed in a moment by a genial gentleman who makes a few remarks in a thick baritone. "This is KGX," he observes. "Stand by, stand by! Stand by for a weather report, and then some news bulletins and then Miss Maria Altenbrite, the famous soprano, will sing for us."

There is a moment of silence. Nobody has answered him back; most of his ten or twenty thousand hearers, or whatever the number happens to be tonight, could not if they wanted to, having only listening-stations—which must be a sad plight for an argumentative man. KGX—the initials are not his own, but the arbitrary combination assigned to him and duly listed in the government's annual directory of stations—proceeds to tell as about the weather. Then he reads a few bulletins of news, which sound exactly like the things they chalk up in front of newspaper offices. Another pause, and "Stand by, stand by! KGX speaking, KGX! Miss Maria Altenbrite will now sing 'Dreaming of You.'" Which she does, in just the manner you would expect from the singer of a song with that title. The human voice is rather louder and clearer than the phonograph record, though the subdued crackle of the static in the background makes it still sound somewhat tinny.

Perhaps our faces indicate a too critical attitude; for our friend and mentor twists a knob and chokes off Miss Altenbrite in the middle of a phrase. As we jump out of her wavelength into a higher one, she ends with the squawk of a decapitated chicken. However, this is the sort of concert from which one may make his exit and not hurt the singer's feelings. If the whole audience "signed off" (disconnected the instruments) Miss Altenbrite would be none the wiser, and would send her trills just as sweetly through ninety thousand square miles of night.

Up we go through the wavelengths; and across the crackling static, we suddenly hear the hissing of a methodical dot-and-dash wireless telegraph message. "That's Norfolk, Virginia, talking to a ship at sea somewhere," we are told, and when we want to know what Norfolk has to say, "Oh, it's just, commercial stuff—a list of items in a shipment, I guess. . . . Talking about six cases of shoes from the Excelsior Manufacturing Company, of Lynn, Massachusetts, right now."

Up another thousand meters or so. A second telegraph message, a higher note, and a faster tempo. "I guess that's press stuff from Paris to London," says the man at the knobs. "We usually pick them up about this time of night." Does it not seem like high impropriety to sit in New York and eavesdrop on the transmission of news between Paris and London? Not to the experts, who are quite calm about it. "We pick up Moscow now and then," says our friend. "When they opened the new Sayville station, very high power, they think the first signal went, around the world and back into their own instrument, but it's hard to be sure. It only takes a thirtieth of a second to cross the Atlantic."

Is there no end to these marvels? We learn, in language condescendingly fitted to our ignorance, that there are at least 250,000 amateur radio operators in the United States, most of whom can listen but cannot transmit. Five thousand are added every month or so. You can get a practical outfit for $25 [about $300]; a first-rate one for $75 to $250 [about $925 to $3,100]. Amateurs are restricted to two hundred meter wavelengths or less, and are supposed to operate over short distances only. However, on the historic night of December 7, 1921, when the great transatlantic tests were made by American, English and Scotch amateurs, 26 Americans, most of them using homemade equipment, made their code signals heard in Scotland. These were in telegraphic form; voice transmission is still limited to a few hundred miles. But then, wireless telegraphy itself is only eighteen years old, telephony perhaps a third of that.

The Bureau of Markets, Department of Agriculture, is broadcasting by radio (telegraph) crop, weather and market news every day throughout the country. These messages will soon be caught in every state, and transmitted again by radio-telephone to as many fanners as want them and will spend a few dollars for equipment. This service, a year old, is already used by 25,000 listeners, including producers, shippers, dealers, brokers, commission men, warehousemen, banks and others. Several newspapers are giving nightly radio telephone programs of news, music, and lectures to listeners in their vicinity. There are nine magazines devoted to radio and any quantity of books. The United States Public Health Service is broadcasting two lectures on health every week. On Tuesdays at 4:15 p.m., Washington time, 1,100 meter wavelength, and Fridays at 9 p.m., Washington time, three hundred and fifteen meter wavelength, you may tune up to the proper pitch and hear sage remarks on the undesirability of overeating, wet feet, and gastritis. You may write questions to the U. S. P. H. S., and perhaps at the end of a Friday evening's chat you—and a few thousand others—will hear the answer. (Too personal queries might well, one would think, be avoided.) The policemen in Chicago are being equipped with pocket radio, with wires inside their coats. Headquarters will soon be able to reach every one of them with a message in a few minutes' time. . . .

But with all this talk we are missing the program. Trenton will be signing off soon; wouldn't we like some more music? The ether stands ready to oblige.

We think not, thanks; we prefer to stumble downstairs and out again into the silent lanes to meditate on the civilization of 1930, when there will be only one orchestra left on earth, giving nightly world-wide concerts; when all the universities will be combined into one super-institution conducting courses by radio for students in Zanzibar, Kamchatka and Oskaloosa; when instead of newspapers, trained orators will dictate the news of the world day and night, and the bedtime story will be told every evening from Paris to the sleepy children of a weary world; when every person will be instantly accessible day or night to all the bores he knows, and will know them all; when the last vestige of privacy, solitude and contemplation will have vanished into limbo.

78. Joseph Riley, "Five Minutes of Radio for a Nickel"
Radio News, April 1926, 1433

One of the favorite pastimes of the American people is dropping coins in a slot. There are the familiar weighing machines in every railroad station, which for the sum of one cent will indicate your correct weight. There are machines scattered all over the country that dispense chewing gum, candy and other eatables for the same amount. If your boots need shining, there is no need to wait for the shoeshine artist; go to the nearest shine machine and place your shoes in its care.

Not to be behind the trend of the times, the radio slot machine has made its appearance. If you forget to bring your pocket receiver with you, and there is a program on the air that you are particularly anxious to hear, just walk into a store that has one of these radio receiver slot machines, drop a nickel in the slot, set the two dials of the set—and your station will be heard from the loudspeaker in the top machine.

How It Operates

This slot machine made its appearance recently in Philadelphia and consists of a five-tube radio frequency receiver, having one tuned R.F. [radio frequency], one stage of fixed R.F., detector and two stages of audio frequency amplification. There is also a timing mechanism which limits the reception to five minutes. On the side of the machine next to the slot in which the nickels are deposited, is a table showing the times when stations are broadcasting and also the necessary dial settings of the receiver.

The small knob below the slot is turned after the nickel is deposited. This starts the motor for which operates the timing mechanism. After four minutes of music a red electric lamp lights in the front of the cabinet, warning the listener that if he wishes to continue the reception beyond the period of another minute another nickel must be dropped in the slot. This must be repeated every five minutes. The opening of the loudspeaker horn is behind the grillwork above the dials of the receiver, and the timing mechanism is under it.

Before long, it is possible these machines will be as common a sight as the many different types of vending machines that are familiar to everybody today and then the American boy and girl will have another slogan, "Papa, gimme a nickel, I wanta hear some radio music!"

Early Broadcasts: Performer and Listener Impressions

79. Leon Lichtenfeld, interview by Layne R. Beaty, 29 May 1988

Library of American Broadcasting, University of Maryland, Transcripts AT 1336[10]

We were the first musicians to play for WGN [Chicago]. We didn't earn a penny. There was no union scale yet when we first started with WDAP [Chicago]. We went up because WGN in 1922, we had nothing to do with stock market reports. We had something to do with stockyards, the income of cattle. . . . Now, they would go and give the reports of what came on the air. . . . The stock market would come later, but the stockyard was the most important thing. In between these reports we would play a solo. I would play a different solo, you know, melodies, popular melodies, and the pianist would play something and Mr. Bizery would play something. There was only a trio, and we were called the

Rondoliers. [It was] popular music. You know, by popular music I mean popular classical music like "The Swan" [a movement from Camille Saint-Saëns's *Carnival of the Animals*]. Light classical music we would play. . . .

In the early days of broadcasting there was no such thing called a script. I'd have to write my own announcements and everything else. . . . We were known as the Music Weavers one day, as the Tone Casters another day, as the Rondoliers another day, and the Stone Crushers on another day. We had four different names to go by every day.

Now . . . back early [quoting from a script], "The Music Weavers are heard for the next fifteen minutes in one of their special morning concerts. First they will play a French ballet," which was popular fifty years ago. It was from Galib's *Naille*, from the ballet music of *Naielle*.[11] Imagine a trio were playing. I had this all in trio. Then the next thing we would play would be a little Mozart, a little number by Mozart. Then we'd go along and we'd wait until the next announcements were made, and then we'd play a little tune called "The Ballet of the Flowers." These are the type tunes we didn't play: we didn't play anything like you know today as jazz. Nothing like that at all or what the Beatles would be doing. We were different kinds of instruments and we played a different kind of solo. And this would go on day in and day out, every day. . . .

In the beginning there was no monies paid for our time. . . . I believe our first salary was $25 apiece [about $300 today], $75—get this—for the three of us. Quinn Ryan [WGN announcer] said to me, "All right, Leon, you will be the contractor for the trio." So the check was made out to me in full for the payment for the three men . . . every week. . . . For each we would get for playing every day we were up there, and we finally go the playing. Before when we went up for nothing. We just stood around and just wanted to get on the air. It was public.

80. Leon Alfred Duthernoy, "Singing to Tens of Thousands; Impressions of an Artist during His First Radio Concert"
Radio Broadcast, November 1922, 49–51

What were my impressions when I sang, for the first time, over the Radiophone? What were they not! I ranged the gamut of human emotions, from helplessness to exultation.

Concert singers are all familiar with the complaint known to phonograph record makers as "horn fever," which means a bad case of nerves. That was it with me. It was a blue funk of the deepest indigo. If my knees had had cymbals attached to them, I should have been a whole brass band. Ask any movie actor who has faced the camera for the first time.

It has been my privilege to appear before 7,000 people at the New York Hippodrome, the Chautauqua Assembly Grounds, and the Chicago Auditorium, and I thought I was fairly intimate with mob psychology, but when I realized that there were 400,000 wireless outfits sold in this country, and that possibly 10% of them were being tuned on me, the roof of my mouth puckered up, my tongue felt paralyzed, and my lips were blanched. Caesar may have had his thousands, but I was to have my tens of thousands! The thought went to my head, my feet, and my stomach at one and the same time.

There was I, alone in the wireless studio, except for an unassuring and impersonal accompanist and the radio representative, standing over there at the side, a mode of decorum (not a bit interested in my repressed *mal de mer*), attending strictly to his knitting, said knitting being the care of some electric light bulbs. In front of me was a skinny arm, or skeletonized frame, and from that frame there hung the transmitter. It was a silly-looking little instrument about the size and shape of a ten-cent baked bean can. When I realized that that wretched little tin can was all that stood between me and the world, his wife and his family, there was an acute palpitation around the heart, and a dry blottery feeling in the mouth.

I could think of nothing but that line of [poetry by William Ernest] Henley's from "Invictus," which all baritones love to burble, "Out of the Night that Covers Me," except that I was far from being "the captain of my fate" and "the master of my soul." In my mind I visualized a life-size map of the United States, and in every town, every hamlet, every crossroads, there was *nothing but ears*. And all these countless thousands of ears were cocked and pointed in my direction. I could see ears sticking out from behind library tables, bookcases and sideboards; the handles were ears, the glass knobs were ears, *and they were waiting for me*. Then came a comforting and cheering thought; one that brought a little gulp to my throat and a foolish bit of moistness around my eyes, and it was this: if there were ears on every sideboard and library table, then by the same token there must be people in hospitals, the bedridden folk at home, tubercular patients in sanitariums, old men and women in institutions, and little children in cripples' wards. They, too, must be waiting and tuning in to catch stupid, simple me. It was with a sigh of relief that I thought of these people.

This all happened while that meticulously polite attendant fiddled around with his electric light bulbs. I tell you, it is a great mistake for a radio attendant to leave a professional singer alone to look around just before he is to sing. It is like wheeling a patient who is only half under the ether into the antechamber of an operating room, while the doctor is putting on his operating robe or thumbing the edge of his knives. One of these days the patient is going to get up and walk off, and one of these days when the radio gentleman looks up, he will find his singer has jumped out of the window. An amateur may be led to the slaughter unawares, but when you lead a professional to the dark water, you should keep an eye on your horse and bridle.

While waiting for 8:30 I looked the "studio" over. It was a room of about twenty feet square, and it was perfectly clear that no woman had had a hand in its design. It was furnished for utility, not beauty. Chairs were pushed in a row against the wall which was hung with thousands of yards of yellow burlap. All the potato sacks in the city must have been draped from that ceiling. "Our acoustical engineer designed that," said the attendant, "to deaden all sound." I would have judged it the work of the office boy. To think that all this had been "conceived and deadicated [*sic*]" by a pedigreed gentleman with four years behind him in some technical institution! Education is certainly a wonderful thing. It looked exactly like a jute factory, although the smell was lacking.

Later I was to find that the burlap did precisely what was expected of it: namely, keep out extraneous sounds.

Over in the corner was what appeared to be a telephone switchboard—minus the gum-chewing central. At the side was a handsome grand piano. The room was certainly nothing to write home to one's mother about, although undoubtedly it was practical and efficient. Quiet reigned over all.

Presently the attendant stopped leaning over his insatiable bulbs and looked up and said, "Er-r, it is 8:30. Shall we begin?" He then stepped over to the transmitter and announced in a voice so beautifully modulated that it was almost what actors call Shakespearean, that "Mr. Duthernoy will begin the evening's concert with 'Vesti la giubba' from *I Pagliacci*." He then led me to within three feet of the transmitter, told me to withdraw my head for crescendo, and to step nearer for diminuendi—and abandoned me to the beyondness of the behindness of the nothingness.

I sang the aria to the tiny tin can. When I had finished, the room seemed dead. The piano had stopped reverberating and there was not the slightest sound.

So, that was that Nothing more to it. I asked the courteous attendant if the people 'way off in Council Bluffs, Idaho [*sic*], had heard that aria. He replied that to the best of his knowledge he "fancied they had."

The attendant then went over to the transmitter and announced that I would sing two songs, [Georges] Bizet's *Agnus Dei* and [Giuseppe] Verdi's "Celeste Aida" from the opera *Aida*. This I then proceeded to do. At the end, there was the same dull, empty silence. I would have given anything for even a pathetic pattering of applause. It was my meat and drink, my board bill. But no—not a sound, not a flutter of a program. I felt like a bell tinkling in a vacuum—you know the example we used to have in high school in physics. I swore to myself that of all the stupid experiences, singing through a tin can was the most stupid. While I was catching my breath, the telephone jangled. The attendant picked up the receiver, and said, "Yes, I will try." He then came over to me with the information that "A family up in Logan's Ferry, forty miles away, had just phoned in to ask if you wouldn't please repeat that last song again. They said it was the finest thing they had ever heard." So there was my applause—my encore! Oh, garçon, that was a moment of exaltation! Would I repeat that song? No power on earth, unless the electric juice gave out, could prevent me. That telephone call was better than a salvo of applause, all the claques in the world couldn't make the noise that one phone ring did in my head. When someone takes the trouble to phone in from forty miles away, it means that you scored a hit, that you shot a bull's-eye. No dead-heads in that audience. No "paper" in that house. These people knew what they wanted. Talk about flattery, satisfaction, appealing to one's vanity—it was all rolled up in one telephone call.

I stepped over to the dinky transmitter, and this time it looked as large as the Union Station. I repeated the *Aida* song. Later on in the evening, when I sang "Deep River" and "Swing Low, Sweet Chariot," the phone rang again and asked me to repeat both of them, and then someone called up to enquire if the singer wouldn't sing "Annie Laurie." I knew that all the "press agent stuff" and the three-sheetings were as nothing.[12] These people didn't know whether I was blonde or brunette, whether I wore my hair parted in the middle, side, or in fact if I had any at all; or whether I won people through my "attractive personality" and all the other ridiculous prattle of the profession. Furthermore, they didn't give a tinker's profanation. What they liked was the singing and they wanted more of it. You may believe that they got it.

When unseen and unknown people clamor to hear you sing, it is far more to be desired than the roaring applause in the concert hall. I felt like the Boy Scout who had "done his good deed daily" and had shaken hands with the President.

I never thought much of Benjamin Franklin and his kite-and-key episode, but when I think what he did for mankind by discovering something for little boys and grown men to capture and train, even if they don't know what it is, I genuflect; and when I think of what Westinghouse and Station KDKA [Pittsburgh] have done and are doing for this country, I orientate.[13] It's your old antenna to your Uncle Dudley, that wireless is *the* invention of the age.

81. Helen Keller, letter to the Symphony Society of New York

New York Times, 10 February 1924, §1, part 2, p. 8[14]

I have the joy of being able to tell you that, though deaf and blind, I spent a glorious hour last night listening over the radio to Beethoven's "Ninth Symphony." I do not mean to say that I "heard" the music in the sense that other people heard it; and I do not know whether I can make you understand how it was possible for me to derive pleasure from the symphony. It was a great surprise to myself. I had been reading in my magazine for the blind of the happiness that the radio was bringing to the sightless everywhere. I was delighted to know that the blind had gained a new source of enjoyment; but I did not dream that I could have any part in their joy. Last night, when the family was listening to your wonderful rendering of the immortal symphony some one suggested that I put my hand on the receiver and see if I could get any of the vibrations. He unscrewed the cap, and I lightly touched the sensitive diaphragm. What was my amazement to discover that I could feel, not only the vibrations, but also the impassioned rhythm, the throb and urge of the music! The intertwined and intermingling vibrations from different instruments enchanted me. I could actually distinguish the cornets, the roll of the drums, deep-toned violas and violins singing in exquisite unison. How the lovely speech of the violins flowed and flowed over the deepest tones of the other instruments! When the human voices leaped up thrilling from the surge of harmony, I recognized them instantly as voices. I felt the chorus grow more exultant, more ecstatic, *upcurving swift* and flame-like, until my heart almost stood still. The women's voices seemed an embodiment of all the angelic voices rushing in a harmonious flood of beautiful and inspiring sound. The great chorus throbbed against my fingers with poignant pause and flow. Then all the instruments and voices together burst forth—an ocean of heavenly vibration—and died away like winds when the atom is spent, ending in a delicate shower of sweet notes.

Of course, this was not "hearing," but I do know that the tones and harmonies conveyed to me moods of great beauty and majesty. I also sensed, or thought I did, the tender sounds of nature that sing into my hand—swaying reeds and winds and murmur of streams. I have never been so enraptured before by a multitude of tone-vibrations.

As I listened, with darkness and melody, shadow and sound filling all the room, I could not help remembering that the great composer who poured forth such a flood of sweetness into the world was deaf like myself. I marveled at the power of his quenchless spirit by which out of his pain he wrought such joy for others—and there I sat, feeling with my hand the magnificent symphony which broke like the sea upon the silent shores of his soul and mine.

Let me thank you warmly for all the delight which your beautiful music has brought to my household and to me. I want also to thank Station WEAF [New York City] for the joy they are broadcasting in the world.

With kindest regards and best wishes, I am

Sincerely yours,

(Signed) Helen Keller.

82. George McClelland, head of sales, WEAF [New York City], memorandum for Mr. J. A. Holman, manager of broadcasting, March 1924

National Broadcasting Company Archives, box 5, folder 1,
Wisconsin Historical Society, Madison[15]

This memorandum is being written in order that we may have in definite form for file or other purposes experiences resultant of our trip to Providence and Pawtucket, R.I., with S. L. Rothafel and his artists.[16]

The first intimation of the widespread interest in this trip was the receipt by Mr. Rothafel of hundreds and hundreds of postal cards from an organization known as the Town Criers welcoming him to Providence, and the day before he left he received a great number of postal cards with special delivery stamps on them from what is known as "The Eleventh Hour Men," further indicating the welcome which awaited him.

Just before he left for the train he was presented with a beautiful traveling case completely filled with cigars, cigarettes and candy for the comfort of the gang on their trip.

We arrived in Providence early Sunday morning March 16th about 7:00 a.m. and went to the hotel. There, at the foot of the marble stairway, were two cutouts about four feet in height representing Town Criers across which in large letters was the greeting "Welcome to Roxy and His Gang."

In the morning a delegation of six men, including judges, business men, lawyers, etc., arrived at the Hotel from Fall River, Mass., to formally request Roxy and His Gang to visit Fall River.

At noon a luncheon was served in one of the private dining rooms and just as it got under way a Town Crier in full regalia entered the room and officially welcomed the gang and described the historical and beautiful parts of Providence which they were going to see after the luncheon in an automobile trip which they had arranged for them.

Following this trip of an hour or more the group left for the Majestic Theatre for their first performance under the auspices of the Shriners of Providence. This theater, one of the largest in Providence, has a capacity of 2,700 people and it was packed. The performance was very successful and the artists were enthusiastically received.

Following this performance Roxy and His Gang were guests at a reception given by the Shriners at which a beautiful platinum Howard watch and chain was presented to Mr. Rothafel as a token of their appreciation.

The evening performance which was given again in the Majestic Theatre to a capacity house was beyond description. As each lady soloist stepped forward to perform her number, she was presented with a beautiful bouquet of roses. In the middle of the entertainment a silver loving cup was presented to Roxy and His Gang by the radio fans of Attleboro, Mass. The performance from beginning to end was perfect. The audience during the feature numbers such as Evelyn Herbert was absolutely spellbound. The entire audience of 2,700 was silent in all that the word implies; not a movement, not a cough nor a rustle disturbed the perfect hypnotism of the audience.

Following the performance a little informal supper was given to the gang and they were free until noon the next day. At this time they were guests of honor at the Town Criers at a luncheon at the Hotel Biltmore. About 450 people were seated at the tables. At the speakers' table was the Mayor of the city, the two Mr. Samuels of the Outlet Company, Mr. Holman and Mr. McClelland. There, at each place, was a little vanity case for the ladies altogether with a bouquet of flowers and at the place of the men a silver match case. The guests were entertained by a takeoff of Roxy giving a radio concert with a burlesque of every artist present including Roxy which was very cleverly and successfully carried out. Here again the gang and each individual of the gang was received with tremendous enthusiasm.

Following the luncheon accompanied by a police escort the group left for a public reception at the Outlet Company Store. At one end of the building a large platform was erected on which were placed floor lamps, a piano, living room furniture etc. In front of this was a large railed off space to permit the crowd to file past and greet them. Seventeen police held the crowed estimated at 50,000 in check. For over an hour and a half this mob stood in the crush and pushed and shoved and literally fought for the opportunity of seeing them. No performance was given, no speeches made; it was simply to see Roxy and His Gang. Perspiring women carrying babies, men, the young and the age, crowded their way before the artists. Woman after woman came to Mr. Rothafel and said that he could not appreciate what they had gone through for the privilege of seeing him, but you had only to look at them to gain an idea of what they had gone through.

Finally at 4:00 o'clock when there was no sign of any diminution of the crowd the police simply shut off the crowd and through a jammed lane, broken open by the police, they fought their way back to the cars and back to the hotel. This demonstration was thrilling to a point beyond description.

Following this reception a dinner was served at one of the private dining rooms of the hotel and just as it got under way it was interrupted (interruptions were the general rule) and the La Tausca Pearl Company presented each artist with a string of pearls in a beautiful jewel case. The whole spirit of the town was that of giving; one trying to outdo the other in showering effects upon them.

Leaving the Hotel the cars went to Rhodes, a small edition of our Madison Square Garden where a large Shrine fair was to be opened. It was announced that Roxy and His Gang would appear at 7:00 o'clock, and at 7:00 o'clock, an unusually early hour, the place was packed. It was impossible to estimate the number of people but very conservatively it was several thousand. Here again his appearance was the signal for another ovation. No performance was given here but each of the gang was introduced to the crowed and received enthusiastic applause.

Thence by automobile they went to Pawtucket to the Strand Theatre, seating about 2,200 people, where the success of the former two appearances was repeated. On this occasion the first thirteen rows of the orchestra were sold at $5.00 a ticket [about $60 today]. Once again the house was jammed, every seat and every inch of standing room allowed by the Fire Department was occupied. Here a large bouquet of roses, fully 2½ feet tall was presented to Roxy and His Gang and following the concert a buffet supper was served.

Following this they left for their train to Washington. It must be borne in mind that all of this attention was showered on them despite the fact that in

Providence they were paid $2,500.00 for their appearance [about $30,400 today] and in Pawtucket $1,500.00 [about $18,240 today] and yet from their attitude it was easily seen that he was conferring a favor upon them by coming to them.

The artists' exemplary deportment made them even more loved and popular if that were possible. In this short digest it is impossible to convey the big feature of this whole trip and that was the hugeness and spontaneity of favorable reaction which surrounded them wherever they went. Evidences of their popularity and the love with which they were held by the radio fans were shown at every turn. It was a trip on which thrill after thrill was the order of the day.

[Signed]

G. McClelland

Radio in Everyday Life

83. "Wireless Music and News for the Roller Chair Passenger"
Scientific American, 7 August 1920, 131

Asbury Park, N.J., has the unique distinction of being the first city in which boardwalk roller chairs have been equipped with wireless telephone and telegraph receiving apparatus so that the passengers are enabled to hear talking and musical concerts from distant stations while the chair rolls merrily along.

W. Harold Warren, who some time ago demonstrated that it is possible to receive wireless telephone and telegraph signals within a steel and concrete bank vault with both inner and outer doors closed and with no external connections to the instruments, is responsible for this new innovation that has already proven so popular at this charming seaside resort.

A small flat "loop" replaces the ordinary aerial and ground connections, and the whole apparatus is so compact that three persons can sit with it comfortably in the chair. The most interesting part of the installation is the fact that the vibrations of the roller chair in motion have no effect whatever on the reception of the signals.

The directional effect of the "loop" is most pronounced, the strongest signals being received when the vertical plane of the "loop" is in the direction of the transmitting station. Signals from stations over 200 miles distant are received with the apparatus.

84. "Very Latest in Wireless; Union College Students Find a 'Universal Lullaby' for Babies"

New York Times, 11 May 1921, 12

SCHENECTADY, N.Y., May 10.—Student members of the Union College Radio Club here think they have found a way to provide what might be called a universal lullaby for American babies.

With a couple of light poles and a few wires the students recently rigged up a wireless receiving station on an ordinary baby carriage, with a small megaphone attached to throw sounds under the carriage hood. With a baby loaded for the occasion by a sympathetic mother, a student trundled the carriage through the old "Blue Gate," down Union Street and into the business section of the city.

As the carriage started a young woman at the Radio Club's sending station in the college grounds began singing a lullaby. Her song was caught and distinctly reproduced by the receiver on the baby carriage all through the business district, more than a mile distant, and the reports of the experiment say that the baby was "as good as could be," soothed by the lullaby from start to finish of the novel wireless experiment.

85. "Radio Now Heard on Buses in New York City"

Radio World, 27 May 1922, 29

The Fifth Avenue Coach Company has broadcasted this interesting information:

Music was received on one of its buses while the vehicle was traveling at its top speed. There was no antenna reaching upward or a ground wire trailing behind to trip up pedestrians. The aerial was the metal rail of the bus and by attaching the ground wire of the radio set to the rail of the bus stairway, a counterpoise grounding was accomplished.

The bus used for the test is a new one known as "Peter's Paradise," because it is a double-decker with a roof over the upper deck. Joseph Conniff, mechanical foreman of the company's garage, No. 4, and William Zimmerman were the men who conducted the experiment. They used a Westinghouse senior set, audion detector-bulb, and headpieces.

Zimmerman held the set in his lap and enjoyed the noon broadcasting from WJZ [Newark]. Conniff tooled the bus along Riverside Drive at a speed that, at times, exceeded twenty miles an hour. There was no interference either from the trees that border the drive or the factory noises that waft across the Hudson

River from the Jersey side. Even the occasional bumping of the bus whenever it hit the customary "Thank-ye-ma'am" brought no interruption.[17] The company intends to make further experiments in the hope of eventually making radio reception a regular feature of a bus ride.

86. "Advance Seat Sale for Radio Concerts"
Popular Radio, October 1923, 528

In a family that owns only one receiving set, it has been necessary to reduce the receiving schedule to a system of advance reservations. A schedule sheet is kept for each evening hour for a week or two ahead. When Mother reads in the paper that a song she especially wants to hear is to be sent out by a certain station at nine o'clock Tuesday evening she reserves that hour on the sheet. That holds the hour for that station and for her against claims of other members of the family. Sister may reserve Thursday evening for jazz from her favorite band and invite in her friends, secure in the knowledge that no one else will have pre-empted the set that evening for a missionary lecture or the report of a prizefight.

87. Bess B. Harris, letter to the editor
Radio Broadcast, April 1924, 528, 530

> *Editor*, Radio Broadcast
> Doubleday, Page & Co.,
> Garden City, L.I. [Long Island, New York]
> Dear Sir:

No one denies the benefits of "radio culture." And since the craze for wireless has spread with even greater speed than an epidemic, and unlike an epidemic, been welcomed with joyful acclamation; high and low, rich and poor have hastened to the nearest carpenter, plumber, and electrician for the makin's.

The mysterious nomenclature of the science has invaded our speech so that we "stand-by," "sign off," "tune-in" or "fade out" without a qualm of a conscience hitherto devoted to pure English.

The most maddening, the most humiliating of all the jargon connected with the use of an active radio set is the warning "sh-ssh" of the interested operator. And so I rise to remark that we are slowly but surely becoming a nation of the speakers and the speechless. The art of conversation is doomed to desuetude, and our eager college boys will flock to courses in after dinner speaking and announcing, while their sisters assiduously devote themselves to bed-time stories in the hope of sometime broadcasting their melodious tones and attractive personality to the wide world.

There is not an hour in the 24 when the average receiving set can not reach out its electrical fingers and clutch a jazz orchestra, a pipe organ, grand opera, a talk on How to Cook Fish, or a bed-time story, out of the ether; to say nothing of the tremolo sopranos, soulful contraltos, and jovial basso profundos, wrestling with the "Rosary," "The Road to Mandalay," or "Pale Hands."

Now all of this outside entertainment insinuating its charms into the average family life around the evening lamp has a strong tendency to discourage family discussion, helping Betty with her homework, checking up the grocery account—all of which are necessary to maintain peace and balance in the family life and exchequer.

But when the head of the family is tuning in and whistles are flying thick and fast, each signaling a station clamoring to be heard, a deathlike silence must prevail in the family circle. To break in on an announcement is a positive crime! And so the prattle of the children is hushed, necessary questions are answered in stealthy whispers, for if we all become too boisterous, father, with a muttered blessing, grabs the headphones, shuts off the loudspeaker and retires into his shell literally speaking. Then mother and the children, properly subdued and shown their place in the scheme of things, wait humbly until the station is successfully captured, when they are allowed to hear the results.

So, instead of discussing the League of Nations, Jim's need for a pair of shoes or a spanking, we all sit speechless while a symphony concert gives place to a market report, and that in turn, to an after-dinner speech from the annual banquet of the Laundrymen's Association—then, a jazz band, with its reiterated tom-tom—one scene from a play now running at the Regent, but not now appearing to arrive anywhere—truly a hodge-podge of information, amusement, and moral suasion. And all punctuated with whistles, groans, static, and fading.

One of the most important of radio developments is the radio widow. When the children are in bed, the local station finished with its program, father goes fishing for those elusive long distance stations, which ought to be heard, but somehow, never are. Wife sits mum, consoling herself with a book, or solitaire, having at least the chill comfort of his physical presence, though his soul goes marching on.

Bess B. Harris
Belle Vernon, Pena

88. "'Sing Down the Cattle' by Radio"

Popular Radio, October 1926, 615

Another one of the traditional customs of the old West seems headed toward extinction—the cowboy habit of "singing the cattle down," as the night herder's crooning melody to quiet the herd is described. The most picturesque fan letter received by Station WGES [Chicago] was from Tom Blevins, a Utah cowman, who wrote that he had set up a portable radio out on the range and treated the cows to metropolitan dance music.

"It sure is a big saving on the voice," Blevins wrote. "The herd don't seem to tell the difference. Don't put on any speeches, though. That'll stampede 'em sure as shootin'."

89. "Wedding Has Radio Music; Orchestra at WAAM Fills Gap Left by Missing Players"

New York Times, 1 January 1927, 7

BELLEVILLE, N.J., Dec. 31.—A wedding march by radio marked the wedding here last night of Miss Jean Muriel Anderson, daughter of Mr. and Mrs. Alexander Anderson of 68 Rutgers Street, to Frederick Jackson of Newark.

The Minister, the Rev. J. Garland Hammer Jr., pastor of the Reformed Church of West Caldwell, was waiting at the home of the bride's parents to perform the ceremony. But the orchestra hired for the occasion had not appeared.

The bridesmaid, Miss Alice Jackson, a sister of the bridegroom, telephoned to Station WAAM of Newark and requested the orchestra there to play a wedding march. As soon as Mr. Anderson tuned in the wedding ceremony proceeded. After a wedding supper the couple left for a honeymoon in the South.

Healing

90. "Maimed and Sick Forget Pain in Model Radio-Equipped Ambulance"

Radio Digest, 3 June 1922, 2

FORT SMITH, ARK.—Now it's the Radio-equipped ambulance! On a test recently made here with a Radio-equipped ambulance, strains of soothing music were administered to a patient being rushed from a train to the hospital. The music was broadcast from Station WCAC [Fort Smith, Ark.], owned and operated by the John Fink Jewelry Company of this city.

The ambulance, which is the first to be so equipped, was fitted with a standard two-stage amplifier receiver with loudspeaker, and had an antenna mounted on its top, while the frame of the car was used as a ground. The antenna consisted of one hundred feet of stranded copper wire. On account of the success of the test, the ambulance, owned by the Putman Undertaking Company, is being permanently equipped.

The photograph [not reproduced] shows the ambulance with the patient, a lady who was taken from an incoming train. The ambulance is shown at the hospital after the trip had been made. In the picture the patient has not yet been removed from the ambulance. Music was furnished all the way from the train to the hospital.

91. Ward Seeley, "Radio Relief for the Ailing"

Wireless Age, August 1922, 35

Have you ever been ill in a hospital?

Not ill enough to be oblivious of your surroundings, as no one ever is for more than a comparatively few hours at a time, but just ill enough to be kept in your bed.

Do you remember how bored and disgruntled you were, how slowly the hours passed, how you slept as much as you could, just to pass the time away, how you wished you could do nothing but sleep and forget your troubles until it was time to get up and go home?

Perhaps you have been ill at home and had the same experience there.

It was a red-letter day when you were declared well enough to get up walk about a bit, and see something of the world outside of the four walls that had hemmed you in, imprisoned you in body and mind.

If you have gone through a long siege of sickness, as nearly everyone has, you will understand what the radio telephone now means to those who are confined to their beds day after day. It brings the news and music of the world to them. It gives entertainment, diversion, occupation. It actually hastens recovery.

Doctors for years have known that music is beneficial in many maladies. The mind has a powerful influence on the body, and often the patient's own mental condition is the chief obstacle to an early recovery. The body is willing, but the mind, from too long dwelling on misery, is unable to comprehend the fact that health is at hand. The mind after thinking of disease for weeks does not turn of its own accord to thoughts of health.

Radio changes all this. It gives patients from outside, bringing the happy cheerful busy world to the ears of the sick, giving them other things to think about than their own condition. In many homes today the radio telephone is a great aid to sufferers, shortening their hours of tedium, lessening the period of their convalescence.

Hence it is that progressive doctors in all parts of the country, and particularly those in charge of hospitals, are eagerly taking advantage of radio.

Dr. W. F. Jacobs, Medical Superintendent of the Cumberland Hospital, Brooklyn, N.Y., said to the writer: "Radio deserves to be ranked with the best mental therapeutic agencies. In fact, for hundreds of cases the radio telephone can be prescribed as the one best treatment."

The Cumberland Hospital is a city institution, most of its patients being charity cases. Since last September Dr. Jacobs has been experimenting with radio for them, having installed several sets at his own expense in the original old hospital, now being evacuated as the new structure nearby is completed. The new building is being completely equipped with loudspeakers and connections for headsets in all its wards. "Think what it will mean," continued Dr. Jacobs, "for some poor devil, friendless, homeless, laid up with a broken back, never receiving any visitors, with nothing to do from one day to another but look at the wall and think. I have put headsets over the ears of many such men, and have seen them transformed in a few minutes from creatures that were just dully existing to the intelligent, interested men they once were and now soon will be again, permanently, and much quicker because of the interest, the life, the health that radiates from radio."

Dr. Jacobs has been a radio fan for about a year, and has gone through all the stages from a crystal set to his present one with radio and audio frequency amplification. He had an interesting experience last winter, in the days when good headsets were hard to secure. He scoured the city for a headset of a particular make, and finally located one in a large department store. The clerk refused to sell it, saying that it was the only one in the store, was "stock" and was not for sale.

"But I've just got to have that headset," said the Doctor. "Who is head of the department?"

The clerk reluctantly named the manager of the radio department, and added the information that he was "hard boiled."

Undaunted, and full of the enthusiasm and determination that are characteristic of him, Dr. Jacobs bearded the lion in his den.

"You have a headset," he declared, "that means life and death to some of my patients. I don't ask you to give it to me, though it is a matter of big-hearted charity, to relieve the suffering of some poor mortals who think that the world has forsaken them. I can prove to them that it hasn't—with that headset. I can show them that it is worthwhile to get well—with that headset. Whether or not they recover is up to them now, for medicine has done all it can. They will have to do the rest. Radio coming through that headset will induce them to think of the joy of living instead of the pains of sickness; of life instead of death; it will banish their despair and bring them hope, faith and the determination to get well. Radio has done all that for many of my patients, and I want to give it to all who need it. And I have many who need it badly. Will you sell me that headset?"

The manager looked at the doctor.

"The headset is yours," he said.

Doctors in charge of other hospitals also realize the great benefits of radio, and, further, its peculiar selective quality, in that by the use of headphones it can be made available only to those who are able. This makes it highly suitable for use in wards, so that patients who can benefit from the daily concerts can listen to them without disturbing others who may be so ill that the music would be of no value.

Easily Adaptable

This feature is to be used in the new Cumberland Hospital, where a loudspeaker is to be put in every ward, and beside it a control switch and a jack. In wards where every case can benefit, the loudspeaker will be used, while in others in which there are cases of various degrees of seriousness, the earphones will be used. This system has been in use in the old building for several months, with sometimes startlingly beneficial results. At the time Dr. Jacobs was interviewed, the radio apparatus was dismantled for moving into the new building, where a large room has been provided as a control station for the entire radio receiving equipment.

Funds for this installation are being collected privately by Dr. Jacobs, as New York City as yet has not appropriated money for the purpose. The Department of Public Welfare, is enthusiastic, from Commissioner Bird Coler down to the newest intern, and it is probable that in time city funds will be provided, but not after a delay of possibly several years. In the meantime, patients in the city hospitals and in fact in most of the others as well, must rely upon private charity for the radio equipment they need so much.

Work of Charity

Several of the hospitals in New York City already have interested philanthropists in radio, and are installing instruments. The Bronx Hospital is one of them. Maurice Dubin, superintendent, said: "The hospital is negotiating for the installation of a radiophone on the Roof Garden, for concerts to be given to the convalescent patients. We are also planning to have a receiving station in the wards for those who are bedridden. In connection with this work we intend to utilize the telephone receivers in order not to disturb patients who may desire to rest.

"I personally feel that radio can be of great service in hastening convalescence."

The Manhattan Eye, Ear and Throat Hospital probably is the best situated of all the New York hospitals, in its radio possibilities, as it already has an annunciator system with loudspeakers in all wards and corridors, for calling the doctors. Reuben O'Brien, superintendent, now has a regenerative set with two stages of audio frequency amplification, and the sum of $100 [about $1,240 today] has been provided for the purchase of a loudspeaker. This is to be placed in front of the main transmitter of the annunciator system, which thus will spread radio concerts, news and sermons throughout the building. Inasmuch as the patients are well classified in the wards according to the seriousness of their cases, it is entirely possible to provide radio entertainment only to those whom it will benefit. Comparatively little interruption is expected due to the necessity of using the annunciators for calling purposes.

A Complete Installation

Another hospital that will use radio to the full is the Beth Israel, in the center of the crowded East Side. This is being provided with a new building that will have 500 beds, and the plans call for the installation of a radio receiving set with loudspeakers in the auditorium, solarium, children's wards and in the open wards. Each private room is to be provided with a headset.

This radio service will be part of the hospital treatment, and will be given without extra charge.

L. J. Frank, superintendent, states: "The effect on the patient is bound to be good, and will in my opinion facilitate his recovery. It will be of special value to those patients who will be in separate rooms, as it will obviate lonesomeness when there are no visitors. It will also be of help to cases of chronicity, where the patients are required to remain in the hospital for a long time.

The New York Post-Graduate Medical School and Hospital likewise intends to utilize radio. S. H. Wadhams, executive office told me: "Steps have been taken to install a radio service for the use of the patients in our wards. How extensive this installation will be will depend on the generosity of the benefactor who has volunteered to pay for the installation. You may depend upon the Hospital's interest in the possibilities of the radiophone as an assistance in solving a feature of the nursing problem that confronts it."

Dr. A. J. Barker Savage, superintendent of the Broad Street Hospital, told me that a complete radio installation is to be made in the new building for which the hospital recently secured funds. "We want to do anything that will add to the patients' happiness," said Dr. Savage, "and radio will do it as nothing else can. I am very much in favor of it." The hospital is located in the financial center of New York City, and its list of directors is an imposing one, including some internationally known names of prominent financiers. The expense of the radio equipment for the new hospital will be borne by three directors, who pledged their support after listening to a vigorous plea by Dr. Savage at a recent meeting of the board.

Many of the government hospitals in which are wounded and disabled veterans consider radio to be vital in improving the mental condition of their patients. The Fox Hills Hospital was one of the first to utilize radio, securing a Signal Corps set, and other hospitals in all parts of the country followed suit. The local posts of the American Legion in many cases raised the funds for the radio equipment. In El Paso, Tex., the Veterans of Foreign Wars only recently provided the William Beaumont Hospital there with receiving equipment.

Probably there is but one handicap to radio from the doctor's point of view. That is the fact that the best and most interesting concerts are broadcast after eight o'clock at night. Several doctors told me that this was just the hour when they expected their patients to be settling for a long sleep. "Give us more concerts in the afternoon," they pleaded, in substance. "The phonograph records are fine, and they come over well, but the major interest is in the personal performances that take place in the evening. In many cases the effect on the patient is well worth an extra hour or so of sleep, but if that effect could be had in the afternoon instead of the evening it would be even greater."

Which is respectfully submitted here to the broadcasting stations, with the hope that they may increase their already great humanitarian work for those who are ill.

92. "Jazzing the Deaf by Radio"

Popular Radio, March 1926, 296

Bitter opponents of jazz are faced with a counter-claim now that the pronounced rhythm of this class of music emphasized by beating of the drums and piercing notes of the "hot" cornet playing have humanitarian value—that through certain strains vibrations are set up which enable the deaf to hear. This information has been conveyed to Paul Ash, orchestra leader and radio star of KYW [Chicago] in letters from several women who explain that these are the only sounds they have been able to hear and that they enjoy the jazz music although otherwise deaf. A famous ear specialist of Chicago has become interested in the subject, it is reported, and is conducting a series of tests to determine the possibilities of utilizing this means of "bone conduction" of sound so that those who have lost normal hearing may through radio have the pleasures of music. When the unique investigation has been completed the renowned specialist promises the issuance of a report and a test program over the air is to be given with deaf persons asked to "listen in" and to report what they "hear."

Economics of Radio Broadcasting

93. Laurence Blackhurst, "Radio Music Fund Committee Appeals to Listeners-In for Contributions"

Radio World, 1 March 1924, 12

The first serious attempt to have listeners-in pay for broadcast programs was inaugurated last week when an appeal was made through the daily newspapers in New York by the Radio Music Fund Committee. This committee, according to a statement supplied to the press, consists of Clarence H. Mackay, Felix M. Warburg, Frederic A. Juilliard, and A. D. Wilt, Jr. all well known for their support of musical activities.

They have selected Station WEAF [New York City] to broadcast the proposed concerts by grand opera and other musical stars. The actual expense of broadcasting will be borne by the American Telephone & Telegraph Company, owners of WEAF. The committee invites from the radio public contributions to the Radio Music Fund of one dollar upwards to be sent to the Central Union Trust Company of New York, subject to the order of the committee. If the contributions received are not sufficient, in the opinion of the committee, to warrant going ahead with the plan, all contributions will be returned by the trust company. If, after starting the broadcasting program, the committee deems it advisable to discontinue the concerts, whatever balance remains of the fund may be returned to the contributors "or disposed of for musical or educational purposes as may be determined by the committee." The members of the committee, as now or hereafter constituted, do not assume personal responsibility nor guarantee personally any radio music concerts under their present plans or as they may be later modified.

The statement concludes: "The success of the plan depends entirely upon the cooperation of the radio audience in making possible to themselves the best radio programs obtainable. Although any radio listener may avail himself of these programs, unless the response is instantaneous and widespread, it will be impossible to present the great artists now contemplated. The public benefits; it should respond promptly."

Officials of Station WEAF were quoted in the daily press as saying that from $100,000 to $200,000 [about $1.22–$2.44 million today] would be required to insure twice-a-week concerts for a season of grand opera stars. They expect listeners-in to contribute enough to pay for a few fine programs and then decide whether to give enough more to provide a program for next season. There is no intention of broadcasting grand opera, only concert programs by grand opera stars and well-known concert singers.

A writer in *The New York Times* expresses these views:

"It is not easy to see how collections are to be made from the listeners or fees exacted. They go to no ticket office, pass through no turnstile, and disclose the possession of a receiving set to no authority. That they should pay something for what they want and get seems only right; but unless all pay, any payment is unfair or at best a sort of charity, and the number who will pay for what they can so easily get for nothing, once it is put 'on the air,' cannot, without exaggeration, be called great."

An editorial in *The Sun and The Globe* offers this opinion:

"Radio is too strong to be incapable of a demonstration such as the committee call for. Yet it is quite plain that the voluntary basis of support cannot be a permanent basis. There must be some method of making delivery contingent upon payment. At present this is physically impossible—the noises of the air are to be had for the gathering. Yet with the problem of making them exclusive and vendable clearly needing solution, the scientists and inventors will probably find a way to make a song flung upon the air as safe from the unpaying listener as an aria at the Metropolitan is from the passer-by outside on Broadway."

94. "How Much Should Good Radio Program Cost? Most Frequently Asked Question Is Hardest to Answer"
Broadcast Advertising, January 1930, 6–7

How much will it cost?

That is one of the first, if not the first, questions asked by the potential sponsor of a commercial broadcast—and one of the most difficult to answer.

The cost of the facilities, i.e., for the time on the station or network of stations chosen, is a simple matter to estimate, for the rates are fixed, but the problem of talent is another thing. The cost depends upon the type and class of program that the firm wishes to sponsor and how much it wishes to put into it. For the success of radio advertising, like almost anything else, largely depends upon the amount of effort put into it. As was pointed out in this magazine in December, there is a lot of difference between just another radio program and a radio program with personality and individuality, and the percentage of return depends to a great extent upon the type of appeal made to the radio audience.

Can Pay $100 or $100,000

If the commercial sponsor is looking for a couple of radio salesmen such as Amos 'n' Andy, he can well expect to pay in excess of $100,000 [about $1,245,000 today] a year for his talent. On the other hand, if he merely wants a small orchestra, he can probably buy them for as little as $100 [about $1,245 today] a show, depending again on the size and quality of the group.

It throws some light on the matter to know that the average cost of talent on programs heard through the National Broadcasting Company is in excess of $1,000.00 [about $12,450] a show. Such well-known successes as Seiberling Singers, Firestone, Westinghouse Salute, and programs of that caliber cost more than $2,000.00 [about $24,900 today] per show for talent.

Reputations Mean More Money

Dance bands of moderate size with established reputations can be bought from $500.00 to more than $1,500.00 [about $6,225 to $18,700 today], depending again upon the reputation and size of the band and upon the amount of work involved in the broadcasts. Such programs as Clicquot Club Eskimos, Ipana Troubadours, and Rudy Vallée may vary from somewhat under $1,000.00 a broadcast to slightly more. Of course, there is the union scale to be paid for musicians in every case, and in the case of bands with a notable reputation this amount is somewhat increased. The leader, whose reputation established that of the band, naturally, gets the larger amount.

Dramatic shows, such as Real Folks, the Keystone Chronicle, Conoco Adventurers (a new feature) and others of like scope depend largely upon the size of the cast, reputation of the actors, the fee of the dramatist and incidental music it used. For example, a show such as Real Folks would involve a cost of about $2,000.00 a broadcast because of the talent used and the reputation of the author, while a less pretentious script show could be produced effectively for as little as $500.00 a broadcast for the talent and script.

Chicago Symphony Worth $3,000

Symphony and concert orchestras also vary in price according to their size, reputation, length of program and length of contract. Such a well-known organization as the Chicago Symphony Orchestra can demand, and get, as much as $3,000.00 [about $37,360 today] a program, while a symphony of like size but of less reputation could probably be built for half that amount.

The estimator of program costs must also take into consideration the cost of special musical arrangements, cost of continuities and special production costs.

But the cost of a program, after all, depends upon what the sponsor wishes to spend.

Advertising

95. "Radio Broadcast Advertisements;
Airphone Advertising Will Kill Fan Interest"
Radio Digest, 24 June 1922, 10

You will remember the days when you paid your money to see a motion picture show and between "acts" you were compelled to read over, or sit with your eyes closed to prevent reading over, a whole lot of local still picture advertisements. Then along came the "bright idea" fellow and put across a movie film with the same sort of "kill time on your money" advertisements. Do you recall how bitterly you were opposed to such a thing? It really hurt a number of movie theaters, and the owners wondered what was the trouble.

The same propaganda now confronts the Radiophone broadcasts. Do you wish to tune up your receiving set and sit back to take in a good concert or listen to something interesting and instructive and get for your trouble, "You can save dollars if you trade at Wanacoopers."

Suppose a delightful soprano voice has just sung your favorite song—"Kiss Me Again," "Little Gray Home in the West," or whatever it may be—and you are just drawing a deep breath, sorry it's over, and you are saying to yourself, "Gosh that was a dandy! Made me think of someone I used to know who sang that song." And then, all of a sudden, a voice says, "Good morning! Have you used Hare's Soap? Be sure to buy Goodberry's Facial Cream. Save the surface and you will keep that schoolgirl complexion!"

Do you like the idea? Something must be done about it—government regulation perhaps. Maybe you have found an answer to the question of who will eventually pay for broadcasting when the saturation point in sales of instruments is reached and if advertising is prohibited. The right place to stop anything dangerous is just before it starts. The broadcasting of advertising matter comes in the "dangerous" class and it must be nipped in the bud.

96. *Davey Tree Hour* [script from 5 January 1930]
J. Walter Thompson Company Archives, Hartman Center: Rare Book, Manuscript, and Special Collections Library, Duke University, Durham, North Carolina[18]

(NOTE TO ANNOUNCER: Make local announcements every 15 minutes except on dramatic programs which depend on a succession of thought)

WEAF   TIME:

DAVEY TREE HOUR
5:00–6:00 p.m.   JANUARY 5, 1930   SUNDAY

      1. (JUST A SONG AT TWILIGHT — THEME — CHANDLER
      GOLDTHWAITE — ORGAN)

BACH: I think that I shall never see
      A poem as lovely as a tree

A tree whose hungry mouth is pressed
Against the earth's sweet flowing breast
A tree that looks to God all day
And lifts her leafy arms to pray
A tree that may in summer wear
A nest of robins in her hair
Upon whose bosom snow has lain
Who intimately lives with rain
Poems are made by fools like me
But only God can make a tree.

(MUSICAL INTERLUDE)

BACH: Think of your own beautiful, priceless trees! Living, breathing—yet,
like all living things, sometimes in danger of starvation, of sickness
or death!

Half a century ago a man who loved trees as <u>you</u> love them developed a new science . . . tree surgery. "If a fine old tree dies," he
said, "We have lost a friend—beautiful trees are priceless." And so
he found a way to save trees.

Today, the methods he developed are yearly saving thousands of
trees from the dangers that threaten them.

The man was John Davey, the father of Tree Surgery. It is fitting,
that this, our first program, is given on the first Sunday in 1930, the
fiftieth anniversary of his founding of Tree Surgery. To his science,
his philosophy, his ideal, this weekly program . . . the Davey Tree
Surgery Golden Anniversary Hour—is dedicated.

(MUSIC SWELLS AND CONCLUDES, BUT BEGINS AGAIN VERY
SOFTLY UNDER ANNOUNCER'S VOICE)

BACH: The Davey Ensemble presents the familiar Sextette from Lucia!

2. (SEXTETTE FROM LUCIA—CHANDLER GOLDTHWAITE—
VIOLIN—CELLO—DAVEY SEXTETTE)

BACH: An old melody of the sunny South! One of Stephen Foster's best-
loved songs is presented by the Davey Organist, Chandler Goldthwaite!

3. (SWANEE RIVER—CHANDLER GOLDTHWAITE)

BACH: Songs of long ago! It is the hope of the Davey organization that this program of old songs will bring happy memories. The quartet sings next. Perhaps they will remind you of the days when you were . . . "Seeing Nellie Home."

4. (SEEING NELLIE HOME—DAVEY QUARTET)

BACH: A thousand years ago, the story goes, an acorn fell in the soil where the town of Hartford was to be. And as the oak grew, the Indian signal-fires upon the hills were seen less often, for the white man had come to found the colony that was called Connecticut. And now a thriving colony has sprung up. There is a bustling town. There are broad meadows where the cattle graze, and pleasant, flourishing gardens, with broad golden fields of grain. And the little acorn has become a sturdy oak, a tree that towers above its fellows, a landmark for the traveler, and a trysting place for lovers.

It is the year of 1687. Today there is a stir about the town . . . men ask each other questions, and shrug their shoulders . . . shake their heads.

Says one, "An evil day has come upon the Colonies, for the cruel Sir Edmund Andros is appointed Governor General of New England, and is to come to the council tonight to demand us to surrender the priceless charter of our liberties."

But now a new note comes into men's voices, their eyes grow bright. They have devised a plan. They know what they will try to do. We are in the council chamber now. Sir Edmund is here, a cold, hard man with a steely glint in his eye. The colonists pretend that they are ready to submit. They have the charter with them, but first they wish to settle many matters of debate. A farmer rises now to speak. It is the signal. Lights go out. Confusion. Shouts. A scuffle. The lights come on. The charter is gone. But it is safe. The rights of the colonists are safe. For two brave men in the confusion, have made their way out into the night . . . have journeyed far . . . have ridden the Charter where Andros will never find it . . . it is concealed in the mighty oak.

Two years go by. The charter is still safe. And then, at last, Sir Edmund Andros is deposed. The Charter can be brought to light. It is taken from the oak . . . a tree which comes to be known, from that day to this, as Charter Oak. And so the crisis is past . . . there is peace and prosperity and happiness. And travelers as they pass by, or lovers, as they keep their tryst, think of the way this fine old tree came by its name—the Charter Oak.

(PAUSE)

All this took place more than two hundred years ago. Today the Charter Oak has gone, but its story will live on for centuries. It is one of the many trees that have helped to make history.

(PAUSE)

BACH: A magnificent organ. A master organist. And a well loved melody! The Davey Organist brings you Anitra's Dance, by Edvard Grieg!

5. (ANITRA'S DANCE—GRIEG—CHANDLER GOLDTHWAITE)

BACH: This is the Davey Tree Surgery Golden Anniversary Hour.

(STATION ANNOUNCEMENTS)

BACH: Another melody to stir old echoes in your heart! Perhaps the memories themselves will be as pleasant as the song. The Davey Chorus!

6. (CARRY ME BACK TO OLD VIRGINNY—DAVEY QUARTETTE—SOPRANO—CHANDLER GOLDTHWAITE)

BACH: Or livelier thoughts! Flurries of snow! And a one horse open sleigh! The Davey Ensemble brings them back to mind with . . . "Jingle Bells!"

7. (JINGLE BELLS—CHANDLER GOLDTHWAITE—VIOLIN— CELLO—DAVEY SEXTETTE)

BACH: The hours I spent with thee, dear heart
Are as a string of pearls to me
I count them over, every one apart
My Rosary . . . My Rosary!

8. (ROSARY—NEVIN—CHANDLER GOLDTHWAITE— VIOLIN—CELLO)

BACH: Liebesfreud! Love's joy! This favorite old melody . . . a composition of Fritz Kreisler . . . is now brought to you by Chandler Goldthwaite, the Davey Organist.

9. (LIEBESFREUD—KREISLER—CHANDLER GOLDTHWAITE)

[handwritten] STA. ANN

BACH: This hour of familiar songs is sent you as a reminder that the Davey Tree Surgeons are the men to whom you should entrust the care of your priceless trees.

BACH: And each heart thinks a different name. But all sing . . . "Annie Laurie."

10. (ANNIE LAURIE—SCOTT—DAVEY QUARTET)

[handwritten] Introduction to Mr. Davey

11. (TREES—MARTIN L. DAVEY) [speech not reprinted]

BACH: Thank you, Mr. Davey. Ladies and gentlemen, you have been listening to Martin L. Davey, President of the Davey Tree Surgeons.

[handwritten] STATION ANN.

BACH: And now the stirring "Soldiers' Chorus" from Faust—presented by the Davey Ensemble.

12. (SOLDIERS' CHORUS FROM FAUST—GOUNOD—
DAVEY ENSEMBLE)

BACH: Judson House, well-known tenor soloist, now brings you an old Irish ballad known and loved the world over. Mr. House!

13. [handwritten] (WHEN YOU & I WERE YOUNG MAGGIE)

BACH: And now another song of the long ago . . . another song that may be full of memories . . . it is presented by the Davey Male Quartette!

14. (WHEN JOHNNY COMES MARCHING HOME AGAIN—
DAVEY MALE QUARTETTE)

BACH: And now a song that typifies, we hope, the spirit of this hour. A song of old friendships, old memories . . ."Auld Lang Syne."

15. (AULD LANG SYNE—BURNS—ENSEMBLE)

ANNOUNCER:

For fifty years now, increasing numbers of property owners have come to see the wisdom of entrusting the care of their priceless trees to no one but scientifically trained experts . . . men whom they can trust with a feeling of confidence and satisfaction. They know that the Davey Tree Experts, by their personal qualities, and by training are the men who can best give the professional and conscientious service that will safeguard their trees. More than twenty-one thousand clients were served by the Davey Tree Surgeons last year.

The work of the Davey Tree Surgeons is surprisingly low in cost, and is available in your vicinity. The Tree Surgeon is almost as convenient as your own dentist or doctor. Your nearest Davey Tree Surgeon will gladly examine your own trees without cost or obligation. If your trees are in good condition, he will tell you so, and it will cost you nothing to have this assurance. You can get full details about this service by writing the Davey Tree Surgeons either at Kent, Ohio, or in care of this station to which you are listening.

Remember! There is no half-good in tree-surgery. You can trust the Davey Tree Surgeons!

16. (JUST A SONG AT TWILIGHT—CHANDLER GOLDTHWAITE—)

BACH: I think that I shall never see
A poem as lovely as a tree
A tree whose hungry mouth is pressed
Against the earth's sweet flowing breast
A tree that looks to God all day
And lifts her leafy arms to pray
A tree that may in summer wear
A nest of robins in her hair
Upon whose bosom snow has lain
Who intimately lives with rain
Poems are made by fools like me
But only God can make a tree.

(MUSIC FADES UNDER READING, AND DIES AWAY SHORTLY AFTER THE ANNOUNCER'S LAST WORDS, AND THE HOUR IS AT AN END)

The Davey Tree Hour has come to you from the New York Studios of the National Broadcasting Company.

97. J. Walter Thompson Company, staff meeting minutes, 14 January 1930

Hartman Center: Rare Book, Manuscript, and Special Collections Library, Duke University, Durham, North Carolina

MR. WM. RESOR:[19] Mr. Reber hasn't been with us for some weeks and I am going to give him five minutes to tell us anything potent that he has to say about the Radio Department.

MR. REBER:[20] We have thirty-one programs a week on the radio now and I am told that the reputation of our programs around the broadcasting companies is that they are all very successful from a business point of view. Obviously we get criticisms of one sort and another, but as nearly as we can tell, they are really doing an advertising job. I won't go through the statistics of each one of them this morning but they do seem to be working.

A new one that was started recently is an hour on Sunday, from five to six o'clock, for the Davey Tree Institute. Just as an example of the success of that program, the first week we received something like 600 letters, all of them unsolicited, which in the most glowing terms expressed genuinely heartfelt thanks for the program and for the speech that Mr. Davey made. Never before, by the way, have we had letters of such a high quality; they were even considerably higher quality than those received as a result of one classical music program that we had. The stationery, the English and the evidences of culture on the part of the writers were decidedly higher than the average.

This is an unusual response: [the] Atwater Kent [program] may put on [operatic tenor Beniamino] Gigli, as they did last Sunday, and if they get twenty letters thanking them for the program, that will be a great many. Of course, they make no effort to get letters; they ask no one to send in any, so that twenty or as many as a hundred is just unheard of; consequently, the 600 received from the Davey program made us feel quite good.

MR. CHERINGTON: What was the nature of that program? Was it a musical program?

MR. REBER: It was a musical program, with organ music and mostly old-fashioned songs with a talk of about five minutes in the first half about a famous tree—the one in the first program was the "Charter Oak" to a background of music—and in the second half, a ten-minute talk by Mr. Davey on some subject that has to do with trees. The first was "The Romance of Trees" and the second was "How Trees Breathe." Those talks, especially Davey's talks, have been very successful. Most all of the letters say "thank goodness, we don't have to hear any more jazz" and the outstanding feature is Davey's talk which is really excellent. . . .

98. Martin L. Davey, letter to E. P. H. James, sales promotion manager, National Broadcasting Company, 1 September 1931

National Broadcasting Company Archives, box 3, folder 5,
Wisconsin Historical Society, Madison[21]

September 1st, 1931.
Mr. E. P. H. James, Sales Promotion Manager,
National Broadcasting Company, Inc.
711 Fifth Avenue,
New York City.

Dear Mr. James:

At the beginning of 1930, and after the depression had started, we made use of radio largely as a supplemental form of advertising to stimulate sales in that period of doubt and agitation. I was somewhat surprised to see how powerful and far-reaching it is. There is not time or space in which to recite the innumerable incidents that prove its force. But it is sufficient to say that I run into the effects of our radio advertising everywhere I go, both as to individuals whom I meet and groups of people whom I address. Furthermore, our sales representatives and our field men meet the beneficial effects of radio times without number.

We have encountered a new and delightful friendliness among people generally. Previous to our radio advertising, those who knew of the Davey Company respected us. Today, not only are there vastly more people who know us, but a distinct friendliness has been added to their respect. People feel acquainted, now. We are closer to them rather than being a far-off, impersonal institution.

Of course it goes without saying that radio advertising must be well done in order to deliver its best results. It must be pleasing to the public as a whole, and it must omit the offensive forms of advertising. But it is a powerful instrumentality, and it has demonstrated its supreme value in our own business beyond our expectations, not only in the advertising effect but also in the actual volume of our business and in the increasing ease with which that volume is done.

With cordial good wishes, I remain

Sincerely yours,

[signed]
Martin L. Davey, President,
THE DAVEY TREE EXPERT COMPANY

99. Martin L. Davey, "Secrets of a Successful Radio Program; Tastes and Sensibilities of Listeners Always Respected; Sponsor's Salesmen Find Welcome, Easier Orders"
Broadcasting, 1 July 1932, 9

THE DAVEY TREE program, with which this article deals, was one of several radio features named by Senator C. C. Dill, of Washington, in an address before the A.A.A.A. [American Association of Advertising Agencies] recently as being a "natural" program.[22] The commercial announcement, he said, is effective and inoffensive despite its length. The author of this article is a former member of Congress and at one time was a candidate for the governorship of Ohio. His views on the effectiveness of radio and advertising and the rights of the listeners are interesting and convincing.

We have abundant reason for the belief that our radio programs have had a powerful influence in maintaining our business through this difficult period.

Probably the most important evidence comes from our salesmen. They tell me that a substantial majority of the people on whom they call speak to them favorably about the Davey radio programs. They tell me also that they encounter a much more pronounced friendliness, that almost everyone whom they contact knows about the Davey Company in a favorable way in contrast with a much more limited knowledge of the company previously, that radio has served to personalize our business and bring it much closer to the people, that they find a much greater and more general confidence in the Davey Company and respect for the institution, and that orders are actually easier to secure.

We began broadcasting the first Sunday in January, 1930, a short time after the stock market crash, and we continued for six months. During the first five months of 1930 our volume ran 20% ahead of the same period in 1929. The business in June, 1930, was equal to that for June, 1929. During the last half of 1930 we encountered a moderate decline in volume, but the total amount for the year 1930 was a little over $3,000,000 [about $37.4 million today]. Or almost the same amount that we did in the boom year of 1929.

Thanks for Advertising

During the year 1931 we experienced a moderate decline in volume, although we served just as many clients as we did in the preceding year. It simply meant that the average order was somewhat smaller than in 1930. Even in this bad year of 1932 we are serving almost as many clients as we did last year, although the average size of the order is again somewhat smaller.

There is no doubt that our radio programs have had a powerful effect in maintaining a very fair volume of business during this period. I do not know of anything that could have produced the same results in creating the obvious friendliness, in selling a name and an idea so broadly, and in making it easier for our salesmen to secure orders. I never before thought that people would take the trouble to thank someone for any kind of an advertisement, but we have had tens of thousands of letters from all over the country thanking us wholeheartedly for our radio programs, a very considerable percent of them on private stationery.

Contrary to the generally accepted theory at the time when we began broadcasting we had decided to build our programs around the old familiar melodies. We believed that the public had been more or less satiated with jazz. I believe that the average person enjoys a reasonable amount of jazz, but that too much of it is like an excessive amount of salt and pepper and vinegar.

On the other hand, we believed that a very small percent of the people really understood and appreciate classical music of the more difficult sort. It is true that there are some melodious classics that are popular—not because they are classics but because they are melodious. Therefore, we decided to use the old familiar songs which combine both melody and harmony. These songs remain popular not only because they sound good to the ear, but also because they are familiar to the people. My observation has been that the average person greatly prefers music that is familiar to him.

Program Stirs Memories

Then again it is doubtful if there are very many of these old familiar songs that do not arouse very precious memories in the minds of many people. Each song has its own special following, and has within itself a variety of reasons why it stirs memories. In my judgment there is absolutely no piece of current music, however good it may be, that has any pull comparable to the memories that the old songs arouse.

Of course, we were very careful not to use any one particular type of song: we wanted a pleasing variety. We made use of a few of the melodious classics, quite a few light opera selections, a considerable number of the relatively modern melodious pieces, many folk songs and others of good racial origin, and a still larger number of the old standard popular songs.

We considered it of very great importance to achieve variety in every conceivable way. We built each program with a constant succession of type as above indicated. We made sure that every other piece was fast and every other piece was slow. We made an effort to have a variety of songs of racial origin, including English, Scotch, Irish, Welsh, German, Italian, etc., as well as many of the old American songs and those with a distinctly southern flavor. We were careful to have a constant variety of rendition, mixing up ensemble work with male quartet and mixed-quartet and solos and instrumental numbers. I believe that the average listener feels the effect of this constant changing variety, and in most cases does not realize the cause of it. He may be equally unconscious of a lack of variety and find a program monotonous without knowing just why. It is the task of the program builder to provide ample variety, but he should be careful to guard against any violently conflicting types close together.

We carefully avoided everything that is vulgar and everything that would be objectionable to people of refined taste. I believe that the majority of American people, whether or not they are highly educated, are naturally refined, and that they like the kind of entertainment that does not grate on their sensibility. It would be an entirely different proposition if you were putting on a show where the people could come of their own volition, but with radio entertainment you are going right into the home and it is your duty to respect the feelings and taste of the better class of citizens. We tried to make our programs just as entertaining and as interesting as possible, but also refined. We attempted to maintain an atmosphere of respect and dignity without being highbrow. The response of the public has amply justified our hopes.

Music That Soothes

Another result which we sought to achieve was restfulness. The constant jar and rasping of irritating sound that is sometimes called music has a tendency to put the nerves on edge. If one turns his radio on for a whole evening and hears nothing but slam-bang jazz, his nervous system is likely to be in rebellion. It seems to me that one of the most desirable qualities of a radio program is restfulness, which causes one to lean back in his chair and be comfortable while listening to the music. A little stimulant is all right, but modern people need a larger proportion of the soothing qualities of entertainment.

The radio is a national form of entertainment. The only fair way to build a program is to base it on the tastes and conditions of the average homes. Those average homes are neither lowbrow nor highbrow, but they have the elements of culture, either in the matter of education or else in their instincts. A program that is capably built to please and satisfy the great average of American homes will win the approval and support of the vast majority of people.

Among the tens of thousands of letters we receive regarding programs, we have almost never received a flippant or disrespectful letter. A majority of them come from people of education and culture, but we have received a very large number of letters written on cheap paper and in poor English. Yet all of them come from intelligent people, even though they are not well educated. All of the letters that we have received have expressed sincere appreciation and profound pleasure. Most of them are grateful that we use no jazz; nearly all of them are delighted with the old familiar songs. Their letters breathe the spirit of respect and genuine pleasure. There are certainly other kinds of radio entertainment that have proved successful. I would not assume that ours is the only type that is worth using, but there is abundant evidence that our programs have been an outstanding success.

100. Justine Magee, undated fan letter to Martin L. Davey

Kent State University, Davey Tree Expert Company, Records, box 21, folder 15, Davey Tree Company: Radio Programs: 1930–32

Dear Mr. Martin Davy—

First, I want to tell you how very much I have missed your delightful talks, and the Davy Program. I think of them very often and in memory have treasured many of the interesting things I learned from you, about trees.

Shortly after you left the air my husband passed away, and as he was my all, I am utterly alone. (I shall be obliged to make this letter a little personal so that my point be made clearer)[.]

I have not been able to live in that part of Plymouth, where beautiful trees and flowers exist and now, as things have grown steadily harder for me, have had to become a dependent, upon the town.

They allow one, only very cheap rent of course, and I have had to choose between two realities in which to live.

My acquaintances, have all advised my taking the one, where I would be in the house with another family (as I am often sick and no one to speak to) but I have made my decision in favor of the lonely house because there was a beautiful <u>elmtree</u> in the next yard. I have not mentioned to any one before, why I decided thus, for I have lived to learn that my friends call me sentimental, but I feel as if you would understand, my great love for a tree. You know there are moments in our lives so tragic, that we reach out to find one understanding heart.

Please do not think me queer for writing but I was impressed to do so.

Hoping that you are well and happy I am just a friend.

Justine Magee

156 Court St.

Plymouth, Mass.

Music on the Radio

Con

101. A.J.M., "Radio Just Another Blight; A Plaint from East Orange [N.J.] on the Tendencies of the Time" [letter to the editor]

New York Times, 31 December 1925, 14

To the Editor of the New York Times:

Your editor note anent radio "request turns" recalled to my mind the fact that my own radio has not been in use for the past six months, and started a mental query as to the why therefor.

One's sensual appetite is satiated to nausea by the modern stage; but one need not buy theatre tickets. Second childhood is hastened—or rather now begins coincident with the ending of the first—by the infantilism of the "movies"; but one can stay away. One's self-respect is insulted by the demoralizing flap-doodle of the churches; but one need not go to church. The magazines may not shock our already case-hardened sensibilities, although this grossness adds its fillip to the general rout; but one need not buy the magazines.

We cannot blame the play producers, the "movie" magnates, the clergy or the publishers for "listening with the ears to the ground" or what the public will pay for, for the echo of the mass mind. No! If fault there be, it lies with you and me, the common people, for buying their wares.

Who buys a radio set destroys the last refuge of a soul hunted and harried by the bestial ministrations to the mass mind of this decadent day.

With a radio in the home, one's peace is at the mercy of the whole household. Without warning, one is pursued by the raucous inanities of the Gold Dust Boys or Happiness Twins.[23]

The radio vividly presents what a horrible thing is the mass mind. Whose soul the gods would destroy they now blight by radio.

I shall not have my expensive radio set repaired, nor yet shall I sell it or give it away. I shall keep it in desuetude, lest in some future evil moment I be bewitched into buying another.

A.J.M.

East Orange, N.J., Dec. 29, 1925

102. Paul Kempf, "Thomas A. Edison Sees a Menace for Music in the Radio"

Musician, January 1927, 1

Thomas A. Edison invented the phonograph in 1876—fifty years ago. Many of us can remember our first reactions to this amazing device. We can recall standing eagerly before an upright cabinet in some waiting room or amusement resort and, having first adjusted two rubber tubes to our ears and deposited a coin in the slot, hearing Cal Stewart's (Uncle Josh) droll, nasal recitations of rural experience.

As the wax cylinders began to reflect messages of greater tonal complexity—brass bands, orchestras, choruses, instrumental and vocal solos—the phonograph became musically important. It brought music of all kinds into the very home life of the people, at a time, certainly, when the opportunities to hear original performances were pitifully meager.

This type of mechanical sound reproduction has passed through many transformations during the half-century of its existence. Today, in its most exalted state, it offers us at one sitting a complete symphony of some forty minutes' duration. It is welcomed in the studio and schoolroom by our best teachers as an indispensable agent in musical training, and is rated by our leading educators and critics as a potent force in the spread of musical knowledge and appreciation.

Intimate associates of Mr. Edison tell me that of all his revolutionary inventions the phonograph remains his pet, his hobby. He does not regard it as his most important contribution to human welfare; yet his unflagging interest in the development of sound reproduction is to him the most engaging of his manifold creative experiments.

The opportunity was given to me the other day to secure, for the benefit of readers of *The Musician*, Mr. Edison's opinions regarding fourteen topics more or less pertinent to the phonograph and its relationship to our musical life. In deference to the veteran inventor's distrust of the oral interview, these views were expressed as answers to a series of typewritten questions.

Readers of *The Musician*, we now present Mr. Edison, who submits himself to our examination, in this manner:

1. Q. To what extent has the phonograph influenced the musical taste of the public?

A. Don't know.

2. Q. Do you consider music a study of cultural value worthy of being taught along with other academic subjects in our public schools?

A. Yes.

3. Q. Do you think that present-day composers are turning out music as good as that of past generations? Will a limit ever be reached in the invention of new melodies?

A. Considered mathematically, an enormous number of melodies are still possible.

4. Q. To what extent will your 40-minute record affect the musical status of the phonograph?[24]

A. That is to be found out. The reaction of the public in anything can never be predicted, but it is to be assumed that a person would rather have a complete symphony on a single record than to have it in a bulky album, especially when they can get it for at least one-half the cost.

5. Q. Which one of your various inventions do you consider as having had the most pronounced effect on the progress of mankind?

A. Electric power and lighting system.

6. Q. Which musical instrument reproduces most naturally in the phonograph?

A. If you listen to an Edison you will find all instruments are reproduced naturally. Even piano records have been used in Tone Test recitals, but I am not yet satisfied with my piano reproduction.[25] Troubles in piano recording arise from the percussion of the hammers.

7. Q. Of the various singers who have made records for you which one, in your opinion, makes the most nearly perfect record?

A. In her younger days, Elizabeth Spencer.

8. Q. Do some voices which sound well to the ear fail to reproduce well in the phonograph? If so, why?

A. I have given over 3,000 public performances before large audiences where the singer and the record proved there was no difference. Any defect shown in the phonograph was shown to be in the voice of the singer.

9. Q. What is your favorite musical composition?

A. I have several: "The Sweetest Story Ever Told," "Kathleen Mavourneen," "When I'm Gone You'll Soon Forget," "I'll Take You Home Again, Kathleen," "That We Two Were Maying."

10. Q. Which of the old standard songs has proved the most popular with the public as judged by the demand for records?

A. "I'll Take You Home Again, Kathleen."

11. Q. Do you think musicians generally would benefit by studying the science of sound?

A. It would improve the technique of music greatly. It is astonishing, for instance, that a violinist doesn't know that the playing of octaves produces agonizing discord, especially on high strings—he cannot correct for pitch, as he would do two separate things simultaneously.

12. Q. Do you think that the public is influenced by the importance of a musical artist's name more than it is by the inherent value of a musical performance as recorded? Would a superlatively fine singing or violin record, equal in every respect to those made by world-famed artists, enjoy a considerable demand purely on the merits of the record?

A. The public is influenced by the reputation of the singer even after the voice is almost gone. People hear what they are told to hear. They are self-hypnotized by reputation.

13. Q. Do you think that the best available radio reception of a musical performance can excel in quality, so far as the auditor is concerned, the best available reproduction on the phonograph of a similar performance? In what respect does either excel?

A. If you listen to an Edison phonograph and a radio side by side, with the same tune, singer or instrumentalist, you will appreciate the distortion of radio music and decide the case yourself.

14. Q. What, do you think, will be the economic effect on the musical profession of radio broadcasting?

A. Bad. Undistorted music in time will sound strange to those brought up on radio music and they will not like the real thing. . . .

103. John C. Freund, Excerpts from an address broadcast from WJZ [Newark]

Wireless Age, May 1922, 36

What's the great world crying for today? It is "We want a better life!" That cry comes from the harassed so-called captain of industry bowed under his burdens as it comes from the harassed wage-earner trying to make both ends meet with falling wages and the rising cost of living.

What are you all getting out of life anyway?—Life!—God's greatest gift to man? You go from home to office or store or factory on foot, by car, by subway, or elevated, over a ferry perhaps; in the middle of the day you take a little time off to swallow a meal which may be a good one or may only consist of a sandwich or some ice cream, and if you are female, you lighten it up with a powder puff and a lipstick. Then back to work and home again by car, by subway, or elevated, over a ferry and by the time you are home, most of you haven't the pep left to enjoy the leisure that you have won and so many of you instead of indulging in some rational social life or going to hear some good music or a good play, off you go to the movies, a vaudeville show or a cabaret where you shimmy and foxtrot to the music of the jazz, preferably with somebody else's girl or wife.

You haven't yet been educated to realize that the end and aim of life should not be work, work all the time but leisure, leisure to spend a little time with your family, if you are married, to get acquainted with your own children instead of telling mother to put the kids to sleep as you smoke a pipe, read the latest murders and suicides in the evening papers and so to bed to prepare for the next day's monotonous toil, for monotonous it is for nearly all of us—same faces, same stunt, same roll-top desk, same job at the factory, same stenographer to look at, pretty or otherwise, as you dictate if you are a business man your ever-increasing monotonous replies to the correspondence you receive which generally begins: Dear Sir: Yours of the tenth duly to hand, et cetera, et cetera—and so it goes.

The great facilities of travel and living, the great inventions are making all our lives more and more monotonous. Do you realize that?

Formerly a shoemaker made a shoe, the whole shoe. If he was in a small town, he was the center of the scandal and the news. He knew your corns and your bunions and your troubles.

Today, through labor-saving machinery, a man or a woman stands or sits at a machine and does one little job eight hours a day, six days a week, fifty-two weeks in the year. Soul-benumbing labor. Do you realize how awful that is?

It is to escape this monotony that men try to smoke themselves to death while playing penny ante while the women murder one another's reputations at sewing circles or mothers' meetings, while the young people get out into the streets and pair off like the birds, go ice-creaming and tangoing as if that was the best way to prepare them for life or their work.

Wherever you go, you find human energy expended just after the day's work is done in an endless number of ways that are positively infernal because of their stupidity. Of all the things that can help make life unreal, it is the movies which must have the happy end where after several acts of villainy, all is well when someone taps the villain on the back and tells him to be a good boy in the future.

Music can help you!

Hitherto good music has been looked upon as something just for the educated few who go to hear the symphonies, the operas, the great artists.

Music belongs to all!

It begins where words end — it whispers to us of immortality.

And it came out of the mass soul in the shape of the folks' songs, the song of the people.

It didn't start as an art.

That's why some of us are trying to give it back to the people, to democratize it.

Some believe that classical music is the only good music.

Rats!

Good music may be a lovely waltz by a great composer or a homely ballad or a quartet or a chorus, though a chorus must not be a drinking song, for, like some of the rivers, we have gone dry, that is those of us who are so by conviction or under doctor's orders.

The main thing with music is to have it in the home, not alone in the church or in the concert halls but in the home whether it comes in the shape of a talking machine, a player piano or a radio set.

Let me tell you mothers and fathers, that with music in the home, the boy will bring in a better type of girl and the girl will certainly bring in a better type of boy. To you girls, let me say that if you have any fellow who threatens to be a "steady" and who can't stand a little good music, take an old man's advice and — fire him.

Did you know that a multimillionaire one day passing along the street heard the sound of violin playing. Curiosity brought him into the place and he found a little, fat, freckled boy scraping away. He became interested in the boy, gave him a chance. That boy later became a multimillionaire himself and one of the great characters of these United States. The name of the man was Andrew Carnegie and the fat, freckled boy is Charles M. Schwab, head of the Bethlehem Steel Works, where at times they have from fifteen to twenty thousand employees. It was his music which gave him a chance.

Let us not forget the radio which already has millions of auditors and will be a most potent force to bring music home to the masses.

104. Lee de Forest, "Opera Audiences of Tomorrow; America to Become a Music-loving Nation through Radio Broadcasting"
Radio World, 5 August 1922, 13

Our recent national awakening to the art of radio and to the possibilities of transmitting music on the Hertzian waves, brings the subject of radio broadcasting very close to the music lovers of America. Certainly, notwithstanding very crude attempts in broadcasting Broadway jazz, the time has come when we may give immediate concern to the opportunity offered by radio in making known the beauties of orchestral and grand-opera music.

We Americans are by no means a musical people—that is, in such measure as are most of the European nations. Familiarity with and liking for operatic music unfortunately is limited to a very small percentage of Americans. Every effort heretofore attempted to make opera at popular prices self-sustaining has met with failure in almost every instance. Excellent organizations, like the Gallo Grand Opera Company, fail to draw even fair houses for longer than a few weeks in any city.

To turn Americans into an opera-loving people, notwithstanding the yearly influx from Europe, would, in the natural course of events, require decades perhaps centuries. Not that we cannot quickly learn to appreciate good music; but to induce the audiences to go first to hear, and then again to hear, then to appreciate, to understand, to love good music is the great difficulty.

So, to one whose greatest joy and relaxation was to hear good opera, this ability of the radiophone to bring into every home—not second-class opera, not phonographic reproductions—but the actual voices of the highest-salaried artists of the Metropolitan and Chicago Opera companies, appealed to me with strange fascination and aroused a faith which today is as keen, as strong, as when the idea was born.

When, in 1907, I first prophesied the era of radio broadcasting, I laid prime stress on what it would mean to the public generally, and to producers of grand opera especially, to send this form of inspiring music to every corner of the land.[26]

Opera impresarios and directors do not, should not, fear that if their productions are heard in every home in New York or Chicago their box office receipts will suffer one whit. For every 20 who thus hear the arias and more or less fragmentary gems at home, without seeing the gorgeous stage pictures which accompany them, one, at least, who would never otherwise know what beauty he is missing, will be constrained to go to grand opera. Thus the number of opera goers and lovers will be greatly increased. Nationwide education in the best of opera, repeated familiarity with the actual voices of the best artists, cannot immensely benefit opera.

I am certain therefore, that, when the time arrives, opera directors will be ready to cooperate to their utmost to place in the wings and in the orchestra pits the properly designed sound-collectors which will convert the music into perfectly modulated telephone-currents, to be transmitted by wire to the distant high-power radiophone transmitter; say, to four or five scattered throughout the United States. The United States should set aside a special zone of wavelengths — reserved exclusively for opera and symphony orchestras — so that, on every night of the musical season, a listener may tune in to the Metropolitan or Chicago operas, or to the Boston, Philadelphia, New York, Philharmonic, Kansas City, or San Francisco symphony program — and, at his own fireside, drink in the very best of the world's music.

If this were the only application of the radiophone, its ability to educate the people in good music, that alone would amply justify the government, or our musical societies, in endowing and maintaining such a service as I have just described. In this field of opera and symphony, of high-class concert and chamber music, secrecy of radiophone transmission is quite unthinkable. The better the music, the more general its value, the more the necessity for making the service quite free to all who can hear. The musical organizations which give freely of their product will suffer no loss; on the contrary, they will earn the grateful interest of multitudes who would otherwise never learn of this superb art. And from these new ranks will flock new patrons, new recruits, new lovers of music who will next seek to hear and to know their newfound friends face to face.

What will this exquisite musical service mean to the American people, hitherto strangers for the most part, to that fine element in life and education? Maintain this service for ten years and we shall see a national musical awakening the like of which history cannot record! Then, and not until then, will we see a genuine American opera—one worthy to rank with those of Verdi, Bizet, or Puccini—one destined to live!

105. "Programs Lauded by Bandmasters"
New York Times, 12 September 1926, §11, p. 2

Prominent bandmasters, many of whom refused to "go on the air," in the early days of radio, are now convinced that the microphone and its associated apparatus sends music into millions of homes with entire fidelity. They say that broadcasting is creating a greater appreciation of music.

By John Philip Sousa
Radio's power to educate and entertain the public is without limit. For an invention that cannot give visual personality its achievements are remarkable. In my opinion it has come to stay forever. If it pays a proper reward to the composers whose works it uses its life will not only be long but merry.

By Walter Damrosch
Director New York Symphony Orchestra
From my standpoint of a musician and educator the importance of the radio cannot be overestimated.

Last February I conducted a concert with the New York Symphony Orchestra over the radio in which I conducted various symphonic selections of the great masters and by request of WEAF interpolated the selections with some explanatory comment. The music as well as my speaking voice were heard distinctly over a radius of thousands of miles and I received letters of commendation from nearly all quarters of the United States as well as Canada and Cuba. Some of the contents of these letters were amazing.

By Nikolai Sokoloff
Director Cleveland Symphony Orchestra
The only words I have for radio broadcasting are words of praise. To say that I think it is wonderful is superfluous. The effect that radio has had on the American public is even more marvelous than the feat of broadcasting itself. One of its

greatest results, and the one which affects me more than any of its many others, is that it is educating the American public to appreciate good music.

It is a fact that all people have an inborn love for music, but before the advent of radio the ordinary man in the street did not have the time or the opportunity of cultivating his longing for the better things in the musical world. Jazz was thrown at him from all sides. He learned to like it or at least to bear it. But classical music has been hard to get. The man in the street did not have the easy opportunity of hearing the better things in music until radio came along, when classical music became just as readily available as jazz. What is the result? After only five years of broadcasting, the general public is acquiring a working knowledge and appreciation of good music. On all sides you hear the great masters discussed with an ever-growing intimacy and understanding. If radio did nothing else, it should go down in history as one of the greatest helps to humanity. That's what I think of radio!

By Willem van Hoogstraten
Conductor New York Philharmonic Orchestra

As a means of developing a great appreciation of music I consider the radio to be a tremendous potential force.

This great force should be handled carefully. Appreciation of good music cannot be developed by listening in to a cheaper kind of merely entertaining musical sounds. They, of course, have nothing whatever to do with the development of a taste and appreciation of music as art. I can only express my profoundest admiration for those radio stations which are already broadcasting symphonic concerts and solos by first-rate artists; because this certainly is, as I see it, a long step toward cultivating a general understanding and love of good music.

By Edwin Franko Goldman
[prominent band conductor and composer]

Radio has a greater opportunity than all individual musicians or all the musical organizations of the world for developing a greater appreciation of music. During the past few years it has rendered notable service, but as it is still in its infancy its possibilities for future development are unlimited.

By Henry Hadley
Associate Conductor New York Philharmonic Orchestra

To say that I am in favor of radio broadcasting would indeed be putting it mildly—I am enthusiastic.

The public has already learned to appreciate good music and they want more. They are beginning to show an intimate knowledge of the musical classics which was formerly only found among the wealthy classes who could afford to hear the operas and big orchestras—yes, even go abroad for their musical education. With radio, in a few years, you will find the same knowledge and appreciation of the classics in even the humblest home with its radio receiver that formerly were only found in the circles of the wealthy and what has been referred to as "the intelligentsia."

Of course, the American public is broader and better for it. Good music broadens and strengthens the soul. I must give full credit to radio for the sudden interest taken in classical music by our public.

Joseph Knecht

It is my opinion that through the medium of broadcasting a greater appreciation of music has been developed throughout the country.

What Do Listeners Want?

106. E. F. McDonald Jr., "What We Think the Public Wants"
Radio Broadcast, March 1924, 382–84

There has always been a considerable division of opinion about what the public really wants in radio broadcasting. Many broadcasters thought most listeners wanted jazz, and others felt that a predominance of classical music would be most pleasing to their listeners, and so on. A survey of the daily radio programs gave proof that the station owners or operators had widely differing notions. They must have arrived at their judgments by some mysterious individual speculation. As for ourselves, we knew no just estimate could be arrived at through the desultory method of making inquiry here and there; nor could we rely much on the daily hundreds of letters from listeners. Constructive suggestions in letters were all too few.

So the idea of a scientific investigation developed among the three Chicago broadcasters. It was decided to put the question up to the entire radio audience.

What kind of radio entertainment do you prefer? The three Chicago stations, Westinghouse Electric and Manufacturing Company Station KYW, the Chicago Board of Trade Station WDAP and the Zenith-Edgewater Beach Hotel Broadcasting Station WJAZ joined in the undertaking. Concretely the test took the form of "The Listeners' Vote Contest" and was staged during the recent Chicago Radio Show.

The public displayed interest which quite surprised all of us. It had an opportunity to make its wants known, and did so in no uncertain fashion. For a period of 12 days, at frequent intervals, during each daily broadcasting period, the listening audience was asked their choice of classical, popular, jazz, instrumental, vocal music; of religious, political, educational talks, etc. Active participation on all sides was invited on the ground of influence which the general vote would have, not only on radio programs for the time being, but on the future of radio. That was the major inducement. The three stations also offered another incentive to the listener in many prizes such as complete radio sets and radio parts. A veritable flood of responses deluged the three stations. The personnel gasped at the tons of mail that had to be counted and sorted, tabulated and analyzed in several different ways. Office help was multiplied twenty times and mail order house activity reigned those twelve days where before had been the quiet repose and dignified atmosphere of the musical studio. A careful count places the number of letters received by all three stations at 263,410.

One Listener out of 50 Answered

Conservative advertising men of broad experience with whom counsel was taken, agreed that not more than one person in 50 will respond to the most attractive advertisement or prize contest. Accordingly, the listening audience of the three large Chicago broadcasting stations may be safely estimated at 13,170,500. WJAZ, the Zenith-Edgewater Beach Hotel Broadcasting Station, claims the largest audience — 8,534,950. The number of replies received by this station alone was 170,699 of the total of 263,410. In one day this station received 20,152 pieces of mail, representative of an army of listeners upward of a million, scattered in all directions, but yet, considering both intensity of population and degree of distance, pretty well represented every state of the union, the Islands, Canada, Greenland, Central and South America.

What the Vote Showed

An analysis of the vote revealed several things which surprised us. Perhaps the most outstanding is the marked taste of our "voters" for classical music. The partisans of classical music exceeded only by 6% (of the total voters) those who preferred the popular. More men than women voted. The proportion was 67.4% men and 32.6% women. This gives some color of reality to the frequently asked question of the irrepressible cartoonist as to whether the women of the land prefer their husbands at the club until midnight or at home listening to the radio until two.

In none of the announcements of the vote contest was reference made to old songs, yet 5.7% of the votes specifically asked for them in preference to all else.

Independent deductions can be made from following tabulation of the vote.

    2.7% desire Band Music
   24.7% desire Classical music
    2.9% desire Dance music
     .3% desire Dramatic music
    1.0% desire Hawaiian Music
   18.4% desire Jazz
     .3% desire Mexican music
     .3% desire Male solos
    5.7% desire Old-time songs
    1.7% desire Grand opera
     .9% desire Orchestra
     .5% desire Pipe organ
   29.0% desire Popular music
     .3% desire Quartette instrumental
     .2% desire Male quartettes
     .8% desire Mixed quartettes
     .5% desire Religious music
    2.1% desire Sacred music
     .7% desire Saxophone
     .6% desire Symphony music
    2.1% desire Vocal selections

At WJAZ, we have from the first felt that a well-balanced program over-emphasizing no one thing and one which gave particular attention to the best in music, was what the public, or at least our public wanted. And our previous estimate, together with the figures from the test vote shows that desire for the better music is growing stronger. Like a good book, good music unfolds additional beauty and charm in the repetition. The flimsy character of jazz and most of the cabaret type of music we generally acknowledge. All the music in that category serves its purpose, such as it is, and probably will never lose popularity of a sort. But the real substance, what may well be called the meat and potatoes of the musical menu, is that which appeals to the higher intelligence and finer emotions. Thus we reasoned from the very inception of station WJAZ. The recent vote proved we were pretty nearly right. From its first day "on the air," the Crystal Studio of WJAZ was devoted entirely to the best in music, and eventually became known as one of the dependable sources of classical music in the realm of radio. The Oriole Orchestra in the Marine Dining Room which alternates with the Crystal Studio supplies entertainment in lighter vein, and furnishes whatever popular "relief" the program needs.

Greater familiarity with good music is developing partiality for it. The talking machine [phonograph] has been an important factor in music's advance. Popular bands insinuating better music at every opportunity have helped much. And now radio with its all-pervasive influence, more than any other agency, is bringing classical music into its own. In former days, when only the well-to-do could afford to hear so-called artistic music, they alone evinced any general desire for it. But now radio gives equal opportunity to people in all walks of life, no matter how lowly, to hear the best music, there is a commensurate growth of general appreciation for it. When Miss Florence Macbeth of the Chicago Civic Opera sang a series of operatic selections on Saturday evening, December 23, more than 5,000 letters of thanks were written to her.

Here is a sample program from our station:

Sample program from radio station WJAZ

1.	"Sobbing Blues"	
	"Faded Love Letters"	Orchestra
2.	"My Lovely Celia" (Old English) — Munro	
	"The Pretty Creature" (Old English) — Storace	Baritone Solos
3.	*Souvenir de Moscou* — Wieniawski	
	Mazurka — Mlynarski	Violin Solos
4.	"Where 'Ere You Walk" — Handel	Baritone Solo
5.	Berceuse — Chopin	
	Ballade — Chopin	Piano Solos
6.	"Silvery Moon"	
	"Marchela"	Orchestra
7.	"Do Not Go My Love" — Hageman	
	"Minor and Major" — Spross	Contralto Solos

8. Sonata, D Major—Mozart	Violin Solo
9. "Sunshine of Mine"	
"Pekin"	Orchestra
10. "My Heart at Thy Sweet Voice" (*Samson et*	
Delilah)—Saint-Saëns	Contralto Solo
11. *Liebestraum*—Liszt	
Etude—Chopin	Piano Solos
12. "Retreat"—LaForge	
"Pirate Song"—Gilbert	Baritone Solos
13. "Londonderry Air"—Kreisler	
Rondine—Beethoven-Kreisler	Violin Solos
14. "Susie"	
"Wonderland of Dreams"	Orchestra

Twenty years ago this program would have been branded as highbrow, and as intended solely for the ears of high society. Now it is everyday diet, for the consumption of the radio audience in the lumber camps, on the plains, in the rural districts, in the tenements, and homes, and clubs of the city dwellers, the largest number of whom within the influence of the Chicago broadcasting stations, we think, pay radio allegiance to Station WJAZ. And we are sure our judgment of programs is responsible.

Even before the Listeners' Vote Contest, we had thousands of testimonial letters from all parts of the country, some written in aristocratic hand and on crested stationery; some on the letterhead of the business or professional man; some in pencil on soiled paper in illiterate fashion, but all giving testimony of how the human heart whether in the mansion or in the hovel beats response to good music. Those letters gave lively encouragement to us to continue as we had set out. But it could not be affirmed that these letters were representative of the majority opinion. Our judgment of popular approval, however, was definitely substantiated by the acid test, the Listeners' Vote Contest.

Crooning

107. Floyd Gibbons School of Broadcasting, correspondence course, lesson 19: "How to Train a Singing Voice for Broadcasting: The Art of Crooning," 1932, 16–17

The art of crooning furnishes a good opportunity for the lower voices. This branch of musical production has been roundly criticized, not because it is displeasing if properly done, but because such a great proportion of it has been badly done. Crooning should be exactly what its name implies—soft, light production—the kind that is associated with lullabies. Properly used, it is very effective. It furnishes excellent contrast with the more vociferous outpourings of classic singing.

Crooning should be confined to songs whose words and music lend themselves to light singing, low volume level of tone. The vocal organs are called upon for considerable shading within a narrow range of volume. It is therefore necessary to have a well-trained, fully controlled and flexible voice to do good crooning. There must be the same capacity for fullness and roundness of tone as is required in operatic work. The mere fact that the volume is held at a lower level does not mean that everybody can do it. In crooning the singer stands very close to the microphone, the mouth almost touching the instrument and the face usually at right angles to the line of direct pickup. Thus the singer is very close to the listener, and every sound made or uttered is heard distinctly.

The intake of the breath is a very important matter to the crooner. It must be absolutely noiseless.

The gasping sound of an improper inspiration of breath, magnified perhaps by the amplifying apparatus, has caused the failure of many otherwise gifted aspirants for broadcasting fame. The student is urged to practice the silent breathing exercises diligently, and to experiment on methods of in-breathing until he is certain he has eliminated all possibility of its being heard through the microphone.

108. Martha Gellhorn, "Rudy Vallée: God's Gift to Us Girls"
New Republic, 7 August 1929, 310–11[27]

Standing room only. That's all there ever is for Rudy Vallée, New York's treasure, the country's newest and nicest beloved. But why?

The Brooklyn Paramount is a leviathan amongst movie houses. The first floor shames the Champs de Mars. Balconies rise endlessly to a remote ceiling. Gilt scrolls and gimcracks glare and glitter all around. In contrast the stage is very simple. Rudy Vallée's revue is on. This week we're pretending to be dough-boys. A large orchestra, a nondescript group of male walk-ons, a funny man, with an unfinished sort of face, a girl whose voice is strong rather than beauti-ful, and Rudy himself, make up the cast. The plot—if revues do have plots—is of no importance either to actors or audience. The orchestra plays occasionally, and their jazz is no worse than any other jazz. The jokester says things that make you think you might laugh, if you put your mind to it. The girl, who is irksome because she is neither young, nor pretty, hands doughnuts to the "boys," and sings a lush love song.

And now the fun begins. The song—of the I'm-crazy-about-you kind—demands that the lady cotton up to and cleave unto one gentleman after an-other. In the course of this vocal, and uninspiring, flirtation, she babbles the you're-the-only-man line to Rudy and encircles him with her masterful arms. Rudy is unquestionably an actor. At first, he seems embarrassed and confused; the audience giggles. Then he looks about like a shamefaced little boy, and, sat-isfying himself that he and she are alone beneath the stars (as I believe she is assuring him at the top of her lungs, betimes) he warms to his task, grins, and hugs her quite convincingly. The audience, except for the few uncomfortable males present, goes mad. A murmur of delight rises like a tidal wave, becomes an envious moan, pants into a yearning sob, and dies down. The revue con-tinues—but alas, drearily. One wishes that it would end; or that Rudy Vallée would do something besides lead his jazz-lads carelessly, with one hand. We wish he would either get into the spirit of the thing or get off the stage. His shy, I-can't-imagine-why-I'm-here pose is tiring. We almost decide to go home.

Suddenly Rudy picks up a megaphone, stands quietly at the corner of the stage, and begins to sing. The audience holds its breath, in joy, in adoration. The orches-tra plays softly, slowly. He has chosen "I Kiss Your Hand, Madame." It was a wise choice. His voice is low, pleasant, natural. It slides along—that is the only way to describe it. He misses the beat of the orchestra, and drops into a slower tempo, with a rhythm of his own. The words drift from the megaphone like a caress, a *billet doux* for each gasping female in the vast theater. The music is charm-ing—thanks to Vienna—and the words are not so gummy as those we are ac-customed to. He sings the piece twice. And he is good. We needn't quibble about that. Crooning "I Kiss Your Hand, Madame," he is even better than good. He is swell. When he stops, the audience's breath, held in an exquisite agony of waiting, is unleashed. And with it comes pounding applause. The woman in the next seat murmurs, "Isn't he the sweetest ever?" Another, behind us, sighs, "That's too lovely to be true." His only other contributions to the gayety of the evening are two more songs: "I'll Get By" and "You Are the Girl of My Dreams." But the first fine frenzy is lost. He should have stuck to "I Kiss Your Hand, Madame."

The audience, however, does not slacken in its turbulent enthusiasm. It is enraptured, fanatical. It has been carried up Parnassus on this insinuating, wooing voice. He is their darling, their Song Lover. He is the best yet. Rudy Valentino wasn't in it.[28] The dead are forgotten, anyhow. Nobody's in it. Give us Rudy Vallée. Give us this tall, slender, simple boy, with his blond, wavy hair, his tanned face, his blue eyes and his gentle voice that makes love so democratically to everyone. He is, indeed, the best yet!

It has been reported that, in one of his revues, Rudy appeared nattily clad in a white linen suit, in splendid solitude against black velvet backdrops. Stealing John Barrymore's thunder, neatly. And when he stepped forth, so young, so beautiful, so calm, the house trembled with the ecstasy of his worshippers. A New York department store, which indiscreetly advertised a sale of Vallée records, quivered and shook, tottering on its foundations, so great a stampede was caused by Rudy's luring, if only mechanical, voice. John Wanamaker's [department store] invited Rudy in to sing one morning at ten-thirty—a forlorn hour, at best. The crowd which surged in to hear, see, and clamor its devotion made the fall gatherings, in the Yale Bowl, seem a wistful handful. All the city papers—and especially the ubiquitous *Daily Mirror*—have paid their compliments, or snarled, in the direction of Mr. Vallée. One cannot ignore such a fervently acclaimed personage. And finally, *Vanity Fair*—that Salute to Success— in its current issue, runs a full-page picture of Rudy, megaphone at mouth, saxophone at side. (For, of course, he plays the saxophone. So many people do.) This photograph portrays our hero in a mood both Byronic and relaxed. The old-style jazz singer, the speed maniac of St. Vitus movements, has passed on to a better world. Rudy Vallée sets another fashion: tasteful simplicity in dress— consider the blatant chequered habits of our former vaudeville hits—dignity, and blond youthfulness. It is not to wonder, particularly. After all, we have been overfed on sleek, dark movie villains who turned out to be, to our growing disgust, heroes in the end. And perhaps Colonel Lindbergh unwittingly started the vogue of men with Nordic physiognomies.

The only surprise in this human cyclone of success is his speaking voice and choice of words. His audiences in Brooklyn are not the "cultured minority." Professors, philanthropists, artists, and philosophers do not gather in that ugly theater at Flatbush and DeKalb Avenues. Rudy's followers are just a movie audience. And to them Rudy Vallée, in a carefully modulated, well-bred voice, announces that the next act is an acrobatic stunt arranged by some Germans "whose dexterity and skill I am sure you will find worthy of admiration"—or words to that academic effect. It doesn't look so startling on paper, but it fair bowls you over in the Brooklyn Paramount Theater.

What can be the reason for Rudy Vallée's meteoric rise? Is it subconscious nationalism on the part of thousands of women? For Rudy is undoubtedly the personification of Clean Young American Manhood. Is it due to the much-vaunted American energy? Do we revel in burning up our cells on hero-worship? But if that were the cause for Mr. Vallée's popularity, why did New York, to say nothing of the innumerable radio owners throughout our lovely land, decide to pin their passionate affection on Rudy rather than on someone else? Is Rudy's voice the key to the riddle? It might be, because it is a respectable voice, and it is a relief to have a man sing like a human being and not like an hydraulic drill. Perhaps the secret lies in the Vallée type of beauty, which reminds one of the Lifebuoy Soap advertisements, or the Sloan's Liniment pictures in their better moments. That too is possible, but radio audiences cannot see their hero's face. No. It would seem that American women—this has all the drawbacks of any generalization—want a beau. Their husbands are busy earning the money that sends the ladies to the movies, or buys them radios. The poor men can't be expected to come home from work, hurry through a shower, gussy up in white linens, and start singing in a languid, cajoling way, "I Kiss Your Hand, Madame." They can't be expected to, but the ladies want it, anyhow. And Rudy fills the bill. He is perfect proof of that good old axiom: supply and demand. He is young, he is handsome, and tenderly, coaxingly he sings love-songs to every romance-silly female in these U. S. A. And *that* is that.

109. "Cardinal Denounces Crooners as Whiners Defiling the Air"
New York Times, 11 January 1932, 21

Boston, Jan. 10.—William Cardinal O'Connell took to task radio crooners and pagan plays in an address today before 3,000 men of the Holy Name Society. He styled the crooners "whiners and bleaters defiling the air," and went on:

"I desire to speak earnestly about a degenerate form of singing which is called crooning. No true American would practice this base art."

"I like to use my radio, when weary. But I cannot turn the dials without getting these whiners, crying vapid words to impossible tunes."

"If you will listen closely when you are unfortunate enough to get one of these you will discern the basest appeal to sex emotions in the young. They are not true love songs, they profane the name. They are ribald and revolting to true men."

110. Whitney Bolton, "Mr. Bolton Queries 'When Was a Crooner a Man in Love?'; Applauds Cardinal; Thinks Stand Well Taken"
Morning Telegraph, 12 January 1932, 2

Up Boston way William Cardinal O'Connell, a Prince of the Church in whose pronouncements I always take profound interest and benefit, is revolted by the radio singing of certain young men commonly known as "crooners." In his status as man, prelate and thinker, Cardinal O'Connell finds that from any point of view radio crooning is supremely distasteful. As a man it makes his blood boil, as a prelate it offends his sense of decency and as a thinker it lacerates his usually calm opinions.

Heretofore there have been sporadic public attacks upon crooners, as artists and men. Mostly, so firmly entrenched were the boys, they laughed the attacks off and went right on crooning. This time, I fear me, they will have difficult even a wan smile in their brave attempt to pretend that attack doesn't hurt. Cardinal O'Connell, God be good to him, has called them practitioners of "a degenerate form of singing," champions of "a base art," performers of "immoral and imbecile slush" and, if that wasn't enough to hammer their croons into walls of anguish, the good Cardinal let it be known that "Of course, they aren't men." This last likely scald is the one that will send the boys scurrying for cover.

Something to It
It has been the admittedly false custom to attribute certain bullock qualities to our crooners. That is every crooner of advanced fame was believed by vast hordes of frustrated women to be a pretty warm young man. Just why what Cardinal O'Connell calls "whining" should suggest to love-starved women that the crooner is a ravening he-man has never been clear and, being privy to certain items in the private lives of some of the boys, the matter has now reached bewildering proportions. What is it in the soft croon of a radio star that prompts thousands of women to write him for a rendezvous?

Crooning and wenching are curious comrades, neither sensibly nor psychologically to be linked up. The boy genuinely aglow with gender is the boy who either sings not at all or else does his singing in a voice neatly combined between a rusty foghorn and a moose call trumpet. There is no choice therefore but to align with Cardinal O'Connell and inquire "What's all the crooning about?"

Naturally the boys will have to make a reply to this attack. In simple defense, they must stand right up and cry aloud that it isn't so. They must assert their manhood, deliver themselves of the stain of immortality and rid themselves of the implication that what they sing is both imbecile and slush. The last count on the Cardinal's strong indictment will be more difficult to expunge than the counts involving gelding tendencies and vice.

Songs Nonsensical

Has anyone, excerpt Cardinal O'Connell, myself and a man in Great Neck [New York] who doesn't like radios at all, has any one except us three ever sat down and analyzed the verse and chorus of the typical crooner's song? It is a sad, frustrated, unhealthy, slightly maniacal and certainly vertiginous combination of words, mostly directed toward two themes: he needs her and will have her, even though she has given herself to another; he is overwhelmed by love because it is deep night and the bats are flying. Neither theme makes sense.

I applaud Cardinal O'Connell for the vigor, soundness and decency of his righteous complaints. And, lest he be running out of solid support for his theories, let me volunteer a case note for the records: A certain crooner of no small stature in his little world recently met a personable and intelligent young woman. The next morning, his voice betraying his confidence that she was pining for him, he telephoned her. She hung up on him promptly, wanting none or any part of him or his songs. Ten minutes later he telephoned again and this time just sang to her. She hung up again. Three times he did this and finally she broke in and, with profanity which under the circumstances I believe the Cardinal will forgive, she told him she hated crooners, detested their songs, miraculous as it might seem, she detested this particular crooner and closed with the suggestion that he shoot himself and rid a long-suffering world of a malignant pest. The poor fellow was so astonished by the rebuff that he fainted.

That, sir, proves your excellent points.

111. "Crooners Cover Up; Pass Well Known Buck"

Morning Telegraph, 13 January 1932, 2

Our better crooners were lifted right back on their eyebrows by Cardinal O'Connell's churchman-like comment that "crooning is a degenerate, low-down sort of interpretation of love." Tracked down at their varied activities, some of them came up with statements of self-defense.

As most of the nation's prominent ballad warblers belong to the same church as Cardinal O'Connell, they were polite and restrained in their answers. But they made it evident that they will defend crooning to the last gurgle—that surely the Cardinal must mean "scat singers" instead of crooners.

A scat singer is one who inserts "hi-de-hi-de-ho" and "trickeration" into his red-hot renditions. Crooners look upon scat singing with elevated brows, just as scat singers are inclined to think crooning is effeminate.

No Crooner on Air

Strangely enough, officials of the two national broadcasting firms looked over their respective payrolls today after reading the Cardinal's criticism and found that they haven't a single crooner in their employ. They use a different designation for that type of artist known in theatrical circles as a "slob singer."

Rudy Vallée, popularly credited with having invented crooning, had little to say about Cardinal O'Connell's description of his art.

"I don't want to get into any controversy with the Cardinal," said the wavy-haired Rudy. "I'll leave it to the public to decide."

"The Cardinal evidently doesn't understand the problems of radio. The soft voice registers much better than the harsh voice. Radio crooners have adapted themselves to that requirement. It ought not to be a sin for a man to seek technical perfection."

Russ Columbo, more recent addition to the ranks of crooning, also thinks Cardinal O'Connell is unjust.[29]

"Why," said the handsome Russ, "crooning is absolutely the original form of singing. Mothers from time immemorial have crooned to their babes, and nothing is sweeter than that."

Vin for Cardinal

Vincent Lopez, orchestra leader who always has a crooner in his band, is inclined to see the Cardinal's side of the matter.

"Crooning," said Lopez, "never has seemed to me to be an adequate form of singing, and I can understand why the Cardinal finds it inartistic."

"I do not believe crooning is purposely vulgar, but it is an insinuating form of song presentation, utterly devoid of cultural aspects."

Morton Downey, approached just as he was preparing to sing for radio audiences in seven European countries, barked: "Don't you call me a crooner or I'll put the sock on ya."[30] Kate Smith likewise denied affiliation with the crooner school and declined to make a statement.[31]

112. "Crooning Comes by Nature" [editorial]
New York Times, 24 February 1932, 20

When Cardinal O'Connell called the crooning of the most popular radio entertainers "a degenerate form of singing," he won the hearts of all admirers of the trained voice. There is no organization of audiences for good singing to congratulate him on his statement, but one group has come out with an endorsement for him. The New York Singing Teachers' Association joins him in condemning the half-suppressed, muffled voices of crooners who daily soothe millions of listeners. It has more reason than most of us could summon for disliking them, for they need no teaching. They sing like that because they can't help it. When they step up to the microphone, throw their heads back, thus tightening the throat muscles in the most disapproved fashion, open their lips ever so little and murmur the sweet nothings of popular love songs, they enchant a multitude of radio fans. It sounds natural to them, simple, untrained, nothing highbrow about it—"just folks."

This is a sad time to speak severely to the crooners. Their style of singing is beginning to go out of fashion. Some of them are already showing that they know it by attempting the newer fad. No one knows how these things get started, though there are always a few who claim the honor. But once started, the fashion of the moment speedily becomes obsolete. For a time the "boop-a-doop" type of song enjoyed the highest favor. "Vo-deo-do" singing pushed it off the radio map. Then came the crooners. Now they are being driven away by the boys and girls who intersperse the vapid lines of the chorus with a medley of monotonous, meaningless syllables which defy print. These interpolations sound as if the singer had forgotten the words of the ditty and had to fill in with a tra-la. Sometimes they vary it with a whistled bar or two. They have undoubtedly caught on, as the most recent hit of the musical comedy stage has its hero imitating their manner.

Except as it relieves their feelings, reproving crooners is futile for singing teachers or any one else. Crooners will soon go the way of tandem bicycles, mahjong and midget golf.

Radio behind the Scenes

Getting on the Air

113. James H. Collins, "How to Get on a Radio Program"
Popular Radio, February 1925, 109–17

How can you get on the radio program?

The simplest thing in the world, Brother—or Sister. All you need is "the goods." And latchstrings hang out at practically every broadcasting station—every one that I have been able to investigate among the hundreds scattered over the United States. And it isn't necessary to go to a great musical center like New York or Chicago if you happen to live in what theatrical people call "the sticks," because there are opportunities at your local station, and if you make a place for yourself on the program, your performance will travel far.

How must you go about getting on the radio program—call at the station personally or apply by letter?

What sort of performers are the broadcasting directors looking for?

What are the restrictions—what is taboo?

Are any tests or rehearsals necessary?

Are performers paid by the station—or must the performer pay to appear? Hundreds of inquiries like this come to the editor of *Popular Radio* from musicians, singers, lecturers and other artists—including press agents, who are certainly artists in their line.

"Write an article and answer them," directed the editor.

So I put on my hat and went out to call upon the folks who directed the programs at the big stations in and around New York.

Are you an artist with "temperament," sensitively shrinking from contact with uncomprehending businessmen? Do you hesitate about offering your talent because you think the programs are directed by engineers and electricians?

Know then, right at the start, that you will deal with fellow artists, because most of the program directors are musicians, in many cases professionals. More than one regularly steps into his own program to fill gaps. There has been an influx of artists and their agents from the phonograph field, particularly, into radio.

You can start things with a letter, or by calling upon a program director himself. Many artists telephone—a good way, too. And the response will be not only cordial but in most cases you get the feeling that the director or his assistants have been expecting to hear from you and are sincerely anxious—even eager—to find out whether you have them there same "goods!"

"What! I thought the broadcasting stations had waiting lists with hundreds of artists, and were turning thousands away!" you may say.

Yep—that's right. But they're not turning away anybody with the goods! Many apply, but not so many qualify by demonstrating program ability. For radio gives opportunity to thousands of amateur performers and students who are not yet able to land paid engagements, and who may never be able to do so, and naturally many of them must study and practice further to make their place on the programs. But the demand for radio talent is so great that anybody with ability is certain to get a hearing.

"What tests or rehearsals are required of the artist?" I asked directors in and around New York, and also fired a volley of questions at some of the distant stations. We will imagine that a composite program director is answering for all of them, because, while the requirements differ at various stations, the same general trend is found in all.

"We ask a few questions about the applicant's artistic experience," said this imaginary director, "and if it is satisfactory and the inquiry has been made by letter or telephone he is invited to come in for a hearing. He sings, plays, or speaks into a live microphone under distance conditions, and the director not only determines the quality of his performance, but finds out where to place him with relation to the microphone and the accompanist. Rehearsals before a dead microphone may follow, so the artist who has demonstrated program quality may grow accustomed to broadcasting conditions. If the applicant is a speaker, most stations require the submission of a typewritten copy of his talk beforehand, and read it in order to be certain that there are no objectionable features. If his talk is technical—say something like popular science or every day health hints that take a medical slant—it may be submitted to authorities in that particular field, who pass upon its accuracy and the professional standing of the speaker. A well-known speaker, however, will usually be given his head, because upon that same head, not the station, will fall any criticism aroused by his talk.

"If a singer or an instrumentalist is well known, tests and rehearsals are usually not required, but we advise him or her to take them. For example, imagine our joyous feeling if an artist like [operatic soprano Amelita] Galli-Curci telephoned in and expressed a desire to sing from our station! We'd put her on the program immediately, before she changed her mind, and require no preliminary hearing. But even an artist of her standing, singing in the microphone for the first time, would gain by a rehearsal beforehand, and by the director's suggestions. As a matter of fact, when Galli-Curci made her first phonograph records she was so concerned with the artistic shortcomings apparent to her own ear that she made a profound study of the phonograph as a medium and mastered it, and it is characteristic of great artists that they study the technical requirements of radio beforehand and practice to master the microphone. [Silent film stars] Mary Pickford and Douglas Fairbanks had a microphone installed in their hotel room several days before talking by radio the first time."

"What kind of program numbers are you looking for?"

"Why, look over the programs for a week and use your imagination!" said the director. "We want good soloists and ensembles, vocal and instrumental, education talks, household suggestions, children's entertainment, symphony and dance orchestras, monologues, organ recitals—there's absolutely no limit if the entertainment can be broadcast. The theatrical manager makes up his vaudeville or moving picture program for a week, and it is repeated several times a day for seven days. But the radio program director gives about fifty hours of entertainment weekly, never repeating a number, so he wants quantity and variety as well as quality. Entertainment must come up to the standard of the station. That standard is high, and constantly growing higher. And he welcomes good novelties, numbers with a really original idea. One of the big eastern stations has a radio gymnasium class at seven every morning, with an instructor and music. That was a real idea. Another eastern station has a children's hour from nine to ten every Sunday morning, with clowns, and talks by comic-strip artists and characters—it is an advertising feature for a string of newspapers, but it was a real idea."

"Some of the radio critics complain that there are too many soprano and baritone soloists on the air."

"They do outnumber other artists—and yet we do not find too many good ones! Some directors think there are too many soloists of all kinds, and are making up their programs with vocal and instrumental ensembles, orchestra numbers, talks and other material."

"The radio critics are ridiculing the instructive talk too—will that be eliminated as well?"

"We like criticism. Sometimes it cuts pretty deep, but it keeps us on our toes.

"A good many of the radio speakers have been dull because they talk on business or technical subjects, and are not practiced speakers. If the talk was about banking or life insurance, we got somebody who was an authority in his line, and his speaking ability came second. Then, there has been considerable publicity seeking in such talks—the expert telling the radio public how to simplify its income tax return, probably turned out to be a professional accountant who sought income tax clients in that way. But look over the good programs and you will see that these numbers are decreasing, and the radio critics have nothing but praise for the kind of talks we are broadcasting nowadays. Instead of going to the First National Bank for a speaker, we go to the Zoo, or Aquarium, or the Museum of Natural History, or Art Institute, and get specialists who can talk entertainingly about head hunters, gorillas, white Indians, or Egyptian tombs. And we are right on the heels of the man or woman who has done something to get into the day's news—a man like Lieutenant Maugham who eats breakfast in New York and supper in San Francisco, keeping pace with the sun in his airplane."[32]

"I hear that good humorous numbers are very scarce."

"That's true, for the reason that good humorous phonograph records are scarce. Some stations broadcast vaudeville numbers direct from the stage. In vaudeville, funny acts are plentiful, but few get over on the air, because the fun must be seen as well as heard. Drop the curtain between the vaudeville audience and the stage, and give your funny act, and see how many laughs you get, and you will understand the difficulties in the way of radio humor. We have just a little more flexibility than the phonograph records, because our acts can be longer. A ten-inch phonograph record plays between three and three and a half minutes—just long enough to cook a soft-boiled egg. In that short time the humorist must raise twenty or thirty laughs. We can give him more time, and a little more scope for his personality, but he must still work through the single sense of hearing. That's why good radio humor is scarce. It is also hard to get clean high-class humor—so much of it is of the slapstick kind, and borders on the vulgar."

"That brings up the question of what is taboo."

"For the speaker, everything likely to arouse religious or political controversy, offend good taste, be unfit for children to hear or not in keeping with the character we maintain for the station. Among the speakers, too, anything in the nature of concealed advertising—paid publicity agents are constantly trying to use our facilities for their own ends, and we also have the enthusiast anxious to speak by radio for his particular cause or movement. The world is full of propaganda and controversy, but we manage to eliminate it by requiring speakers to submit a written talk beforehand and holding them to it on the air. In music, we put the ban on suggestive songs, as well as compositions not up to a certain artistic standard. Also certain compositions that are rather overdone by radio artists. We'd be glad to have John McCormack sing "Mother Machree," or [pianist/composer Sergei] Rachmaninoff play his famous "Prelude," but when the unknown artist makes such frequently played compositions prominent on his or her program, we advise other selections for the sake of variety—and it may be that the unknown artist will play something else better."

He had other, practical suggestions to make to people ambitious to get on the air—little sidelights growing out of his program experience.

For instance, it occurred to me that if sopranos and baritones are too abundant, and solo numbers are becoming unpopular, that the superfluous baritone and soprano might join hands with a contralto and a basso, forming a vocal quartette. The director said that would be fine from his standpoint, but if you look at it as an artist—not so good. One poor singer in a quartette would spoil three good voices. Or a good soprano might get into bad company all around, the other three singers being poor. Then, even if all four were good, it takes months of practice to create ensemble quality, either vocal or instrumental. When they have it, the directors welcome them, but creating this quality is strictly the artists' risk, and can be attained only by careful selection of fellow artists and many months of practice together.

He said some interesting things about music teachers on the radio program. The individual instructor, vocal and instrumental, as well as the school and conservatory director, quickly saw the advertising possibilities in radio and are among the applicants.

He doesn't care a cat whisker whether you are a teacher or not, nor worry about any possible advertising you may get by a radio appearance. It is what you can do as an artist that he considers. Not every teacher, however capable, is also an artist. Many of the successful radio artists are also teachers, as that is a secondary occupation. Music teachers figure on the radio program in another way—they may not be artists themselves, but they seek a hearing for pupils who, if successful in getting on the program, give the teacher indirect advertising. Especially if the pupil is a child prodigy. There was a regular epidemic of child pianists violinists and other marvels in New York about a year ago, but they are not now so often on the air. The radio public grew tired of prodigies. Making an actual appearance, their childish "cuteness" helps out musical ability, but on the air something is lacking. However, the good child prodigy is still welcome. Musical schools and conservatories frequently give pupils' programs lasting an hour or more, but these are being carefully restricted to institutions whose pupils really have ability, the publicity-seeking school being eliminated.

So far as I have been able to find out, no broadcasting station in the country—and that includes Canada—pays the artist or makes any charge. Some stations pay orchestras that play regularly, just as they pay their regular accompanists, announcers and other employees, but the artist's performance is voluntary. One great eastern station charges ten dollars a minute for the broadcasting of publicity talks and acts, but the artists in this case are engaged on salary by the business concern doing such advertising, and are usually well-paid professional performers, because, unless the advertising stunt is entertaining in itself, people tune out and listen to something else. This station has many more numbers by volunteer artists on its programs, and they are, of course, charged nothing for their appearance.

"Then what does the artist get out of it?" I asked, finally. "At last accounts, there were more than five hundred commercial broadcasting stations throughout the country, and the programs more than half volunteer numbers—talks, instrumental recitals, vocal recitals, reading, bedtime stories, lectures, sports talks and the like. Allow only five volunteer numbers on the daily program of each station, and count them all as soloists—no duets, quartettes or ensembles. Between fifteen thousand and twenty thousand performers at least, are appearing weekly, the programs are constantly changing, and there is a waiting list. What is there in it for the artist?"

First, publicity that makes reputation and leads to paid engagements or permanent positions.

It is a common experience for artists to receive letters offering engagements at home musicales, club and lodge entertainments, as well as opportunity to become stage professionals. Something in the performer's ability or personality makes an impression on the "cash customer" in the ether, and it often happens that a telephone call offering an engagement comes in before the performer leaves the studio. The dance orchestra is hired for dances, the organist gets a movie position, the monologist is invited to a phonograph tryout. Wonderful things are happening in American music nowadays. Fifteen years ago, exceptional talent and hard study might land the musician in a narrow professional field. There were opera, recitals, orchestra and chorus, and that was about all. The native artist suffered under the handicap of being an American. If the world of professional music was not controlled by foreigners, the snobbish American musical public, made up of highbrows, looked down upon native talent. Besides ability and work, the artist needed money to pay managers and agents, and for advertising in the musical press which was pretty close to blackmail.

The moving pictures changed all that. There are at least ten thousand picture theaters in the United States that employ artists, and the demand is so great that even the amateur may secure paid engagements while he or she is studying. No agents, critics or other interlopers stand in the way—the moving-picture manager's door is open to anyone who wishes to ask for a tryout. And now, on top of these new opportunities, comes radio, offering a greater audience, a hearing and a chance to make a reputation. No more highbrow prejudice to be overcome, and no traveling to a few big cities where the world of music centers. The radio audience is "just folks," it is everywhere, and the broadcasting station and the opportunity may be right around the corner, even if the aspiring artist lives a thousand miles from New York, Chicago, or San Francisco.

Besides the publicity of the ether, radio artists get that of the printed word. When the program director accepts you after the tryout, he hands you a blank to be filled out for the publicity department. You tell who you have studied with, where you have performed before, what musical organizations you belong to, and so on, also listing the selections to be broadcast, with the time required for each number. This is turned in with a photograph of yourself, and the publicity department sends press notices to the newspapers. Even if none of the "write-ups" are published, your name will appear in printed programs published by several hundred papers for a local station, and several thousand for one of the big stations. If you perform at a station operated by newspaper—and there are more than half a hundred of them—the publicity generally runs several days, with a preliminary notice the day before you appear, a picture and sketch on "the day," and a review the day after. It may also be your luck to have one of the "columnists" praise your performance. And if enough listeners write in, the program director will invite you to appear again and again—many popular artists become fixtures on the programs.

It may be that you care nothing for paid engagements or a professional career. Very well—but how about reputation or social prestige? Many amateur artists who have sung or played only for friends, find through the radio program a new circle of friends running into the millions, and to be known and appreciated is their kind of reward. Finally, there is the incentive of doing something for the cause of music. When Theodore Thomas and Dr. Leopold Damrosch were struggling to establish symphony orchestras in the United States, less than fifty years ago, they had to sweeten their programs with "popular" numbers.[33] Real musical appreciation in America was limited to a few cities with German colonies. Gradually the symphony orchestra created its public until today there are good orchestras in most of our large cities. The phonograph and player piano created a wider public for good music, and the moving-picture theater helped further. Radio is reaching out still more widely. Eventually, it will reach everybody. But, for the present, its most interesting developments are found in the local stations. Again and again, the past three or four years, a new station has been opened in some community far from the big musical centers. In the beginning, the program director had a hard job. It was necessary to hunt for performers and urge them to appear, and the programs were often pretty thin in quality and length. But before long the director had a waiting list, because radio creates artists just as it creates appreciative listeners, and as the latter develop in musical taste, so the station's artists develop in ability and new ones appear.

Getting on to the radio program is, therefore, getting into the greatest of all musical and educational movements.

114. Audition form, National Broadcasting Company, c. 1930

National Broadcasting Company Archive, box 2, folder 82,
Wisconsin Historical Society, Madison[34]

AUDITION

    Name
    Address
    Telephone
    Type of Artist

_____

    Introduced by
    Rating

_____

APPOINTMENT FOR AUDITION:

    Date   Hour
    Heard by
    Intonation

Quality

Diction

Technique

Appearance

Personality

Musicianship

Remarks

Please describe fully your experience in the following lines, stating <u>when</u> and <u>where</u> you have appeared:

Vaudeville

Musical Comedy

Dramatics

Do you dance?

Concert

Opera

Church

What full Operatic Roles do you know?

Radio?

Have you had a Movie-Tone Test?[35]

If so, when and where?

Height   Weight   Blonde or Brunette

Date of birth

Professional experience note covered above may be listed here.

115. Olive Palmer, "Requirements of the Radio Singer"

Etude, December 1931, 849–50[36]

So many letters are sent to me from singers and students wanting to know about "radio technic," "radio voice," "how to break into radio," "how to sing a song over the radio" and the various other details of the radio artist's work that I am glad to take this opportunity through the pages of *The Etude* of answering some of these questions.

First I should like to say something about the possibilities of radio and incidentally tell about my own background and training for the work. When I first began singing over the radio—and I was one of the pioneers—I did not realize what a gigantic development it was to become, affecting literally the lives of all of us. In its first stages radio was considered by the majority of people as merely a fad. Serious artists would have nothing to do with it. But gradually, as the means of transmission improved, they were won over one by one until now there is hardly a famous singer or instrumentalist who has not made a radio debut. The quality of music has improved constantly. Radio has made it possible for literally millions of people to hear good music capably performed. As a result the people are becoming more and more discriminating in their tastes. This is quite apparent to me, comparing the letters I first received with those I get today.

The Stirring Lion

Radio is awakening slumbering desires in people, desires to know more about music, desires to learn to play and sing. It will eventually bring about a musical renaissance in this country. With television coming on, we shall probably develop a characteristic type of American opera. This unseen force will bring to light new talent and will provide an increasing opportunity for the American singer. I feel this way about radio since I have watched its development from the inside. Now as for some of my own preparation and training for the work.

I have sung at the least provocation ever since I was five and a half years old. At a Sunday School entertainment at the Fourth Avenue Methodist Church of Louisville, Kentucky, I first appeared in public. I sang a little song, using what I thought to be appropriate gestures and acquitting myself to my own satisfaction, at least, although to the disgust of my older brother. He thought I was "putting on" and said so in no uncertain terms.

Piano lessons were among my first studies; I have always been glad my mother insisted on these. It is such an advantage for a singer to be able to play the piano. Later when we moved to Des Moines, Iowa, I attended Drake University with its Conservatory of Music. I found plenty to do as president of the Girls' Glee Club, taking part in musical shows, acting as soloist in the University Church of Christ and carrying the prescribed work of the conservatory. After graduation I went abroad to study further and acquire operatic experience.

A Telephone Audition

One day, after I had returned home, I read in the paper that William Wade Hinshaw was planning to revive twenty operas in New York.[37] This news seemed to spell opportunity to me. If I could only see Mr. Hinshaw! Then a happy thought occurred. I would telephone him over long distance. So a call was put through. After a time Mr. Hinshaw was located, and I became quite excited when I heard his voice coming over the intervening miles. But my hopes were soon dashed when he said that his casts were all full and that there was no use in my coming to New York. I felt my opportunity slipping away, and I did so want to sing for him. Since there was no other way I asked him if he would not listen to me sing over the telephone. He could not well refuse since I was paying the bill; so I launched into the "Bell Song" from [Léo Delibes's 1883 opera] *Lakmé*. I waited breathlessly after I had finished, and finally a quiet voice came back.

"Get the first train you can for New York."

I was simply overcome with joy. My career had really begun in this country. Then followed opera, concert singing and the making of phonograph records. Someone once asked me in the phonograph recording studio why I did not try the newest medium of sound transmission, the radio, since I had all the qualifications. I did, and have been appearing "on the air" ever since. I give this brief recital of my own experiences since many letters inquire how I "got a start."

The "Radio Voice"

Now as to some of the requirements of the radio singer. There have been many misconceptions regarding singing over the radio. We frequently hear such terms as "radio technic," or a "good radio voice," phrases seeming to imply that the microphone requires special vocal qualifications. In fact, many people thinking to pay me a compliment say, "You have a perfect radio voice."

These misconceptions are no doubt due to the fact that it is possible to "fake," as we call it, over the radio. One may get close to the microphone and sing so softly that it is barely audible in the studio. This singing is then mechanically swelled out to the desired volume. Crooning, however, is possible only over the radio or through a megaphone and has no doubt given rise to the idea of a special radio voice. But the crooner would not be heard ten feet in an auditorium. And I have it from my teacher, Douglas Stanley, who has spent ten years in research on voice production and transmission, that crooning, if persisted in, will eventually ruin the voice since it constricts and closes the throat and puts the muscles of the neck in tension.

In reality, any voice that is properly produced and of good quality is a good radio voice. Singing that is broadcast need not be different from that heard in concert or opera. In fact, it should have all the color, contrast and expression of the concert singer. The radio is capable of transmitting a high percentage of tone that is swelled from soft to loud. Swelling out on a tone is one of the thrilling things about singing anyway. But the crooner sings only on a dead level.

Broadcasting Technic

While, as intimated, there is no particular radio voice except that of the crooner, there are features about broadcasting which might be considered individual to it. It is well for the aspirant to understand these.

A singer, for instance, may be a huge success in concert or opera and be a decided failure over the radio. In fact, the singer accustomed to a visible audience finds all the little accouterments of her art shorn from her when she steps before the microphone. In the first place, there is no visible audience to provide the inevitable stimulus. There are no pretty dresses, smiles, gestures, facial expressions—all those concomitants which go to make up personal charm and magnetism. The singer must get down to the bare fundamentals of tone, and this, after all, is far from easy. Tone is of the greatest importance to the microphone which picks up all imperfections in the voice with disconcerting accuracy and seemingly magnifies them.

I am frequently asked whether it is possible to project personality through the voice alone. I suppose it depends on the individual. I do know that the test of a radio singer is whether he can convey to others through the voice what he feels. A tear, for instance, must carry over to the unseen listener, or else the song is ineffective. A smile, a bit of whimsy, of rollicking good humor, longing, tenderness, a caress—all these and many more must register on the listener through the ear solely. The singer simply stands quietly before the microphone and offers up his song to the world at large. There is very little glamour attached, and some singers find the medium decidedly ungrateful.

The Near Audience

A well-known opera and concert singer once confessed to me that her first appearance on the air was a perfect nightmare. "It was all so cold!" she said. "I missed the audience which always warms a singer. Before my first number was over, I was covered with perspiration and felt that I was doing rather miserably. Between numbers I pulled myself together and decided that I must use my imagination. I had not considered the microphone as a person but as a mechanical contrivance. I must think of it as a person to whom I am singing, and it is really the composite person of some millions of listeners, I even called up a picture of some friends whom I knew to be listening in and decided to sing to them. This made a wonderful difference in my next number. All the warmth returned to my voice. I felt it and I know my unseen audience felt it. After that I always considered the microphone as a person and not a machine."

In our weekly broadcasts the presence of an audience in the studio, numbering some three hundred, gives a more personal touch. In fact, the audience is there chiefly for that reason. We do not sing to them, however, but to the auditors who are unseen. Personally I can feel the presence of this vast unseen audience and find singing for them quite thrilling. Radio singing demands the very best an artist has to give.

The Motley Throne

Then, too, singing for literally everybody brings with it a heavy responsibility in the selection of songs. The people who come to a hall to hear a concert singer usually have fairly well-defined tastes, and making a program for such an audience is not so difficult. The radio artist, however, singing to a cross section of humanity, finds it necessary to choose selections to please the majority. For the response of the listeners is evidenced by the letters they send. They are the final arbiter of whether the radio singer succeeds or fails. The letters — or the lack of them — tell the tale.

For my own presentation over the *Palmolive Hour*, I choose three solos each week, and it is a problem, since I am allowed only two repeats a year. Quite often I am guided by requests which come in letters. My selections are made up of operatic arias, new songs, old songs "everybody knows," selections from light opera. I have noticed a gradual improvement in taste. People are requesting more operatic arias than formerly because they are beginning to know them. They like particularly songs with considerable opportunity for coloratura. They also like the familiar songs, the melodic numbers that will never grow old.

Preparation and Rehearsal

Perhaps you would like to know how a broadcast such as the *Palmolive Hour* is prepared and rehearsed. The average person has little conception of the great amount of work necessary to present one of these hours.

First I submit the three solos I have selected to the program department well in advance so that, if orchestrations are necessary, they can be made. A considerable staff is required to make these orchestrations. Then permission must be secured from the copyright owners. On a recent occasion this was not secured, and at the very last minute I had to sing some other numbers without rehearsal. The program is then laid out in its entirety. There follow several rehearsals with piano. The radio performer must calculate very closely with Father Time. A large-faced clock is usually in evidence. While you are singing a staff member may appear and hold up one or two fingers indicating how many minutes to go. So the first rehearsals are measured for time limits. On the night of the broadcast there is a rehearsal from 6–8 p.m., with orchestra, before the microphone. After which I rush home, grab a bite to eat, dress and rush back to the studio by 9:30 for the broadcast. The long rehearsal is held on the night of the broadcast because then the program will be fresh and more apt to go as intended.

Broad Musicianship

Speaking of rehearsals, they are an important consideration to anyone who would broadcast. A rehearsal with a large body of musicians is expensive. So rehearsals are held to a minimum and made only as long as is absolutely necessary in covering the ground. This means that the radio singer must have qualities of musicianship as well as those of voice. He must be able to read almost anything at sight. In ensemble work he must be particularly apt. The question of musicianship is a stumbling block to many singers. They think a lovely voice is all that is needed, whereas it is but one of the requirements. The radio singer may be called upon to take a part at a moment's notice in an ensemble, say, to rehearse the part in the afternoon and broadcast it in the evening. A director has no time to stop a costly rehearsal and correct a singer who stumbles over time or notes. Such a singer is soon eliminated no matter how excellent the voice may be. A solid musical training is well nigh essential.

In addition the singer should have the gift of song—that is, song should be the natural means of expression. Perfect pitch is of next importance.[38] In a vocal duet, if one of the singers is off pitch, blasting results. Then comes the control of color in a musical phrase. The color determines the expression. And, lastly, comes articulation, since upon this depends whether the auditors will understand the words.

Blasting

Undoubtedly the one greatest fault of radio singers is overloading the microphone, which causes blasting. Nine out of ten of those who seek auditions blast and are therefore quickly eliminated. There is a common misconception about blasting to the effect that volume, particularly on high notes, causes it. That is one reason we have so much soft singing. But I have found that a high note properly produced will not blast no matter how much volume is used, whereby a shrill note will do it invariably. It is seldom possible to overload the microphone in the lower register, but there is always that possibility in the high register unless the tone is clear cut and resonant. There are tricks to avoid blasting such as moving back from the microphone, turning away and others, but I never resort to them. I stand about arm's length from the microphone, remain in that position and sing just as I would on the concert stage.

A plan which I have found helpful is to finish on the last note with the orchestra. In concert, if the singer finishes first, he at least retains his position on the stage until the accompaniment ceases. But, in radio, if the singer finishes first, he is rather ruthlessly blotted out of the picture. So I try and hold on wherever possible.

The radio aspirant would do well to acquire some experience at one of the smaller stations before applying to the larger ones. There are a number of small stations scattered throughout the country, which at least offer a good opportunity of becoming acquainted with the microphone. Then, if the singer feels sufficiently prepared, he might try one of the larger stations.

To Obtain an Audition

A letter requesting an audition, stating qualifications and so forth, is the first step. The audition granted, a time is set and the aspirant comes to the studio with an accompanist and a few songs of his own choosing for a microphone test. This is much like a screen test in the motion pictures, the idea here being to see how well the voice "comes over." It is well to bring songs to the audition with which one is thoroughly familiar, and it is far better to sing a simple song and do it well than to choose a difficult operatic aria which lies a little out of bounds. The candidate then sings into the microphone while the judges hear the result in another room. If there is blasting, the candidate is counted "out" at once.

But, if the first test is promising, another is given in sight reading. If this one is passed satisfactorily the singer is put on the payroll and is subject to call at any time. While the pay is not large at first, it is adequate. The big point is that the doors of opportunity are thereby thrown open.

It is frequently said that only those with "pull" are accepted on the big chains [networks]. I have never found that to be the case. I do not know of any of the radio stars today who got their opportunity through "pull." In fact, many of them simply wandered into the studio unknown and took their audition as anyone would. If a singer did get in by "pull" he would not hold his place long unless he made a success with the public. For the public is always the final court of appeal.

116. Myda Adams, letter to John Royal, program director, National Broadcasting Company, 11 January 1932

National Broadcasting Company Archive, box 6, folder 38,
Wisconsin Historical Society, Madison

[The following was handwritten on stationery from the Hotel Lincoln, New York City.]

Jan 11/32
Mr John Royal
National Broadcasting Co.
Dear Sir:—For quite some time I have been trying to get in communication with some one over in your offices who might enlighten me in regard to an audition for your studio.

Perhaps I had better tell you I am a blues singer, have done some very nice things in clubs and theaters, and also have sung over numerous stations outside of New York. Right now I am very interested in Radio work and would like an opportunity to sing for you or who ever has charge of your auditions.

I would appreciate it greatly if you would be so kind as to answer me on this for I know I have the type of voice that is seemingly in demand at the present time.

I hope you will not think me to bold in writing you, but I have tried so many other ways, so I thought Id take another chance
Thanking you, I am Very Truly Yours
Miss Myda Adams
Lincoln Hotel

117. "Have You a Radio Voice?" [advertisement]

Radio Guide, 28 January 1932, 9

Have you ever wanted to enter radio work? Do you think you have that spark of genius that can win you fame and fortune as a broadcast star? Here's your opportunity.

Radio Guide, in conjunction with the local broadcasting stations given below, will give you the opportunity to take a microphone test, and, if your talent warrants it, at least one broadcast.

This is not a contest; it is a search for new radio talent.

Everyone is eligible, provided only that he or she has never broadcast before. Singers, instrumentalists, soloists, duos, trios, and so on up to chorus groups and orchestras—any sort of talent—all is welcome.

The only stipulations are that singers must bring their own accompanists; artists must bring their own music and instruments (except pianos); there will be no studio rehearsals, and your act must be timed to exactly four minutes.

If you want a chance at a real radio tryout, write to "Radio Auditions," RADIO GUIDE, 475 Fifth Avenue, N.Y. State briefly what you do, and give your reason for feeling that you should be among the first to have a real studio tryout. Then watch this paper to see when and where you are scheduled to appear for your audition.

Station officials (who will be the only judges) will listen in at the monitors, and those applicants that pass the exacting tests will be notified by mail when they may appear for a broadcast.

Please do not write to this paper or to station officials, after your application has been sent in. Necessary arrangements will naturally take time, and needless delay to you and other applicants must result from unnecessary correspondence.

WRNY [New York City] and WOV [New York City] are cooperating with *Radio Guide* in this series of tests.

Talent

118. Harvey B. Gaul, "The Vicissitudes of a Radio Impresario"
Wireless Age, September 1922, 53

If your nerves can stand it, being a radio impresario is one of the greatest little indoor sports of the day. First, wireless was invented, and then improved into the radiophone, and no sooner were the glad tidings picked out of the air than every son and daughter of old Adam conceived the idea that a waiting world was clamoring for the sound of his or her voice. Therefore every person who could twang, pick or scrape a string, every person who could touch or pound a keyboard, and anyone at all who was not tongue-tied became possessed of the idea that he must be heard over radio.

Little Wilfred, who recited [Felicia Dorothea Browne Heman's poem] "Casablanca" so dramatically last Friday morning during the assembly exercises writes, "My teacher says I have a big voice and I never skip a word. I would like to recite over the wireless for you."

Youthful Elmer, who is just learning to use the violin bow and is now studying the first position, but who, nevertheless, promises to be the future Fritz Kreisler [violin virtuoso], invites us a note to the effect that he "would like to play the 'Jolly Farmer's Return' over the radio."

Mme. Dufranne-Ducault who (many years ago) once sang an operatic aria, phones in that she "would consent to sing over the wireless" provided we would "give her an exclusive program." She will sing such art works as "Just a Song at Twilight," "At Dawning," and other seldom-heard canzoni.

Happy Hazel, the child wonder of Squirrel Hill, who could play "Chop Sticks" when she was three, and who has had all of one year's tuition at teasing the clavier, has her fond mother write us: "Our little girl is an infant prodigy. She plays the 'Dance of the Toad Stools' in a heavenly manner. We have just installed a radio and would like to hear her."

One woman is the mother of a child preacher, a lad who has stirred thousands to walk in the straight and narrowing path. This lad must be given a chance to convert the nation. Politicians who have a "message" for their constituents want to make "stump speeches" in our studio.

Then, there is Maestro Rudolfo Kzbyck, the Hungarian who plays the Hawaiian guitar better than anyone else in his mining town. He wants to make himself heard.

Emil Dopper, who has played a mouth-organ ever since he was knee-high to a milk bottle, likewise is crazy to prove his prowess.

And so it goes. Everyone who has his little gift is not anxious to hide his talent under a basket, but is most generous in wanting to share it with the world at large—by radio. Even the professional has his and her peculiarities—often the trouble has but begun when a famous artist is placed on a program, whether at her own request or at our suggestion.

Let me catalogue a few of the diversions of this phase of radio program making. Mme. Raznor-Hazlitt, the celebrated cantatrice, is going to sing. Her secretary (who is her husband) phones in that the diva's accompanist is sick and cannot accompany madame. You are regretful, but in order to save a program that has been advertised in 500 newspapers, from Massachusetts to Mexico, you send another accompanist to madame. Two hours later the phone rings and the secretary is sorry to inform you that the famous artiste cannot sing "because the accompanist you sent was not *en rapport* with madame." It makes no difference that the accompanist has played for almost everybody under the sun, she is not *"en rapport"* and as you very well know, if you are not that, life is *nothing!*

Miss Cooper, who holds quite an enviable position at the Third Presbyterian Church, gives you a ring as she says "Not to be catty, but why am I placed on the same program with that dreadful contralto from the Sixth United Presbyterian Church? I won't stand for it." This means that someone has to be juggled and someone else has to be placated.

The prime difficulty of the radio impresario's life, however, is in getting talent of the proper caliber. That artists are temperamental and sometimes peculiar seems to be inevitable. Dealing with these peculiarities is part of the job, often amusing, and never dull. Discovering the artist who has both temperament and talent is the big difficulty, for while the famous performers are well known, programs cannot be made up exclusively of international names. Local talent must be used, but only if it is really accomplished.

In order to determine the availability of unknown performers, we sent each applicant a questionnaire. It asks for name, address, phone number, nature of performance, whether vocal, instrumental or recitation, experience, musical connections, dates available, and space for suggested program.

While it is not always possible to tell from a suggested program just how meritorious the concert will be, yet one can tell something of the capability of the performer by glancing over his proposed list. A singer who offers Puccini, Handel, or Gounod arias, or lieder by Strauss, Hugo Wolff, or Brahms, is almost certain to have had some technical experience.

To be sure, we are taking a chance on some of these unknown performers, and while we try to protect our vast audience as much as is possible by demanding references and recommendations, occasionally there is a slip. One night we had a woman who professed to have all possible experience. She had sent in a program of Schubert, Franz, and Grieg. It looked good and we booked her. When she arrived at the studio she shifted her program and sang "Old Black Joe," "Kathleen Mavourneen," and a number of other demi-semi-demi classics. She sang two numbers and the operators shut down the transmitter.

To canvass the territory and to make up a list for future reference, a new scheme is now being tried. Two nights a week, at the *Pittsburgh Post* studio, try-outs are being held for instrumentalists, singers, and reciters who are over 14 years of age, and who are not professionals. This scheme is being tried, not because the professional field has been exhausted—as a matter of fact, it has hardly been scratched—but because we feel that there are a great many talented youngsters, and not a few "oldsters" who can sing, play and recite in a pleasurable manner, and should be given a hearing, first, that the next generation of musicians may be stimulated, and second, to aid radio. A critic passes judgment on the performer's ability, and if he comes up to 80% in tone, diction, phrasing and quality, he is given an opportunity to perform over wireless.

The percentage of musical talent in any commonwealth is astonishingly large. Almost everyone has some slight musical training, and when you combine this training with native ability, the result is often quite amazing. It is this same half-hidden, half-blossomed talent that makes choral organizations and amateur orchestras flourish. Say what you will, radio is stimulating and encouraging the young musical generation.

The one difficulty in preparing radio programs is the securing of sufficient instrumental material. Abraham Lincoln once said: "God must have loved the common people; he made so many of them," and by the same token there must have been a tremendous amount of affection spent upon singers as there are proportionately so few instrumentalists. In making up KDKA's [Pittsburgh] programs, we try to obtain a capable instrumentalist for each concert. Violinists are numerous, but cellists, clarinetists, flutists, cornetists and the other instrumentalists that compose the orchestra are scarce, due to the fact that most of the players have theatrical or orchestral engagements.

If at times you feel that inner urge, the desire to obey that impulse, to sit down and send in a black-hand letter telling us how "rotten the program was last night," don't do it. We have professional listeners in who tell us, and they don't sign their names "pro bono publico" nor yet "Well-wisher." A famous editor once said to me, "People complain to me about how poor the stuff is that is in our journal. If they only knew how much worse the stuff is that we keep out, they would be grateful." Something like that is the experience of a radio impresario. We are the original, simon-pure "conscientious rejectors."[39]

Production behind the Scenes

119. Gustav Klemm, "Putting a Program on the Air"
Etude, March 1933, 163–64

When the average listener goes to his radio, turns it on and idly spins the knob that brings him first one station and then another, he has little or no conception of the work, the energy, the care and the manifold talents going into the making of the various programs he so lightly considers and dismisses by a move of the dial. It is safe to say that every half-hour program as finally broadcast over the air represents, very often, as much as fifteen hours in preparation, this preparation including the creation of the program "idea," its working into concrete form, the selection of the musical numbers, the writing of the continuity and, after all these and more have been taken care of, the endless rehearsing of the vocalists or other participants. If the same average listener referred to above could "follow through" on a radio program from its very conception until it is put on the air, we are quite sure he would have a greater understanding and appreciation of the sincere, skilled efforts to entertain him by means of his radio.

The Cost of a Half Hour

Let us trace the course of a single half-hour commercial program from the time the client, having gone carefully over his budget, decides he is going in for some radio advertising. Such advertising is not cheap. If his product is nationally known, he will naturally want wide coverage and to this end will buy time on the key station of a national network. In the evening, that is, from six to midnight, a half-hour program will cost him, for one broadcast, over three thousand dollars, this including the key station and a large number of stations closely affiliated with the key station, the whole being an inseparable unit known as "the basic group." For each additional station or group outside of the *basic* group, which carries his program, the prices vary, according to the size, power and importance of the stations. Add to this, of course, the high fee he pays for talent appearing on his program and you have a fair idea of the sum represented by an elaborate program.

Operating on a smaller scale, as contrasted to the national advertiser, is the local advertiser. Since it would be foolish for him to buy national broadcasting privileges for a product known only in a particular region, he uses a local station. The rates are considerably lower and, while the price for a half-hour varies greatly (there are many fifteen-minute programs and a few hour ones, but the average program length is thirty minutes), he will pay in the neighborhood of one hundred and fifty dollars for "station time," as it is called. This is for a single broadcast only. His talent charge will be in addition to this but will naturally cost him less than at the key stations, located in big cities, of national networks. The contracts are usually made for periods covering thirteen programs, this custom having started in the early days of radio when the average advertiser put on his program once a week. In a year, this would amount to 52 programs; a half-year contract would call for 26 and a quarter-year for 13 programs.

The Typical Client

As our imaginary client, let us settle on a manufacturer of coffee distributed to a large but limited locality. Since his coffee reaches a good bit beyond the bounds of the city covering his main operations, he selects a station of considerable power. After the commercial department of this station his shown him just how far the station reaches, which counties receive its programs most satisfactorily, how many radio sets are in these counties and a thousand and one other things that are rather dull to the man on the street but of great importance to the client, the contracts are drawn up and signed. All that now remains to be done is to design a program that will please the client. Here's where the real work starts. And it never stops!

Usually the client has no ideas at all for his program. He places his trust in the program department of the radio station and it is its members' responsibility to produce. As the first step in this direction, a round-table conference is held whereat everyone present submits whatever ideas occur to him. In attendance at this are representatives from the commercial department, the program department, often the director of the station and, occasionally a member from the engineering staff, the latter to solve any mechanical difficulties that may arise. From this round-table discussion, the program head and his various associates select the wheat from the chaff and start working.

Since dance orchestras, or programs of dance music interspersed with vocal soloists and quartets, have been done literally "to death," an effort is made to find something new. (The client always clamors for "something new.") He never gets it, of course, the trick being to take the old and make it *seem* new. Now, let's see—coffee. Where does it come from? Arabia, South America, Central America, Dutch West Indies? South America. Perhaps a colorful program featuring South American music? This sort of national-music program, however, is apt to become tiresome over a long period; so some provision will have to be contrasted character. The coffee to be advertised is a quality product; so the program must be of high caliber and not cheapened by anything of doubtful value. So, here we are—reasonably convinced that there should be South American music. By way of contrast we shall have, perhaps, some lush American foxtrots. And quality. These are ideas, but *not* a program.

The Advertiser's Motif
About this time, the question of a theme song or signature comes up. No program is complete without one and much depends on it. A tango? Too obvious. Pencils are chewed and heads are scratched. Meanwhile, one mind quicker than the rest has been working furiously. "Why not 'Rolling Down to Rio'"? Our client's coffees (as was revealed at the round-table conference) come from Rio, and slowly but surely the wisdom of the suggestion becomes apparent. Here is a neat tie-up. The number is a rousing, rollicking one and should, of course, be sung. Now, who would sing it? Who would "roll to Rio"? A sea captain, perhaps. Why not the captain of a sea vessel bearing our client's coffees? And, furthermore, why not call him Captain Clayton, thus working in the name of the coffee?[40]

From this point on, the program almost builds itself. The central figure is to be Captain Clayton, a lusty old sea dog who will be a sort of master of ceremonies on the program. He, by nature of his calling, will confine himself largely to singing songs of the bounding main and the sort of things you expect from a gruff old sea dog. Each program will take Captain Clayton to some South American port, thus allowing for the South American music. But it seems, so the program department decides, that he has fondness for American foxtrots which he brings South with him on his trips so that the orchestras may play them and remind him of his beloved native United States. Thus the desired contrast in music.

Just about now, someone remembers that the client expressed a wish for a female voice (soprano) on the program, if possible. That's easy. She will be the vocal entertainer at the various dance halls and cabarets the captain visits, and she can sing the colorful, exotic songs one expects to hear in such places.

Amassing the Material
While the literary department starts amassing information on coffee, South America, the customs of the natives and all the other material needed to create a colorful, accurate background, the musical wing of the program department starts working on the instrumentation of the orchestra and the musical numbers going into the first program. Much depends on the orchestra and the

instruments employed. Just the ordinary concert group would hardly be satisfactory for such a program and neither would a straight "dance combination." Do not forget that there must be an orchestra capable of handling the desired American foxtrots as well as the true South American music, especially the songs to be sung by the soprano. In order to get some "color" into the instrumentation the program head, working with the orchestra leader selected for the program, decides to use a marimba and a guitar, these two instruments to be located near the microphone in order that they may be heard to good advantage when they are used. The rest of the group, as finally agreed upon, is to consist of three violins, one cello, one string bass, three saxophones, one piano, one trumpet and a drummer with a complete equipment of percussion instruments—gourd, rattles, tambourines, castanets, and so forth—usually heard in the rumbas and tangos.

As for the numbers to be used, this lineup, designed to get the greatest contrast, is settled on:

Theme—"Rolling Down to Rio"
Opening announcement
South American number (lively)   orchestra
Vocal number (South American)   soprano
American foxtrot   orchestra
Vocal number (sea song)   baritone
South American number (rumba)   orchestra
Midpoint announcement (over theme)
Vocal number (South American)   soprano
American foxtrot orchestra   orchestra
Vocal number (sea song)   baritone
South American number (lively)   orchestra
Vocal duet   soprano and baritone
Closing announcement (over theme)

Assembling the Musicians

With this frame before him and bearing in mind all suggestions given him by the program department, the orchestra leader picks out numbers of the type desired, giving a rough timing to each selection. The program director acts, in all such program building, as a link between the vocal soloists and the orchestra leader, the program head usually having a broad knowledge of vocal literature, the soloists' repertoires and their capabilities. Where there is no orchestral accompaniment to a song selected, the number has to be arranged. The duet, placed at the end of the program to serve as a climax, will also have to be arranged for the two voices, in the case of a song written as a solo.

By this time, the literary department is already working on the script, embodying the numbers selected. (Every program presented on the air uses a prepared script, neatly typed, a bit of information that may be news to those people who seem to imagine that all talking on the radio is impromptu.) It has been decided to work in a lot of nautical terms (for the captain) and Latin American ones (for the café entertainer). This means, especially in the latter case, looking up pronunciations and being sure that idioms used are correct.

While the continuity writers are busy on the script, the vocalists are being rehearsed. In these days, clients want their talent to talk as well as sing; so appropriate dialogue is written and this also must be rehearsed. At the early rehearsals, the vocalists sing to a piano accompaniment. The orchestra leader (usually the piano accompanist), the program director and, often, the writer of the continuity are customarily present. The songs are carefully timed and, when the songs are too long, they are, if possible, cut. The conductor has also timed all his orchestra numbers to the second.

Timing to the Second
The entire program is checked for time. It is of prime importance that our program gets off the air at the exact moment. In a half-hour period, the program must have completed itself and arrived at the final signature (which can continue until fading into the next program), at, say, 29:30 minutes. There is a slight variation at the stations of different networks. Armed with this information, the orchestra leader works *back* through the program from the end. So if the closing announcement is a half-minute in length, and the duet two and a half minutes, he should start it at 26:30. In this way, he works back to the beginning, taking into consideration the dialogue and "business" between each number. It takes a lot of juggling before the thing is finally arranged, and one acquires skill in timing only by doing it often.

When the leader finally shapes his program, copies are made and given to the announcer, production man (if any) and others on the program. It probably starts like this (by the way our program goes on the air at eight in the evening): theme—8:00:00; opening announcement—8:01:00; South American number—8:02:00; vocal number (soprano)—8:05:00, and so on to the end.

At the advance rehearsal, at which everyone concerned is present, including the full orchestra, the numbers are rehearsed individually and everything smoothed out satisfactorily; the program is then run through for time. All sorts of difficulties come to light at this rehearsal—that is why rehearsals are held—and, what with the various temperaments involved, occasional clashes occur. But when the heat of battle has died down, a better program than was originally conceived is the result. Some numbers may be thrown out and others put in; the instrumentation may be changed; the orchestration may be "tricked up"; instruments may be moved to different positions. As we said in an earlier article, in radio it is what is heard that counts; things that look good on paper and should sound well are promptly thrown out if they *don't*.

The Dress Rehearsal

On the night of the broadcast, another dress rehearsal is held immediately preceding the broadcast, in this case from 7:30 to 8:00. The entire program is run through and last-minute touches are given to the various numbers. The timing is also checked again. At two minutes before eight, all activity in the studio ceases. There is a dead silence and everyone prepares himself for the nerve-racking ordeal ahead. This may seem a strong term but it well describes the agonies endured by those in charge of the program whose one concern, all others having been settled, is time. Anything is liable to happen. The whole timing scheme is thus thrown out of joint and some fast thinking and rearranging has to be done right in the midst of the program, all this, of course, unknown to the listener outside who sits back calmly and enjoys what he feels to be a smooth-running program. It is—over the air!

At the stroke of eight and immediately upon receiving a signal from the announcer, the conductor brings down his baton (which had been pointed in the air awaiting the signal) and the orchestra starts the signature, also sung by the baritone. The program is on the air! For the next thirty minutes, everyone is on his toes (where one always remains at a radio station). The conductor watches his orchestra, his time chart and the announcer. According to schedule, the opening announcement is read at 8:01:00 and the first South American number is started at 8:02:00. And so it goes throughout the program. But, as often happens, this or that number goes more quickly or more slowly than at rehearsals; so what is lost here must be picked up there and vice versa. After the midpoint announcement which, though it should have been read at 8:15:00 is actually read at 8:16:30, the conductor realizes he is back one and a half minutes, and it is up to him to take care of this. During the second half of the program, the production man or announcer keeps signaling the conductor just how far ahead or back of schedule the program is. This often causes changes in numbers. Where, for instance, two choruses of a song may have been rehearsed, only one will be used. The conductor usually has a stack of placards near at hand and holds the desired one up for the men to see. They may read *one chorus, coda, cut, theme,* and so forth. The latter is held up to warn the men at the midpoint and closing announcements which, on this program, are to be read over the signature, played lightly.

The Relaxing Finale

By 8:29:00 the program is completely through and the orchestra is playing the theme, which it will continue to play until the program fades off the air and the next program, from another studio, is begun. During the playing of the closing theme, one can sense the relaxation of nerves; worried frowns have disappeared and smiles are cropping up (if everything went well!). When the program is finally through and the lights in the studio dim, the orchestra musicians stop playing at once. A great sigh goes up. After such intense silence for a half-hour, it is difficult to start talking again. But a buzzing gradually gets under way and before the first or second hushed minute has passed, there is an excited exchange of opinions on this or that feature of the program, some remark that draws laughter, a query from the conductor as to why the baritone took the low instead of the optional high ending of a certain song, and so on. Meanwhile the musicians are putting away their instruments and the studio is being put in readiness for a later program.

The conductor may give the vocalists their music for next week's program and make arrangements for the first rehearsal the next day. He may even run over the songs then and there to give the soloists an idea of what he wants. The script for the second broadcast is already typed. In fact, the whole program had been prepared, complete in every detail, probably a week before the first broadcast was presented. All that lies ahead during the intervening week is the same endless routine of rehearsals. The conductor of the coffee program may also have a half-dozen other programs during the week, all of them surrounded by the same care, detail and other radio incidentals. Likewise the soloists are probably working on several other programs. As for the program director, it is his duty to lend an attentive, patient ear and give constructive advice and quick opinion to all the various conductors on the radio staff, the singers and the literary department, to see that the client's wishes, in the case of a commercial program, are completely embodied in the program representing him, to urge all hands concerned to do their best, to smooth ruffled temperaments—in other words, to be a slave like his associates, in constant attendance on His Majesty, the Microphone. A wearing life, in all truth, but a fascinating one!

120. Herbert Devins, "A Glimpse 'behind the Mike' during the *Palmolive Hour*"
Radio Revue for the Listener, December 1929, 27

Nine-thirty, Wednesday night. To millions of radio fans from coast to coast, it means a pleasant circle about the family loudspeaker for another *Palmolive Hour*.

To ushers and page boys at the New York studios of the National Broadcasting Company, it means another problem in higher mathematics, to make the Cathedral Studio's 400 chairs accommodate twice that number of applicants — all eager to catch a glimpse of the nationally famous Palmolive entertainers actually working before the mike.

For visitors in New York have learned the way to NBC's secluded studios, high above Fifth Avenue near Central Park. Every night brings new crowds of the curious. But the greatest number by far, week after week, storms the sound-proof doors precisely at 9:30 on Wednesday night.

Those, who are fortunate enough to be among the first 400 applicants for the cards admitting them to the studio, quietly take their places a few minutes before 9:30. At 9:29 the doors are closed and stalwart guards take their positions before every entrance.

Guards Not Mere Ornaments
The guards are not mere ornaments. There is the task of quieting the crowd of tardy arrivals and those who failed to obtain admissions in advance. A signal flashes. 9:30. "On the air!" Under no circumstances may the door be opened now. The murmur in the corridor subsides as the disappointed gather at the windows. All they see, however, is row upon row of smiling faces. These are the early ones, now watching intently some scene invisible to those outside.

Inside, the scene is colorful and bright, as gay lights concealed within the studio diffuse a warm glow around the crowd of performers and orchestra. Just a few inches beyond the first row of audience seats is the director's stand, with a full symphony orchestra ranged before it. Between the director's desk and the semicircle of first violins is an open space. Here are two microphones, one to catch the music of the orchestra, the other for vocal solos and novelty instruments.

Standing at the announcer's microphone on a platform at the far end is Phillips Carlin, master of ceremonies for the *Palmolive Hour*. As the second hand of a clock ticks 9:30, he lifts his arm—and Director Gustave Haenschen, his back to the audience, raises his baton.

"Good as a play," whispers one woman to her neighbor. A uniformed usher immediately tiptoes over and, with finger on lips, cautions her to silence. The slightest sound is apt to record on the sensitive microphones now connected with millions of American homes from the Atlantic to the Pacific.

Fast Pace Must Be Maintained

The baton in Haenschen's fingers swoops down, and a surge of melody from the orchestra swings into a marching rhythm. This creates immediately a sensation of speed and movement, setting a pace that must not lag for the next sixty minutes.

Out in the corridors, the disappointed ones wonder what causes a general grin on the faces of seat-holders inside. The grin is caused by the antics of Director Haenschen, who by this time has dropped his baton and is now leading with elbows, knees and feet, as well as his fingertips.

Haenschen cuts a graceful figure on the stand. He is tall and curly-haired, with shoulders that are a joy to his tailor. He combines an air of authority with irrepressible boyishness, the latter heightened by his "Charleston" and "Black Bottom" technique in leading the orchestra.

Before the orchestra has finished, Paul Oliver and Olive Palmer, two of the highest-salaried singers on the air, take their places before the microphone for their first duet. They stand quietly while the orchestra ends the overture, and wait for Phillips Carlin to introduce their opening contribution. Carlin drops his arm in signal, and the two bring their lips within a few inches of the microphone as Haenschen again lifts his hand over the orchestra in accompaniment.

Audience in Studio Amazed

The visible audience in the studio is amazed. Why, they can hardly hear the two familiar voices above the music of the orchestra! How is it that the voices sound so clearly over the air, with the orchestra but a dim accompaniment? The answer lies on the secret of distances from the microphone, and a set of black knobs on the mixing panel to be seen in the "monitor board" beyond.

Meanwhile, all eyes are glued on the faces of the soloists. Paul Oliver, garbed in neat evening clothes, stands as imperturbably as a Brahmin at the mouth-piece of the mike, his face a perfect mask as he puts all the expression and color into his voice alone—that rich tenor comparable only to McCormack's. He holds one hand nipped over his ear. But look! Olive Palmer too holds her hand in the same curious way, although her body sways more in time and her features reflect the expressions carried through the ether by her voice. What mean these strange gestures? It is a professional trick of radio—one that found its origin in the phonograph recording laboratories. It enables the soloist to sing softly close to a microphone, and still hear his own voice above the louder orchestra behind.

As the last notes of the duet fade away, Phillips Carlin again switches in from his microphone in the corner. While he tells what beauty experts say about "that schoolgirl complexion," the star singers move away from the central space to make way for four young men in dinner jackets and gleaming, starched shirt-fronts. There is a rustle in the audience. It recognizes that quartet, which is none other than the famous Revelers, recently returned from fresh triumphs abroad.

Frank Black at the Piano

Before the Revelers begin their inimitable close harmony, all four glance toward the piano, which is placed within arm's length of their place. This calls attention to the pianist, who has gone unnoticed until now. The dark Mephistophelean countenance and angular figure proclaim him Frank Black, who makes the Reveler's special arrangements, and, in addition, conducts orchestras on other programs. Before this program is over, Director Haenschen will consult him for sound musical advice on how to handle a number for which the time has grown too short.

But the Revelers begin, and they are again the center of all eyes. A glance ranges across the four faces, assuring the beholder that they are there in person—Lewis James and Jimmie Melton, tenors; Elliott Shaw, baritone, and the only Wilfred Glenn, basso profundo. This summer Paris audiences yelled for nine encores, made them take fourteen curtain calls—and then cried for "Speech!" France likes the Revelers more every year.

As the quartet completes its number and moves away from the mike, Director "Gus" steps down from the dais. Simultaneously a dozen handpicked jazz-men in the big orchestra stand up and bring their instruments closer. Haenschen now stands in profile towards the audience. All the feminine members lean forward in their chairs.

Then Haenschen starts his men on a madcap tune by means of a series of contortionist waves. His whole body moves now, and he is never on more than one foot at a time. Is he skipping rope or leading the jazz group? Listen to the sounds, and receive an answer. A wide grin wreaths his own youthful face as he remounts the stand at the end of the number.

Olive Palmer Sings a Solo

Next a solo by Olive Palmer, displaying the coloratura ability which was lost to grand opera when radio gained a star.[41] Another concert selection by the orchestra—or perhaps a symphonic fragment. Then the most curious assortment of all steps before the microphone.

Andy Sannella, virtuoso of many instruments, stands closest to the mike with a Hawaiian guitar slung across his chest. Behind him stands Murray Kellner, no longer the dignified first violin but now a jazz fiddler. Nearby is Larry Abbott, "one of the sweetest alto saxes in New York"—but that is no saxophone he holds. It is an ordinary comb, with tissue paper wrapped over the side nearest his lips. At a nod from Haenschen they go into action, this weird assortment—and what action. Sannella leaps like a jumping jack with the guitar on his chest, making sounds for which no guitar was intended. But this music cannot be described. A gleam lights the faces of the audience as they see the solution of the puzzling music they had heard in other *Palmolive Hours*. They knew it was somewhat different but they couldn't tell why or how.

And so the minutes fly, with a rapid succession of solos and combination vocal and instrumental groups that maintain the swift pace set by the opening rhythmic selection. A grand finale by the whole company brings the hour to its climax and finish—and there is a deathly pause while Phillips Carlin makes the closing announcement. He holds his arm in warning for several seconds, and then with a throw of a switch drops his arm. Another grin lightens his face as he releases the audience from its bond of silence with the cheerful call: "Party's over!"

Composing for the Radio

121. Viva Liebling, "Creating Scores for Radio"
Musical Courier, 20 January 1944, 9

Radio is producing the great daily output of creative music ever known—and very little of it is heard on musical programs. In fact, a good deal of it is written in the hope that it will not be *consciously* heard at all. The music in question, composed for radio's dramatic and documentary shows, serves many purposes, the least of which is to impress itself on the listener purely as music.

Take a show like Columbia's *The Man behind the Gun*. This is a half-hour drama based on some authentic story from the fighting fronts. It is very much the he-man type of thing, packs plenty of punch and action, and is, of course, highly topical. Musical director for the program is Nathan Van Cleave, who composes, arranges and conducts the music for the show. Because of rapidly changing war conditions, the script cannot be written more than a few days in advance, or it might find itself outdated. Therefore, Van Cleave has approximately two days in which to do the music.

In sitting down to the job, he bears in mind that there are about six different ways in which the music will be used. They can be roughly classified as follows: as a framework or theme marking the general outline; to carry scenes of action from one sequence to another as a bridge of time, place and mood; to back (play behind) a scene and enhance it by creating or intensifying a mood; to appear in a scene realistically as a part of the dramatic story as an arbitrary studio device; to cushion a show and take up slack or time; and, finally, as sound effect to create general all-over moods, periods or settings.

It may be seen from the foregoing that, to put it briefly, music is used in radio drama to create a third dimensional illusion. Whereas stage and screenwriters can depend on the endless magic of scenery and lighting to bring their brain children to life, radio dramatists can fall back only on the cold, spoken word.

Radio, someone once remarked, is for the blind. Whatever visual illusion is conjured up in the imagination is due to the skill with which words and music are combined.

Music Intensifies Drama

Tune in to any dramatic show, and try to imagine it without its musical accompaniment. Think how abrupt the transition from one scene to another would seem, how difficult it would be for the mind to shift its train of thought so quickly without music to help it along. In *Man behind the Gun*, one of its shows tried to picture a phase of an imaginary invasion of Europe, based on stories of actual commando raids. Action shifted rapidly back and forth from the hullabaloo of the men preparing for the raid to the quiet emotional intensity of two of the men discussing their beliefs and feelings about the war. Merely a chord or two made the transition natural, effortless, and the mind's eye followed the packed mass of men back to the two standing alone with no difficulty.

Of course, the all-over theme music of the show differs from the mood changes, just as backing a scene (that is, the old reliable "soft music" of the movies) is again different from the extra bars thrown in to use up time. When you realize that these complete changes of mood and setting must take place in a few seconds, you can understand something of the composer's problem. He considers himself lucky if he has four or five bars to reset a scene from the downward plunge of a screaming, death-spewing high-powered plane, back to the quiet street the pilot knew as home.

Then, too, the composer must be careful not to have a single unnecessary sound, since it might destroy the pace or distract the listener. Many a time, music is written for a scene which in theory seemed to demand a mood setting. Yet in rehearsal it was found that the simple words conveyed sufficient meaning; or perhaps a sound effect was substituted for the music. Each chord must have significance, be so shrewdly prepared and flow so naturally and realistically from the text that the listener accepts without question the authentic justice of including it in the dramatic pattern. Often the narrator on such programs says but one word, which is developed by the music into a complete thought or setting for the following dramatic bit. Yet everything must be kept subordinate to the dramatic action of plot thread.

Varying the Theme
While the script for a show like *The Man behind the Gun* is pretty much of a piece, keeping to a fairly consistent line, a show like *Radio Reader's Digest* presents an entirely different problem. Two or three dramatic skits are given during the half hour which may range from a satirical bit on ancient Greece, to the story of quinine, to almost anything else you can name. The composer, Don Bryan, may have to use a dozen different styles of music. Or a show like *March of Time*, on NBC, the most topical of them all, which works as much as possible with the story behind today's headlines, but also jumps around from subject to subject.

Here the composer-conductor, Don Voorhees, has approximately a day and a half to do the music. He picks up the script Wednesday morning, works on it all day and half the night, and Thursday spends most of the day, sometimes until a few minutes before actual performance time at rehearsal, changing, revising, rewriting. The toughest problem is when a big newsbreak comes on a Thursday and half of the script is thrown out to make room for the new event. If Hitler gets killed some late Thursday afternoon it's going to be something of a strain on the *March of Time* outfit.

It is vital to such programs that original music be written. For a long time, it was the custom of most conductors who did this type of show to draw on the immense network musical libraries for what they wanted and have it arranged to fit each script. But slowly they began to realize that this was impracticable. Most of the music already written had been composed to follow a certain line of thought or action. It never quite fit the specific requirements of the program. So gradually they started writing their own music, and out of this a whole new profession in music has grown.

Split-Second Work

The men who are in it must have behind them lives crowded with experience that make for the excellent split-second work demanded by such highly specialized programs. A conductor must have made a thorough study of all composers' techniques so that they are instantly available from the storehouse of his mind. He must have had years of experience not only playing, but in all phases of musical study including harmony, composition, arranging, etc., and have a sufficient mental retention of all kinds of music from jive to symphonic to make their themes appeal to the musically uneducated as well as the musical experts. Being a conductor on such programs also demands a thorough knowledge of the physics of sound because everything must have a proper balance. It is the most deft of musical combinations that give the dramatic accents and yet still subordinate to the plot as a whole. Then too, he must have an instinctive feeling for drama so that he can work well with the show's producers. Many a producer knows little or nothing about music, but knows exactly the effect he wishes to achieve. The conductor-composer must be able to grasp what the producer is unable to describe in musical terms and translate it into the desired mood or effect.

Double Duty

The majority of these men double as conductor and composers, and many of them orchestrate the scores. Some of them employ arrangers and orchestrators. But using an outside conductor would mean too much loss of time. Most conductors in radio have done this type of work. Frank Black has written hundreds of such scores and is currently doing the *Words at War* show, which dramatizes bestsellers of the moment. All these men have a wide background of experience. To cite only a few of the many, Van Cleave was for many years one of the outstanding arrangers in radio; Don Bryan was one of the top trumpeters of the country, studied with Edwin Franko Goldman, played with the New York Philharmonic and has been conducting since 1927; Don Voorhees started conducting when he was seventeen, has led many big Broadway musical shows, is permanent conductor of the *Telephone Hour* and has been in radio since 1928, arranging, conducting and composing; Lee Kempinsky did movie scores for many years.

They all differ on whether great music will emerge from any of these dramatic shows. The themes employed are all necessarily short and incomplete, and the scores cannot be sufficiently integrated to stand alone, except in rare instances, such as Frank Black's score for Alice Duer Miller's *White Cliffs of Dover*. However, many of the composers would like eventually to explore the larger fields of composition and believe that many of the scores they are doing may some day serve as sketches or idea reservoirs for other things.

122. Rose Heylbut, "The Background of Background Music; How NBC's Experts Fit Music to the Mood and Action of Dramatic Shows"
Etude, September 1945, 493–94

"We once put on a story about Abraham Lincoln," Dr. [Thomas] Belviso [Head of NBC's Music Library Division] relates, "in the middle of which Ann Rutledge was introduced as coming back to life and telling of her love for Lincoln. A scene of such a nature was very effectively backed with music throughout. Ann's talk was set against music, and the music was in no wise disturbing because it served a particular use in establishing mood. We wanted to convey to the audience that this was a supernatural condition, and also one of tender emotion. We asked the composer to furnish two minutes of tender and slightly sad melody, moving against harmonies of supernatural effect. On another occasion, we had a narration (spoken by Graham McNamee) describing a then-current scene of exciting values which was contrasted, through flashback, to the Minute Men. Here again we used background music calculated to set off the two separate moods. We asked for a theme of eerie quality, through which was heard, as in the distance, "Yankee Doodle" played by fife and drum.

Peculiar Difficulties
Back in 1931, we did a drama called *Skyscraper* which had a man fall from a skyscraper and review his entire life, and its values, as he fell. I wrote the music for that myself, and endeavored to stress the various emotional values of the things he remembered. Oddly enough, we revived that show in 1944; this time,

Mr. Kempinski did the music for it—and although his themes were entirely different from mine, he stressed the same emotions! Thus, the test for background music is not so much the melodic value as the emotional enhancement. The worth of background music, then, depends on how well it fits the script. An excellent piece of music, as music, may be of no use whatever if it fails to underscore the drama; on the other hand, music that is less valuable, as music, may do a superb job as a background blending of moods.

Messrs Kempinski and Mamorsky agree that the radio composer has his troubles. When a script is assigned for production, the composer, the author, and the producer discuss how much music is to be used, what kind of music, and the exact spot where it is to go. Then the composer times the specified passages with a stopwatch and writes suitable cues or bridges of desired length. Then rehearsals begin—and it can happen that necessary changes in the script play havoc with both the length and mood of the music! A scene that ended in a strong "punch line" may be rewritten or revised on no notice at all.

"All sorts of situations arise," Mr. Mamorsky observes. "I did the music for a sketch called *The Creightons*, a comedy involving the adventures of a rather mad family, all bound up in the arts. The sketch was comedy and the music had to reflect comedy—which is always a job, since funny music is greatly limited whereas dramatic or tragic music is much more free. Finally we hit on the idea of supplying the show with musical gags, based on lines in the script. If, for instance, the fantastic father cried out about his love of life and living, we backed up the speech with a comedy-parody of *I Love Life*. The assignment developed into supplying original bridges and suddenly steering them into parodies of very well-known tunes that everyone could recognize."

"No two shows, require exactly the same treatment," according to Mr. Kempinski. "Some scripts, by their nature, need much musical backing, and some need comparatively little. The show *Battle-Stations*, on which I worked, was a half-hour production, fully twenty minutes of which needed cues. *Arthur Hopkins Presents*, a radio adaptation of well-known plays, used music chiefly as curtains. As a rule, adaptations take less music than productions originating in radio and making use of all radio's vast facilities."

Both gentlemen agreed, and with fervor, that they would far rather prepare a long score, backing twenty or twenty-five minutes of a half-hour program and thus more or less continuous throughout it, than a series of 12 or 15 unconnected, unrelated thematic bridges. The continuous work permits of freer development, freer thought, and stands more solidly as music—"though," Mr. Mamorsky put in, "it must always be remembered that radio music is not absolute music.[42] The composer in radio accommodates himself, first, last, and all the time, to the needs of the script. He doesn't write as he would a symphony. When he has a symphony in his mind that has to be set down, he does it in his own time. In radio, the show comes first."

"Background music," agreed Mr. Kempinski, "is actually an obbligato.[43] It should never take attention away from the script itself—either for its goodness or its badness! If for any reason, the music outshines the story, it isn't good background music. Thus, the composer must familiarize himself with the script and steep himself in its mood."

After composer, author, and producer have ironed out preliminary adjustments, the music goes to the copyist, and at last to the conductor. Sometimes the composer conducts his own score. Whoever conducts, however, the first task is to go over the score with the musicians and perfect its performance values. Then joint rehearsals begin, the producer taking the dramatic actors through their lines, and the composer sitting by, stopwatch in hand, to time (and if necessary adjust) the coinciding of his cues with the dramatic entrances. When the audience hears the show, a few bars of background music (of which the listeners may not even be specially conscious) have involved hours of the most careful and detailed work.

Perhaps you ask, why is background music specially written for each and every dramatic air-show that uses music at all? Why not use the March from [Giuseppe Verdi's 1871 opera] *Aida* in a military scene, Brahms's *Lullaby* in a gentle-evening-at-home scene, and so on? The answer is that the great works of classic repertory stand independently as music, and could not blend so effectively with the specific emotions of given dramatic passages. Besides, the question of timing is important, five seconds of martial music might cut off *Aida* at the wrong point. Even if it were possible, by dint of long research, to compile and combine bits of existing music ("printed" music in radio jargon) into a satisfactory background score, the researcher would find that he had still another problem on his hands. The very familiarity of familiar music would tend, unconsciously, to distract attention from the dramatic continuity of the play. Each individual has associations of his own for [Richard Wagner's 1882 opera] *Parsifal*, the Seventh Symphony [of Beethoven], anything at all; and if such works were used in a dramatic setting that did not correspond to the individual's association, he would feel jolted, his attention would be taken away from the play, and some of his pleasure would be spoiled.

The business of background music in radio is to do just the reverse of what Brahms and Beethoven do. Brahms and Beethoven rivet your attention. Radio music, if it serves the purpose for which it is meant, keeps your attention on something else—the emotional and dramatic value of the play. When we feel a (perhaps slight) sense of hominess in a play, the right amount of "hominess music" intensifies that feeling. That's why it's there! If you have dreams of writing music for radio, concentrate on the emotional value of scripts. And the next time you hear two seconds of love melody in an otherwise nonmusical show, dedicate a bit of mental applause to the gifted and experienced men who make background music possible.

How to Listen to Music on the Radio

123. Peter W. Dykema, "Music as Presented by the Radio"
New York: Radio Institute of the Audible Arts, 1935[44]

No other single item of the varied offerings which radio presents is accorded so much attention as music. Not only are there many periods which are devoted entirely to music, but practically every program, whatever its main content may be, makes use of music to some extent as introduction or close, as a feature here or there, or as an incidental accompaniment throughout. The tendency, moreover, seems to me to provide even greater quantities of music and to make the offerings increasingly important. He who listens to radio will hear music, and he will increase the satisfaction from his listening as he grows in appreciation of the message of music.

Radio Is Revolutionizing Listening to Music
Radio with its remarkable offerings has created almost a revolution in the status of music in our country. Twenty-five years ago, music in its higher forms was heard and enjoyed by only a small portion of our people—the musical elite. Today there is no type of music which cannot be heard by anyone who has access to this marvelous invention. Those who a quarter of a century ago satisfied their love of music with the simple forms which could be produced in the home, the modest offerings of the churches, and the occasional concerts which were available in the larger centers of population, now have the resources not only of our own country, but, in an increasing degree, of the world, at their beck and call. Neither travel nor riches at the opening of this century could command what today the turn of a dial brings to humble but discriminating music lovers.

Soloists, quartets, choruses, light and grand opera groups, oratorio societies, a cappella choirs, small vocal ensembles and corresponding offerings in a wide variety of instrumental music—all these and more stand ready week after week to present the results of careful preparation.

But what has been carefully prepared is not always quickly assimilated. Fine music is made up of many details nicely balanced. All solid culture or appreciation is slow in its development. It is not surprising that radio listeners who have had slight opportunity for musical guidance and education often feel that they fail to get the full musical content of what the air waves bring to them from great artists and great ensembles. It is the purpose of this series of booklets to discuss in friendly, intimate and non-technical manner suggestions which may help listeners who are desirous of gaining more from music as presented by the radio.

It Is Smart to Know Music
Being mindful of what we may expect frequently sharpens our attention and helps us to obtain what might otherwise escape us. Let us then consider briefly some of the benefits which may be expected from keen listening. First of all, keeping abreast with the world, musically. It is astonishing how much general information, common knowledge of what is going on in musical circles, is taken for granted in ordinary conversation. Without it one frequently is at a loss to contribute his part in everyday discussions. Significance and point can be given to conversations about musical activities only when they are reinforced by actual acquaintance with music. Talking about music without the background of actual experience with music is not only meager and threadbare, but is often so filled with errors as to be ludicrous. The radio is doing for music what the printing press did for literature—making it available for everybody. In fact, the musical offerings on the radio may well be compared to the fare which the daily newspaper provides for the reader. All of us who mingle with others feel that we must devote a certain amount of time each day to becoming acquainted with what is common property through the medium of the newspaper; we are fast approaching the time when, in musical affairs, the same attitude will be general toward music which has been heard over the radio. The printing press, books, and newspapers have made people literate regarding material which can be recorded bywords; the radio is making people literate regarding what may be recorded or transmitted by sound.

Listen for Pleasure

Second, using music as a pastime, a pleasure. This, which is a natural condition—for everybody is born with a love of music in some of its forms—has frequently been corrupted or destroyed by unfortunate circumstances, especially by unwise attempts to force people to study or to like music for which they are not ready. Many of us have developed repugnance for certain articles of food, because of some unfortunate contacts, but we still have not lost our interest in eating. So we should remember that early lack of pleasure in music does not shut us out forever from the enjoying of the art in one or more of its phases. While there are other benefits from music besides simply responding pleasurably to it, this is one that must never be overlooked. In fact, all other accomplishments with music, some of which will be discussed below, rest upon genuine pleasure in the music which one hears. Since pleasure is an individual matter, each person must decide for himself what gives him pleasure. If he is wise, if he wishes his pleasure to continue and to grow, he will be absolutely honest with himself. He will say, frankly and fearlessly, "This is what I like now, and this is what I intend to hear." Let no one fear that this will prevent growth and development. It simply emphasizes the fact that interest is at the base of all learning. Before long any listener will be discussing his likes and dislikes with other listeners, and thus the way will be opened for growth and development.

Increase Your Sympathies

Third, the extending of one's sympathies. One cannot listen to music without giving himself to it more or less completely, and this carries with it the necessity of accepting the mood or point of view embodied in the music. This identifying of oneself with the music is not only the best way to grasp its message, but it is also the best way to obtain rest and relaxation. In the process, as is always the case when one takes the point of view of someone else, understanding and sympathy arise. One of the reasons why, in times of war, the music of the enemy nation is forbidden is that the use of it would tend to develop feelings of kindliness toward the enemy. It was not mere chance that, during the Great War, the period of fraternizing between the rival troops at Christmas time was marked by the singing of the same song by men on both sides of the trenches. Singing together, or listening together, to the same music makes, or tends to make, us take on the mood of the music instead of clinging to the feelings we had before the music began. Music keeps our hearts responsive and extends our sympathies.

Music as Medicine
Fourth, listening to music may act as an outlet or safety valve for undesirable emotional states. If, as mentioned above, we can, by listening to the right kind of music take on its mood and get rid of the less desirable ones which have been controlling us, the time may come when we may use this as medicine, much more consciously and effectively than we now do. When this condition prevails it is easy to conceive how a person in discouragement or anger or grief might turn on the radio to a program which would so move him that these emotions would be drained off and swallowed up in the mood of the music heard. Many a thinker has pondered upon the possibility of finding substitutes for the feelings that are now frequently expressed in undesirable conduct or even crime. George Bernard Shaw has said, "If young men had music and pictures to interest them, to engage them, and to satisfy many of their impulses, they would not go to the low pleasures of the street; they would be too fastidious to do so, for they would have an alternative."

Keep Company with Good Music
Fifth, music is good company. We hear so much of the contamination which comes to us from contact with debasing things that we forget the truth of the opposite, namely, uplifting by contact with the fine and lovely. In an address by Superintendent W. D. Webster of the Minneapolis Public Schools, made a few years ago, this significant statement is found: "Music is not so much a thing to be explained and talked about as a thing to be exposed to. Man loves not because he knows; man loves because he has been exposed to beauty, whether it be a simple flower, a lovely woman, a haunting melody. As the object of his love is beautiful, so his soul assumes the beauty it looks upon." Most of us forget the responsibility we have for controlling ourselves by controlling our environment. When we put ourselves in contact with good music, such as we may often, especially on Sundays, hear over the radio, we are submitting ourselves to the possibility of "catching" goodness to inoculating ourselves with beauty. Good company is a powerful influence in making good people.

Be Yourself with Music
Sixth, while listening to music, as just stated, makes us realize that we have much in common with other people who are making the music or who are listening to it, the radio also gives remarkable advantages for developing the individual because by means of it he can control the music he hears. When we go to a concert we are largely bound by what some one else has decided. It is some-

times impossible, and always difficult, to rise and walk out of the hall just because we do not like a particular piece or the way it is being presented; even if we did, there would probably be no other concert, more to our liking, we could attend. With the radio, all we have to do is turn the dial until we come to something else which is satisfactory or until we decide there is nothing so good as being by ourselves. The radio can do much to develop individuality of taste, because it allows us such a large choice without disturbing anyone else—providing the family doesn't object, or each one of us has an individual instrument!

Soar with Music

Seventh, listening to music stimulates the imagination. Music and the other arts are available not only for the pleasure of the moment, not only for that immediate consciousness of beauty which we may have, but for that great unconscious general stimulation of the whole being which is akin to warmth and comfort and feeling of sympathy. Much music, like the Mendelssohn composition "On Wings of Song," might for many people when listening, be called "On Wings of Imagination." As the tones pour in to us over the radio with no actual presence of conductor to distract us, with no audience coughing or whispering, with none of the many distractions of the concert hall, then we are in the presence of music in a pure form, and our imagination may rise and fall with the strains of the music. In a later brochure we shall examine some of the uses to which various listeners, businessmen, for example, have put this stimulating of the imagination by means of music.

Music Widens Our World

Eighth, music satisfies our longings. Various limitations make it impossible for any of us to obtain everything we long for. We cannot, physically speaking, be in both China and France at the same time. We cannot have the sober maturity of age and the joyous freedom of childhood and youth. We cannot have the ease of wealth and the stimulus of poverty. But aside from incompatible longings, there are many that are possible of realization through the aroused spirit. Art and music enable us to have in our minds and hearts much of the pleasure and satisfaction which the limitations of space, time, and money deny to us. All of us live in two worlds, one that of the earthbound here and now, the other that of all space, all time, all bodies, all desires. This is the realm of ideas and ideals. To a large extent the real world is made for us, while the ideal world is one we create for ourselves. Music through its stimulation tends to satisfy our longings.

Growing in Music

We are all of us body, mind, and spirit and we grow unevenly in our various aspects. Music may do something for us physically, more for us intellectually, and, if we treat it well, most for us emotionally and spiritually. It will meet us on almost any plane and respond to almost any need we feel, and it apparently makes no complaint. But the great lovers and friends of music believe that there is much more sweet joy and inspiration in music than most people realize and that all of us can get greater satisfaction from it than we now do.

Let him who would gain more from music remember that he must be honest and sincere. Let him like what he likes today and be enthusiastic about it, knowing that as he grows his taste will grow. So great is the power of music that anyone who puts himself in touch with it in its various manifestations will inevitably grow in the appreciation and love of it.

Notes

General Introduction: Music Technologies in Everyday Life

1. See Lynn Dumenil, *The Modern Temper: American Culture and Society in the 1920s* (New York: Hill and Wang, 1995) for a useful history of the 1920s.

2. Frederick Lewis Allen, *Only Yesterday: An Informal History of the 1920's* (New York: Harper and Row, 1931), 11.

3. Lizabeth Cohen, *Making a New Deal: Industrial Workers in Chicago, 1919–1939* (New York: Cambridge University Press, 1990), 103.

4. For important writings on the early advertising industry, see Stuart Ewen, *Captains of Consciousness: Advertising and the Social Roots of the Consumer Culture* (New York: McGraw-Hill, 1976); Jackson Lears, *Fables of Abundance: A Cultural History of Advertising in America* (New York: Basic Books, 1994); and Roland Marchand, *Advertising the American Dream: Making Way for Modernity, 1920–1940* (Berkeley: University of California Press, 1985).

5. *Supreme Court of the District of Columbia in Equity No. 37623, United States of America Petitioner v. Swift & Company, Armour & Company, Morris & Company, Wilson & Co., Inc., and the Cudahy Packing Co., et al., Defendants, on Petitions of Swift & Company, and Its Associate Defendants, and Armour & Company, and Its Associate Defendants, for Modification of Decree of February 27, 1920, Petitioning Defendants Statement of the Case* (Washington: Press of Byron S. Adams, 1930), quoted by Cohen, *Making a New Deal*, 106.

6. For studies of consumption in American culture, see Gary Cross, *An All-Consuming Century: Why Commercialism Won in Modern America* (New York: Columbia University Press, 2000); and Charles F. McGovern, *Sold American: Consumption and Citizenship, 1890–1945* (Chapel Hill: University of North Carolina Press, 2006).

7. For a study of the player piano and music as a commodity, see Timothy D. Taylor,

"The Commodification of Music at the Dawn of the Era of 'Mechanical Music,'" *Ethnomusicology* 51 (spring–summer), 281–305. For a broader study of the rise of the commercial music industry, see David Suisman, *Selling Sounds: The Commercial Revolution in American Music* (Cambridge: Harvard University Press, 2009).

8. Erik Barnouw, *A Tower in Babel: A History of Broadcasting in the United States to 1933* (New York: Oxford University Press, 1966), 125.

9. Cohen, *Making a New Deal*, 120.

10. Ibid., 125.

11. Orange Edward McMeans, "The Great Audience Invisible," *Scribner's Magazine*, April 1923, 411.

12. See Bruce Lenthall, *Radio's America: The Great Depression and the Rise of Modern Mass Culture* (Chicago: University of Chicago Press, 2007).

13. Loren H. B. Knox, "Our Lost Individuality," *Atlantic*, December 1909, 818, 824, quoted by T. J. Jackson Lears, "From Salvation to Self-Realization: Advertising and the Therapeutic Roots of the Consumer Culture, 1880–1930," in *The Culture of Consumption: Critical Essays in American History, 1880–1980*, edited by Richard Wightman Fox and T. J. Jackson Lears (New York: Pantheon, 1982), 8; emphasis in original.

14. *Printers' Ink: A Journal for Advertisers, Fifty Years: 1888–1938* (New York: Printers' Ink, 1938), 397.

15. Two technologies from after the Second World War that significantly shaped people's relationships were the Sony Walkman, introduced in 1980, and the Apple iPod, introduced in 2001. These devices further complicated the public-private dichotomy, making it possible to listen privately to one's own music—in public. See Shuhei Hosokawa, "The Walkman Effect," *Popular Music* 4 (1984), 165–80; Michael Bull, "No Dead Air! The iPod and the Culture of Mobile Listening," *Leisure Studies* 24 (2005), 343–55; and Michael Bull, ed., *Sounding out the City: Personal Stereos and the Management of Everyday Life* (New York: Berg, 2000).

16. Jonathan Sterne, *The Audible Past: Cultural Origins of Sound Reproduction* (Durham: Duke University Press, 2003).

17. Claude S. Fischer, *America Calling: A Social History of the Telephone to 1940* (Berkeley: University of California Press, 1992), 5. Thanks are due Colleen Dunlavy for informing me of this book.

18. Marilyn Strathern, Foreword, in *Consuming Technologies: Media and Information in Domestic Spaces*, edited by Roger Silverstone and Eric Hirsch (New York: Routledge, 1992), viii.

19. Rena Domke, quoted by Cohen, *Making a New Deal*, 105.

20. For general treatments by music specialists, see René T. A. Lysloff and Leslie Gay Jr., eds., *Technoculture and Music* (Middletown, Conn.: Wesleyan University Press, 2003); Paul D. Greene and Thomas Porcello, eds., *Wired for Sound: Engineering and Technology in Sonic Cultures* (Middletown, Conn.: Wesleyan University Press, 2004); Timothy D. Taylor, *Strange Sounds: Music, Technology and Culture* (New York: Routledge, 2001); and Paul Théberge, *Any Sound You Can Imagine: Making Music/Consuming*

Technology (Hanover, N.H.: University Press of New England, 1997). On the phonograph, see Michael Chanan, *Repeated Takes: A Short History of Recording and Its Effects on Music* (New York: Verso, 1995); Timothy Day, *A Century of Recorded Music: Listening to Musical History* (New Haven: Yale University Press, 2000); Roland Gelatt, *The Fabulous Phonograph*, 2nd ed. (New York: Macmillan, 1977); John Harvith and Susan Edwards Harvith, eds., *Edison, Musicians, and the Phonograph: A Century in Retrospect* (Westport, Conn.: Greenwood, 1987); Mark Katz, *Capturing Sound: How Technology Has Changed Music*, rev. ed. (Berkeley: University of California Press, 2010); William Howland Kenney, *Recorded Music in American Life: The Phonograph and Popular Memory, 1890–1945* (New York: Oxford University Press, 1999); James P. Kraft, *Stage to Studio: Musicians and the Sound Revolution, 1890–1950* (Baltimore: Johns Hopkins University Press, 1996); Andre Millard, *America on Record: A History of Recorded Sound* (Cambridge: Cambridge University Press, 1995); and Oliver Read and Walter L. Welch, *From Tin Foil to Stereo: Evolution of the Phonograph*, 2nd ed. (Indianapolis: Howard W. Sams, 1976). On the radio, see Erik Barnouw, *A Tower in Babel*; Susan J. Douglas, *Inventing American Broadcasting, 1899–1922* (Baltimore: Johns Hopkins University Press, 1987), and *Listening In: Radio and the American Imagination, from Amos 'n' Andy and Edward R. Murrow to Wolfman Jack and Howard Stern* (New York: Times Books, 1999); Michele Hilmes, *Radio Voices: American Broadcasting, 1922–1952* (Minneapolis: University of Minnesota Press, 1997); Michele Hilmes and Jason Loviglio, eds., *Radio Reader: Essays in the Cultural History of Radio* (New York: Routledge, 2002); Alice Goldfarb Marquis, "Written on the Wind: The Impact of Radio during the 1930s," *Journal of Contemporary History* 19 (1984), 385–415; Susan Smulyan, *Selling the Air: The Commercialization of American Broadcasting, 1920–1934* (Washington: Smithsonian Institution Press, 1994); and Timothy D. Taylor, "Music and the Rise of Radio in Twenties America: Technological Imperialism, Socialization, and the Transformation of Intimacy," in Greene and Porcello, *Wired for Sound*, 245–68. On film, see Richard Abel and Rick Altman, eds., *The Sounds of Early Cinema* (Bloomington: Indiana University Press, 2001); Evan William Cameron, ed., *Sound and the Cinema: The Coming of Sound to American Film* (Pleasantville, N.Y.: Redgrave, 1980); Donald Crafton, *The Talkies: American Cinema's Transition to Sound, 1926–1931* (Berkeley: University of California Press, 1997); Claudia Gorbman, *Unheard Melodies: Narrative Film Music* (Bloomington: Indiana University Press, 1987); Sarah Kozloff, *Invisible Storytellers: Voice-over Narration in American Fiction Film* (Berkeley: University of California Press, 1988); James Lastra, *Sound Technology and the American Cinema: Perception, Representation, Modernity* (New York: Columbia University Press, 2000); and Elizabeth Weis and John Belton, eds., *Film Sound: Theory and Practice* (New York: Columbia University Press, 1985).

21. Some significant works in these new fields include Karin Bijsterveld, *Mechanical Sound: Technology, Culture, and Public Problems of Noise in the Twentieth Century* (Cambridge: MIT Press, 2008); Karin Bijsterveld, and José van Dijck, eds., *Sound Souvenirs: Audio Technologies and Cultural Practices* (Amsterdam: Amsterdam University Press, 2009); Alain Corbin, *Village Bells: Sound and Meaning in the Nineteenth-Century French*

Countryside, translated by Martin Thom (New York: Columbia University Press, 1998); James H. Johnson, *Listening in Paris* (Berkeley: University of California Press 1995); Panayotis Panopoulos, "Animal Bells as Symbols: Sound Hearing in a Greek Island Village," *Journal of the Royal Anthropological Institute* n.s. 9 (2003), 639–56; Trevor Pinch and Karin Bijsterveld, "'Should One Applaud?' Breaches and Boundaries in the Reception of New Technology in Music," *Technology and Culture* 44 (2003), 535–59; Trevor Pinch and Frank Trocco, *Analog Days: The Invention and Impact of the Moog Synthesizer* (Cambridge: Harvard University Press, 2002); Leigh Eric Schmidt, *Hearing Things: Religion, Illusion, and the American Enlightenment* (Cambridge: Harvard University Press, 2000); Bruce R. Smith, *The Acoustic World of Early Modern England: Attending to the O-Factor* (Chicago: University of Chicago Press, 1999); Mark M. Smith, *Listening to Nineteenth-Century America* (Chapel Hill: University of North Carolina Press, 2001); Sterne, *Audible Past*; and Emily Thompson, *The Soundscape of Modernity: Architectural Acoustics and the Culture of Listening in America, 1900–1933* (Cambridge: MIT Press, 2002).

22. See, for example, Merete Lie and Knut Holtan Sørensen, *Making Technology Our Own: Domesticating Technology into Everyday Life* (Oslo: Scandinavian University Press, 1996); and Nelly Oudshoorn and Trevor J. Pinch, eds., *How Users Matter: The Co-Construction of Users and Technology* (Cambridge: MIT Press, 2003).

Part I. Sound Recording: Introduction

1. Arthur Sullivan, recorded 5 October 1888, London. Recording preserved at the Edison National Historic Site, object catalogue number E-2439-7. The recording may be heard online at http://www.nps.gov/edis/photosmultimedia/very-early-recorded-sound.htm.

2. For an exploration of the differences between live and recorded music and the influence of recording technology, see Mark Katz, *Capturing Sound: How Technology Has Changed Music*, rev. ed. (Berkeley: University of California Press, 2010).

3. Patrick Feaster, "'The Following Record': Making Sense of Phonographic Performance, 1877–1908" (Ph.D. diss., Indiana University, 2007), 2. Feaster also maintains a website, phonozoic.net, that includes a substantial collection of early documents related to sound recording. There is relatively little overlap between the documents reproduced here and Feaster's collection, which is particularly strong in its representation of articles from newspapers and non-music journals.

4. In fact, Edison was not even the first to record sound. In 1860 the French typesetter Édouard-Léon Scott de Martinville made a ten-second recording of a woman singing "Au clair de la lune" using a device he called a phonautogram. Scott's work on recording had long been known, but it was not until 2008 that the recording was discovered and the sound on it reproduced. See Jody Rosen, "Researchers Play Tune Recorded Before Edison," *New York Times*, 27 March 2008. Online at http://www.nytimes.com/2008/03/27/arts/27soun.html.

5. For detailed accounts of the invention and early history of the phonograph, see Raymond Wile, "The Edison Invention of the Phonograph," *ARSC Journal* 14 (1982),

5–28; Patrick Feaster, "Speech Acoustics and the Keyboard Telephone: Rethinking Edison's Discovery of the Phonograph Principle," *ARSC Journal* 38 (spring 2007), 10–43.

6. Photograph courtesy of the Edison National Historic Site. See http://www.nps.gov/archive/edis/edisonia/graphics/29110013.jpg.

7. Some early phonographs were equipped with batteries or electric motors as a power source, but these were relatively rare. Before 1925 most phonographs operated with spring motors (or were hand-cranked like the first machines).

8. It should be remembered that the acoustic era—from which the majority of the documents here come—lasted nearly fifty years, and that there were many technological developments during that time. (Two examples are the spring motor, introduced in the early 1890s, which meant that users no longer had to turn a crank continuously to keep the music playing, and the internal horn machine in 1906, which eliminated the large bell-shaped horns that many consumers found unwieldy.) A discussion of these developments is beyond the scope of this volume. For more, see David L. Morton, *Sound Recording: A Life History of a Technology* (Baltimore: Johns Hopkins University Press, 2006), and Oliver Read and Walter L. Welch, *From Tin Foil to Stereo: Evolution of the Phonograph*, 2nd ed. (Indianapolis: Howard W. Sams, 1976).

9. Patrick Feaster has argued that Edward Johnson, a business associate of Edison and a fellow inventor, had considerable input into this article, and perhaps even drafted it for Edison. Even given Johnson's collaboration we can assume that the article represents Edison's thinking. See Feaster, "Speech Acoustics and the Keyboard Telephone."

10. For an informative look into the issues facing the business use of the phonograph, see *Proceedings of the 1890 Convention of Local Phonograph Companies* (Milwaukee: Phonograph Printing Co., 1890; repr. Nashville: Country Music Foundation Press, 1974). The reprint edition includes useful contributions by the historians Raymond Wile, Oliver Read, and Walter L. Welch. See also *ARSC Journal* 26 (fall 1995), a special issue devoted to cylinder records and the cylinder industry, with articles by Steve Smolian, Peter Shambarger, Raymond Wile, and Bill Klinger.

11. See Raymond R. Wile, "The Automatic Phonograph Exhibition Company and the Beginnings of the Nickel-in-the-Slot Phonograph," *ARSC Journal* 33 (spring 2002), 1–20.

12. For more on the Berliner's gramophone, see Emile Berliner, "The Gramophone: Etching the Human Voice," *Journal of the Franklin Institute* 125 (1888), 426–46; and Raymond Wile, "Etching the Human Voice: The Berliner Invention of the Gramophone," *ARSC Journal* 21 (1990), 2–22.

13. For other early predictions about the future of recorded sound, see J. Armory Knox, "The Future of the Phonograph," *Electrical Review*, 12 April 1888, 1; Edward Bellamy, "With the Eyes Shut," *Harper's New Monthly* 79 (1889), 736–45; and Thomas H. MacDonald, "Past and Future of the Talking Machine," *Musical Age* 56 (1909), 261–62.

14. See, for example, "Phonograph for Band at Wedding," *New York Times*, 26 December 1905, 2; "Phonograph at Funeral," *New York Times*, 18 December 1910, 1; O. Henry, "The Phonograph and the Graft," *McClure's* 20 (1903), 428–34 (slightly different version in *Cabbages and Kings* [New York: A. L. Burt, 1904], 92–112).

15. Frank Swinnerton, "A Defence of the Gramophone," *Gramophone* 1 (1923), 52–53.

16. The figure greeting the hostess is likely Don Pasquale from Donizetti's opera of the same name. Among the other characters seem to be Isolde (from Wagner's *Tristan und Isolde*), Aida (from Verdi's *Aida*), and Rigoletto (from Verdi's *Rigoletto*). Selections from the aforementioned operas were available on Victor records. My thanks to John Nádas and James Haar for identifying these figures. For a useful compendium of reproductions of early phonograph advertising, see James N. Weber, *The Talking Machine: The Advertising History of the Berliner Gramophone and Victor Talking Machine* (Midland, Ont.: Adio, 1997).

17. Disc-playing machines, which superseded cylinder phonographs, were not generally equipped for recording. For a collection of early home recordings, see *I'm Making You a Record: Home and Amateur Recordings on Wax Cylinder, 1902-1920*, Phonozoic compact disc 001, phonozoic.net.

18. Recital program, 6 June 1905, Warshaw Collection of Business Americana, National Museum of American History.

19. According to one account, "The first [gramophone] society was started at Cricklewood, the North-West London, in September 1911." William J. Robins, "Gramophone Societies," *Gramophone* 9 (November 1931), 248–49. The activities of these organizations are described in *Gramophone* 1 (1923); *Phonograph Monthly Review* 1 (1926); A. Coeuroy and G. Clarence, *Le Phonographe* (Paris: Kra, 1929); and E. T. Bryant, "The Gramophone Society Movements: A History of Gramophone Societies in Britain, Including Their Links with Public Libraries" (M.A. thesis, Queen's University of Belfast, 1971).

20. "Mainly about Phones," *Sound Wave*, December 1909, 54.

21. Felix Machray, "My Phonograph Entertainment," *Talking Machine News* 3 (1905), 400. For another example, see W. Montgomery, "How to Give a Christmas or New Year's Party," *Talking Machine News and Journal of Amusements*, January 1911, 66.

22. "Die Hausmusik und ihr Programm," *Die Stimme seines Herrn*, March 1912, 46–47.

23. Robert Haven Schauffler, "Canned Music—The Phonograph Fan," *Collier's*, 23 April 1921, 10–11, 23–24.

24. Mrs. John P. Walker, "The Dance Craze of the Present Day," *Musical Monitor and World*, June 1914, 285.

25. Fay Compton, "The Power of the Needle," *Gramophone* 1 (1923), 32.

26. Victor Talking Machine Company, *Three Modern Dances: One-Step, Hesitation, Tango* (Camden, N.J.: Victor Talking Machine Company, 1914).

27. Maurice Abrahams and Grant Clarke, *They Start the Victrola (And Go Dancing Around the Floor)* (London: Francis, Day and Hunter, 1914).

28. In the nineteenth century, the primary goal had been to teach students how to *make* music, particularly through singing. For more on music appreciation and the changing priorities of American music education, see Waldo S. Pratt, "New Ideals in Musical Education," *Atlantic*, December 1900, 826–30; Edward Dickinson, *The Education of a Music Lover* (Boston: Charles Scribner's Sons, 1914), 1–15; Edward Bailey Birge,

"Music Appreciation—The Education of the Listener," *Papers and Proceedings of the Music Teachers' National Association* 17 (1923), 189–93.

29. A. E. Winship, "The Mission of School Music," *Journal of Education*, 21 September 1916, 260. For more on the phonograph in the rural school, see M. D. Gordon, "How Mechanical Instruments Bring the Best Music into the Country," *Countryside*, November 1918, 253–54; and W. Arthur B. Clementson, "The Sound Reproducing Machine in the Country School," *Etude*, November 1928, 840.

30. C. M. Tremaine, "Music Memory Contests," *Journal of the National Education Association*, February 1926, 43–44. Another source put the number of participating cities in 1926 at 1,083. Edward Bailey Birge, *History of Public School Music in the United States*, rev. ed. (Boston: Oliver Ditson, 1939; repr. Reston, Va.: Music Educators National Conference, 1988), 214–15. For more on the music memory contest, see Peter W. Dykema, "The Music Memory Contest and the Course of Study," *School Music*, September–October 1922, 12–17; and Will H. Mayes, "How to Conduct a Music Memory Contest," *Etude*, March 1923, 153.

31. See, for example, the rules and repertoire for the 2011–2012 contests sponsored by the University Interscholastic League of Texas, posted online at http://www.uil.utexas.org/aplus/events/aplus-music-memory. The UIL has been sponsoring contests since the early 1920s.

32. Here I refer specifically to the United States and to a lesser extent England.

33. Richard J. Magruder, "Manufacturing Music Lovers," *Disques*, March 1931, 17.

34. "Who Buys Phonographs?," *Sonora Bell*, October 1919, 1–6.

35. Harold Randolph, "The Feminization of Music," *Papers and Proceedings of the Music Teachers' National Association* 17 (1923), 196, 197. See also Edith Brower, "Is the Musical Idea Masculine?," *Atlantic*, March 1894, 332. For a recent discussion of the issue that cites a wealth of primary sources, see Gavin James Campbell, "Classical Music and the Politics of Gender in America, 1900–1925," *American Music* 21 (winter 2003), 446–73.

36. *Munsey's Magazine* (1905), advertising section. Clipping from the George H. Clark Radioana Collection, Series 126, Box 524A, National Museum of American History, Behring Center, Smithsonian Institution.

37. For more on gender and recording in the early twentieth century, see William Howland Kenney, "The Gendered Phonograph: Women and Recorded Sound, 1890–1930," in *Recorded Music in American Life: The Phonograph and Popular Memory, 1890–1945* (New York: Oxford University Press, 1999), 88–108; Jonathan Sterne, *The Audible Past: Cultural Origins of Sound Reproduction* (Durham: Duke University Press, 2003); and Katz, *Capturing Sound*, 57–61.

38. For period articles from the German and English perspectives, see Paul Lindau, "Musik im Kriegszeiten," *Die Stimme seines Herrn* 6 (December 1914), 4–5; Friedrich Krafft, "Briefe aus dem Felde," *Die Stimme seines Herrn* 8, nos. 6–7 (1916), 56, 59; Edmond Symons, "The Gramophone Banishes the Horrors of War," *Voice*, May 1919, 9; Percy A. Scholes, "Gramophonic Adventures: Some Notes of War Experiences," *Voice*, July 1919,

8–9. For more recent discussion of the phonograph and the First World War, see Curt Riess, "Krieg," in *Knaurs Weltgeschichte der Schallplatte* (Zurich: Droemer, 1966), 153–71, and Eric Charles Blake, *Wars, Dictators, and the Gramophone* (York, England: William Sessions, 2004).

39. Phonograph ads made the point as well. For example, an ad for the Columbia Grafonola in 1918 explains that supplying records and machines to off-duty soldiers at home is "Columbia's war-work over here." *Saturday Evening Post*, 23 November 1918, 80.

40. Figures and quotation from Roland Gelatt, *The Fabulous Phonograph*, 2nd ed. (New York: Macmillan, 1977), 191, 194.

41. "15,000 Enroll in Phonograph Drive," *New York Times*, 27 October 1918, 35.

42. Frances Hodgson Burnett, *Little Lord Fauntleroy* (New York: Charles Scribner's Sons, 1889). For more on the life of Vivian Burnett, see Tom McCarthy, "The Real Little Lord Fauntleroy," *American Heritage*, February 1970.

43. See "'Stage Fright' Produced by the Phonograph," *Phonogram* 1 (1891), 39; and "The Science of Making Canned Music," *Literary Digest*, 28 September 1918, 24–25.

44. For more on the Stroh violin, see Dick Donovan, "The Stroh Violin," *Strand Magazine*, January 1902, 89–91; and Cary Clements, "Augustus Stroh and the Famous Stroh Violin," 2 parts, *Experimental Musical Instruments*, June 1995, 8–15; September 1995, 38–39.

45. Nellie Melba, *Melodies and Memories* (New York: H. Doran, 1926), 252–53.

46. For more on the impact of recording on early jazz, see Katz, *Capturing Sound*, 72–84.

47. For more commentary from musicians about sound recording, see John and Susan Edwards Harvith, eds., *Edison, Musicians, and the Phonograph: A Century in Retrospect* (New York: Greenwood, 1987).

48. For an interesting adjunct to this excerpt, see "The Salesman and the Singing Course," *Talking Machine Journal*, November 1917, 16. Other teachers published similar methods for piano and clarinet. See Hazel Gertrude Kinscella, "The Subtle Lure of Duet-Playing," *Musician*, January 1924, 8, 15; and Gustave Langenus, *The Langenus Clarinet Correspondence School with Talking Machine Records* (New York, 1915).

49. For example, the first recordings of music by Stravinsky and Ravel—*Firebird* (excerpts only) and *Jeux d'eau*—appeared in 1917 and 1920, respectively; the music of Schoenberg and Bartók was first recorded in 1924 and 1925, with the former's *Verklärte Nacht* and the latter's String Quartet no. 2.

50. See Jerrold Moore, *Elgar on Record: The Composer and the Gramophone* (London: Oxford University Press, 1974).

51. "Nos amis et nos adversaires," *L'Édition Musicale Vivante*, December 1927, 18–19; and "Nos amis et nos adversaires," *L'Édition Musicale Vivante*, February 1928, 23–24. These statements were originally published in French.

52. For another discussion of recording by a composer who made recordings, see Aaron Copland, "The World of the Phonograph," *American Scholar* 6 (1937), 27–38.

53. Musique concrète, developed by the French composer Pierre Schaeffer in the late

1940s, was a compositional method in which fragments of recorded sound (initially on disc but largely using magnetic tape) were arranged and manipulated to create musical works. In the United States, a similar approach, employed by John Cage, Vladimir Ussachevsky, and others, was called tape music. Digital sampling, which was developed in the 1970s and flourished in the 1980s and 1990s, is also based upon the manipulation of recorded sound, though the sound has been digitized—rendered into data consisting of strings of 0s and 1s. For more on musique concrète, see Peter Manning, *Electronic and Computer Music*, rev. ed. (New York: Oxford University Press, 2004); on digital sampling, see Katz, "Music in 1s and 0s: The Art and Politics of Digital Sampling," in *Capturing Sound*, 137–57.

54. For more on the early use of sound recording as a compositional tool, see Katz, "The Rise and Fall of *Grammophonmusik*," in Katz, *Capturing Sound*, 99–113.

55. Part of Sousa's attack on sound recording is clearly motivated by his worries about copyright protection for composers. Before the landmark Copyright Act of 1909, no royalties were paid to the copyright holders of published musical works when the music was recorded on disc or player-piano roll. Sousa later softened his tone. In 1923 he remarked, "The effect of hearing a record of a performer who has passed on, such as Caruso, almost gives me the shivers. Only a few years ago it was impossible for the public to hear more than a few of the world's great artists. Now, thanks to [the phonograph], these artists can be heard in the humblest homes." "A Momentous Musical Meeting: Thomas A. Edison and Lt. Comm. John Philip Sousa Meet for the First Time and Talk upon Music," *Etude*, October 1923, 663. For more on the significance of the 1909 Copyright Act and its impact on sound recording, see Lisa Gitelman, "Reading Music, Reading Records: Musical Copyright and the U.S. Copyright Act of 1909," *Musical Quarterly* 81 (summer 1997), 265–90.

56. Horace Johnson, "Department of Recorded Music: Phonographs in the Home," *Etude*, February 1922, 88.

Part I. Sound Recording: Readings

1. "In propria persona" is a legal term referring to the act of representing oneself in a court proceeding without a lawyer; here, it simply means that Edison is speaking on his own behalf. Ironically, however, it may well be that Edison's associate Edward Johnson drafted this article on Edison's behalf. See note 5 of the introduction to part I.

2. Adelina Patti (1843–1919) was one of the most famous opera singers of the day.

3. This article cites a number of famous orators and preachers of the day. Thomas De Witt Talmage (1832–1902) was an American Presbyterian minister whose sermons were widely reprinted at the time. Others include Wendell Phillips (1811–1884), American abolitionist and orator; Robert G. Ingersoll (1833–1899), American abolitionist preacher; Senator Roscoe Conkling of New York (1829–1888); and Henry Ward Beecher (1813–1887), a prominent American clergyman and reformer.

4. A reference to Thomas Edison's laboratory in West Orange, New Jersey, where he

and his associates invented the phonograph and had recording facilities. It is now preserved as the Edison National Historic Site by the U.S. National Park Service.

5. This is true only in theory; early recordings did not stand up to repeated plays in the manner of later formats.

6. In 1889 Thomas Edison sent Theodore Wangemann to Boston to record a concert by Hans von Bülow (1830–1894), a famous German conductor. It is not known what became of these cylinders, or even if they were actually made.

7. In fact, Wagner's Ring Cycle, *Der Ring des Nibelungen*, consists of four operas: *Das Rheingold* (1854), *Die Walküre* (1856), *Siegfried* (1871), and *Götterdämmerung* (1874).

8. A hugely popular song written by H. P. Danks in 1872, based on a poem by Eben Rexford.

9. The scrapbook contained clippings of concert reviews featuring the musicians whose recordings were available to those taking the Edison Realism Test, along with photographs of those musicians.

10. A reference to Karl Friedrich Hieronymus, Freiherr von Münchhausen (1720–1797), infamous for his tall tales.

11. Edison preferred the term RE-CREATION (almost always spelled in capital letters) to describe his company's recordings.

12. Benedict was a telegrapher for the Colorado and Southern Railroad.

13. According to various historical inflation calculators, what cost $265 in 1921 would cost in 2011 between about $3,200 and $3,400.

14. The American classical violinist Albert Spalding.

15. A popular American contralto, known for her performances of "Abide with Me." An Edison cylinder recording of that song made in 1913 can be heard through the website of the library at the University of California, Santa Barbara, http://cylinders.library.ucsb.edu/mp3s/0000/0521/cusb-cylo521d.mp3.

16. Among the patents Lonk refers to below is one for a "Carpet Stiffener," which he received in 1921. Lonk was also the author of *"The Original" Complete Seventy-two Part Manual of Hypnosis and Psychotherapeutics, and also Mysteries of Time and Space*, which was self-published in at least three editions up to 1947.

17. In a box party, typically the girls of a school would bring boxes of lunch with their names on the inside. The boxes were auctioned off to the boys, who then had the privilege of eating lunch with the girls who brought those particular boxes.

18. This is likely a misidentification. The correct title is "Gently Fall the Dews of Eve," which is the name of a mid-nineteenth-century hymn and is identified in a 1925 Victor catalogue as a trio by the Italian composer Saverio Mercadante.

19. See part I, introduction, figure 3, for this image.

20. This is the opening line of the popular sentimental song "Ben Bolt" (published 1848) by Nelson Kneass, after a poem by Thomas Dunn English.

21. A reference to George DuMaurier's novel *Trilby* (1894).

22. These refer to units of British currency; one guinea equaled 21s, or shillings.

23. A character in Max Beerbohm's popular novel *Zuleika Dobson, or, an Oxford Love Story* (1911), who frequently remarks, "I don't know anything about music really, but I know what I like."

24. A popular nineteenth-century Scottish folksong.

25. A reference to the YMCA.

26. The Knights of Columbus, a charitable organization.

27. Burnett wrote the song "When I Hear That Phonograph Play"—see item 21.

28. King Oliver's Creole Jazz Band comprised Joseph "King" Oliver and Louis Armstrong, cornets, Honoré Dutrey, trombone, Johnny Dodds, clarinet, Lil Hardin Armstrong, piano, Bill Johnson, banjo, and Baby Dodds, drums.

29. Lincoln Gardens, a popular dance hall in Chicago where Oliver's band was in residence between 1922 and 1924.

30. [Footnote in original:] Gennett record: never issued (master lost or destroyed).

31. A pioneering jazz pianist, bandleader, and composer.

32. A small town in Germany where Wagner's specially designed opera house is located.

33. In this case "tremolo" refers to an unwanted tremor or vibrato in the voice.

34. A German city that held an annual new music festival.

35. Cowell is referring to a group of Italian futurists, including F. T. Marinetti and Luigi Russolo, who promoted the use of noise and noisemakers as the future of music.

36. Jove is another name for the Roman god Jupiter.

37. "Punch and Judy" is a popular puppet show with roots in sixteenth-century Italy.

38. Louis C. Elson, *The History of American Music* (New York: Macmillan, 1904), 1.

39. The ancient name for Great Britain.

40. "The Girl I Left Behind Me" was a popular folksong, "Dixie" refers to the famous American song by Daniel Emmet, and "Stars and Stripes Forever" is a composition by Sousa himself.

41. This is the opening verse from the Scottish folksong "Annie Laurie."

42. Sousa is referring to a then familiar military anecdote about the Battle of Fontenoy (1745) between the French and the English. When the two armies approached one another, it is said that the English commander Lord Charles Hay called out, "Gentlemen of the French guards, shoot," whereupon the Count d'Auteroches replied, "Sir, we never shoot first, please to fire yourselves."

43. The legislation Sousa discusses here led to the landmark Copyright Act of 1909. An important provision of that act established a compulsory mechanical license for sound recordings, which stipulated that royalties must be paid to the copyright holder of any work of music when that work is recorded. Sousa testified before Congress in support of copyright protections for composers.

44. A graphophone was a type of phonograph developed in the 1880s by Charles Sumner Tainter and Chichester Bell.

Part II. Cinema: Introduction

1. See Eileen Bowser, *The Transformation of Cinema, 1907–1915* (New York: Charles Scribner's Sons, 1990).

2. This historical trajectory of audience composition, from immigrant and working-class audiences in the nickelodeon period to middle-class patrons for the movie theaters of the 1920s, has been the subject of some debate by early cinema scholars. In his "Introduction: Reconstructing American Cinema's Audiences," Melvyn Stokes outlines a few of the challenges to this "founding myth" of film history, with a number of scholars offering evidence to support a more complex portrait of social composition from the very beginning. See Melvyn Stokes and Richard Maltby, eds., *American Movie Audiences: From the Turn of the Century to the Early Sound Era* (London: British Film Institute, 1999). For scholarship focused on the class dimensions of movie audiences prior to the First World War, see Steven J. Ross, *Working-Class Hollywood: Silent Film and the Shaping of Class in America* (Princeton: Princeton University Press, 1998). Even if early cinema did not attract the industrial working class exclusively, it is worth noting that, as Douglas Kellner argues, films became "a major force of enculturation" to these segments of the audience in particular, helping to "socialize immigrant and working-class cultures into the emerging forms of the consumer society, teaching them how to behave properly and consume with style and abandon." Douglas Kellner, "Culture Industries," in *A Companion to Film Theory*, edited by Toby Miller and Robert Stam (Malden, Mass.: Blackwell, 1999), 205, 206. For more on the "Americanization" of immigrants through film culture, see Stuart Ewen and Elizabeth Ewen, *Channels of Desire: Mass Images and the Shaping of American Consciousness* (New York: McGraw-Hill, 1982), especially part 3: "City Lights: Immigrant Women and the Rise of the Movies."

3. For example, Lauren Rabinovitz, *For the Love of Pleasure: Women, Movies, and Culture in Turn-of-the-Century Chicago* (New Brunswick, N.J.: Rutgers University Press, 1998), Janet Staiger, *Bad Women: Regulating Sexuality in Early American Cinema* (Minneapolis: University of Minnesota Press, 1995), and Miriam Hansen, *Babel and Babylon: Spectatorship in American Silent Film* (Cambridge: Harvard University Press, 1991).

4. Mary Carbine, "'The Finest Outside the Loop': Motion Picture Exhibition in Chicago's Black Metropolis, 1905–1928," in *Silent Film*, edited by Richard Abel (New Brunswick, N.J.: Rutgers University Press, 1996), 255. See also Gregory A. Waller, "Another Audience: Black Moviegoing, 1907–16," *Cinema Journal* 31 (winter 1992), 3–25.

5. Donald Crafton, *The Talkies: American Cinema's Transition to Sound, 1926–1931* (Berkeley: University of California Press, 1999), 42, 10. On the various experimental attempts to combine cinema and radio in the 1920s, see especially chapter 2: "Electric Affinities." See also Paul Young, *The Cinema Dreams Its Rivals: Media Fantasy Films from Radio to the Internet* (Minneapolis: University of Minnesota Press, 2006).

6. René Clair, "The Art of Sound" (1929), in *Film Sound: Theory and Practice*, edited by Elisabeth Weis and John Belton (New York: Columbia University Press, 1985), 95.

7. Recent scholarship constructing a reception model of spectatorship and the movie-

going experience includes the four-volume series edited by Melvyn Stokes and Richard Maltby: *American Movie Audiences: From the Turn of the Century to the Early Sound Era* (London: British Film Institute, 1999); *Identifying Hollywood's Audiences: Audiences and Cultural Identity* (London: British Film Institute, 1999); *Hollywood Spectatorship: Changing Perceptions of Cinema Audiences* (London: British Film Institute, 2001); and *Hollywood Abroad: Audiences and Cultural Exchange* (London: British Film Institute, 2004). See also *Moviegoing in America: A Sourcebook in the History of Film Exhibition*, edited by Gregory A. Waller (Malden, Mass.: Blackwell, 2002); Mark Jancovich and Lucy Faire with Sarah Stubbings, *The Place of the Audience: Cultural Geographies of Film Consumption* (London: British Film Institute, 2003); and Janet Staiger, *Media Reception Studies* (New York: New York University Press, 2005).

8. Rick Altman, *Silent Film Sound* (New York: Columbia University Press, 2004), 19. For an earlier treatment of this "new, nonlinear approach to film history," see Rick Altman, "The Silence of the Silents," *Musical Quarterly* 80, no. 4 (winter 1996), 688–89, and Altman, "Deep-Focus Sound: *Citizen Kane* and the Radio Aesthetic," *Quarterly Review of Film and Video* 15, no. 3 (1994), 21–22.

9. Richard Abel and Rick Altman, eds., *The Sounds of Early Cinema* (Bloomington: Indiana University Press, 2001), xiii.

10. Andre Gaudreault, "Showing and Telling: Image and Word in Early Cinema," translated by John Howe, in *Early Cinema: Space, Frame, Narrative*, edited by Thomas Elsaesser with Adam Barker (London: British Film Institute, 1990), 274 (emphasis in original). See also Rick Altman, "Film Sound—All of It," *iris* 27 (spring 1999), 31–48.

11. See Hansen, *Babel and Babylon*. For more on the film lecturer, see Tom Gunning, "An Aesthetic of Astonishment: Early Film and the [In]Credulous Spectator," in *Viewing Positions: Ways of Seeing Film*, edited by Linda Williams (New Brunswick, N.J.: Rutgers University Press, 1995), Gunning, "'Now You See It, Now You Don't': The Temporality of the Cinema of Attractions," in Abel, *Silent Film*, 71–84, and Gunning, "The Scene of Speaking: Two Decades of Discovering the Film Lecturer," *iris* 27 (spring 1999), 67–79. On the role of the itinerant showmen exhibitors in early American cinema, see Charles Musser with Carol S. Nelson, *High-Class Moving Pictures: Lyman H. Howe and the Forgotten Era of Traveling Exhibition, 1880–1920* (Princeton: Princeton University Press, 1991), Musser, "Introducing Cinema to the American Public: The Vitascope in the United States, 1896–7," in *Moviegoing in America: A Sourcebook in the History of Film Exhibition*, edited by Gregory A. Waller (Malden, Mass.: Blackwell, 2002), 13–26, and Edward Lowry, "Edwin J. Hadley: Traveling Film Exhibitor," in *Film before Griffith*, edited by John L. Fell (Berkeley: University of California Press, 1983), 131–43. See also *iris* 22 (autumn 1996), special issue on "The Moving Picture Lecturer," in particular the memoir of the Dutch film lecturer Max Nabarro, "This Is My Life," 183–200.

12. Rick Altman, "The Sound of Sound: A Brief History of the Reproduction of Sound in Movie Theaters," *Cineaste*, special supplement on "Sound and Music in the Movies," 21, nos. 1–2 (1995), 68. See also Altman's *Silent Film Sound*, especially chapter 9, "Films That Talk."

13. See Gillian B. Anderson, *Music for Silent Films, 1894–1929: A Guide* (Washington: Library of Congress, 1988). See also Martin Miller Marks, *Music and the Silent Film: Contexts and Case Studies, 1895–1924* (New York: Oxford University Press, 1997), and Paul Fryer, *The Opera Singer and the Silent Film* (Jefferson, N.C.: McFarland, 2005). For more specific examples of various roles music played in this era, see Norman King, "The Sound of Silents" (31–44), and Mary Carbine, "'The Finest Outside the Loop': Motion Picture Exhibition in Chicago's Black Metropolis, 1905–1928" (234–62), both in Abel, *Silent Film*; see also Tim Anderson, "Reforming 'Jackass Music': The Problematic Aesthetics of Early American Film Music Accompaniment," *Cinema Journal* 37, no. 1 (fall 1997), 3–22.

14. As Charles Musser points out regarding the release of these films, "The Edison catalog urged exhibitors to use some kind of verbal clarification to motivate the character's actions and the relationship between the shots: 'the music and words accompanying are explanatory and can be either sung or spoken.'" Charles Musser, *Before the Nickelodeon: Edwin S. Porter and the Edison Manufacturing Company* (Berkeley: University of California Press, 1991), 150. See also Anderson, *Music for Silent Films*, xiii. These "song films" were also sometimes advertised as illustrated songs, a practice that included the song-slide format in which the projection of lantern slides was accompanied by either phonograph recordings or live singers who would lead the audience in song, apparently to fill in space between reels. See David Nasaw, *Going Out: The Rise and Fall of Public Amusements* (New York: Basic Books, 1993), 165–66, Lowry, "Edwin J. Hadley," 133, and Richard Abel, "That Most American of Attractions, the Illustrated Song," in Abel and Altman, *The Sounds of Early Cinema*. For more on lantern shows, see David Robinson, *From Peepshow to Palace: The Birth of American Film* (New York: Columbia University Press, 1996).

15. Messter, who had demonstrated several sound films at the St. Louis Exposition in 1904, first utilized the Auxetophone, an apparatus designed in 1902 by Charles Parsons, who had outfitted a gramophone with an air valve to amplify sound. See David L. Parker and Burton J. Shapiro, "The Phonograph Movies," ARSC *Journal* 7, nos. 1–2 (1975), 6–9. See also Raymond Fielding, "Hale's Tours: Ultrarealism in the Pre-1910 Motion Picture," in Fell, *Film before Griffith*, 120. For a brief notation on the Parsons Auxetophone, see V. K. Chew, *Talking Machines, 1877–1914: Some Aspects of the Early History of the Gramophone* (London: Her Majesty's Stationery Office, 1967), 68–73. "From the beginning," as Gillian Anderson maintains, "Thomas Edison saw the mechanical reproduction of sound and image as inextricably bound" (*Music for Silent Films*, xiii). Hence, an Edison film catalogue from 1894 listing some fifty-three motion pictures includes this note: "We can furnish specially selected Musical Records for use on the Kineto-Phone, for nearly all of the films in the foregoing list. Price, each, $1.50." Reprinted as an appendix in Terry Ramsaye's classic history of the cinema *A Million and One Nights: A History of the Motion Picture* (New York: Simon and Schuster, 1926; repr. 1964), 838–39.

16. Rick Altman, "Introduction: Four and a Half Film Fallacies," in Altman, *Sound Theory/Sound Practice* (New York: Routledge, 1992), 36. On "the dozens of experiments

with sound-on-disc synchronization," see Altman, "The Sound of Sound"; Bowser, *The Transformation of Cinema, 1907–1915*; and Douglas Gomery, "The Coming of Sound: Technological Change in the American Film Industry," in Weis and Belton, *Film Sound: Theory and Practice*, 5–24. Against Gomery's contention that Gaumont's Chronophone failed because it "lacked the necessary amplification" to carry sound across a large hall, among other inherent problems, Alan Williams asserts that "the early Gaumont sound films were presented to audiences of 5000 (!) patrons at the Gaumont Palace in Paris, using an amplification system based on compressed air." Williams, "Historical and Theoretical Issues in the Coming of Recorded Sound in the Cinema," in Altman, *Sound Theory/Sound Practice*, 127–28. Finally, Arthur Kingston, a technician who worked on talking pictures for Pathé Frères in 1907, claimed to have utilized a gramophone equipped with "pneumatic sound boxes" that produced "terrific amplification": "In those days we synchronized the disc with the projector. We would take a ready-made disc, and artists would mime to it while we photographed them. The synchronization was a complicated and very clever device, completely automatic. We got perfect lip sync — provided the artist miming the record was doing his job properly." Quoted in Kevin Brownlow, *The Parade's Gone By* (Berkeley: University of California Press, 1968), 567. On the briefly successful resuscitation and popularity of Edison's kinetophone in 1913–14, see Rosalind Rogoff, "Edison's Dream: A Brief History of the Kinetophone," *Cinema Journal* 15, no. 2 (spring 1976), 58–68.

Part II. Cinema: Readings

1. Edison is referring to Eadweard Muybridge and Etienne-Jules Marey, both nineteenth-century pioneers in the use of photography for early time-motion studies.

2. A tube designed to display electrical phenomena.

3. Sir Harry Lauder (1870–1950), Scottish singer, songwriter, and vaudeville star, made several early sound films.

4. Charles K. Harris (1867–1930) was a famous songwriter and publisher, best known for his song "After the Ball" (1891).

5. All of these plays were major literary successes in the nineteenth century.

6. The Flatiron Building is a famous skyscraper in New York City.

7. "Programme music" refers to instrumental music involving some kind of story.

8. *The Birth of a Nation* is a famous film directed by D. W. Griffith and released in 1915.

9. Geraldine Farrar (1882–1967) was a famous opera singer and film actress.

10. Obbligato is a technical term for an essential instrumental part, second in importance to the melody.

11. Sigmund Spaeth (1885–1965) was a well-known popularizer of classical music.

12. The Canadian-born Mary Pickford (1892–1979) was married to Douglas Fairbanks Sr. and was one of the most famous stars of the silent era.

13. Gloria Swanson (1899–1983) was one of the most famous stars of the silent era.

14. The Polish-born Pola Negri (1894–1987) was a silent film star who had trouble in the Hollywood transition to sync-sound cinema.

15. The references are to the French composer Gabriel Fauré (1845–1924), the British documentary filmmaker and writer John Grierson (1898–1972), and the German theatrical and film director Max Reinhardt (1873–1943).

16. The Italian-born Rudolph Valentino (1895–1926) was a major star and sex symbol in the silent era.

Part III. Radio: Introduction

1. George Burns, *Gracie: A Love Story* (New York: Putnam, 1988), 86–87.

2. There are, however, some useful articles on particular radio stations and musicians, and some nonscholarly histories: Frank Biocca, "Media and Perceptual Shifts: Early Radio and the Clash of Musical Cultures," *Journal of Popular Culture* 24 (fall 1990), 1–15; Pamela Grundy, "'We Always Tried to Be Good People': Respectability, Crazy Water Crystals, and Hillbilly Music on the Air, 1933–1935," *Journal of American History* 81 (March 1995), 1591–1620, and "From *Il Trovatore* to the Crazy Mountaineers: The Rise and Fall of Elevated Culture on WBT-Charlotte, 1922–1930," *Southern Culture* 1 (1994), 51–73; Louis M. Kyriakoudes, "The Grand Ole Opry and the Urban South," *Southern Cultures* 10 (spring 2004), 67–84; Tracey E. W. Laird, *Louisiana Hayride: Radio and Roots Music along the Red River* (New York: Oxford University Press, 2005); Allison McCracken, "'God's Gift to Us Girls': Crooning, Gender, and the Re-Creation of American Popular Song, 1928–1933," *American Music* 17 (winter 1999), 365–95; Kristine M. McCusker, "'Dear Radio Friend': Listener Mail and the *National Barn Dance*, 1931–1941," *American Studies* 39 (summer 1998), 173–95; Kathy M. Newman, *Radio Active: Advertising and Consumer Activism, 1935–1947* (Berkeley: University of California Press, 2004); Susan Smulyan, "Branded Performers: Radio's Early Stars," *Timeline* 3 (December 1986–January 1987), 32–41; Derek Vaillant, "Sounds of Whiteness: Local Radio, Racial Formation, and Public Culture in Chicago, 1921–1935," *American Quarterly* 54 (March 2002), 25–66. Nonscholarly histories include Thomas A. DeLong, *The Mighty Music Box: The Golden Age of Musical Radio* (Los Angeles: Amber Crest, 1980), and Philip K. Eberly, *Music in the Air: America's Changing Tastes in Popular Music, 1920–1980* (New York: Hastings House, 1982).

3. Susan J. Douglas, *Listening In: Radio and the American Imagination . . . from Amos 'n' Andy and Edward R. Murrow to Wolfman Jack and Howard Stern* (New York: Times Books, 1999); Michele Hilmes, *Radio Voices: American Broadcasting, 1922–1952* (Minneapolis: University of Minnesota Press, 1997); Michele Hilmes and Jason Loviglio, eds., *Radio Reader: Essays in the Cultural History of Radio* (New York: Routledge, 2002); and Susan Smulyan, *Selling Radio: The Commercialization of American Broadcasting, 1920–1934* (Washington: Smithsonian Institution Press, 1994). See also Ray Barfield, *Listening to Radio, 1920–1950* (Westport, Conn.: Praeger, 1996).

4. See Susan J. Douglas, *Inventing American Broadcasting, 1899–1922* (Baltimore: Johns Hopkins University Press, 1987), for a useful discussion of radio as a male domain in its earliest usages.

5. Douglas, *Listening In*, 64.

6. Ibid.

7. Erik Barnouw, *A Tower in Babel: A History of Broadcasting in the United States to 1933* (New York: Oxford University Press, 1966), 91; Frederick Lewis Allen, *Only Yesterday: An Informal History of the 1920s* (1931; repr. New York: Harper Perennial, 1964), 137.

8. The baby-carriage experiment generated an editorial in the *New York Times*: "Anyhow, Baby Was Good," 12 May 1921, 16, and was also reported in "A New Use for Radio," *Radio News*, June 1921, 856. Cornell University students attempted the same experiment: see "Now for a Radio Milk Bottle!," *Radio Digest*, 29 April 1922, 4. Around the same time as these experiments, radio programs devoted to lullabies at bedtime were common.

9. Hugo Gernsback, "The 'Pianorad,'" *Radio News*, November 1926, 493; G. B. Ashton, "Building the 'Tomborad,'" *Radio News*, April 1927, 1237; Patrick Whelan, "The New Radio Violin," *Popular Radio*, July 1926, 229; R. F. Starzl, "The Giant-Tone Radio Violin," *Radio News*, April 1927, 1236; and Georges Desilets, "Music by Radio Spark Tones," *Radio Amateur News*, June 1920, 681. See also "Runs a Radio Piano," *Radio World*, 12 April 1924, 15.

10. See Smulyan's excellent *Selling Radio* for this history.

11. "Metropolitan Broadcasts First Full Opera; Hailed as a Success as Millions Listen In," *New York Times*, December 26, 1931, 1.

12. See William Barlow, "Black Music on the Radio during the Jazz Age," *African American Review* 29 (summer 1995), 325–28.

13. See Ross Melnick, "Rethinking Rothafel: Roxy's Forgotten Legacy," *Moving Image* 3 (2003), 62–95.

14. See Smulyan, "Branded Performers."

15. Especially the chapter "The Zen of Listening."

16. Many scholars of radio have argued this point. For a few useful sources, see Douglas, *Listening In*; Jason Loviglio, *Radio's Intimate Public: Network Broadcasting and Mass-Mediated Democracy* (Minneapolis: University of Minnesota Press, 2005), and "Vox Pop: Network Radio and the Voice of the People," in Hilmes and Loviglio, *Radio Reader*; and Roland Marchand, *Advertising the American Dream: Making Way for Modernity, 1920–1940* (Berkeley: University of California Press, 1985), especially the chapter "Abandoning the Great Genteel Hope: From Sponsored Radio to the Funny Papers."

17. For lengthier histories of crooners, see Douglas, *Listening In*; McCracken, "'God's Gift to Us Girls'"; and Michael R. Pitts, *The Rise of the Crooners: Gene Austin, Russ Columbo, Bing Crosby, Nick Lucas, Johnny Marvin, and Rudy Vallee* (Lanham, Md.: Scarecrow, 2002).

18. This song is collected in Rudy Vallée, *Heigh-ho Everybody!*, Pavilion Records PAST CD 7077, 1995.

19. John Webster, "The Radioman's Love Song," *Radio World*, 9 September 1922, 12.

20. "Perfectly Satisfied" (cartoon), *Radio World*, 10 February 1923, 26.

Part III. Radio: Readings

1. Lee de Forest (1873–1961) was the inventor of the Audion vacuum tube and a famous inventor of the period.

2. Hudson Maxim (1853–1927) was an inventor and chemist.

3. David Sarnoff (1891–1971) was a Russian-born immigrant to the United States who was a pioneer in broadcasting and communications technologies. He founded the National Broadcasting Company and worked in a variety of capacities at Radio Corporation of America for many years. This memo is a reconstruction that Sarnoff made in 1920 of the original from 1916, which is lost.

4. In a later memo to E. W. Rice Jr., president of the General Electric Company, dated 3 March 1920, Sarnoff estimated that one million "Radio Music Boxes" could be sold over a period of three years, 100,000 the first year, 300,000 the second, and 600,000 the third, generating sales revenue of $75 million (David Sarnoff, *Looking Ahead: The Papers of David Sarnoff* [New York: McGraw-Hill, 1968], 33–34). The actual sales figures proved to be $83.5 million, according to E. E. Bucher, *Radio and David Sarnoff*, 234–35 (cited in Sarnoff, *Looking Ahead*, 34).

5. Bruce Bliven (1889–1977) was a leading journalist and editor in chief of the *New Republic* from 1930 to 1953.

6. The opera's full title is *Lucia di Lammermoor*.

7. Jimmy Valentine was a fictitious safecracker who first appeared in a short story by O. Henry that was turned into a play and later adapted for film.

8. John Philip Sousa (1854–1932), band conductor and composer, was one of the most famous musicians of his day.

9. Enrico Caruso (1873–1921) was an Italian tenor and a classical music superstar in his era.

10. Lichtenfeld was a cellist associated with WGN in Chicago beginning in 1924, with Leon Benditsky, piano, and Armand Bizery, violin. In the early days it was common for the announcer to act as producer, so the announcer Quinn Ryan's offer to pay Lichtenfeld was not unusual. In general, the practice of paying "talent" began in 1925.

11. The transcript of this interview has a marking saying "phonetic"; I think Lichtenfeld is referring to Léo Delibes's *La Source*, or *Naila* (1866).

12. "Three-sheeting" was a practice of actors loitering about near their advertising posters ("three-sheets") in theaters.

13. Station KDKA in Pittsburgh, the first radio station in the country, began broadcasting in 1920.

14. Helen Keller (1880–1968) was a deaf, blind, and mute woman who became a major inspirational figure to many Americans.

15. From NBC Archives, courtesy of NBC Universal, Inc.

16. Samuel L. Rothafel (1882–1936), known affectionately by radio listeners as "Roxy," was an early radio star on station WEAF, the flagship station of the National Broadcasting Company.

17. A "thank-ye-ma'am" was a small plateau carved into a road on a hill so that horses could rest.

18. The Davey Tree Company of Ohio was founded in the late nineteenth century; the president at the time of this broadcast, Martin L. Davey, later went on to become the fifty-third governor of Ohio in 1934.

19. William Resor was the grandson of the president of the J. Walter Thompson Company, Stanley Resor.

20. John U. Reber was the powerful head of the radio department at the J. Walter Thompson Company.

21. These kinds of testimonials from advertisers were commonly solicited by broadcasters and distributed to potential advertisers.

22. Clarence Dill (1884–1978) was a Democratic senator from Washington who sponsored the Radio Act of 1927, which created the Federal Communications Commission, and the Communications Act of 1934, which established the commercial funding mechanism for broadcasting still familiar today.

23. *The Gold Dust Twins* was an early musical variety program aired over WEAF in New York City from 1923 to 1926, sponsored by Gold Dust Powder, a cleaner; and Happiness Boys, the well-known song and comedy duo of Billy Jones and Ernest Hare, first broadcast in 1921 on WJZ, Newark, for Happiness Candy.

24. Edison was attempting to market a forty-minute record beginning in 1927; 78 rpm recordings could only contain three to five minutes of sound per side.

25. A "Tone Test Recital" was an event at which audiences would sit in a darkened hall and listen to live music followed by an Edison recording, and then asked if they could tell the difference.

26. This prophecy appeared in an advertisement for the De Forest Radio Telephone Company.

27. Martha Gellhorn (1908–1998) was a journalist and novelist who became one of the great war correspondents of the twentieth century.

28. Rudolph Valentino (1895–1926), was a star of silent films who was renowned for his appeal to women fans.

29. Russ Columbo (1908–1934) was a popular crooner.

30. Morton Downey (1901–1985) was a popular crooner.

31. Kate Smith (1907–1986) was a singer, one of the most popular entertainers in America for decades.

32. This comment refers to Lieutenant Russell L. Maugham, who flew a dawn-to-dusk flight from New York to San Francisco on 23 June 1924.

33. Theodore Thomas (1835–1905) was the founder of the Chicago Symphony Orchestra; Leopold Damrosch (1832–1885), father of Walter, founded the Oratorio Society of New York and the Symphony Society in New York City.

34. From NBC Archives, courtesy of NBC Universal, Inc.

35. A sound film screen test.

36. Olive Palmer, whose real name was Virginia Rea, was given her stage name for the *Palmolive Radio Hour* program, which was on the air from 1927 to 1931.

37. William Wade Hinshaw (1867–1947) was a noted opera singer.

38. Perfect pitch is a person's ability to sing or recognize a pitch without having heard it first.

39. "Simon-pure" means genuinely and completely pure.

40. Klemm is clearly modeling this hypothetical program on the program *Maxwell House Show*, which included as its host the character "Captain Henry." This program aired from 1932 to 1937.

41. A coloratura soprano voice is one that is light and is able to negotiate fast passages.

42. "Absolute music" is a nineteenth-century categorization of music, usually instrumental music, which is not about anything other than itself.

43. Obbligato is a technical term for an essential instrumental part, second in importance to the melody. Kempinski is using a metaphor to describe the relationship between the music as the obbligato and the main "melody," the script.

44. Peter W. Dykema (1873–1951) was a well-known music educator.

References

General Introduction

Abel, Richard, and Rick Altman, eds. *The Sounds of Early Cinema*. Bloomington: Indiana University Press, 2001.

Allen, Frederick Lewis. *Only Yesterday: An Informal History of the 1920's*. New York: Harper and Row, 1931.

Barnouw, Erik. *A Tower in Babel: A History of Broadcasting in the United States to 1933*. New York: Oxford University Press, 1966.

Bijsterveld, Karin. *Mechanical Sound: Technology, Culture, and Public Problems of Noise in the Twentieth Century*. Cambridge: MIT Press, 2008.

Bijsterveld, Karin, and José van Dijck, eds. *Sound Souvenirs: Audio Technologies and Cultural Practices*. Amsterdam: Amsterdam University Press, 2009.

Bull, Michael. "No Dead Air! The iPod and the Culture of Mobile Listening." *Leisure Studies* 24 (2005), 343–55.

———, ed. *Sounding out the City: Personal Stereos and the Management of Everyday Life*. New York: Berg, 2000.

Cameron, Evan William, ed. *Sound and the Cinema: The Coming of Sound to American Film*. Pleasantville, N.Y.: Redgrave, 1980.

Chanan, Michael. *Repeated Takes: A Short History of Recording and Its Effects on Music*. New York: Verso, 1995.

Cohen, Lizabeth. *Making a New Deal: Industrial Workers in Chicago, 1919–1939*. New York: Cambridge University Press, 1990.

Corbin, Alain. *Village Bells: Sound and Meaning in the Nineteenth-Century French Countryside*. Translated by Martin Thom. New York: Columbia University Press, 1998.

Crafton, Donald. *The Talkies: American Cinema's Transition to Sound, 1926–1931*. Berkeley: University of California Press, 1997.

Cross, Gary. *An All-Consuming Century: Why Commercialism Won in Modern America.* New York: Columbia University Press, 2000.

The Crowd. Directed by King Vidor. 1928.

Day, Timothy. *A Century of Recorded Music: Listening to Musical History.* New Haven, Conn.: Yale University Press, 2000.

Douglas, Susan J. *Inventing American Broadcasting, 1899–1922.* Baltimore: Johns Hopkins University Press, 1987.

———. *Listening In: Radio and the American Imagination, from Amos 'n' Andy and Edward R. Murrow to Wolfman Jack and Howard Stern.* New York: Times Books, 1999.

Dumenil, Lynn. *The Modern Temper: American Culture and Society in the 1920s.* New York: Hill and Wang, 1995.

Ewen, Stuart. *Captains of Consciousness: Advertising and the Social Roots of the Consumer Culture.* New York: McGraw-Hill, 1976.

Fischer, Claude S. *America Calling: A Social History of the Telephone to 1940.* Berkeley: University of California Press, 1992.

Gelatt, Roland. *The Fabulous Phonograph.* 2nd ed. New York: Macmillan, 1977.

Gitelman, Lisa. *Always Already New: Media, History, and the Data of Culture.* Cambridge: MIT Press, 2008.

Gorbman, Claudia. *Unheard Melodies: Narrative Film Music.* Bloomington: Indiana University Press, 1987.

Greene, Paul, and Thomas Porcello, eds. *Wired for Sound: Engineering and Technology in Sonic Cultures.* Middletown, Conn.: Wesleyan University Press, 2004.

Harvith, John, and Susan Edwards Harvith, eds. *Edison, Musicians, and the Phonograph: A Century in Retrospect.* Westport, Conn.: Greenwood, 1987.

Hilmes, Michele. *Radio Voices: American Broadcasting, 1922–1952.* Minneapolis: University of Minnesota Press, 1997.

Hilmes, Michele, and Jason Loviglio, eds. *Radio Reader: Essays in the Cultural History of Radio.* New York: Routledge, 2002.

Hosokawa, Shuhei. "The Walkman Effect." *Popular Music* 4 (1984), 165–80.

Johnson, James H. *Listening in Paris.* Berkeley: University of California Press, 1995.

Katz, Mark. *Capturing Sound: How Technology Has Changed Music.* Rev. ed. Berkeley: University of California Press, 2010.

Kenney, William Howland. *Recorded Music in American Life: The Phonograph and Popular Memory, 1890–1945.* New York: Oxford University Press, 1999.

Kozloff, Sarah. *Invisible Storytellers: Voice-over Narration in American Fiction Film.* Berkeley: University of California Press, 1988.

Kraft, James P. *Stage to Studio: Musicians and the Sound Revolution, 1890–1950.* Baltimore: Johns Hopkins University Press, 1996.

Lastra, James. *Sound Technology and the American Cinema: Perception, Representation, Modernity.* New York: Columbia University Press, 2000.

Lears, Jackson. *Fables of Abundance: A Cultural History of Advertising in America*. New York: Basic Books, 1994.

———. "From Salvation to Self-Realization: Advertising and the Therapeutic Roots of the Consumer Culture, 1880–1930." In *The Culture of Consumption: Critical Essays in American History, 1880–1980*, edited by Richard Wightman Fox and T. J. Jackson Lears. New York: Pantheon, 1982.

Lenthall, Bruce. *Radio's America: The Great Depression and the Rise of Modern Mass Culture*. Chicago: University of Chicago Press, 2007.

Lie, Merete, and Knut Holtan Sørensen. *Making Technology Our Own: Domesticating Technology into Everyday Life*. Oslo: Scandinavian University Press, 1996.

Lysloff, René T. A., and Leslie Gay, Jr., eds. *Technoculture and Music*. Middletown, Conn.: Wesleyan University Press, 2003.

Marchand, Roland. *Advertising the American Dream: Making Way for Modernity, 1920–1940*. Berkeley: University of California Press, 1985.

Marquis, Alice Goldfarb. "Written on the Wind: The Impact of Radio during the 1930s." *Journal of Contemporary History* 19 (1984), 385–415.

McGovern, Charles F. *Sold American: Consumption and Citizenship, 1890–1945*. Chapel Hill: University of North Carolina Press, 2006.

McMeans, Orange Edward. "The Great Audience Invisible." *Scribner's Magazine*, April 1923, 411.

Millard, Andre. *America on Record: A History of Recorded Sound*. Cambridge: Cambridge University Press, 1995.

Oudshoorn, Nelly, and Trevor J. Pinch, eds. *How Users Matter: The Co-construction of Users and Technology*. Cambridge: MIT Press, 2003.

Panopoulos, Panayotis. "Animal Bells as Symbols: Sound Hearing and in a Greek Island Village." *Journal of the Royal Anthropological Institute* n.s. 9 (2003), 639–56.

Pinch, Trevor, and Karin Bijsterveld. "'Should One Applaud?' Breaches and Boundaries in the Reception of New Technology in Music." *Technology and Culture* 44 (2003), 535–59.

Pinch, Trevor, and Frank Trocco. *Analog Days: The Invention and Impact of the Moog Synthesizer*. Cambridge: Harvard University Press, 2002.

Printers' Ink: A Journal for Advertisers, Fifty Years: 1888–1938. New York: Printers' Ink, 1938.

Read, Oliver, and Walter L. Welch. *From Tin Foil to Stereo: Evolution of the Phonograph*. 2nd ed. Indianapolis: Howard W. Sams, 1976.

Schmidt, Leigh Eric. *Hearing Things: Religion, Illusion, and the American Enlightenment*. Cambridge: Harvard University Press, 2000.

Smith, Bruce R. *The Acoustic World of Early Modern England: Attending to the O-Factor*. Chicago: University of Chicago Press, 1999.

Smith, Mark M. *Listening to Nineteenth-Century America*. Chapel Hill: University of North Carolina Press, 2001.

Smulyan, Susan. *Selling the Air: The Commercialization of American Broadcasting 1920–1934*. Washington: Smithsonian Institution Press, 1994.

Sterne, Jonathan. *The Audible Past: Cultural Origins of Sound Reproduction*. Durham: Duke University Press, 2003.

Strathern, Marilyn. Foreword. In *Consuming Technologies: Media and Information in Domestic Spaces*, edited by Roger Silverstone and Eric Hirsch. New York: Routledge, 1992.

Suisman, David. *Selling Sounds: The Commercial Revolution in American Music*. Cambridge: Harvard University Press, 2009.

Taylor, Timothy D. "The Commodification of Music at the Dawn of the Era of 'Mechanical Music.'" *Ethnomusicology* 51 (spring–summer 2007), 281–305.

———. "Music and the Rise of Radio in Twenties America: Technological Imperialism, Socialization, and the Transformation of Intimacy." In *Wired for Sound: Engineering and Technology in Sonic Cultures*, edited by Thomas Porcello and Paul Greene. Middletown, Conn.: Wesleyan University Press, 2004.

———. *Strange Sounds: Music, Technology and Culture*. New York: Routledge, 2001.

Théberge, Paul. *Any Sound You Can Imagine: Making Music/Consuming Technology*. Hanover, N.H.: University Press of New England, 1997.

Thompson, Emily. *The Soundscape of Modernity: Architectural Acoustics and the Culture of Listening in America, 1900–1933*. Cambridge: MIT Press, 2002.

Weis, Elisabeth, and John Belton, eds. *Film Sound: Theory and Practice*. New York: Columbia University Press, 1985.

Part I. Sound Recording

Abrahams, Maurice, and Grant Clarke. *They Start the Victrola (And Go Dancing around the Floor)*. London: Francis, Day and Hunter, 1914.

Bellamy, Edward. "With the Eyes Shut." *Harper's New Monthly* 79 (1889), 736–45.

Berliner, Emile. "The Gramophone: Etching the Human Voice." *Journal of the Franklin Institute* 125 (1888), 426–46.

Birge, Edward Bailey. *History of Public School Music in the United States*. Rev. ed. Boston: Oliver Ditson, 1939. Repr. Reston, Va.: Music Educators National Conference, 1988.

———. "Music Appreciation—The Education of the Listener." *Papers and Proceedings of the Music Teachers' National Association* 17 (1923), 189–93.

Blake, Eric Charles. *Wars, Dictators, and the Gramophone*. York, England: William Sessions, 2004.

Brooks, Tim. *Lost Sounds: Blacks and the Birth of the Recording Industry, 1890–1919*. Urbana: University of Illinois Press, 2004.

Brower, Edith. "Is the Musical Idea Masculine?" *Atlantic*, March 1894, 332–39.

Bryant, E. T. "The Gramophone Society Movements: A History of Gramophone Societies in Britain, including their Links with Public Libraries." M.A. thesis, Queen's University of Belfast, 1971.

Burnett, Frances Hodgson. *Little Lord Fauntleroy*. New York: Charles Scribner's Sons, 1889.

Campbell, Gavin James. "Classical Music and the Politics of Gender in America, 1900–1925." *American Music* 21 (winter 2003), 446–73.

Clements, Cary. "Augustus Stroh and the Famous Stroh Violin." 2 parts. *Experimental Musical Instruments* 10 (June 1995), 8–15; 11 (September 1995), 38–39.

Clementson, W. Arthur B. "The Sound Reproducing Machine in the Country School." *Etude*, November 1928, 840.

Coeuroy, A., and G. Clarence. *Le Phonographe*. Paris: Kra, 1929.

Compton, Fay. "The Power of the Needle." *Gramophone*, June 1923, 32.

Copland, Aaron. "The World of the Phonograph." *American Scholar* 6 (1937), 27–38.

"A Defense of Mechanical Music." *Literary Digest*, 26 March 1927, 70, 72.

Dickinson, Edward. *The Education of a Music Lover*. Boston: Charles Scribner's Sons, 1914.

Donovan, Dick. "The Stroh Violin." *Strand*, January 1902, 89–91.

Dykema, Peter W. "The Music Memory Contest and the Course of Study." *School Music*, September–October 1922, 12–17.

Edison, Thomas A. "The Perfected Phonograph." *North American Review* 146 (1888), 641–50.

Faulkner, Anne Shaw. *Music in the Home: An Aid to Parents and Teachers in the Cause of Better Listening*. Chicago: Ralph Fletcher Seymour, 1917.

Feaster, Patrick. "'The Following Record': Making Sense of Phonographic Performance, 1877–1908." Ph.D. diss., Indiana University, 2007.

———. "Speech Acoustics and the Keyboard Telephone: Rethinking Edison's Discovery of the Phonograph Principle." *ARSC Journal* 38 (spring 2007), 10–43.

"15,000 Enroll in Phonograph Drive." *New York Times*, 27 October 1918, 35.

Gelatt, Roland. *The Fabulous Phonograph*. 2nd ed. New York: Macmillan, 1977.

Gershwin, George. "The Composer in the Machine Age." In *The American Composer Speaks*, edited by Gilbert Chase. Baton Rouge: Louisiana State University Press, 1966.

Gitelman, Lisa. "Reading Music, Reading Records: Musical Copyright and the U.S. Copyright Act of 1909." *Musical Quarterly* 81 (summer 1997), 265–90.

Gordon, M. D. "How Mechanical Instruments Bring the Best Music into the Country." *Countryside*, November 1918, 253–54.

Greenwood, Annie Pike. "The Victor in the Rural School." *Journal of Education*, 26 February 1914, 235.

Harvith, John, and Susan Edwards Harvith, eds. *Edison, Musicians, and the Phonograph: A Century in Retrospect*. New York: Greenwood, 1987.

"Die Hausmusik und ihr Programm." *Die Stimme seines Herrn* 4 (March 1912), 46–47.

Henry, O. "The Phonograph and the Graft." *McClure's* 20 (1903), 428–34. Slightly different version in *Cabbages and Kings*, 92–112. New York: A. L. Burt, 1904.

Hoffmann, Frank, ed. *Encyclopedia of Recorded Sound*. 2nd ed. New York: Routledge, 2005.

Johnson, Horace. "Department of Recorded Music: Phonographs in the Home." *Etude*, February 1922, 88.

Katz, Mark. *Capturing Sound: How Technology Has Changed Music*. Rev. ed. Berkeley: University of California Press, 2010.

Kenney, William Howland. *Recorded Music in American Life: The Phonograph and Popular Memory, 1890–1945*. New York: Oxford University Press, 1999.

Kinscella, Hazel Gertrude. "The Subtle Lure of Duet-Playing." *Musician*, January 1924, 8, 15.

Knox, J. Armoy. "The Future of the Phonograph." *Electrical Review*, 12 April 1888, 1.

Krafft, Friedrich. "Briefe aus dem Felde." *Die Stimme seines Herrn* 8, nos. 6–7 (1916), 56, 59.

Langenus, Gustave. *The Langenus Clarinet Correspondence School with Talking Machine Records*. New York, 1915.

Lindau, Paul. "Musik im Kriegszeiten." *Die Stimme seines Herrn* 6 (Christmas 1914), 4–5.

MacDonald, Thomas H. "Past and Future of the Talking Machine." *Musical Age* 56 (1909), 261–62.

Machray, Felix. "My Phonograph Entertainment." *Talking Machine News* 3 (1905), 400.

Magruder, Richard J. "Manufacturing Music Lovers." *Disques*, March 1931, 14–18.

"Mainly about Phones." *Sound Wave*, December 1909, 54.

Manning, Peter. *Electronic and Computer Music*. Rev. ed. New York: Oxford University Press, 2004.

Mayes, Will H. "How to Conduct a Music Memory Contest." *Etude*, March 1923, 153.

McCarthy, Tom. "The Real Little Lord Fauntleroy." *American Heritage*, February 1970.

Melba, Nellie. *Melodies and Memories*. New York: H. Doran, 1926.

Milhaud, Darius. "Les Ressources nouvelles de la musique." *L'Esprit Nouveau* 25 (1924), n.p.

"A Momentous Musical Meeting: Thomas A. Edison and Lt. Comm. John Philip Sousa Meet for the First Time and Talk upon Music." *Etude*, October 1923, 663.

Montgomery, W. "How to Give a Christmas or New Year's Party." *Talking Machine News and Journal of Amusements*, January 1911, 66.

Moore, Jerrold. *Elgar on Record: The Composer and the Gramophone*. London: Oxford University Press, 1974.

Morton, David L. *Sound Recording: A Life History of a Technology*. Baltimore: Johns Hopkins University Press, 2006.

"Nos amis et nos adversaires." *L'Édition Musicale Vivante*, December 1927, 18–19.

"Nos amis et nos adversaires." *L'Édition Musicale Vivante*, February 1928, 23–24.

"Organize a Music Memory Contest." *Talking Machine Journal*, March 1919, 8.

"Phonograph at Funeral." *New York Times*, 18 December 1910, 1.

"Phonograph for Band at Wedding." *New York Times*, 26 December 1905, 2.

Pratt, Waldo S. "New Ideals in Musical Education." *Atlantic*, December 1900, 826–30.

Proceedings of the 1890 Convention of Local Phonograph Companies. Milwaukee: Phonograph Printing Co., 1890. Repr. Nashville: Country Music Foundation Press, 1974.

Randolph, Harold. "The Feminization of Music." *Papers and Proceedings of the Music Teachers' National Association* 17 (1923), 194–200.

Read, Oliver, and Walter L. Welch. *From Tin Foil to Stereo: Evolution of the Phonograph.* 2nd ed. Indianapolis: Howard W. Sams, 1976.

Rehrig, Harold W. "Impressions from the Recording Room." *Phonograph Monthly Review*, May 1928, 284–86.

Richards, Grant. "Against the Gramophone." *Gramophone*, June 1923, 36.

Riess, Curt. "Krieg." In *Knaurs Weltgeschichte der Schallplatte.* Zurich: Droemer, 1966.

Robins, William J. "Gramophone Societies." *Gramophone*, November 1931, 248–49.

Rosen, Jody. "Researchers Play Tune Recorded Before Edison." *New York Times*, 27 March 2008. http://www.nytimes.com/2008/03/27/arts/27soun.html.

"The Salesman and the Singing Course." *Talking Machine Journal*, November 1917, 16.

Schauffler, Robert Haven. "Canned Music—The Phonograph Fan." *Collier's*, 23 April 1921, 10–11, 23–24.

Scholes, Percy A. "Gramophonic Adventures: Some Notes of War Experiences." *Voice*, July 1919, 8–9.

Schünemann, Georg. "Produktive Kräfte der Mechanischen Musik." *Die Musik*, January 1932, 246–49.

"The Science of Making Canned Music." *Literary Digest*, 28 September 1918, 24–25.

Seegers, J. C. "Teaching Music Appreciation by Means of the Music-Memory Contest." *Elementary School Journal*, November 1925, 215–23.

"'Stage Fright' Produced by the Phonograph." *Phonogram* 1 (1891), 39.

Sterne, Jonathan. *The Audible Past: Cultural Origins of Sound Reproduction.* Durham: Duke University Press, 2003.

Swinnerton, Frank. "A Defence of the Gramophone." *Gramophone*, August 1923, 52–53.

Symons, Edward. "The Gramophone Banishes the Horrors of War." *Voice*, May 1919, 9.

Tremaine, C. M. "The Music Memory Contest, Etc." *Proceedings of the Music Supervisors' National Conference* 11 (1919), 99–107.

———. "Music Memory Contests." *Journal of the National Education Association*, February 1926, 43–44.

Victor Talking Machine Company. *Three Modern Dances: One-Step, Hesitation, Tango.* Camden, N.J.: Victor Talking Machine Company, 1914.

Walker, Mrs. John P. "The Dance Craze of the Present Day." *Musical Monitor and World*, June 1914, 285.

Weber, James N. *The Talking Machine: The Advertising History of the Berliner Gramophone and Victor Talking Machine.* Midland, Ont.: Adio, 1997.

"Who Buys Phonographs?" *Sonora Bell* 2 (October 1919), 1–6.

Wile, Raymond. "The Automatic Phonograph Exhibition Company and the Beginnings of the Nickel-in-the-Slot Phonograph." *ARSC Journal* 33 (spring 2002), 1–20.

———. "The Edison Invention of the Phonograph." *ARSC Journal* 14 (1982), 5–28.

———. "Etching the Human Voice: The Berliner Invention of the Gramophone." *ARSC Journal* 21 (1990), 2–22.

Winship, A. E. "The Mission of School Music." *Journal of Education*, 21 September 1916, 260.

Part II. Cinema

Abel, Richard. "That Most American of Attractions, the Illustrated Song." In *The Sounds of Early Cinema*, edited by Richard Abel and Rick Altman. Bloomington: Indiana University Press, 2001.

Altman, Rick. "Deep-Focus Sound: *Citizen Kane* and the Radio Aesthetic." *Quarterly Review of Film and Video* 15 (1994), 1–33.

———. "Film Sound-All of It." *iris* 27 (spring 1999), 31–48.

———. "Introduction: Four and a Half Film Fallacies." In *Sound Theory/Sound Practice*, edited by Rick Altman. New York: Routledge, 1992.

———. "The Silence of the Silents." *Musical Quarterly* 80 (winter 1996), 648–718.

———. *Silent Film Sound*. New York: Columbia University Press, 2004.

———. "The Sound of Sound: A Brief History of the Reproduction of Sound in Movie Theaters." *Cineaste* 21 (1995), 68–72.

Anderson, Gillian B. *Music for Silent Films, 1894–1929: A Guide*. Washington: Library of Congress, 1988.

Anderson, Tim. "Reforming 'Jackass Music': The Problematic Aesthetics of Early American Film Music Accompaniment." *Cinema Journal* 37 (fall 1997), 3–22.

Bowser, Eileen. *The Transformation of Cinema, 1907–1915*. New York: Charles Scribner's Sons, 1990.

Brownlow, Kevin. *The Parade's Gone By*. Berkeley: University of California Press, 1968.

Carbine, Mary. "'The Finest Outside the Loop': Motion Picture Exhibition in Chicago's Black Metropolis, 1905–1928." In *Silent Film*, edited by Richard Abel. New Brunswick, N.J.: Rutgers University Press, 1996.

Chew, V. K. *Talking Machines, 1877–1914: Some Aspects of the Early History of the Gramophone*. London: Her Majesty's Stationery Office, 1967.

Clair, René. "The Art of Sound." In *Film Sound: Theory and Practice*, edited by Elisabeth Weis and John Belton. New York: Columbia University Press, 1985.

Crafton, Donald. *The Talkies: American Cinema's Transition to Sound, 1926–1931*. Berkeley: University of California Press, 1999.

Ewen, Stuart, and Elizabeth Ewen. *Channels of Desire: Mass Images and the Shaping of American Consciousness*. New York: McGraw-Hill, 1982.

Fielding, Raymond. "Hale's Tours: Ultrarealism in the Pre-1910 Motion Picture." In *Film before Griffith*, edited by John L. Fell. Berkeley: University of California Press, 1983.

Fryer, Paul. *The Opera Singer and the Silent Film*. Jefferson, N.C.: McFarland, 2005.

Gaudreault, Andre. "Showing and Telling: Image and Word in Early Cinema." Translated by John Howe. In *Early Cinema: Space, Frame, Narrative*, edited by Thomas Elsaesser with Adam Barker. London: British Film Institute, 1990.

Gomery, Douglas. "The Coming of Sound: Technological Change in the American Film

Industry." In *Film Sound: Theory and Practice*, edited by Elisabeth Weis and John Belton. New York: Columbia University Press, 1985.

Gunning, Tom. "An Aesthetic of Astonishment: Early Film and the [In]Credulous Spectator." In *Viewing Positions: Ways of Seeing Film*, edited by Linda Williams. New Brunswick, N.J.: Rutgers University Press, 1995.

———. "'Now You See It, Now You Don't': The Temporality of the Cinema of Attractions." In *Silent Film*, edited by Richard Abel. New Brunswick, N.J.: Rutgers University Press, 1996.

———. "The Scene of Speaking: Two Decades of Discovering the Film Lecturer." *iris* 27 (spring 1999), 67–79.

Hansen, Miriam. *Babel and Babylon: Spectatorship in American Silent Film*. Cambridge: Harvard University Press, 1991.

Jancovich, Mark, and Lucy Faire, with Sarah Stubbings. *The Place of the Audience: Cultural Geographies of Film Consumption*. London: British Film Institute, 2003.

Kellner, Douglas. "Culture Industries." In *A Companion to Film Theory*, edited by Toby Miller and Robert Stam. Malden, Mass.: Blackwell, 1999.

King, Norman. "The Sound of Silents." In *Silent Film*, edited by Richard Abel. New Brunswick, N.J.: Rutgers University Press, 1996.

Lowry, Edward. "Edwin J. Hadley: Traveling Film Exhibitor." In *Film before Griffith*, edited by John L. Fell. Berkeley: University of California Press, 1983.

Marks, Martin Miller. *Music and the Silent Film: Contexts and Case Studies, 1895–1924*. New York: Oxford University Press, 1997.

Musser, Charles. *Before the Nickelodeon: Edwin S. Porter and the Edison Manufacturing Company*. Berkeley: University of California Press, 1991.

———. "Introducing Cinema to the American Public: The Vitascope in the United States, 1896–7." In *Moviegoing in America: A Sourcebook in the History of Film Exhibition*, edited by Gregory A. Waller. Malden, Mass.: Blackwell, 2002.

Musser, Charles, with Carol S. Nelson. *High-Class Moving Pictures: Lyman H. Howe and the Forgotten Era of Traveling Exhibition, 1880–1920*. Princeton, N.J.: Princeton University Press, 1991.

Nabarro, Max. "This Is My Life." *iris* 22 (autumn 1996), 183–200.

Nasaw, David. *Going Out: The Rise and Fall of Public Amusements*. New York: Basic Books, 1993.

Parker, David L., and Burton J. Shapiro. "The Phonograph Movies." *ARSC Journal* 7 (1975), 6–9.

Rabinovitz, Lauren. *For the Love of Pleasure: Women, Movies, and Culture in Turn-of-the-Century Chicago*. New Brunswick, N.J.: Rutgers University Press, 1998.

Ramsaye, Terry. *A Million and One Nights: A History of the Motion Picture*. New York: Simon and Schuster, 1926. Repr. 1964.

Robinson, David. *From Peepshow to Palace: The Birth of American Film*. New York: Columbia University Press, 1996.

Rogoff, Rosalind. "Edison's Dream: A Brief History of the Kinetophone." *Cinema Journal* 15 (spring 1976), 58–68.

Ross, Steven J. *Working-Class Hollywood: Silent Film and the Shaping of Class in America.* Princeton: Princeton University Press, 1998.

Staiger, Janet. *Bad Women: Regulating Sexuality in Early American Cinema.* Minneapolis: University of Minnesota Press, 1995.

———. *Media Reception Studies.* New York: New York University Press, 2005.

Stam, Robert. *Film Theory: An Introduction.* Malden, Mass.: Blackwell, 2000.

Stokes, Melvyn, and Richard Maltby, eds. *American Movie Audiences: From the Turn of the Century to the Early Sound Era.* London: British Film Institute, 1999.

———. *Hollywood Abroad: Audiences and Cultural Exchange.* London: British Film Institute, 2004.

———. *Hollywood Spectatorship: Changing Perceptions of Cinema Audiences.* London: British Film Institute, 2001.

———. *Identifying Hollywood's Audiences: Audiences and Cultural Identity.* London: British Film Institute, 1999.

Waller, Gregory A. "Another Audience: Black Moviegoing, 1907–16." *Cinema Journal* 31 (winter 1992), 3–25.

———, ed. *Moviegoing in America: A Sourcebook in the History of Film Exhibition.* Malden, Mass.: Blackwell, 2002.

Williams, Alan. "Historical and Theoretical Issues in the Coming of Recorded Sound in the Cinema." In *Sound Theory/Sound Practice*, edited by Rick Altman. New York: Routledge, 1992.

Young, Paul. *The Cinema Dreams Its Rivals: Media Fantasy Films from Radio to the Internet.* Minneapolis: University of Minnesota Press, 2006.

Part III. Radio

Allen, Frederick Lewis. *Only Yesterday: An Informal History of the 1920's.* New York: Harper and Brothers, 1931. Repr. New York: Harper Perennial, 1964.

"Anyhow, Baby Was Good" [editorial]. *New York Times*, 12 May 1921, 16.

Ashton, G. B. "Building the 'Tomborad.'" *Radio News*, April 1927, 1237.

Barfield, Ray. *Listening to Radio, 1920–1950.* Westport, Conn.: Praeger, 1996.

Barlow, William. "Black Music on the Radio during the Jazz Age." *African American Review* 29 (summer 1995), 325–28.

Barnouw, Erik. *A Tower in Babel: A History of Broadcasting in the United States to 1933.* New York: Oxford University Press, 1966.

Biocca, Frank. "Media and Perceptual Shifts: Early Radio and the Clash of Musical Cultures." *Journal of Popular Culture* 24 (fall 1990), 1–15.

Burns, George. *Gracie: A Love Story.* New York: Putnam's, 1988.

DeLong, Thomas A. *The Mighty Music Box: The Golden Age of Musical Radio.* Los Angeles: Amber Crest, 1980.

Desilets, Georges. "Music by Radio Spark Tones." *Radio Amateur News*, June 1920, 681.

Douglas, Susan J. *Inventing American Broadcasting, 1899–1922*. Baltimore: Johns Hopkins University Press, 1987.

———. *Listening In: Radio and the American Imagination . . . from Amos 'n' Andy and Edward R. Murrow to Wolfman Jack and Howard Stern*. New York: Times Books, 1999.

Eberly, Philip K. *Music in the Air: America's Changing Tastes in Popular Music, 1920–1980*. New York: Hastings House, 1982.

Gernsback, Hugo. "The 'Pianorad.'" *Radio News*, November 1926, 493.

Grundy, Pamela. "From *Il Trovatore* to the Crazy Mountaineers: The Rise and Fall of Elevated Culture on WBT-Charlotte, 1922–1930." *Southern Culture* 1 (1994), 51–73.

———. "'We Always Tried to Be Good People': Respectability, Crazy Water Crystals, and Hillbilly Music on the Air, 1933–1935." *Journal of American History* 81 (March 1995), 1591–1620.

Hilmes, Michele. *Radio Voices: American Broadcasting, 1922–1952*. Minneapolis: University of Minnesota Press, 1997.

Hilmes, Michele, and Jason Loviglio, eds. *Radio Reader: Essays in the Cultural History of Radio*. New York: Routledge, 2002.

Kyriakoudes, Louis M. "The Grand Ole Opry and the Urban South." *Southern Cultures* 10 (spring 2004), 67–84.

Laird, Tracey E. W. *Louisiana Hayride: Radio and Roots Music along the Red River*. New York: Oxford University Press, 2005.

Loviglio, Jason. *Radio's Intimate Public: Network Broadcasting and Mass-Mediated Democracy*. Minneapolis: University of Minnesota Press, 2005.

———. "Vox Pop: Network Radio and the Voice of the People." In *Radio Reader: Essays in the Cultural History of Radio*, edited by Michele Hilmes and Jason Loviglio. New York: Routledge, 2002.

Marchand, Roland. *Advertising the American Dream: Making Way for Modernity, 1920–1940*. Berkeley: University of California Press, 1985.

McCracken, Allison. "'God's Gift to Us Girls': Crooning, Gender, and the Re-Creation of American Popular Song, 1928–1933." *American Music* 17 (winter 1999), 365–95.

McCusker, Kristine M. "'Dear Radio Friend': Listener Mail and the *National Barn Dance*, 1931–1941." *American Studies* 39 (summer 1998), 173–95.

Melnick, Ross. "Rethinking Rothafel: Roxy's Forgotten Legacy." *Moving Image* 3 (2003), 62–95.

"Metropolitan Broadcasts First Full Opera; Hailed as a Success as Millions Listen In." *New York Times*, December 26, 1931, 1.

Newman, Kathy M. *Radio Active: Advertising and Consumer Activism, 1935–1947*. Berkeley: University of California Press, 2004.

"A New Use for Radio." *Radio News*, June 1921, 856.

"Now for a Radio Milk Bottle!" *Radio Digest*, April 29, 1922, 4.

"Perfectly Satisfied" (cartoon). *Radio World*, 10 February 1923, 26.

Pitts, Michael R. *The Rise of the Crooners: Gene Austin, Russ Columbo, Bing Crosby, Nick Lucas, Johnny Marvin, and Rudy Vallee*. Lanham, Md.: Scarecrow, 2002.

"Runs a Radio Piano." *Radio World*, 12 April 1924, 15.

Sarnoff, David. *Looking Ahead: The Papers of David Sarnoff*. New York: McGraw-Hill, 1968.

Smulyan, Susan. "Branded Performers: Radio's Early Stars." *Timeline* 3 (December 1986–January 1987), 32–41.

———. *Selling Radio: The Commercialization of American Broadcasting, 1920–1934*. Washington: Smithsonian Institution Press, 1994.

Starzl, R. F. "The Giant-Tone Radio Violin." *Radio News*, April 1927, 1236.

Vaillant, Derek. "Sounds of Whiteness: Local Radio, Racial Formation, and Public Culture in Chicago, 1921–1935." *American Quarterly* 54 (March 2002), 25–66.

Vallée, Rudy. *Heigh-ho Everybody!* Pavilion Records PAST CD 7077, 1995.

Webster, John. "The Radioman's Love Song." *Radio World*, 9 September 1922, 12.

Whelan, Patrick. "The New Radio Violin." *Popular Radio*, July 1926, 229.

Index

"Meet Me Tonight in Dreamland" (song), 181–82

"Meine Stellung zur Schallplatte" (Stravinsky), 113

Melba, Nellie, 25, 374

Melchior, Lauritz, 92–94

Melton, Jimmie, 353–54

Mendelssohn, Felix, 47, 66, 99, 115, 176, 219, 365

Mendoza, David, 224–25

Menjou, Adolph, 233–34

Mercadante, Saverio, 376n18

Messter, Oskar, 142, 380n15

Metronome (magazine), 202–5, 212–20, 223–29

Milano Films, 182–88

Miller, Alice Duer, 358

Min and Bill (film), 235

Miracle Man, The (film), 197

Mitchell, Theodore, 209

Modern Electronics (magazine), 258–59

Modern Music (journal), 104–7, 110–13

Monsieur Beaucaire (film), 192

Morning Telegraph, 320–22

Morton, Jelly Roll, 91–92

movie attendance, rise of mass culture and, 3–5, 137–38

Movietone sound-on-film format, 142, 234

Moving Picture World (magazine), 148–52, 153–71, 173–88

Mozart, Wolfgang Amadeus: phonograph and, 47, 110, 115; radio broadcasting and, 267, 315; silent cinema and, 185, 193

Munn, Frank, 247, 249

Murphy, John T., 258

Musical Courier (magazine), 209–11, 221–23, 354–58

musical sound recordings: cinema and, 139–44; commercial development of, 14; cultural impact of, 39–44, 123–26; Edison's predictions of, 35–37; educational uses for, 19–20, 26–27; Great War and, 22–23, 78–84, 374n39; illustrated song slides and, 45, 142, 153–73; mass

culture and, 3–5; in nickelodeon theaters, 171–72; public suspicion of, 16–19; quality issues of, 24–26; radios and, 243–54, 301–24; recording technology and, 13–16; telephone lines and, 255–57

music appreciation: phonograph and, 65–70, 129–33; radio broadcasting and, 309–11

Musician (magazine), 85–88, 302–4

musicians: auditioning for radio, 324–31, 347–48; conducting and scoring, 200–211; recording and, 39–44, 84–94; on radio, 244–54; radio broadcasts and, 266–67; silent cinema performance and, 173–211; talking pictures and, 226–29

music memory contests, phonography recordings and, 20, 67–70, 373n31

Music Monitor and World (journal), 19

music pedagogy: phonograph recordings and, 26, 28, 94–104; talking pictures and, 226–29

musique concrète, 27, 374n53

Muybridge, Edward, 145, 381n1

"My Highland Laddie" (song), 176

Nally, Edward J., 259–60

National Broadcasting Company, 246, 251–52, 254, 272–75, 287, 339, 384n3; audition form for, 331–32; radio music arrangement at, 358–61

National Bureau for the Advancement of Music, 67–70

National Music Monthly, 129–33

National Phonograph Company, 18

"National Phonograph Records Recruiting Corps," 22–23

Nazimova, Alla, 202

Negri, Pola, 226, 382n14

New Moon (film), 234

New Republic (magazine), 260–65, 316–19

news coverage, radio and, 240–54, 264–65, 275–76

New York Times: on early sound technology, 13, 37–39; popular culture and,

212–25; sound recording and, 40–42, 48, 51, 93–94, 128

Pickford, Mary, 219

Picture Play (magazine), 233–36

"Picture Songs," 142

player piano, 3, 19, 26, 79, 95–99, 105–6, 117, 127, 129–33, 217, 306, 331, 375n55

Poet and Peasant (von Suppé), 203

popular culture: early cinema and, 137–44, 378n2; impact of radio on, 239–54; recorded music and, 39–44, 123–26; rise of, 2–5; talking pictures and, 229–36

popular magazines, mass culture and, 3–5

popular music: advertising on radio and, 288–89; crooning and, 247, 250–54, 316–24; early recordings of, 26–27; guidelines for listening to, 361–66; radio broadcasts of, 246–54, 287–88, 309–11; radio listeners and, 311–15; silent cinema and, 175–76, 204–5, 209–11, 218–19, 223–25

Popular Radio (magazine), 277, 279, 324–31

"Prelude to the Deluge" (Saint-Saëns), 198

Printers' Ink (magazine), 4–5

production of radio programming, 344–54

QSL cards, 240–41

"race orchestras," 138

radio: advertising and impact of, 239–54, 287–301; auditioning for, 324–40; on buses, 276–77; composing for, 354–61; cost issues in, 287–88, 344–45; early broadcasts of, 266–75; economics of broadcasting, 285–88; in everyday life, 254, 275–79; evolution of, 139–41, 144; guidelines for listening to, 361–66; healing effects of, 244, 279–85, 364; history of, 239–54; home use of, 53–56; listener surveys for, 311–15; mass culture and, 3–5; nickel slot machines for, 265–66; program development and production for, 324–61; talent development for, 340–43; technology for, 255–66; telephone technology and, 255–66

Radio Act of 1927, 385n22

Radio Broadcast (magazine), 267–71, 277–78, 311–15

Radio Digest, 279–80, 288–89

Radio Film, early cinema and, 139

Radio Guide (magazine), 339–40

"Radioman's Love Song, The" (Webster), 252

Radio Music Fund Committee, 285

Radio News, 265–66

Radiophone technology, cinema and, 139

Radio Reader's Digest, 356

Radio Revue for the Listener, 351

Radio World (magazine), 276–77, 285–87, 307–9

Rea, Virginia, 247, 249

reading, sound technology and, 39

Real Folks (radio program), 288

Reber, John U., 246

recorded music: composers and, 104–13; educational uses for, 19–20, 26–27; live music *vs.*, 11–12, 16–19; parties for creation of, 48–51; performance and, 84–94; over telephone lines, 255–57

Re-Creations, 59–61, 376n11

Refuge, The (film), 181–82

Reliance picture company, 182

Reproducer (Edison product), 59

research methodology: document selection, 7–8; on radio, 240–54

Resor, Stanley, 246, 295–96

Resor, William, 246, 295–96

Respighi, Ottorino, 105–7

Revelers, 353–54

Rhoads, W. M., 164

Riesenfeld, Hugo, 198, 209–11, 230

Riley, Joseph, 265–66

Roberts, Charles J., 213

Robinson, Adolf, 43

Rogers, Buddy, 234

Romance (film), 235

Root, Frederic W., 100–101

Rosenfield Manufacturing Co., 45

Rossini, Gioacchino, 183

Stravinsky, Igor, 27, 104–13, 374n49; silent
  cinema music by, 220
Stroh, Augustus, 24
Stroh violins, 24–26
Sullivan, Arthur, 11
surveys of listeners, radio broadcasting
  and, 311–15
Swanson, Gloria, 221–23
Szeminanyi, L., 189–90

talking machine: business applications for,
  13, 33–37; home uses for, 55–56; musical pedagogy and, 99–100; support for,
  126–29
Talking Machine Journal, 20, 22, 67–75,
  78–80
Talking Machine News, 18
talking pictures (talkies): actors and, 164–
  66; American vs. British, 235–36; introduction of, 139–44; mass culture and,
  3–5, 138–44; music in, 226–29; popular
  culture and, 229–36; singing in, 234–36
Talmage, Thomas De Witt, 37, 375n3
tape music, 374n53
taste: impact of radio on, 246–54; silent
  cinema musical accompaniment and,
  211–25
Taylor, Deems, 204
Taylor, Frederick Winslow, 4
Taylor, Timothy, D. 1–8, 239–54
telegraph: phonograph technology and, 12,
  36–37; radio technology and, 263–65
telephone: development of, 6–7; phonograph technology and, 12, 36–37; radio
  technology and, 240–51, 255–66
Telephone Hour (radio program), 358
Telephone (magazine), 255–57
Tel-musici Company, 256–57
Thanhouser film company, 182
Thérémin, Leon, 111–13
"They Start the Victrola (And Go Dancing
  around the Floor)" (song), 19
Thief of Bagdad, The (film), 192

Thomas A. Edison, Inc.: film catalogue for,
  151–52, 380n15; picture songs by, 142,
  380n14; questionnaire and employee
  responses, 56–65
Tibbett, Lawrence, 234
"Times and Seasons" (Williams), 45–47
tinfoil phonograph, 12–13
Toch, Ernst, 106–7
"Tone Test Recital," 385n25
"Tonight You Belong to Me" (song), 224–25
Tosti, Francesco Paolo, 176
toys, phonographs as, 35–37
Transactions of the Society of Motion Pic-
  ture Engineers (journal), 205–9, 229–32
Tremaine, C. M., 20, 67–70
Trenton, Dinah, 236
Triadic Ballet (Hindemith), 106–7
Truette, Everett E., 102
"Turkey in the Straw" (song), 197

Ussachevsky, Vladimir, 374n53

Valentino, Rudolph, 232
Vallée, Rudy, 251–52, 288, 316–19, 322
Van Hoogstraten, Willem, 310
Vanity Fair (magazine), 70–71
vaudeville, impact of radio on, 239
Victor Salon Orchestra, 24
Victor Talking Machine Company, 15, 19,
  65–67, 85, 103–4
Victrola advertisements, gender targeting
  of, 70
Vidor, King, 1–2, 4
Vila, Josephine, 209–11, 221–23
Violinist (magazine), 84–85
violin playing: phonograph and, 41–44; for
  silent cinema, 173–76, 189–90, 212–25
Vitaphone, 142, 233–34
vocal training, recording technology and,
  26, 103–4
voice: on radio, 334–40; silent cinema and
  role of, 140–44, 153, 169–71; in talking
  pictures, 233–36

A portion of the introduction to part III is based on Timothy D. Taylor's essay "Music and the Rise of Radio in Twenties America: Technological Imperialism, Socialization, and the Transformation of Intimacy," in *Wired for Sound: Engineering and Technology in Sonic Cultures,* ed. Paul Greene and Thomas Porcello (Middletown, Conn.: Wesleyan University Press, 2004).

Timothy D. Taylor is a professor of ethnomusicology and musicology at the University of California, Los Angeles. He is the author of many articles and several books, most recently *The Sounds of Capitalism: Advertising, Music, and the Conquest of Culture*, published by the University of Chicago Press.

Mark Katz is an associate professor of music at the University of North Carolina, Chapel Hill. He is the author of *Capturing Sound: How Technology Has Changed Music* and *Groove Music: The Art and Culture of the Hip-Hop DJ* and editor of the *Journal of the Society for American Music*.

Tony Grajeda is an associate professor of cultural studies in the department of English at the University of Central Florida. He is the coeditor (with Jay Beck) of *Lowering the Boom: Critical Studies in Film Sound* (2008) and the guest coeditor of a special issue on "The Future of Sound Studies" for the journal *Music, Sound, and the Moving Image*.

. . . . .

Library of Congress Cataloging-in-Publication Data
Music, sound, and technology in America : a documentary history of early phonograph, cinema, and radio / edited by Timothy D. Taylor, Mark Katz, and Tony Grajeda.
p. cm.
Includes bibliographical references and index.
ISBN 978-0-8223-4927-3 (cloth : alk. paper)
ISBN 978-0-8223-4946-4 (pbk. : alk. paper)
1. Popular music—Social aspects—United States—20th century.
2. Popular culture—United States—History—20th century.
3. Phonograph—United States—History—20th century. 4. Radio broadcasting—United States—History—20th century. 5. Motion picture music—United States—History—20th century. 6. Mass media—Technological innovations—United States—History—20th century.
I. Taylor, Timothy Dean. II. Katz, Mark, 1970– III. Grajeda, Tony, 1960–
ML3917.U6M89 2012
781.49—dc23   2011038524